The Works of John Taylor

The Works

of

John Taylor

The Mediation and Atonement

The Government of God

Items on Priesthood

Succession in the Priesthood

On Marriage

The Origin and Destiny of Woman

Compiled by David Hammer

© 2010 David Hammer

All Rights Reserved. No part of this book my be reproduced in any form or by any means without permission in writing from the publisher, Eborn Publishing.

NOTE:
The numbers scattered throughout the text in brackets, i.e. [28], correspond to the beginning of that page, i.e. page 28, in the original.

ISBN: 978-1-60919-592-2

Eborn Publishing, Inc.
2700 W. 3500 S. Ste 120
Salt Lake City, UT

www.ebornbooks.com

CONTENTS

THE MEDIATION AND ATONEMENT........................ 7

THE GOVERNMENT OF GOD.............................. 193

ITEMS ON THE PRIESTHOOD............................ 319

SUCCESSION IN THE PRIESTHOOD....................... 361

ON MARRIAGE.. 381

THE ORIGIN AND DESTINY OF WOMAN................... 389

INDEX.. 393

AN EXAMINATION INTO AND AN ELUCIDATION OF THE
GREAT PRINCIPLE OF THE

MEDIATION AND ATONEMENT

OF

OUR LORD AND SAVIOR JESUS CHRIST

By PRESIDENT JOHN TAYLOR

"Wherefore the fruit of thy loins shall write, and the fruit of the loins of Judah shall write; and that which shall be written by the fruit of thy loins, and also that which shall be written by the fruit of the loins of Judah, shall grow together unto the confounding of false doctrines, and laying down of contentions." (JST Genesis 1:31)

"For I command all men, both in the east and in the west, and in the north and in the south, and in the islands of the sea, that they shall write the words which I speak unto them: for out of the books which shall be written, I will judge the world, every man according to their works, according that which is written. For behold, I shall speak unto the Jews, and they shall write it; and I shall also speak unto the Nephites, and they shall write it; and I shall also speak unto the other tribes of the house of Israel, which I have led away, and they shall write it; and I shall also speak unto all nations of the earth, and they shall write it. And it shall come to pass that the Jews shall have the words of the Nephites, and the Nephites shall have the words of the Jews; and the Nephites and the Jews shall have the words of the lost tribes of Israel; and the lost tribes of Israel shall have the words of the Nephites and the Jews. And it shall come to pass that my people which are of the house of Israel, shall be gathered home unto the lands of their possessions; and my word also shall be gathered in one." (2 Nephi 29:11-14.)

SALT LAKE CITY, UTAH

1882

CONTENTS

CHAPTER 1: Introductory—Christ's Testimony with regard to His Sufferings—Christ came to do the Will of His Father—The Testimony of the Father at His Baptism and Transfiguration.............................. 15

CHAPTER 2: The Testimony of Jesus the Spirit of Prophecy—The Declarations of the Ancient Servants of God—Extracts from the Writings and Testimonies of Moses, Job, David, Isaiah, Zechariah, Micah and Hoses, to be found in the Old Testament, with remarks....................... 20

CHAPTER 3: Extracts from the New Testament, touching the Personal History of the Lord Jesus Christ and the Doctrine of the Atonement—Remarks on the "Times of Refreshing"—Results accruing to the Redeemer through His Death on the Cross, etc................................ 27

CHAPTER 4: Extracts from the Pearl of Great Price and Inspired Translation of Genesis-Record of Moses regarding Adam, Enoch, Noah, Abraham and Joseph, and of their faith in the Coming of the Savior. 41

CHAPTER 5: The Book of Mormon and the Atonement—Extracts from the Books of Ether, Nephi, Mosiah, Alma, Helaman and Mormon.................................... 45

CHAPTER 6: Extracts from the Book of Doctrine and Covenants—

Christ's Testimony of Himself, of His Power and Calling, etc.—Testimony of Joseph Smith and Sidney Rigdon—Record of John the Baptist—Extract from a Sermon by President Brigham Young. 58

CHAPTER 7: Introduction to the Historical Portion of this Treatise—The Dealings of God with Adam, Cain and Abel—The Institution of Sacrifice—The Symbolism of this Rite—The Words of the Angel to Adam—Lucifer—His Rebellion in Heaven—His Conflict with Michael for the Body of Moses—He tempts Christ—He is cast into a Lake of Fire and Brimstone.. 63

CHAPTER 8: Seth—His Sacrifice Accepted—Rebellion in the Heavens—The Gathering of the Patriarchs in the Valley of Adam-ondi-Ahman—Sacrifices Offered There. 69

CHAPTER 9: Enoch, his Life and Translation—References to Him by Paul and Jude—Copious Extracts from His Prophecy—The Prophet Joseph Smith on Enoch and the Doctrine of Translation—The Office of Translated Saints—Enoch's Future Work—Translation and Resurrection—Christ the Creator—Summary of the Results of Enoch's Faith in the Saving Blood of Christ. .... .73

CHAPTER 10: Noah—His Sacrifice—God's Covenant with Him—Melchizedek—His Priesthood—Its Powers—Instances thereof Recorded in the Bible, in the Book of Mormon and in Latter-days—All Power of the Priesthood the Result of Faith in Christ and Impossible without the Atonement—The Power of the Priesthood the Power of God—The Glory of God in the Immortality of Man—Christ the Word, the Creator...................................... 82

CHAPTER 11: Abraham's Record Concerning the Creation—The Council in Heaven—The Father's Plan, the Son's Acceptance, Satan's Rebellion—The Agency of Man—Suggestions Regarding Satan's Plan to Save All Mankind........ 91

CHAPTER 12: Abraham, Isaac and Jacob—Sacrifices Offered by Them—Abraham and the Gospel Covenant—Extracts from the Book of Abraham and the Writings of Paul. 98

CHAPTER 13: Sacrifices in the Days of Moses—The Institution of the Passover and the Exodus—The Symbolism of the Paschal Lamb—The Covenant of the Atonement between Christ and His Father—The Redeemed—Tokens of Covenants—The Rainbow—The Name of Jesus the Only Name—The Levites. 102

CHAPTER 14: History of Sacrifices and the Law of Moses among the Nephites—References to the Books of Nephi, Jacob, Mosiah and Alma—The Testimony of Jesus regarding the Law of Moses. 107

CHAPTER 15: The Offering of Sacrifice in the Times of the Restitution of all Things—Teachings of the Prophet Joseph Smith thereof—The Sons of Levi—Malachi's Prophecy—The Dispensation of the Fulness of Times. 116

CHAPTER 16: Brief Retrospect of the History of Sacrifice and its Symbolism—The Passover and the Lord's Supper—Christ's Relation to both these Ordinances—The Last Supper..120

CHAPTER 17: The Atonement and the Resurrection—Adam and Christ—Why a Law was given unto Adam—The Results of Disobedience to that Law—Testimony of our First Parents—"Adam fell that Man might be"—The Fall a Necessary Part of the Plan of Salvation—God's Plan a Merciful Plan—The Plan of Lucifer—Man's Free Agency—The Chain Complete. 124

CHAPTER 18: Christ, as the Son of God—A Comparison between His Position Glory. etc., and Those of other Sons of God—His Recognition by the Father—Christ called the Very Eternal Father. 131

CHAPTER 19: Man as Man—His Excellency and His Limitations —Salvation and Eternal Progression Impossible without the Atonement—In Christ only can All be made Alive. . . 134

CHAPTER 20: Christ to be Subject to Man—His Descent Below all

Things—Man's Condition had there been no Atonement—The Sons of God—Man's Inability to Save Himself—Christ's Glory before the World Was—Necessity for an Infinite Atonement—The Father and Son have Life in Themselves. 137

CHAPTER 21: The Relation of the Atonement to Little Children—Jesus Assumes the Responsibility of Man's Transgression, and Bears the Weight of his Sins and Sufferings—The Inferior Creatures and Sacrifice—The Terrors and Agonies of Christ's Passion and Death—The Tribulations, Earthquakes, etc., when He gave up the Ghost—Universal Nature Trembles—The Prophecies of Zenos and Enoch—The Testimony of the Centurion—Heirship, and the Descent of Blessings and Curses. 142

CHAPTER 22: The Operations of the Priesthood in the Heavens and upon the Earth, in Time and Eternity—The Heirs of the Celestial Kingdom—Those who Die without Law—The Judges of the Earth—Priests and Kings—Christ the King of Kings—Condition of Patriarch Joseph Smith, Apostle David Patten and Others—Moses and Elias—The Visits of Angels and their Testimonies—Peter, James and John—The Angel in the Book of Revelation. 148

CHAPTER 23: The Laws of God Unchangeable, Universal and Eternal—Examples and Definitions—Evolutionists—Kingdoms and Light—Christ the Creator. etc.—Deviations from General Laws—Every Kingdom has a Law Given. 155

CHAPTER 24: The Results of the Atonement—The Debt Paid—Justice and Mercy—Extracts from the Teachings of Alma and Others. 163

CHAPTER 25: The Resurrection—The Universality of the Atonement—The Promises to those who Overcome—The Gospel—Its First Principles —Faith, Repentance, Baptism and the Gift of the Holy Ghost—Its Antiquity—It is Preached in Various Dispensations, from Adam until the Present—The Final Triumph of the Saints.. 169

APPENDIX: The Ideas of a General Atonement and Redemption, Entertained by Ancient Heathen Nations, Derived Originally from the Teachings of Earlier Servants of God
.. . . .179

THE MEDIATION AND ATONEMENT

OF

OUR LORD AND SAVIOUR JESUS CHRIST

CHAPTER 1

INTRODUCTORY—CHRIST'S TESTIMONY WITH REGARD TO HIS SUFFERINGS—CHRIST CAME TO DO THE WILL OF HIS FATHER—THE TESTIMONY OF THE FATHER AT HIS BAPTISM AND TRANSFIGURATION.

In the last chapter of St. Luke's Gospel is to be found a deeply interesting account of several events that took place on the day that the Redeemer was resurrected. Amongst other incidents, he relates that on that day two of the disciples took a melancholy journey from Jerusalem to the neighboring village of Emmaus. Whilst they walked, the sadness of their hearts found expression on their tongues, and they mournfully rehearsed to each other the story of the crucifixion of their Master. By and by, they were joined by an apparent stranger, who, though none other than the resurrected Savior, was not recognized by them. In answer to His inquiries, they repeated the sad history of the days just passed, and expressed the disappointment that His death had brought, for they trusted that it had been He who should have redeemed Israel. Then Jesus said unto them, "O fools, and slow of heart to believe all that the prophets have spoken! Ought not Christ to have suffered these things, and to enter into His glory? And beginning at Moses, [7] and all the prophets, He expounded unto them in all the scriptures the things concerning Himself." (Luke 24:25-27.)

When they reached Emmaus, with characteristic eastern hospitality, they constrained the stranger to abide with them. He consented, and as they sat at meat He took bread, and blessed it, brake and gave unto them. Then their eyes were opened and they knew Him, and He vanished out of their sight. "And they rose up the same hour, and returned to Jerusalem, and found the eleven gathered together and them that were with them, saying, The Lord is risen indeed, and hath appeared to Simon. And they told what things were done in the way, and how He was known of them in breaking of bread. And as they thus spake, Jesus himself stood in the midst of them, and saith unto them, Peace be unto you." (v. 33-36.)

After the Savior had convinced the disciples then present of His identity, and had partaken of some broiled fish and an honey comb, He said unto them, "These are the words which I spake unto you, while I was yet with you, that all things must be fulfilled which were written in the law of Moses, and in the prophets, and in the psalms, concerning me. Then opened he their understanding, that they might understand the scriptures, and said unto them, Thus it is written, and thus it behooved Christ to suffer, and to rise from the dead the third day: And that repentance and remission of sins should be preached in his name among all nations, beginning at Jerusalem. And ye are witnesses of these things." (v. 44-48.)

One great and very striking statement is here made by the Lord Himself, to the effect that it behooved Christ to suffer, and the question at once presents itself before us, why did it behoove Him? Or why was it necessary that He should suffer? For it would seem from His language, through His sufferings, death, atonement and resurrection, "that repentance and remission of sins" (v. 47) could be preached among all nations, and that [9]consequently if He had not atoned for the sins of the world, repentance and remission of sins could not have been preached to the nations.

A very important principle is here enunciated, one in which the interests of the whole human family throughout all the world are involved. That principle is the offering up of the Son of God, as a sacrifice, an atonement and a propitiation for our sins. Jesus said, He came not to do His will, but the will of His Father, who sent Him. He came, as we are told, to take away sin by the sacrifice of Himself; and not only did He come, but He came in accordance with certain preconceived ideas that had been entertained and testified of by Prophets and men of God in all preceding ages, or from the days of Adam to the days of John the Baptist, the latter being His precursor or forerunner, who indeed, when he saw Him coming, made the declaration, Behold the Lamb of God, who taketh away the sin of the world. At His Baptism the Spirit of God bore witness to this testimony and descended upon Jesus in the form of a dove, or, rather, the form of a dove was the sign of the Holy Spirit; whilst a voice was heard from heaven proclaiming: "This is my beloved Son, in whom I am well pleased." (Matthew 3:17.)

This manifestation of God's acknowledgment of His beloved Son was spoken of by personal witnesses who bore record to the facts.

Matthew testifies: "Then cometh Jesus from Galilee to Jordan unto John, to be baptized of him. But John forbade him, saying, I have need to be baptized of thee, and comest thou to me? And Jesus answering said unto him, Suffer it to be so now: for thus it becometh us to fulfill all righteousness. Then he suffered him. And Jesus, when he was baptized, went up straightway out of the water: and lo, the heavens were opened unto him, and he saw the Spirit of God descending like a dove, and lighting upon him: And lo, a voice from heaven, saying, This is my beloved Son, in whom I am well pleased." (Matthew 3:13-17.) [10]

Whilst Mark relates, "And it came to pass in those days, that Jesus came from Nazareth of Galilee, and was baptized of John in Jordan. And straightway coming up out of the water, he saw the heavens opened, and the Spirit like a dove descending upon him. And there came a voice from heaven, saying, Thou art my beloved Son, in whom I am well pleased." (Mark 1:9-11.)

And John, in his Gospel, states that John the Baptist bare record, saying, "I saw the Spirit descending from heaven like a dove, and it abode upon him. And I knew him not: but he that sent me to baptize with water, the same said unto me, Upon whom thou shalt see the Spirit descending and remaining on him, the same is he which baptizeth with the Holy Ghost. And I saw and bare record, that this is the Son of God." (John 1:32-34.)

We have this great truth of the open recognition of Jesus, by His Father, as His beloved Son, again enunciated when the three Apostles, Peter, James and John, were on the Mount, and Jesus was transfigured before them. It is declared that "a bright cloud overshadowed them: and behold, a voice out of the cloud, which said, This is my beloved Son, in whom I am well pleased; hear ye him." (Matthew 17:5.)

The Son, thus openly acknowledged, came not to earth to do His own will, but the will of His Father. The will of the Father appears to have been that the Son should suffer, for He, Himself, prayed: "O my Father, if it be possible, let this cup pass from me: nevertheless, not as I will, but as thou wilt." (Matthew 26:39.) Or, as the New Translation by the Prophet Joseph Smith has it, "O my Father, if this cup may not pass away from me except I drink it, thy will be done." (JST Matthew 26:39.) The Father did not let it pass from Him; He therefore drank it, and finally, on the cross He said, "It is finished," (John 19:30) and bowed His head and gave up the Ghost.

In regard to this Jesus Himself testifies. First to the Nephites: "Behold, I am Jesus Christ, whom the Pro[11]phets testified shall come into the world; and behold, I am the light and life of the world; and I have drunk out of that bitter cup which the Father hath given me, and have glorified the Father in taking upon me the sins of the world, in the which I have suffered the will of the Father in all things from the beginning." (3 Nephi 11:10-11.)

And again, in this dispensation, He bears witness: "For behold, I, God, have suffered these things for all, that they might not suffer if they would repent, but if they would not repent, they must suffer even as I, which suffering caused myself, even God, the greatest of all, to tremble because of pain, and to bleed at every pore, and to suffer both body and spirit: and would that I might not drink the bitter cup and shrink, nevertheless, glory be to the Father, and I partook and finished my preparations unto the children of men." (D&C 19:16-19.)

The saying of our Savior, to which we have already alluded, "Thus it is written and thus it behooved Christ to suffer," (Luke 24:46) is a very important one, and it would seem to be necessary, in the consideration of our subject, for us to obtain, from the writings of the servants of God that we have, an understanding what these statements were; how extensively they were corroborated by the sacred records; and what is said with regard to the necessity of Christ's sufferings thus referred to: and, furthermore, we may notice the reason why they should be thus necessary.

In making this examination, we will first quote from the writings of the Old and New Testaments, and, although we are informed by later revelations that "many parts which are plain and most precious" (1 Nephi 13:26) have been taken away therefrom, yet there is a large amount of testimony left in this valuable and sacred record, which plainly exhibits that the principle of the atonement was fully understood by the Prophets in former ages. [12]

CHAPTER 2

THE TESTIMONY OF JESUS THE SPIRIT OF PROPHECY—THE DECLARATIONS OF THE ANCIENT SERVANTS OF GOD—EXTRACTS FROM THE WRITINGS AND TESTIMONIES OF MOSES, JOB, DAVID, ISAIAH, ZECHARIAH, MICAH AND HOSES, TO BE FOUND IN THE OLD TESTAMENT, WITH REMARKS.

In the chapter of Luke's Gospel, to which we have already referred, speaking of Jesus, it is written, "Beginning with Moses and all the prophets, he expounded unto them in all the Scriptures the things concerning himself." (Luke 24:27.)

If this be taken in the fullest sense, and we know of no reason why it should not thus be received, there is a great principle developed, which is, that not only Moses, but all the Prophets, testified concerning the coming Redeemer. As elsewhere stated, this must have been the case, for we are told that "the testimony of Jesus is the spirit of prophecy;" (Revelation 19:10) and this being admitted, how, could they have the spirit of prophecy, or be Prophets without having the testimony of Jesus? And we are told further that the Prophets sought "what manner of time the Spirit of Christ which was in them did signify, when it testified beforehand the sufferings of Christ, and the glory that should follow." (1 Peter 1:11.)

These scriptures evidently show that the testimony of Jesus was the very principle, essence and power of the spirit of prophecy whereby they were inspired.

We find a great many statements corroborative of these facts in those portions of the writings and prophecies of the ancient servants of God, that have been handed down to us in the Old Testament, and from these testimonies we select a few to show how various and how detailed have been the inspired utterances regarding the life and death of the Messiah.

"The Lord thy God will raise up unto thee a Pro[13]phet from the midst of thee, of thy brethren, like unto me, [Moses,] unto him ye shall hearken. . . . And the Lord said unto me, They have well spoken that which they have spoken. I will raise them up a Prophet from among their brethren, like unto thee, and will put my words in his mouth; and he shall speak unto them all that I shall command him. And it shall come to pass, that whosoever will not hearken unto my words which he shall speak in my name, I will require it of him." (Deuteronomy 18:15, 17-19.)

"For I know that my Redeemer liveth, and that he shall stand at the latter day upon the earth: And though after my skin worms destroy this body, yet in my flesh shall I see God: Whom I shall see for myself, and mine eyes shall behold, and not another; though my reins be consumed within me." (Job 19:25-27.)

"Why do the heathen rage, and the people imagine a vain thing? The kings of the earth set themselves, and the rulers take counsel together, against the Lord and against his Anointed, saying, Let us break their bands asunder, and cast away their cords from us. He that sitteth in the heavens shall laugh: the Lord shall have them in derision. Then shall he speak unto them in his wrath, and vex them in his sore displeasure. Yet have I set my king upon my holy hill of Zion. I will declare the decree: the Lord hath said unto me, Thou art my Son; this day have I begotten thee. Ask of me, and I shall give thee the heathen for thine inheritance, and the uttermost parts of the earth for thy possession. Thou shalt break them with a rod of iron; thou shalt dash them in pieces like a potter's vessel. Be wise now therefore, O ye kings: be instructed, ye judges of the earth. Serve the Lord with fear, and rejoice with trembling. Kiss the Son, lest he be angry, and ye perish from the way, when his wrath is kindled but a little. Blessed are all they that put their trust in him." (Psalms 2:1-12.)

While the first portion of the above psalm refers to [14] the Anointed of the Lord, and matters that would take place at His first appearing, still many of the things, therein mentioned, have not yet transpired. The same may be said of the following passages from Zechariah, which speak of His being pierced and of His rejection by the Jews as a thing accomplished, when at that time these events had not taken place. But it does prove that His people would reject and pierce Him, and that afterwards when He should come as their deliverer (like Joseph, whom his brethren sold, appeared as their deliverer in Egypt), they should look upon Him whom they had pierced.

"And I will pour upon the house of David, and upon the inhabitants of Jerusalem, the spirit of grace and of supplications: and they shall look upon me whom they have pierced, and they shall mourn for him, as one mourneth for his only son, and shall be in bitterness for him, as one that is in bitterness for his first born." (Zechariah 13:10.)

"And one shall say unto him, What are these wounds in thy hands? Then he shall answer, Those with which I was wounded in the house of my friends." (Zechariah 13:6.)

"For unto us a child is born, unto us a son is given: and the government shall be upon his shoulder: and his name shall be called Wonderful, Counsellor, The mighty God, The everlasting Father, The Prince of Peace. Of the increase of his government and peace there shall be no end, upon the throne of David, and upon his kingdom, to order it, and to establish it with judgment and with justice from henceforth even forever. The zeal of the Lord of hosts will perform this." (Isaiah 9:6-7.)

"Therefore, the Lord himself shall give you a sign; Behold, a virgin shall conceive, and bear a son, and shall call his name Immanuel." (Isaiah 7:14.)

"The Lord said unto my Lord, Sit thou at my right hand, until I make thine enemies thy footstool. The Lord shall send the rod of thy strength out of [15] Zion; rule thou in the midst of thine enemies. Thy people shall be willing in the day of thy power, in the beauties of holiness from the womb of the morning: thou hast the dew of thy youth. The Lord hath sworn and will not repent, Thou art a priest forever after the order of Melchizedek." (Psalms 110:1-4.)

"Thou lovest righteousness, and hatest wickedness: therefore God, thy God, hath anointed thee with the oil of gladness above thy fellows." (Psalms 45:7.)

"And the Redeemer shall come to Zion, and unto them that turn from transgression in Jacob, saith the Lord." (Isaiah 59:20.)

"Behold my servant, whom I uphold; mine elect, in whom my soul delighteth; I have put my Spirit upon him: he shall bring forth judgment to the Gentiles. He shall not cry, nor lift up, nor cause his voice to be heard in the street. A bruised reed shall he not break, and the smoking flax shall he not quench: he shall bring forth judgment unto truth. He shall not fail nor be discouraged, till he have set judgment in the earth: and the isles shall wait for his law. Thus saith God the Lord, he that created the heavens and stretched them out; he that spread forth the earth, and that which cometh out of it; he that giveth breath unto the people upon it, and spirit to them that walk therein: I the Lord have called thee in righteousness, and will hold thine hand, and will keep thee, and give thee for a covenant of the people, for a light of the Gentiles; to open the blind eyes, to bring out the prisoners from the prison, and them that sit in darkness out of the prison house. I am the Lord; that is my name: and my glory will I not give to another, neither my praise to graven images. Behold, the former things are come to pass, and new things do I declare: before they spring forth I tell you of them." (Isaiah 42:1-9.)

"Who hath believed our report? and to whom is the arm of the Lord revealed? For he shall grow up before him as a tender plant, and as a root out of a dry ground: he hath no form nor comeliness; and when [16] we shall see him, there is no beauty that we should desire him. He is despised and rejected of men; a man of sorrows, and acquainted with grief: and we hid as it were our faces from him; he was despised, and we esteemed him not. Surely he hath borne our griefs, and carried our sorrows: yet we did esteem him stricken, smitten of God, and afflicted. But he was wounded for our transgressions, he was bruised for our iniquities: the chastisement of our peace was upon him; and with his stripes we are healed. All we like sheep have gone astray; we have turned every one to his own way; and the Lord hath laid on him the iniquity of us all. He was oppressed, and he was afflicted, yet he opened not his mouth: he is brought as a lamb to the slaughter, and as a sheep before her shearers is dumb, so he openeth not his mouth. He was taken from prison and from judgment: and who shall declare his generation? for he was cut off out of the land of the living: for the transgression of my people was he stricken. And he made his grave with the wicked, and with the rich in his death; because he had done no violence, neither was any deceit in his mouth. Yet it pleased the Lord to bruise him; he hath put him to grief: when thou shalt make his soul an offering for sin, he shall see his seed, he shall prolong his days, and the pleasure of the Lord shall prosper in his hand. He shall see of the travail of his soul, and shall be satisfied: by his knowledge shall my righteous servant justify many; for he shall bear their iniquities. Therefore will I divide him a portion with the great, and he shall divide the spoil with the strong; because he hath poured out his soul unto death: and he was numbered with the transgressors; and he bare the sin of many, and made intercession for the transgressors." (Isaiah 53:1-12.)

"Rejoice greatly, O daughter of Zion; shout, O daughter of Jerusalem: behold, thy king cometh unto thee: he is just, and having salvation; lowly, and riding upon an ass, and upon a colt the foal of an ass." (Zechariah 9:9.) [17]

"And I said unto them, If ye think good, give me my price; and if not, forbear. So they weighed for my price thirty pieces of silver." (Zechariah 11:12.)

"When Israel was a child, then I loved him, and called my son out of Egypt." (Hosea 11:1.)

Regarding which prophecy Matthew writes, "When he arose he took the young child [Jesus] and his mother by night, and departed into Egypt: and was there until the death of Herod: that it might be fulfilled which was spoken of the Lord by the Prophet, saying, Out of Egypt have I called my Son." (Matthew 2:14-15.)

"Thus saith the Lord; A voice was heard in Ramah, lamentation, and bitter weeping; Rachel weeping for her children, refused to be comforted for her children, because they were not." (Jeremiah 31:15.)

The same evangelist refers also to the fulfilment of this prophecy: "Then Herod, when he saw that he was mocked of the wise men, was exceeding wroth, and sent forth, and slew all the children that were in Bethlehem, and in all the coasts thereof, from two years old and under, according to the time which he had diligently inquired of the wise men. Then was fulfilled that which was spoken by Jeremy the prophet, saying, In Ramah was there a voice heard, lamentation, and weeping, and great mourning, Rachel weeping for her children, and would not be comforted, because they are not." (Matthew 2:16-18.)

"But thou, Bethlehem Ephratah, though thou be little among the thousands of Judah, yet out of thee shall he come forth unto me that is to be Ruler in Israel; whose goings forth have been from of old, from everlasting." (Micah 5:2.)

"Therefore my heart is glad, and my glory rejoiceth: my flesh also shall rest in hope. For thou wilt not leave my soul in hell; neither wilt thou suffer thine Holy One to see corruption." (Psalms 16:9-10.)

This expression of the Psalmist evidently refers to the resurrection of the Son of God. It is so quoted by Paul in his sermon at Antioch: "And we declare [18] unto you glad tidings, how that the promise which was made unto the fathers, God hath fulfilled the same unto us their children, in that he hath raised up Jesus again; as it is also written in the second psalm, Thou art my Son, this day have I begotten thee. And as concerning that he raised him up from the dead, now no more to return to corruption, he said on this wise, I will give you the sure mercies of David. Wherefore he saith also in another psalm, Thou shalt not suffer thine Holy One to see corruption. For David, after he had served his own generation by the will of God, fell on sleep, and was laid unto his fathers, and saw corruption, But he, whom God raised again, saw no corruption." (Acts 13:32-37.)

"The Spirit of the Lord God is upon me; because the Lord hath anointed me to preach good tidings unto the meek; he hath sent me to bind up brokenhearted, to proclaim liberty to the captives, and the opening of the prison to them that are bound: to proclaim the acceptable year of the Lord, and the day of vengeance of our God; to comfort all that mourn; to appoint unto them that mourn in Zion, to give unto them beauty for ashes, the oil of joy for mourning, the garment of praise for the spirit of heaviness; that they might be called Trees of righteousness, The planting of the Lord, that he might be glorified." (Isaiah 61:1-3.)

This prophecy is referred to in the following incident in the life of Jesus, narrated by Luke:

"And he came to Nazareth, where he had been brought up: and, as his custom was, he went into the synagogue on the Sabbath day, and stood up for to read. And there was delivered unto him the book of the prophet Esaias. And when he had opened the book, he found the place where it was written, The Spirit of the Lord is upon me, because he hath anointed me to preach the gospel to the poor; he hath sent me to heal the brokenhearted, to preach deliverance to the captives, and recovering of sight to the blind, to set at liberty them that are bruised, to preach the acceptable year of the Lord. And he closed the book, and he gave it [19] again to the minister, and sat down. And the eyes of all them that were in the synagogue were fastened on him. And he began to say unto them, This day is this scripture fulfilled in your ears." (Luke 4:16-21.)

"Lift up your heads, O ye gates; and be ye lifted up, ye everlasting doors; and the King of glory shall come in. Who is this King of glory? The Lord strong and mighty, the Lord mighty in battle. Lift up your heads, O ye gates; even lift them up, ye ever lasting doors; and the King of glory shall come in. Who is this King of glory? The Lord of hosts, he is the King of glory. Selah." (Psalms 24:7-10.)

The above is made much more plain in the inspired version, where it appears as follows:

"Lift up your heads, O ye generations of Jacob; and be ye lifted up; and the Lord strong and mighty, the Lord mighty in battle, who is the King of glory, shall establish you for ever. And he will roll away the heavens, and will come down to redeem his people, to make you an everlasting name, to establish you upon his everlasting rock. Lift up your heads, O ye generations of Jacob; lift up your heads, ye everlasting generations and the Lord of hosts, the King of kings, even the King of glory, shall come unto you; and shall redeem his people, and shall establish them in righteousness. Selah." (JST Psalms 24:7-10.) [20]

CHAPTER 3

EXTRACTS FROM THE NEW TESTAMENT, TOUCHING THE PERSONAL HISTORY OF THE LORD JESUS CHRIST AND THE DOCTRINE OF THE ATONEMENT—REMARKS ON THE "TIMES OF REFRESHING"—RESULTS ACCRUING TO THE REDEEMER THROUGH HIS DEATH ON THE CROSS, ETC.

From the New Testament we will first introduce some texts with regard to the birth of the Savior, followed by testimonies of the Lord Jesus with regard to Himself, and afterwards give extracts from the teachings and epistles of His disciples, etc.

"Now the birth of Jesus Christ was on this wise: When as his mother Mary was espoused to Joseph, before they came together, she was found with child of the Holy Ghost. Then Joseph her husband, being a just man, and not willing to make her a public example, was minded to put her away privily. But while he thought on these things, behold, the angel of the Lord appeared unto him in a dream, saying, Joseph, thou son of David, fear not to take unto thee Mary thy wife: for that which is conceived in her is of the Holy Ghost. And she shall bring forth a son, and thou shalt call his name JESUS: for he shall save his people from their sins. Now all this was done, that it might be fulfilled which was spoken of the Lord by the prophet, saying, Behold, a virgin shall be with child, and shall bring forth a son, and they shall call his name Emmanuel, which being interpreted is, God with us." (Matthew 1:18-23.)

"And in the sixth month the angel Gabriel was sent from God unto a city of Galilee, named Nazareth, to a virgin espoused to a man whose name was Joseph, of the house of David; and the virgin's name was Mary. And the angel came in unto her, and said, Hail, thou that art highly favored, the Lord is with thee; [21] blessed art thou among women. And when she saw him, she was troubled at his saying, and cast in her mind what manner of salutation this should be. And the angel said unto her, Fear not, Mary: for thou hast found favor with God. And behold, thou shalt conceive in thy womb, and bring forth a son, and shalt call his name Jesus. He shall be great, and shall be called the Son of the Highest; and the Lord God shall give unto him the throne of his father David. And he shall reign over the house of Jacob forever; and of his kingdom there shall be no end. Then said Mary unto the angel, How shall this be, seeing I know not a man? And the angel answered and said unto her, The Holy Ghost shall come upon thee, and the power of the Highest shall overshadow thee: therefore also that holy thing which shall be born of thee, shall be called the Son of God. And behold thy cousin Elisabeth, she hath also conceived a son in her old age; and this is the sixth month with her who was called barren: for with God nothing shall be impossible. And Mary said, Behold the handmaid of the Lord, be it unto me according to try word. And the angel departed from her. And Mary arose in those days, and went into the hill-country with haste, into a city of Juda, and entered into the house of Zacharias, and saluted Elisabeth. And it came to pass, that when Elisabeth heard the salutation of Mary, the babe leaped in her womb: and Elisabeth was filled with the Holy Ghost. And she spake out with a loud voice and said, Blessed art thou among women, and blessed in the fruit of thy womb. And whence is this to me, that the mother of my Lord should come to me? For lo, as soon as the voice of thy salutation sounded in mine ears, the babe leaped in my womb for joy. And blessed is she that believed: for there shall be a performance of those things which were told her from the Lord. And blessed is she that believed: for there shall be a performance of those things which were told her from the Lord. And Mary said, My soul doth magnify the Lord, and my spirit hath rejoiced in God my Savior. For he hath regarded the low estate of his handmaiden: for behold, from henceforth all genera[22]tions shall call me blessed. For he that is mighty hath done to me great things; and holy is his name. And his mercy is on them that fear him, from generation to generation. He hath shewed strength with his arm; he hath scattered the proud in the imagination of their hearts. He hath put down the mighty from their seats, and exalted them of low degree. He hath filled the hungry with good things, and the rich he hath sent empty away. He hath holpen his servant Israel, in remembrance of his mercy; as he spake to our fathers, to Abraham, and to his seed, forever." (Luke 1:26-55.)

"And it came to pass in those days, that there went out a decree from Cesar Augustus, that all the world should be taxed. (And this taxing was first made when Cyrenius was governor of Syria.) And all went to be taxed, every one into his own city. And Joseph also went up from Galilee, out of the city of Nazareth, into Judea, unto the city of David, which is called Bethlehem (because he was of the house and lineage of David), to be taxed with Mary his espoused wife, being great with child. And so it was, that while they were there, the days were accomplished that she should be delivered. And she brought forth her first born son, and wrapped him in swaddling-clothes, and laid him in a manger: because there was no room for them in the inn. And there were in the same country shepherds abiding in the field, keeping watch over their flock by night. And lo, the angel of the Lord came upon them, and the glory of the Lord shone round about them; and they were sore afraid. And the angel said unto them, Fear not: for behold, I bring you good tidings of great joy, which shall be to all people. For unto you is born this day, in the city of David, a Savior, which is Christ the Lord. And this shall be a sign unto you; Ye shall find the babe wrapped in swaddling-clothes, lying in a manger. And suddenly there was with the angel a multitude of the heavenly host praising God, and saying, Glory to God in the Highest, and on earth peace, good will toward men. And it came to pass, as the [23] angels were gone away from them into heaven, the shepherds said one to another, Let us now go even unto Bethlehem, and see this thing which is come to pass, which the Lord hath made known unto us." (Luke 2:1-15.)

"When Jesus came into the coasts of Cesarea Philippi, he asked his disciples, saying, Whom do men say that I, the Son of man, am? And they said, Some say that thou art John the Baptist: some, Elias: and others, Jeremias, or one of the prophets. He saith unto them, But whom say ye that I am? And Simon Peter answered and said, Thou art the Christ, the Son of the living God. And Jesus answered and said unto him, Blessed art thou, Simon Bar-jona; for flesh and blood hath not revealed it unto thee, but my Father which is in heaven. . . . Then charged he his disciples that they should tell no man that he was Jesus the Christ." (Matthew 16:13-17, 20.)

Of this same conversation Mark records: "And Jesus went out, and his disciples, into the towns of Cesarea Philippi: and by the way he asked his disciples, saying unto them, Whom do men say that I am? And they answered, John the Baptist: but some say, Elias; and others, one of the prophets. And he saith unto them, But whom say ye that I am? And Peter answereth and saith unto him, Thou art the Christ, And he charged them that they should tell no man of him. And he began to teach them, that the Son of man must suffer many things, and be rejected of the elders, and of the chief priests, and scribes, and be killed, and after three days rise again. And he spake that saying openly." (Mark 7:27-32.)

Whilst Luke testifies, "And it came to pass, as he was alone praying, his disciples were with him; and he asked them, saying, Whom say the people that I am? They answering, said, John the Baptist; but some say, Elias; and others say, that one of the old prophets is risen again. He said unto them, But whom say ye that I am? Peter answering, said, The Christ of God. And [24] he straitly charged them, and commanded them to tell no man that thing, saying, The Son of man must suffer many things, and be rejected of the elders, and chief priests, and scribes, and be slain, and be raised the third day." (Luke 9:18-22.)

"For God so loved the world that he gave his only begotten Son, that whosoever believeth in him should not perish, but have everlasting life. For God sent not his Son into the world to condemn the world; but that the world through him might be saved." (John 3:16-17.)

"And he said unto them, Ye are from beneath; I am from above: ye are of this world; I am not of this world. I said therefore unto you, that ye shall die in your sins: for if ye believe not that I am he, ye shall die in your sins. Then said they unto him, Who art thou? And Jesus saith unto them, Even the same that I said unto you from the beginning. I have many things to say, and to judge of you: but he that sent me, is true; and I speak to the world those things which I have heard of him. They understood not that he spake to them of the Father. Then said Jesus unto them, When ye have lifted up the Son of man, then shall ye know that I am he, and that I do nothing of myself; but as my Father hath taught me I speak these things. And he that sent me is with me: the Father hath not left me alone; for I do always those things that please him." (John 8:23-29.)

"Then answered Jesus, and said unto them, Verily, verily, I say unto you, The Son can do nothing of himself, but what he seeth the Father do; for what things soever he doeth, these also doeth the Son likewise. For the Father loveth the Son, and sheweth him all things that himself doeth: and he will shew him greater works than these, that ye may marvel. For as the Father raiseth up the dead, and quickeneth them; even so the Son quickeneth whom he will. For the Father judgeth no man; but hath committed all judgment unto the Son: that all men should honor the Son, [25] even as they honor the Father. He that honoreth not the Son, honoreth not the Father which hath sent him. . . . But I have greater witness than that of John: for the works which the Father hath given me to finish, the same works that I do, bear witness of me, that the Father hath sent me. And the Father himself which hath sent me, hath borne witness of me. Ye have neither heard his voice at any time, nor seen his shape. And ye have not his word abiding in you: for whom he hath sent, him ye believe not. Search the scriptures; for in them ye think ye have eternal life: And they are they which testify of me. (John 5:19-23, 36-39.)

"Jesus heard that they had cast him out: and when he had found him, he said unto him, Dost thou believe on the Son of God? He answered and said, Who is he, Lord, that I might believe on him? And Jesus said unto him, Thou hast both seen him, and it is he that talketh with thee. And he said, Lord, I believe. And he worshipped him. And Jesus said, For judgment I am come into this world; that they which see not might see, and that they which see, might be made blind." (John 9:35-39.)

"I am the good shepherd, and know my sheep, and am known of mine. As the Father knoweth me, even so know I the Father: and I lay down my life for the sheep. And other sheep I have, which are not of this fold: them also I must bring, and they shall hear my voice; and there shall be one fold, and one shepherd. . . . My sheep hear my voice, and I know them, and they follow me: and I give unto them eternal life; and they shall never perish, neither shall any pluck them out of my hand. My Father, which gave them me, is greater than all;

and none is able to pluck them out of my Father's hand. I and my Father are one." (John 10:14-16, 27-30.)

"And while they abode in Galilee, Jesus said unto them, The Son of man shall be betrayed into the hands of men: and they shall kill him, and the third day [26] he shall be raised again. And they were exceeding sorry." (Matthew 17:22-23.)

Of this same prophecy Mark relates: "And they departed thence, and passed through Galilee; and he would not that any man should know it. For he taught his disciples, and said unto them, The Son of man is delivered into the hands of men, and they shall kill him; and after that he is killed, he shall rise the third day. But they understood not that saying, and were afraid to ask him." (Mark 9:30-32.)

And Luke states, "And they were all amazed at the mighty power of God. But while they wondered every one at all things which Jesus did, he said unto his disciples, Let these sayings sink down into your ears: for the Son of man shall be delivered into the hands of men. But they understood not this saying, and it was hid from them, that they perceived it not, and they feared to ask him of that saying." (Luke 9:43-45.)

"And as they were eating, Jesus took bread, and blessed it, and brake it, and gave to the disciples, and said, Take, eat; this is my body. And he took the cup, and gave thanks, and gave it to them, saying: Drink ye all of it; for this is my blood of the new testament, which is shed for many, for the remission of sins." (Matthew 26:26-28.)

"And as they did eat, Jesus took bread, and blessed, and brake it, and gave to them, and said, Take, eat: this is my body. And he took the cup, and when he had given thanks, he gave it to them: and they all drank of it. And he said unto them, This is my blood of the new testament, which is shed for many." (Mark 14:22-24.)

"And he took bread, and gave thanks, and brake it, and gave unto them, saying, This is my body which is given for you: this do in remembrance of me. Likewise also the cup after supper, saying, This cup is the new testament in my blood, which is shed for you." (Luke 22:19-20.) [27]

"For the Son of man shall come in the glory of his Father, with his angels; and then he shall reward every man according to his works" (Matthew 16:27.)

"Take heed that ye despise not one of these little ones: for I say unto you, that in heaven their angels do always behold the face of my Father which is in heaven. For the Son of man is come to save that which was lost." (Matthew 18:10-11.)

"Then the eleven disciples went away into Galilee, into a mountain where Jesus had appointed them. And when they saw him they worshipped him: but some doubted. And Jesus came and spake unto them, saying, All power is given unto me in heaven and in earth. Go ye therefore and teach all nations, baptizing them in the name of the Father, and of the Son, and of the Holy Ghost; teaching them to observe all things whatsoever I have commanded you: and lo, I am with you alway, even unto the end of the world. Amen." (Matthew 28:16-20.)

"Then said Jesus unto the twelve, Will ye also go away? Then Simon Peter answered him, Lord, to whom shall we go? thou hast the words of eternal life. And we believe, and are sure that thou art that Christ, the Son of the living God." (John 6:67-69.)

"Him, being delivered by the determinate counsel and foreknowledge of God, ye have taken and by wicked hands have crucified and slain: whom God hath raised up, having loosed the pains of death: because it was not possible that he should be holden of it." (Acts 2:23-24.)

"This Jesus hath God raised up, whereof we all are witnesses Therefore being by the right hand of God exalted, and having received of the Father the promise of the Holy Ghost, he hath shed forth this, which ye now see and hear. For David is not ascended into the heavens, but he saith himself, The Lord said unto my Lord, Sit thou on my right hand, until I make thy foes thy footstool. Therefore let all the house of Israel know assuredly, that God hath made that same Jesus [28] whom ye have crucified, both Lord and Christ." (Acts 2:32-36.)

"And now, brethren, I wot that through ignorance ye did it, as did also your rulers. But those things which God before had shewed by the mouth of all his prophets, that Christ should suffer, he hath so fulfilled. Repent ye therefore, and be converted, that your sins may be blotted out, when the times of refreshing shall come from the presence of the Lord; and he shall send Jesus Christ, which before was preached unto you; whom the heavens must receive, until the times of restitution of all things, which God hath spoken by the mouth of all his holy prophets, since the world began. For Moses truly said unto the fathers, A Prophet shall the Lord your God raise up unto you, of your brethren, like unto me; him shall ye hear in all things, whatsoever he shall say unto you. And it shall come to pass, that every soul which will not hear that Prophet, shall be destroyed from among the people Yea, and all the prophets from Samuel, and those that follow after, as many as have spoken, have likewise foretold of these days." (Acts 3:17-24.)

Does it not seem from this that these men, having committed the infamous act of crucifying Jesus, or consenting to His death, although they may have done it ignorantly, could not at that time, even by repentance and conversion, be placed in a state of salvation, but that they would have to wait until Jesus Christ should come again before their sins could be blotted out; when Jesus Christ should be sent, who before was preached unto them and whom they had crucified? Is not this the same condition that the antediluvians were in, when once the long suffering of God waited in the days of Noah, when they were cast into prison and remained there until the time when Jesus went and preached to those spirits in prison? In their day they rejected the offers of mercy through the atonement of Jesus Christ, as the Jews did in their time; but afterwards they had the same Gospel preached to them by Jesus, and those [29] Jews who had participated in those deeds, or who had consented thereto, to whom the Apostle then spake, even if they then repented, would have to wait for forgiveness and salvation until Jesus should come again. Furthermore, the Jews who will live in the times of the restitution in the last days, after the testimony of the Gospel shall have gone to the Gentiles through this same atonement, and the introduction of the Gospel, will again have it preached to them on the earth, and will, through Him, the Elias, or restorer, be gathered again to their own land.

"Be it known unto you all, and to all the people of Israel, that by the name of Jesus Christ of Nazareth, whom ye crucified, whom God raised from the dead, even by him doth this man stand here before you whole. This is the stone, which was set at naught of you builders, which is become the head of the corner. Neither is there salvation in any other: for there is none other name under heaven given among men, whereby we must be saved." (Acts 4:10-12.)

"But he (Stephen), being full of the Holy Ghost, looked up

steadfastly into heaven, and saw the glory of God, and Jesus standing on the right hand of God, and said, Behold, I see the heavens opened, and the Son of man standing on the right hand of God." (Acts 7:55-56.)

"The place of the Scripture which he read was this, He was led as a sheep to the slaughter, and like a lamb dumb before his shearer, so opened he not his mouth: in his humiliation his judgment was taken away: and who shall declare his generation? for his life is taken from the earth." (Acts 8:32-33.)

"Take heed therefore unto yourselves, and to all the flock over the which the Holy Ghost hath made you overseers, to feed the church of God, which he hath purchased with his own blood." (Acts 20:28.)

"The next day John seeth Jesus coming unto him, and saith, Behold the Lamb of God, which taketh away the sin of the world!" (John 1:29.) [30]

"For all have sinned, and come short of the glory of God; being justified freely by his grace, through the redemption that is in Christ Jesus: whom God hath set forth to be a propitiation, through faith in his blood, to declare his righteousness for the remission of sins that are past, through the forbearance of God." (Romans 3:23-25.)

"But for us also, to whom it shall be imputed, if we believe on him that raised up Jesus our Lord from the dead, who was delivered for our offences, and was raised again for our justification." (Romans 4:24-25.)

"But God commendeth his love toward us, in that while we were yet sinners, Christ died for us. Much more then, being now justified by his blood, we shall be saved from wrath through him. For if, when we were enemies, we were reconciled to God by the death of his Son; much more, being reconciled, we shall be saved by his life. And not only so, but we also joy in God, through our Lord Jesus Christ, by whom we have now received the atonement. Wherefore as by one man sin entered into the world, and death by sin; and so death passed upon all men, for that all have sinned." (Romans 5:8-12.)

"For I delivered unto you first of all that which I also received, how that Christ died for our sins according to the scriptures. And that he was buried, and that he rose again the third day according to the scriptures: and that he was seen of Cephas, then of the twelve: after that, he was seen of above five hundred brethren at once; of whom the greater part remain unto this present, but some are fallen asleep. After that, he was seen of James; then of all the apostles. And last of all he was seen of me also, as of one born out of due time. For I am the least of the apostles, that am not meet to be called an apostle, because I persecuted the church of God." (1 Corinthians 15:3-9.)

"To the praise of the glory of his grace, wherein he hath made us accepted in the Beloved: in whom we have redemption through his blood, the forgiveness of [31] sins, according to the riches of his grace." (Ephesians 1:6-7.)

"Giving thanks unto the Father, which hath made us meet to be partakers of the inheritance of the Saints in light: who hath delivered us from the power of darkness, and hath translated us into the kingdom of his dear Son: in whom we have redemption through his blood, even the forgiveness of sins: who is the image of the invisible God, the first-born of every creature. . . . And he is the head of the body, the church: who is the beginning, the first-born from the dead; that in all things he might have the pre-eminence. For it pleased the Father that in him should all fulness dwell; and, having made peace through the blood of his cross, by him to reconcile all things unto himself; by him, I say, whether they be things in earth, or things in heaven." (Colossians 1:12-15, 18-20.)

From the above passage we learn that our redemption is obtained through the blood of Jesus; that He is in the image of God; again, that He is "the first-born of every creature;" also that He is "the first-born from the dead;" and furthermore, that He stands preeminent as the representative of God in the interests of humanity pertaining to this world, or the world which is to come, and that He is the head of the Church, the Grand Medium through which all blessings flow to the human family.

"Beware lest any man spoil you through philosophy and vain deceit, after the tradition of men, after the rudiments of the world, and not after Christ. For in him dwelleth all the fulness of the Godhead bodily. And ye are complete in him, which is the head of all principality and power." (Colossians 2:8-10.)

"For there is one God, and one mediator between God and men, the man Christ Jesus; who gave himself a ransom for all, to be testified in due time." (1 Timothy 2:5-6.)

"For unto which of the angels said he at any time, Thou art my

Son, this day have I begotten thee? [32] And again, I will be to him a Father, and he shall be to me a Son? And again, when he bringeth in the first-begotten into the world, he saith, And let all the angels of God worship him." (Hebrews 1:5-6.)

"Thou hast put all things in subjection under his feet. For in that he put all in subjection under him, he left nothing that is not put under him, But now we see not yet all things put under him: but we see Jesus, who was made a little lower than the angels for the suffering of death, crowned with glory and honor; that he by the grace of God should taste death for every man. For it became him, for whom are all things, and by whom are all things, in bringing many sons unto glory, to make the Captain of their salvation perfect through sufferings." (Hebrews 2:8-10.)

Here we have something said of the results accruing to the Redeemer Himself, through His sufferings and death. He stands next to the Father, "and is on the right hand of God; angels and authorities and powers being made subject unto him." (1 Peter 3:22.) Or as He elsewhere says of Himself, "All power is given unto me, in heaven and in earth." (Matthew 28:18.) And again, it is written that He "forever sat down on the right hand of God; from henceforth expecting till his enemies be made his footstool;" (Hebrews 10:12-13) and "that at the name of Jesus every knee shall bow, of things in heaven, and things in earth, and things under the earth; and that every tongue should confess that Jesus Christ is Lord, to the glory of God the Father." (Philippians 2:10-11.)

"For such an high priest became us, who is holy, harmless, undefiled, separate from sinners, and made higher than the heavens; who needeth not daily, as those high priests, to offer up sacrifice, first for his own sins, and then for the people's: for this he did once, when he offered up himself. For the law maketh men high priests which have infirmity; but the word of the oath, which was since the law, maketh the Son, who is consecrated forevermore." (Hebrews 7:26-28.)

There is something peculiar pertaining to the expres[33]sion here used, "forevermore," which manifestly exhibits an eternal principle. We find the same expression (as elsewhere alluded to) in the Pearl of Great Price. To Adam it was said "Thou shalt do all that thou doest, in the name of the Son. And thou shalt repent, and call upon God, in the name of the Son forevermore." (Moses 5:8.) The same principle continued both on the Asiatic and on this continent; and was recognized by all men of God holding the Melchisedec Priesthood, and will be recognized throughout all time until the final consummation of all things, when every knee shall bow, and every tongue confess that Jesus is the Christ, to the glory of God, the Father.

"Neither by the blood of goats and calves, but by his own blood, he entered in once into the holy place, having obtained eternal redemption for us. For if the blood of bulls and of goats, and the ashes of an heifer sprinkling the unclean, sanctifieth to the purifying of the flesh: how much more shall the blood of Christ, who through the eternal spirit offered himself without spot to God, purge your conscience from dead works to serve the living God? . . . And almost all things are by the law purged with blood; and without shedding of blood is no remission." (Hebrews 9:12-14, 22.)

"By the which will we are sanctified through the offering of the body of Jesus Christ once for all. And every priest standeth daily ministering and offering oftentimes the same sacrifices, which can never take away sins: but this man, after he had offered one sacrifice for sins, forever sat down on the right hand of God: from henceforth expecting till his enemies be made his footstool. For by one offering he hath perfected forever them that are sanctified." (Hebrews 10:10-14.)

Or, as the thirteenth and fourteenth verses are rendered in the inspired translation: "But this man, after he had offered one sacrifice for sins for ever, sat down on the right hand of God; from henceforth to reign until his enemies be made his footstool." [34]

"Elect according to the foreknowledge of God the Father, through sanctification of the spirit, unto obedience and sprinkling of the blood of Jesus Christ: Grace unto you, and peace, be multiplied. . . . Forasmuch as ye know that ye were not redeemed with corruptible things as silver and gold, from your vain conversation received by tradition from your fathers; but with the precious blood of Christ, as of a lamb without blemish and without spot: who verily was foreordained before the foundation of the world, but was manifest in these last times for you." (1 Peter 1:2, 18-20.)

"For Christ also hath once suffered for sins, the just for the unjust, that he might bring us to God, being put to death in the flesh, but quickened by the Spirit: by which also he went and preached unto the spirits in prison; which sometime were disobedient when once the long-suffering of God waited in the days of Noah, while the ark was a preparing, wherein few, that is, eight souls, were saved by water. The like figure whereunto, even baptism, doth also now save us, (not the putting away of the filth of the flesh, but the answer of a good conscience toward God,) by the resurrection of Jesus Christ: who is gone into heaven, and is on the right hand of God; angels, and authorities, and powers, being made subject unto him." (1 Peter 3:18-22.)

"This then is the message which we have heard of him, and declare unto you, that God is light and in him is no darkness at all. If we say that we have fellowship with him, and walk in darkness, we lie, and do not the truth; but if we walk in the light, as he is in the light, we have fellowship one with another, and the blood of Jesus Christ his Son cleanseth us from all sin." (1 John 1:5-7.)

"And if any man sin, we have an advocate with the Father, Jesus Christ the righteous: And he is the propitiation for our sins: and not for ours only, but also for the sins, of the whole world." (1 John 2:1-2.) [35]

Or as it is written in the inspired translation, "But if any man sin *and repent*, we have an advocate," etc.

"And from Jesus Christ, who is the faithful Witness, and the first-begotten of the dead, and the Prince of the kings of the earth. Unto him that loved us, and washed us from our sins in his own blood." (Revelation 1:5.)

"These things, saith the Amen, the faithful and true Witness, the beginning of the creation of God." (*Ibid.* 3:14.)

"And when he had taken the book, the four beasts, and four and twenty elders fell down before the Lamb, having every one of them harps, and golden vials full of odors, which are the prayers of saints. And they sung a new song, saying, Thou art worthy to take the book, and to open the seals thereof; for thou wast slain, and hast redeemed us to God by thy blood out of every kindred, and tongue, and people, and nation; and hast made us unto our God kings and priests: and we shall reign on the earth." (*Ibid.* 5:8-10.)

Thus it would seem that the redeemed of the Lord from all nations and peoples are indebted to the Lord Jesus Christ, through His atonement, for the position that they will occupy in the state of exaltation here referred to; and if they are exalted to be kings and priests unto God, it is through the ordinances which He has appointed for the accomplishment of this object, as the wise will understand. As regards the Book mentioned in the above passage, an explanation thereof will be found in the Key to the Revelation of John. (D&C 77.)

"And it was given unto him [the Dragon] to make war with the Saints, and to overcome them; and power was given him over all kindreds, and tongues, and nations. And all that dwell upon the earth shall worship him, whose names are not written in the book of life of the Lamb slain from the foundation of the world." (Revelation 13:7-8.) [36]

CHAPTER 4

EXTRACTS FROM THE PEARL OF GREAT PRICE AND INSPIRED TRANSLATION OF GENESIS-RECORD OF MOSES REGARDING ADAM, ENOCH, NOAH, ABRAHAM AND JOSEPH, AND OF THEIR FAITH IN THE COMING OF THE SAVIOR.

We shall now introduce some extracts from the Pearl of Great Price and the Inspired Translation of the Book of Genesis, which replace some of those parts, "plain and most precious," (1 Nephi 13:26, 32) which are said to have been taken from the version of the Holy Scriptures known as King James' or the authorized version. These extracts are taken from the revelations and writings of the Prophet Joseph Smith.

"And God spake unto Moses, saying, Behold, I am the Lord God Almighty, and Endless is my name; for I am without beginning of days or end of years; and is not this Endless? And, behold, thou art my son; wherefore look, and I will show thee the workmanship of mine hands, but not all; for my works are without end, and also my words; for they never cease; wherefore, no man can behold all my works, except he behold all my glory; and no man can behold all my glory, and afterwards remain in the flesh on the earth. And I have a work for thee, Moses, my son; and thou art in the similitude of mine Only Begotten; and my Only Begotten is and shall be the Savior, for he is full of grace and truth: but there is no God beside me, and all things are present with me, for I know them all." (Moses 1:3-6.)

"And in that day the Holy Ghost fell upon Adam, which beareth record of the Father and the Son, saying, I am the Only Begotten of the Father from the beginning, henceforth and for ever, that as thou hast fallen thou mayest be redeemed; and all mankind, even as many as will." (*Ibid.* 5:9) [37]

"But God hath made known unto our fathers that all men must repent. And he called upon our father Adam by his own voice, saying, I am God: I made the world, and men before they were in the flesh. And he also said unto him, If thou wilt turn unto me, and hearken unto my voice, and believe, and repent of all thy transgressions, and be baptized, even in water, in the name of mine Only Begotten Son, who is full of grace and truth, which is Jesus Christ, the only name which shall be given under heaven, whereby salvation shall come unto the children of men, ye shall receive the gift of the Holy Ghost, asking all things in his name, and whatsoever ye shall ask, it shall be given you. And our father Adam spake unto the Lord, and said, Why is it that men must repent and be baptized in water? And the Lord said unto Adam, Behold, I have forgiven thee thy transgression in the Garden of Eden. Hence came the saying abroad among the people, That the Son of God hath atoned for original guilt, wherein the sins of the parents cannot be answered upon the heads of the children, for they are whole from the foundation of the world." (*Ibid.* 6:50-54)

"Wherefore teach it unto your children, that all men, everywhere, must repent, or they can in no wise inherit the kingdom of God, for no unclean thing can dwell there, or dwell in his presence; for, in the language of Adam, Man of Holiness is his name; and the name of his Only Begotten, is the Son of Man, even Jesus Christ, a righteous Judge who shall come in the meridian of time. Therefore I give unto you a commandment, to teach these things freely unto your children, saying, That by reason of transgression cometh the fall, which fall bringeth death, and inasmuch as ye were born into the world by water, and blood, and the spirit, which I have made, and so became of dust a living soul, even so ye must be born again into the kingdom of heaven, of water, and of the Spirit, and be cleansed by blood, even the blood of mine Only Begotten; that ye might be sanctified from all sin, and enjoy the words of eter[38]nal life in this world, and eternal life in the world to come, even immortal glory: For by the water ye keep the commandment; by the Spirit ye are justified, and by the blood ye are sanctified; therefore it is given to abide in you; the record of heaven; the Comforter; the peaceable things of immortal glory; the truth of all things; that which quickeneth all things, which maketh alive all things; that which knoweth all things, and hath all power, according to wisdom, mercy, truth, justice, and judgment. And now, behold, I say unto you, This is the plan of salvation unto all men, through the blood of mine Only Begotten, who shall come in the meridian of time." (v. 57-62.)

"And he gave unto me [Enoch] a commandment that I should baptize in the name of the Father, and of the Son, who is full of grace and truth, and the Holy Ghost, which beareth record of the Father and the Son." (Moses 7:11.)

"And behold, Enoch saw the day of the coming of the Son of Man, even in the flesh; and his soul rejoiced, saying, The Righteous is lifted up, and the Lamb is slain from the foundation of the world; and through faith I am in the bosom of the Father, and behold, Zion is with me!" (v. 47.)

"And great tribulations shall be among the children of men, but my people will I preserve; and righteousness will I send down out of heaven; and truth will I send forth out of the earth, to bear testimony of mine Only Begotten; his resurrection from the dead; yea, and also the resurrection of all men." (v. 61-62.)

"And it came to pass that Noah continued his preaching unto the people, saying, Hearken, and give heed unto my words; believe and repent of your sins, and be baptized in the name of Jesus Christ, the Son of God, even as our fathers did, and ye shall receive the Holy Ghost, that ye may have all things made manifest; and if ye do not this, the floods will come in upon you." (Moses 8:23-24.)

"And if thou shalt die, yet thou shalt possess it [39] [the land of Canaan], for the day cometh, that the Son of Man shall live; but how can he live, if he be not dead? He must first be quickened. And it came to pass that Abram looked forth and saw the days of the Son of Man, and was glad, and his soul found rest, and he believed in the Lord; and the Lord counted it unto him for righteousness." (JST Genesis 15:11-12.)

"The sceptre shall not depart from Judah, nor a lawgiver from between his feet, until Shiloh come: and unto him shall the gathering of the people be." (Genesis 49:10.)

"The Lord hath visited me [Joseph], and I have obtained a promise of the Lord, that out of the fruit of my loins the Lord will raise up a righteous branch out of my loins; and unto thee, whom my father

Jacob hath named Israel, a prophet; (not the Messiah who is called Shiloh;) and this prophet shall deliver my people out of Egypt in the days of thy bondage. And it shall come to pass that they shall be scattered again; and a branch shall be broken off, and shall be carried into a far country; nevertheless, they shall be remembered in the covenants of the Lord, when the Messiah cometh; for he shall be made manifest unto them in the latter days, in the spirit of power, and shall bring them out of darkness into light; out of hidden darkness, and out of captivity unto freedom." (JST Genesis 1:24-25.) [40]

CHAPTER 5

THE BOOK OF MORMON AND THE ATONEMENT—EXTRACTS FROM THE BOOKS OF ETHER, NEPHI, MOSIAH, ALMA, HELAMAN AND MORMON.

We next quote from the Book of Mormon, making our selections in chronological order; first from the Book of Ether, and afterwards from the records of the Nephites.

"And when he had said these words, behold, the Lord showed himself unto him [the brother of Jared], and said, Because thou knowest these things, ye are redeemed from the fall; therefore ye are brought back into my presence; therefore I show myself unto you. Behold, I am he who was prepared from the foundation of the world to redeem my people. Behold, I am Jesus Christ. I am the Father and the Son. In me shall all mankind have light, and that eternally, even they who shall believe on my name; and they shall become my sons and my daughters." (Ether 3:13-14.)

"And then cometh the New Jerusalem; and blessed are they who dwell therein, for it is they whose garments are white through the blood of the Lamb; and they are they who are numbered among the remnant of the seed of Joseph, who were of the house of Israel. And then also cometh the Jerusalem of old; and the inhabitants thereof, blessed are they, for they have been washed in the blood of the Lamb; and they are they who were scattered and gathered in from the four quarters of the earth, and from the north countries, and are partakers of the fulfilling of the covenant which God made with their father Abraham." (Ether 13:10-11.)

"Yea, even six hundred years from the time that my father left Jerusalem, a prophet would the Lord God raise up among the Jews; even a Messiah; or, in other [41] words, a Savior of the world. And he also spake concerning the prophets, how great a number had testified of these things, concerning this Messiah, of whom he had spoken, or this Redeemer of the world. Wherefore all mankind were in a lost and in a fallen state, and ever would be, save they should rely on this Redeemer. And he spake also concerning a prophet who should come before the Messiah to prepare the way of the Lord; yea, even he should go forth and cry in the wilderness, Prepare ye the way of the Lord, and make his paths straight; for there standeth one among you whom ye know not; and he is mightier than I, whose shoe's latchet I am not worthy to unloose. And much spake my father concerning this thing. And my father said he should baptize in Bethabary, beyond Jordan; and he also said he should baptize with water: even that he should baptize the Messiah with water. And after he had baptized the Messiah with water, he should behold and bear record, that he had baptized the Lamb of God, who should take away the sins of the world." (1 Nephi 10:4-10.)

"And it came to pass that the angel spake unto me again, saying, Look! And I looked and beheld the Lamb of God, that he was taken by the people; yea, the Son of the everlasting God was judged of the world; and I saw and bear record. And I, Nephi, saw that he was lifted up upon the cross, and slain for the sins of the world." (1 Nephi 11:32-33.)

"He doeth not anything, save it be for the benefit of the world; for he loveth the world, even that he layeth down his own life, that he may draw all men unto him. Wherefore he commandeth none that they shall not partake of his salvation." (2 Nephi 26:24.)

"Yea, I know that ye know, that in the body he shall show himself unto those at Jerusalem, from whence we came; for it is expedient that it should be among them; for it behoveth the great Creator that he suffereth himself to become subject unto man in the flesh, and die for all men, that all men might become subject unto him. For as death hath passed upon all men, to fulfil [42] the merciful plan of the great Creator, there must needs be a power of resurrection, and the resurrection must needs come unto man by reason of the fall; and the fall came by reason of transgression; and because man became fallen, they were cut off from the presence of the Lord." (2 Nephi 9:5-6.)

"Wherefore, I know that thou art redeemed because of the righteousness of thy Redeemer; for thou hast beheld, that in the fulness of time he cometh to bring salvation unto men. And thou hast beheld in thy youth his glory; wherefore thou art blessed even as they unto whom he shall minister in the flesh; for the Spirit is the same, yesterday, to-day, and forever. And the way is prepared from the fall of man, and salvation is free. And men are instructed sufficiently, that they know good from evil. And the law is given unto men. And by the law, no flesh is justified; or, by the law, men are cut off. Yea, by the temporal law, they were cut off; and also, by the spiritual law they perish from that which is good, and become miserable for ever Wherefore, redemption cometh in and through the Holy Messiah; for he is full of grace and truth. Behold, he offereth himself a sacrifice for sin, to answer the ends of the law, unto all those who have a broken heart and a contrite spirit; and unto none else can the ends of the law be answered. Wherefore, how great the importance to make these things known unto the inhabitants of the earth, that they may know that there is no flesh that can dwell in the presence of God, save it be through the merits, and mercy, and grace of the Holy Messiah, who layeth down his life according to the flesh, and taketh it again by the power of the Spirit, that he may bring to pass the resurrection of the dead, being the first that should rise. Wherefore he is the first fruits unto God, inasmuch as he shall make intercession for all the children of men; and they that believe in him shall be saved. And because of the intercession for all, all men come unto God; wherefore, they stand in the presence of him, to be judged of him according to the [43] truth and holiness which is in him. Wherefore, the ends of the law which the Holy One hath given, unto the inflicting of the punishment which is affixed, which punishment that is affixed is in opposition to that of the happiness which is affixed, to answer the ends of the atonement; for it must needs be, that there is an opposition in all things. If not so, my first-born in the wilderness, righteousness could not be brought to pass; neither wickedness; neither holiness nor misery; neither good nor bad. Wherefore, all things must needs be a compound in one; wherefore, if it should be one body, it must needs remain as dead, having no life, neither death, nor corruption nor incorruption, happiness nor misery, neither sense nor insensibility. Wherefore, it must needs have been created for a thing of naught; wherefore, there would have been no purpose in the end of its creation. Wherefore, this thing must needs destroy the wisdom of God, and his eternal purposes; and also, the power, and the mercy, and the justice of God. And if ye shall say there is no law, ye shall also say there is no sin. If ye shall say there is no sin, ye shall also say there is no righteousness. And if there be no righteousness, there be no happiness. And if there be no righteousness nor happiness, there be no punishment nor misery. And if these things are not, there is no God. And if there is no God, we are not, neither the earth; for there could have been no creation of things, neither to act nor to be acted upon; wherefore, all things must have vanished away. And now, my sons, I speak unto you these things, for your profit and learning; for there is a God, and he hath created all things, both the heavens and the earth, and all things that in them is; both things to act, and things to be acted upon. And to bring about his eternal purposes in the end of man, after he had created our first parents, and the beasts of the field and the fowls of the air, and in fine, all things which are created, it must needs be that there was an opposition; even the forbidden fruit in opposition to the tree of life: the one being sweet and [44] the other bitter; wherefore, the Lord God gave unto man that he should act for himself. Wherefore, man could not act for himself, save it should be that he was enticed by the one or the other. And I, Lehi, according to the things which I have read, must needs suppose, that an angel of God, according to that which is written, had fallen from heaven: wherefore, he became a devil, having sought that which was evil before God. And because he had fallen from heaven, and had become miserable for ever, he sought also the misery of all mankind. Wherefore, he said unto Eve, yea, even that old serpent, who is the devil, who is the father of all lies; wherefore he said, Partake of the forbidden fruit, and ye shall not die, but ye shall be as God, knowing good and evil. And after Adam and Eve had partaken of the forbidden fruit, they were driven out of the garden of Eden, to till the earth. And they have brought forth children; yea, even the family of all the earth. And the days of the children of men were prolonged, according to the will of God, that they might repent while in the flesh; wherefore, their state became a state of probation, and their time was lengthened, according to the commandments which the Lord God gave unto the children of men. For the gave commandment that all men must repent; for he shewed unto all men that they were lost, because of the transgression of their parents. (2 Nephi 2:3-21.)

"And now, my brethren, I have spoken plain, that ye cannot err; and as the Lord God liveth that brought Israel up out of the land of Egypt, and gave unto Moses power that he should heal the nations, after they had been bitten by the poisonous serpents, if they would cast their eyes unto the serpent which he did raise up before them, and also gave him power that he should smite the rock, and the water should come forth; yea, behold I say unto you, that as these things are true, and as the Lord God liveth, there is none other name given under heaven, save it be this Jesus Christ of whom I have spoken, whereby man can be saved. Wherefore, for [45] this cause hath the Lord God promised unto me that these things which I write, shall be kept and preserved, and handed down unto my seed, from generation to generation, that the promise may be fulfilled unto Joseph, that his seed should never perish as long as the earth should stand. Wherefore, these things shall go from generation to generation as long as the earth shall stand; and they shall go according to the will and pleasure of God; and the nations who shall possess them shall be judged of them according to the words which are written; for we labor diligently to write, to persuade our children, and also our brethren, to believe in Christ, and to be reconciled to God; for we know that it is by grace that we are saved, after all we can do. And notwithstanding we believe in Christ, we keep the law of Moses, and look forward with steadfastness unto Christ, until the law shall be fulfilled; for, for this end was the law given; wherefore, the law hath become dead unto us, and we are made alive in Christ, because of our faith; yet we keep the law because of the commandments; and we talk of Christ, we rejoice in Christ, we preach of Christ, we prophesy of Christ, and we write according to our prophecies, that our children may know to what source they may look for a remission of their sins. Wherefore, we speak concerning the law, that our children may know the deadness of the law; and they, by knowing the deadness of the law, may look forward unto that life which is in Christ, and know for what end the law was given. And after the law is fulfilled in Christ, that they need not harden their hearts against him, when the law ought to be done away." (2 Nephi 25:20-27.)

The reference, in the above quotation, to the serpent which Moses raised up before the children of Israel in the wilderness, directly confirms the statement of our Savior:

"And as Moses lifted up the serpent in the wilderness, even so must the Son of man be lifted up; that whosoever believeth in him should not perish, but have eternal life." (John 3:14-15.) [46]

We now return to our extracts from the Book of Mormon. King Benjamin teaches:

"For behold, the time cometh, and is not far distant, that with power, the Lord Omnipotent, who reigneth, who was and is from all eternity to all eternity, shall come down from heaven, among the children of men, and shall dwell in a tabernacle of clay, and shall go forth amongst men, working mighty miracles, such as healing the sick, raising the dead, causing the lame to walk, the blind to receive their sight, and the deaf to hear, and curing all manner of diseases; and he shall cast out devils, or the evil spirits which dwell in the hearts of the children of men. And lo, he shall suffer temptations, and pain of body, hunger, thirst, and fatigue, even more than man can suffer, except it be unto death: for behold, blood cometh from every pore, so great shall be his anguish for the wickedness and the abominations of his people. And he shall be called Jesus Christ, the Son of God, the Father of heaven and earth, the Creator of all things, from the beginning; and his mother shall be called Mary. And lo, he cometh unto his own, that salvation might come unto the children of men, even through faith on his name; and even after all this, they shall consider him a man, and say that he hath a devil, and shall scourge him, and shall crucify him. And he shall rise the third day from the dead; and behold, he standeth to judge the world; and behold, all these things are done, that a righteous judgment might come upon the children of men. For behold, and also his blood atcneth for the sins of those who have fallen by the transgression of Adam, who have died, not knowing the will of God concerning them, or who have ignorantly sinned. But wo, wo unto him who knoweth that he rebelleth against God; for salvation cometh to none such, except it be through repentance and faith on the Lord Jesus Christ. And the Lord God hath sent his holy prophets among all the children of men, to declare these things to every kindred, nation. and tongue, that thereby who[47]soever should believe that Christ should come, the same might receive remission of their sins, and

THE MEDIATION AND ATONEMENT 51

rejoice with exceeding great joy, even as though he had already come among them. Yet the Lord God saw that his people were a stiffnecked people, and he appointed unto them a law, even the law of Moses. And many signs, and wonders, and types, and shadows shewed he unto them, concerning his coming; and also holy prophets spake unto them concerning his coming; and yet they hardened their hearts, and understood not that the law of Moses availeth nothing, except it were through the atonement of his blood. And even if it were possible that little children could sin, they could not be saved: but I say unto you they are blessed; nor behold, as in Adam, or by nature they fall, even so the blood of Christ atoneth for their sins. And moreover, I say unto you, that there shall be no other name given, nor any other way nor means whereby salvation can come unto the children of men, only in and through the name of Christ, the Lord Omnipotent. For behold he judgeth, and his judgment is just; and the infant perisheth not that dieth in his infancy; but men drink damnation to their own souls, except they humble themselves and become as little children, and believe that salvation was, and is, and is to come, in and through the atoning blood of Christ, the Lord Omnipotent; for the natural man is an enemy to God, and has been from the fall of Adam, and will be, for ever and ever; but if he yields to the enticings of the Holy Spirit, and putteth off the natural man, and becometh a saint, through the atonement of Christ the Lord, and becometh as a child, submissive, meek, humble, patient, full of love, willing to submit to all things which the Lord seeth fit to inflict upon him, even as a child doth submit to his father. And moreover, I say unto you, that the time shall come, when the knowledge of a Savior shall spread throughout every nation, kindred, tongue, and people. And behold, when that time cometh, none shall be found blameless before God, except it be little children only [48] through repentance and faith on the name of the Lord God Omnipotent." (Mosiah 3:5-21.)

"And now, it came to pass that when king Benjamin had made an end of speaking the words which had been delivered unto him by the angel of the Lord, that he cast his eyes round about on the multitude, and behold they had fallen to the earth, for the fear of the Lord had come upon them; and they had viewed themselves in their own carnal state, even less than the dust of the earth. And they all cried aloud with one voice, saying, O have mercy, and apply the atoning blood of

Christ, that we may receive forgiveness of our sins, and our hearts may be purified; for we believe in Jesus Christ, the Son of God, who created heaven and earth, and all things; who shall come down among the children of men. And it came to pass that after they had spoken these words, the Spirit of the Lord came upon them, and they were filled with joy, having received a remission of their sins, and having peace of conscience, because of the exceeding faith which they had in Jesus Christ who should come, according to the words which king Benjamin had spoken unto them. And king Benjamin again opened his mouth, and began to speak unto them, saying, My friends and my brethren, my kindred and my people, I would again call your attention, that ye may hear and understand the remainder of my words which I shall speak unto you; for behold, if the knowledge of the goodness of God at this time has awakened you to a sense of your nothingness, and your worthless and fallen state; I say unto you, if ye have come to a knowledge of the goodness of God, and his matchless power, and his wisdom, and his patience, and his long suffering towards the children of men, and also, the atonement which has been prepared from the foundation of the world, that thereby salvation might come to him that should put his trust in the Lord, and should be diligent in keeping his commandments, and continue in the faith even unto the end of his life; I mean the life of the mortal body; I say that this is the man who receiveth [49] salvation, through the atonement which was prepared from the foundation of the world for all mankind, which ever were ever since the fall of Adam, or who are, or whoever shall be, even unto the end of the world; and this is the means whereby salvation cometh. And there is none other salvation, save this which hath been spoken of; neither are there any conditions whereby man can be saved, except the conditions which I have told you." (Mosiah 4:1-8.)

"And now Abinadi said unto them, I would that ye should understand that God himself shall come down among the children of men, and shall redeem his people; and because he dwelleth in flesh, he shall be called the Son of God: and having subjected the flesh to the will of the Father, being the Father and the Son; the Father, because he was conceived by the power of God; and the Son, because of the flesh, thus becoming the Father and Son: And they are one God, yea, the very eternal Father of heaven and of earth; and thus the flesh becoming subject to the Spirit, or the Son to the Father, being one God, suffereth temptation, and yieldeth not to the temptation, but suffereth himself to be mocked, and scourged, and cast out, and disowned by his people. And after all this, after working many mighty miracles among the children of men, he shall be led, yea, even as Isaiah said, As a sheep before the shearer is dumb, so he opened not his mouth; yea, even so he shall be led, crucified, and slain, the flesh becoming subject even unto death, the will of the Son being swallowed up in the will of the Father; and thus God breaketh the bands of death, having gained the victory over death; giving the Son power to make intercession for the children of men: having ascended into heaven; having the bowels of mercy; being filled with compassion towards the children of men; standing betwixt them and justice; having broken the bands of death, taken upon himself their iniquity and their transgressions: having redeemed them, and satisfied the demands of justice." (Mosiah 15:1-9.) [50]

"And now it came to pass that after Abinadi had spoken these words, he stretched forth his hand and said, The time shall come when all shall see the salvation of the Lord; when every nation, kindred, tongue and people shall see eye to eye, and shall confess before God that his judgments are just; and then shall the wicked be cast out, and they shall have cause to howl, and weep, and wail, and gnash their teeth; and this because they would not hearken unto the voice of the Lord; therefore the Lord redeemeth them not, for they are carnal and devilish, and the devil has power over them; yea, even that old serpent that did beguile our first parents, which was the cause of their fall: which was the cause of all mankind becoming carnal, sensual, devilish, knowing evil from good; subjecting themselves to the devil. Thus all mankind were lost; and behold, they would have been endlessly lost, were it not that God redeemed his people from their lost and fallen state. But remember, that he that persists in his own carnal nature, and goes on in the ways of sin and rebellion against God, remaineth in his fallen state, and the devil hath all power over him. Therefore he is as though there was no redemption made; being an enemy to God; and also is the devil an enemy of God. And now if Christ had not come into the world, speaking of things to come, as though they had already come, there could have been no redemption. And if Christ had not risen from the dead, or have broken the bands of death, that the grave should have no victory, and that death should have no sting, there could have been no resurrection. But there is a resurrection, therefore the grave hath no victory, and the sting of death is swallowed up in Christ: he is the light and the life of the world; yea, a light that is endless, that can never be darkened: yea, and also a life which is endless, that there can be no more death. Even this mortal shall put on immortality, and this corruption shall put on incorruption, and shall be brought to stand before the bar of God, to be judged of him according to their works, whether they be good [51] or whether they be evil. If they be good, to the resurrection of endless life and happiness, and if they be evil, to the resurrection of endless damnation; being delivered up to the devil, who hath subjected them, which is damnation; having gone according to their own carnal wills and desires; having never called upon the Lord while the arms of mercy were extended towards them; for the arms of mercy were extended towards them; and they would not; they being warned of their iniquities, and yet they would not depart from them; and they were commanded to repent, and yet they would not repent. And now had ye not ought to tremble and repent of your sins, and remember only in and through Christ ye can be saved? Therefore, if ye teach the law of Moses, also teach that it is a shadow of those things which are to come; teach them that redemption cometh through Christ the Lord, who is the very eternal Father. Amen." (Mosiah 16:1-15.)

"But behold, the Spirit hath said this much unto me, saying: Cry unto this people, saying, Repent ye, and prepare the way of the Lord, and walk in his paths, which are straight: for behold, the kingdom of heaven is at hand, and the Son of God cometh upon the face of the earth. And behold, he shall be born of Mary, at Jerusalem, which is the land of our forefathers, she being a virgin, a precious and chosen vessel, who shall be overshadowed, and conceive by the power of the Holy Ghost, and bring forth a son, yea, even the Son of God; and he shall go forth, suffering pains and afflictions, and temptations of every kind; and this that the word might be fulfilled which saith, He will take upon him the pains and the sicknesses of his people; and he will take upon him death, that he may loose the bands of death which bind his people: and he will take upon him their infirmities, that his bowels may be filled with mercy, according to the flesh, that he may know according to the flesh how to succor his people according to their infirmities. Now the Spirit knoweth all things; nevertheless, the Son of God suffereth [52] according to the flesh, that he might take upon him the sins of his people, that he might blot out their transgressions, according to the power of his deliverance; and now behold, this is the testimony which is in me." (Alma 7:9-13.)

"Now Zeezrom said unto the people, See that ye remember these things; for he said there is but one God; yet he saith that the Son of God shall come, but he shall not save his people, as though he had authority to command God. Now Amulek saith again unto him, Behold, thou hast lied, for thou sayest that I spake as though I had authority to command God, because I said he shall not save his people in their sins. And I say unto you again, that he cannot save them in their sins; for I cannot deny his word, and he hath said that no unclean thing can inherit the kingdom of heaven; therefore, how can ye be saved, except ye inherit the kingdom of heaven? Therefore, ye cannot be saved in your sins. Now Zeezrom saith again unto him, Is the son of God the very eternal Father? And Amulek said unto him, Yea, he is the very eternal Father of heaven and of earth, and all things which is them is; he is the beginning and the end, the first and the last; and he shall come into the world to redeem his people; and he shall take upon him the transgressions of those who believe on his name; and these are they that shall have eternal life, and salvation cometh to none else; therefore, the wicked remain as though there had been no redemption made, except it be the loosing of the bands of death; for behold, the day cometh that all shall rise from the dead and stand before God, and be judged according to their works. Now, there is a death which is called a temporal death: and the death of Christ shall loose the bands of this temporal death, that all shall be raised from this temporal death; the spirit and the body shall be re-united again in its perfect form; both limb and joint shall be restored to its proper frame, even as we now are at this time; and we shall be brought to stand before God, [53] knowing even as we know now, and have a bright recollection of all our guilt. Now this restoration shall come to all, both old and young, both bond and free, both male and female, both the wicked and the righteous; and even there shall not so much as a hair of their heads be lost; but all things shall be restored to its perfect frame, as it is now, or in the body, and shall be brought and be arraigned before the bar of Christ the Son, and God the Father, and the Holy Spirit, which is one eternal God, to be judged according to their works, whether they be good or whether they be evil." (Alma 11:35-44.)

"Now I say unto you, that ye must repent, and be born again: for the Spirit saith, If ye are not born again, ye cannot inherit the kingdom of heaven; therefore come and be baptized unto repentance, that ye may be washed from your sins, that ye may have faith on the Lamb of God, who taketh away the sins of the world, who is might to save and to cleanse from all unrighteousness." (Alma 7:14.)

"And the angel said unto me, Look! And I looked, and beheld three generations pass away in righteousness; and their garments were white, even like unto the Lamb of God. And the angel said unto me, These are made white in the blood of the Lamb, because of their faith in him." (1 Nephi 12:11.)

"Therefore they were called after this holy order, and were sanctified, and their garments were washed white, through the blood of the Lamb." (Alma 13:11.)

"And this I know, because the Lord hath said, He dwelleth not in unholy temples, but in the hearts of the righteous doth he dwell; yea, and he has also said, That the righteous shall sit down in his kingdom, to go no more out: but their garments should be made white, through the blood of the Lamb." (Alma 34:36.)

"O then, ye unbelieving, turn ye unto the Lord; cry mightily unto the Father in the name of Jesus, that perhaps ye may be found spotless, pure, fair and white, [54] having been cleansed by the blood of the Lamb, at that great and last day." (Mormon 9:6.)

"Behold, I give unto you a sign; for five years more cometh, and behold, then cometh the Son of God to redeem all those who shall believe on his name." (Helaman 14:2.)

"For behold, he must surely die, that salvation may come; yea, it behoveth him, and becometh expedient that he dieth, to bring to pass the resurrection of the dead, that thereby men may be brought into the presence of the Lord; yea, behold this death bringeth to pass the resurrection, and redeemeth all mankind from the first death—that spiritual death; for all mankind by the fall of Adam, being cut off from the presence of the Lord, are considered as dead, both as to things temporal and things spiritual. But behold, the resurrection of Christ redeemeth mankind, yea, even all mankind, and bringeth them back into the presence of the Lord." (Helaman 14:15-17.)

"Arise and come forth unto me, that ye may thrust your hands into my side, and also that ye may feel the print of the nails in my hands, and in my feet, that ye may know that I am the God of Israel, and the God of the whole earth, and have been slain for the sins of the world." (3 Nephi 11:14.)

"Behold, he created Adam, and by Adam came the fall of man. And because of the fall of man, came Jesus Christ, even the Father and the Son; and because of Jesus Christ came the redemption of man. And because of the redemption of man, which came by Jesus Christ, they are brought back into the presence of the Lord; yea, this is wherein all men are redeemed, because the death of Christ bringeth to pass the resurrection, which bringeth to pass a redemption from an endless sleep from which sleep all men shall be awoke by the power of God when the trump shall sound; and they shall come forth, both small and great, and all shall stand before his bar, being redeemed and loosed from this eternal band of death, which death is a temporal death; and [55] then cometh the judgment of the Holy One upon them, and then cometh the time that he that is filthy shall be filthy still; and he that is righteous shall be righteous still; he that is happy shall be happy still; and he that is unhappy shall be unhappy still. (Mormon 9:12-14.)

CHAPTER 6

Extracts from the Book of Doctrine and Covenants—Christ's Testimony of Himself, of His Power and Calling, etc.—Testimony of Joseph Smith and Sidney Rigdon—Record of John the Baptist—Extract from a Sermon by President Brigham Young.

We now turn to the Book of Doctrine and Covenants:

"Behold, I am Jesus Christ, the Son of God. I am the same that came unto my own, and my own received me not. I am the light which shineth in darkness, and the darkness comprehendeth it not." (D&C 6:21.)

"Behold, I am Jesus Christ, the Son of the living God, who created the heavens and the earth; a light which cannot be hid in darkness." (D&C 14:9.)

"Remember the worth of souls is great in the sight of God; for, behold, the Lord your Redeemer suffered death in the flesh; wherefore, he suffered the pain of all men, that all men might repent and come unto him. And he hath risen again from the dead, that he might bring all men unto him, on conditions of repentance." (D&C 18:10-12.)

"I am Alpha and Omega, Christ the Lord; yea, even I am He, the beginning and the end, the Redeemer of the world. I, having accomplished and finished the will of him whose I am, even the Father, concerning me—[56] having done this that I might subdue all things unto myself." (D&C 19:1-2.)

"I am Jesus Christ; I came by the will of the Father, and I do his will." (D&C 19:24.)

The Mediation and Atonement 59

"For, behold, I will bless all those who labor in my vineyard with a mighty blessing, and they shall believe on his words, which are given him through me by the Comforter, which manifesteth that Jesus was crucified by sinful men for the sins of the world, yea, for the remission of sins unto the contrite heart." (D&C 21:9.)

"Listen to the voice of Jesus Christ, your Redeemer, the great I AM, whose arm of mercy hath atoned for your sins." (D&C 29:1.)

"Be faithful unto the end, and lo, I am with you. These words are not of man, nor of men, but of me, even Jesus Christ, your Redeemer, by the will of the Father. Amen." (D&C 31:13.)

"My son Orson, hearken and hear and behold what I, the Lord God, shall say unto you, even Jesus Christ your Redeemer; the light and the life of the world; a light which shineth in darkness, and the darkness comprehendeth is not; who so loved the world that he gave his own life, that as many as would believe might become the sons of God: wherefore you are my son." (D&C 34:1-3.)

"Listen to the voice of the Lord your God, even Alpha and Omega, the beginning and the end, whose course is one eternal round, the same to-day as yesterday, and forever. I am Jesus Christ, the Son of God, who was crucified for the sins of the world, even as many as will believe on my name, that they may become the sons of God, even one in me as I am in the Father, as the Father is one in me, that we may be one." (D&C 35:1-2.)

"Thus saith the Lord your God, even Jesus Christ, the great I AM, Alpha and Omega, the beginning and the end, the same which looked upon the wide expanse of eternity, and all the serephic hosts of heaven, before [57] the world was made: the same which knoweth all things, for all things are present before mine eyes: I am the same which spake, and the world was made, and all things came by me: I am the same which have taken the Zion of Enoch into mine own bosom; and verily, I say, even as many as have believed in my name, for I am Christ, and in mine own name, by the virtue of the blood which I have split, have I pleaded before the Father for them; but behold, the residue of the wicked have I kept in chains of darkness until the judgment of the great day; which shall come at the end of the earth." (D&C 38:1-5.)

"Hearken and listen to the voice of him who is from all eternity to all eternity, the great I AM, even Jesus Christ, the light and the life of the world; a light which shineth in darkness and the darkness comprehendeth it not: the same which came in the meridian of time unto my own. and my own received me not." (D&C 39:1-3.)

"Listen to him who is the Advocate with the Father, who is pleading your cause before him, saying, Father, behold the sufferings and death of him who did no sin, in whom thou wast well pleased; behold the blood of thy Son which was shed—the blood of him whom thou gavest that thyself might be glorified; wherefore, Father, spare these my brethren that believe on my name, that they may come unto me and have everlasting life." (D&C 45:3-5.)

"To some it is given by the Holy Ghost to know that Jesus Christ is the Son of God, and that he was crucified for the sins of the world; to others it is given to believe on their words, that they also might have eternal life if they continue faithful." (D&C 46:13-14.)

"Hear O ye heavens, and give ear O earth, and rejoice ye inhabitants thereof, for the Lord is God, and beside him there is no Savior: Great is his wisdom, and marvellous are his ways, and the extent of his doings [58] none can find out; his purposes fail not, neither are there any who can stay his hand; from eternity to eternity he is the same, and his years never fail." (D&C 76:1-4.)

"By the power of the Spirit our eyes were opened and our understandings were enlightened, so as to see and understand the things of God—even those things which were from the beginning before the world was, which were ordained of the Father, through his Only Begotten Son, who was in the bosom of the Father, even from the beginning, of whom we bear record, and the record which we bear is the fulness of the gospel of Jesus Christ, who is the Son, whom we saw and with whom we conversed in heavenly vision." (D&C 76:12-14.)

"And while we meditated upon these things, the Lord touched the eyes of our understandings and they were opened, and the glory of the Lord shone round about; and we beheld the glory of the Son, on the right hand of the Father, and received of his fulness; and saw the holy angels and they who are sanctified before his throne, worshiping God, and the Lamb, who worship him for ever and ever. And now, after the many testimonies which have been given of him, this is the testimony last of all, which we give of him, that he lives; for we saw him, even on the right hand of God, and we heard the voice bearing record that he is the Only Begotten of the Father—that by him and through him, and of him the worlds are and were created, and the inhabitants thereof are begotten sons and daughters unto God." (D&C 76:19-24.)

"That he came into the world, even Jesus, to be crucified for the world, and to bear the sins of the world, and to sanctify the world, and to cleanse it from all unrighteousness; that through him all might be saved whom the Father had put into his power and made by him, who glorifies the Father, and saves all the works of his hands, except those sons of perdition, [59] who deny the Son after the Father has revealed him." (D&C 76:41-43.)

"These are they whose names are written in heaven, where God and Christ are the judge of all. These are they who are just men made perfect through Jesus the mediator of the new covenant, who wrought out this perfect atonement through the shedding of his own blood." (D&C 76:68-69.)

"Verily, thus saith the Lord, it shall come to pass that every soul who forsaketh their sins and cometh unto me, and calleth on my name, and obeyeth my voice, and keepeth my commandments, shall see my face and know that I am, and that I am the true light that lighteth every man that cometh into the world; and that I am in the Father, and the Father in me, and the Father and I are one: the Father because he gave me of his fulness, and the Son because I was in the world and made flesh my tabernacle, and dwelt among the sons of men. I was in the world and received of my Father, and the works of him were plainly manifest; and John saw and bore record of the fulness of my glory, and the fulness of John's record is hereafter to be revealed. . . . And I, John, saw that he received not of the fulness at the first, but received grace for grace: and he received not of the fulness at first, but continued from grace to grace, until he received a fulness; and thus he was called the Son of God, because he received not of the fulness at the first. And I, John, bear record, and lo, the heavens were opened, and the Holy Ghost descended upon him in the form of a dove, and sat upon him, and there came a voice out of heaven saying, This is my beloved Son. And I, John, bear record that he received a fulness of the glory of the Father; and he received all power, both in heaven and on earth, and the glory of the Father was with him, for he dwelt in him." (D&C 93:1-6, 12-17.)

"But, behold, I say unto you, that little children are redeemed from the foundation of the world through mine Only Begotten." (D&C 29:46.) [60]

"Every spirit of man was innocent in the beginning, and God having redeemed man from the fall, men became again in their infant state, innocent before God." (D&C 93:38.)

"And then shall the Lord set his foot upon this mount, and it shall cleave in twain, and the earth shall tremble and reel to and fro, and the heavens also shall shake, and the Lord shall utter his voice, and all the ends of the earth shall hear it; and the nations of the earth shall mourn, and they that have laughed shall see their folly, and calamity shall cover the mocker, and the scorner shall be consumed, and they that have watched for iniquity shall be hewn down and cast into the fire. And then shall the Jews look upon me and say, What are these wounds in thine hands and in they feet? Then shall they know that I am the Lord; for I will say unto them, These wounds are the wounds with which I was wounded in the house of my friends. I am he who was lifted up. I am Jesus that was crucified. I am the Son of God. And then shall they weep because of their iniquities; then shall they lament because they persecuted their King. And then shall the heather nations be redeemed, and they that knew no law shall have part in the first resurrection; and it shall be tolerable for them; and Satan shall be bound that he shall have no place in the hearts of the children of men." (D&C 45:48-55.)

From a discourse by President Brigham Young, August 8, 1852:

"Christ is the Author of this Gospel, of this earth of men and women, of all the posterity of Adam and Eve, and of every living creature that lives upon the face of the earth, that flies in the heavens, that swims in the waters, or dwells in the field. Christ is the Author of salvation to all this creation, to all things pertaining to this terrestrial globe we occupy." (Journal of Discourses, 3:80-81.) [61]

CHAPTER 7

Introduction to the Historical Portion of this Treatise—The Dealings of God with Adam, Cain and Abel—The Institution of Sacrifice—The Symbolism of this Rite—The Words of the Angel to Adam—Lucifer—His Rebellion in Heaven—His Conflict with Michael for the Body of Moses—He tempts Christ—He is cast into a Lake of Fire and Brimstone.

Having thus gathered in one numerous testimonies from the writings of the ancient inspired servants of God who dwelt on either hemisphere, and joined there—with extracts from the revelations of the present dispensation, with regard to the fore-ordination, mission, life-work and death of the Only Begotten Son, we shall now proceed to trace, from the sacred volumes, the revelation of our Savior, and the prophecy of his advent from the earliest ages of recorded history, until He fulfilled in Himself all, even all that, as offering, sacrifice, sacrament, vision or prophetic word, had foreshadowed His appearing, or typified the mystery of His all-atoning blood.

We shall commence this portion of our subject by showing that sacrifices have been offered from the very earliest times, and that when performed under divine instruction, they prefigured and typified the sacrifice of the Son of God, and that it was with this view these sacrifices were offered up.

It is recorded in the fourth chapter of the Book of Genesis that,

"Adam knew Eve, his wife; and she conceived, and bare Cain, and said, I have gotten a man from the Lord. And she again bare his brother Abel: and Abel was a keeper of sheep, but Cain was a tiller of the ground. And in process of time it came to pass, that Cain brought of the fruit of the ground an offering unto the Lord. And Abel, he also brought of the firstlings of his flock, and of the fat thereof. And the Lord [62] had respect unto Abel, and to his offering: but unto Cain, and to his offering, he had not respect." (Genesis 4:1-5.)

As these sayings found in King James' translation of the Bible are very limited, and somewhat obscure, we will here refer, as a starting point on this subject, to the account given of these events in the Pearl of Great Price, which is a selection from the revelations, translations and narrations of Joseph Smith, the Prophet, Seer and Revelator of the Church of Jesus Christ of Latter-day Saints. For in that translation it is stated that Adam, previous to these acts of Abel and Cain, offered up a sacrifice by the direct command of God. It is there written that the Lord gave unto Adam and Eve "commandments, that they should worship the Lord their God; and should offer the firstlings of their flocks for an offering unto the Lord. And Adam was obedient unto the commandments of the Lord. And after many days, an angel of the Lord appeared unto Adam, saying, Why dost thou offer sacrifices unto the Lord? And Adam said unto him, I know not, save the Lord commanded me. And then the angel spake, saying, This thing is a similitude of the sacrifice of the Only Begotten of the Father, which is full of grace and truth; wherefore thou shalt do all that thou doest in the name of the Son. And thou shalt repent, and call upon God, in the name of the Son, for evermore." (Moses 5:5-8.) We are further informed that "Adam and Eve blessed the name of God; and they made all things known unto their sons and their daughters." (v. 12.)

From the above it would seem that Adam, until instructed by the angel, did not know the reasons for the offering up of sacrifices, nor the object that the Lord had in view in requiring this offering at his hands; for, being asked by the angel why he performed this rite, he said, "I know not, save the Lord commanded me;" (v. 6) and the object of the visit of this holy being to Adam evidently was to show him why he was called to offer a sacrifice to the Lord, as, on Adam expressing his [63] ignorance of the intent of this offering, the angel stated very explicitly that this thing was "a similitude of the sacrifice of the Only Begotten of the Father." (v. 7.) We have here given a reason why Adam offered up this sacrifice. We may hereafter explain why it was necessary that the sacrifice of the Son of God should be made.

These sacrifices, which were similitudes of the sacrifice of the Only Begotten, were continued from that time until, as is stated in the Scriptures, Jesus came to offer "his own body once for all." (Hebrews 10:10.)

We will now return to the sacrifices offered by Cain and Abel, and give the statement in relation thereto contained in the Pearl of Great Price. It is as follows:

"And Cain loved Satan more than God. And Satan commanded him, saying, Make an offering unto the Lord. And in process of time it came to pass, that Cain brought of the fruits of the ground an offering unto the Lord. And Abel, he also brought, of the firstlings of his flock, and of the fat thereof; and the Lord had respect unto Abel, and to his offering; but unto Cain, and to his offering, He had not respect. Now Satan knew this, and it pleased him. And Cain was very wroth and his countenance fell. And the Lord said unto Cain, Why art thou wroth? Why is thy countenance fallen? If thou doest well, thou shalt be accepted, and if thou doest not well, sin lieth at the door, and Satan desireth to have thee, and except thou shalt hearken unto my commandments, I will deliver thee up, and it shall be unto thee according to his desire; and thou shalt rule over him, for from this time forth thou shalt be the father of his lies. Thou shalt be called Perdition, for thou wast also before the world, and it shall be said in time to come, that these abominations were had from Cain, for he rejected the greater counsel, which was had from God; and this is a cursing which I will put upon thee, except thou repent. And Cain was wroth, and listened not any more to the voice of the Lord, neither to Abel his brother, who walked in holiness before the Lord." (Moses 5:18-26) [64]

From the above it would appear that Satan, or Lucifer, was "also before the world," (v. 24) and that the term "also" refers to another personage, and that personage was the Messiah, the Christ, the Well Beloved Son, who, we are told, was the Lamb slain from before the foundation of the world; and it is obvious that Lucifer, who is elsewhere called the Son of the Morning, had an important role to play upon the earth as well as the Messiah, and that he occupied a very prominent position before the world was, and still occupies that position in opposition to his Heavenly Father, to the Son of God, and to the interests of humanity; which opposition will continue, we are informed, until he shall not only be bound, but cast into the bottomless pit; as stated by the Apostle John in the Book of Revelations:

"And I saw an angel come down from heaven, having the key of the bottomless pit and a great chain in his hand. And he laid hold on the dragon, that old serpent, which is the Devil, and Satan, and bound him a thousand years, and cast him into the bottomless pit, and shut him up, and set a seal upon him, that he should deceive the nations no more, till the thousand years should be fulfilled; and after that he must be loosed a little seasons." (Revelation 20:1-3.)

And a little further on we read that after the thousand years have passed, "Satan shall be loosed out of his prison," and shall go out to deceive the nations and gather them to battle against the Saints, when fire from heaven will devour them.

"And the devil that deceived them was cast into the lake of fire and brimstone, where the beast and the false prophet are, and shall be tormented day and night for ever and ever." (Revelation 20:10.)

The operations of Satan in opposition to the designs and purposes of God are frequently noticed in Holy Writ. Reference has already been made to his control over Cain and the results thereof, and unfortunately for them, Cain was not the only one in that early age of the world's history over whom Satan gained the mastery. [65] For he went abroad amongst the inhabitants of the earth, saying, "I am also a son of God; . . . and they loved Satan more than God. And men began, from that time forth, to be carnal, sensual, and devilish." (Moses 5:13.) And so they continued increasing in wickedness, until "all flesh had corrupted its way upon the earth," (*Ibid.* 8:29) and the waters of the flood had to accomplish the work which the preaching of Noah could not effect

In later years we hear of Satan contending with the archangel, Michael, for the body of Moses. Jude writes: "Yet Michael, the archangel, when contending with the devil, he disputed about the body of Moses, durst not bring against him a railing accusation, but said, The Lord rebuke thee." (Jude 1:9.)

This is again exhibited in the part he took in tempting the Savior, after His baptism and recognition by His Heavenly Father. Of this event it is written:

"Then was Jesus led up of the Spirit into the wilderness to be tempted of the devil. And when he had fasted forty days and forty

THE MEDIATION AND ATONEMENT 67

nights, he was afterward an hungered. And when the tempter came to him, he said, If thou be the Son of God, command that these stones be made bread. But he answered and said, It is written, Man shall not live by bread alone, but by every word that proceedeth out of the mouth of God. Then the devil taketh him up into the holy city, and setteth him on a pinnacle of the temple. And saith unto him, If thou be the Son of God, cast thyself down, for it is written, He shall give his angels charge concerning thee, and in their hands they shall bear thee up, lest at any time thou dash thy foot against a stone. Jesus said unto him, It is written again, Thou shalt not tempt the Lord thy God. Again, the devil taketh him up into an exceeding high mountain, and showeth him all the kingdoms of the world, and the glory of them; and saith unto him, All these things will I give thee if thou wilt fall down and worship me. Then saith Jesus unto him, Get thee hence, Satan: for it is written. Thou [66] shalt worship the Lord thy God, and him only shalt thou serve. Then the devil leaveth him; and behold, angels came and ministered unto him." (Matthew 4:1-11.)

Or to give the words of the inspired translation: "Then Jesus was led up of the Spirit into the wilderness, to be with God. And when he had fasted forty days and forty nights, and had communed with God, he was afterwards an hungered, and was left to be tempted of the devil. And when the tempter came to him, he said, If thou be the Son of God, command that these stones be made bread. But Jesus answered and said, It is written, Man shall not live by bread alone, but by every word that proceedeth out of the mouth of God." (JST Matthew 4:1-4.)

"Then Jesus was taken up into the holy city, and the Spirit setteth him on the pinnacle of the temple. Then the devil came unto him and said, If thou be the Son of God, cast thyself down, for it is written, He shall give his angels charge concerning thee, and in their hands they shall bear thee up, lest at any time thou dash thy foot against a stone. Jesus said unto him, It is written again, Thou shalt not tempt the Lord thy God." (v. 5-7.)

"And again, Jesus was in the Spirit, and it taketh him up into an exceeding high mountain, and showed him all the kingdoms of the world and the glory of them. And the devil came unto him again, and said, All these things will I give unto thee, if thou wilt fall down and worship me. Then said Jesus unto him, Get thee hence, Satan; for it is written, Thou shalt worship the Lord thy God, and him only shalt thou serve. Then the devil leaveth him." (v. 8-10.)

Again, John in the Revelations, when referring to the latter days, exclaims, "Wo to the inhabitants of the earth, and of the sea! for the devil is come down unto you, having great wrath, because he knoweth he hath but a short time." (Revelation 12:12.) And by and by the same writer tells us, in a passage already quoted, that Satan's time is finished, and he is bound and cast into the bottomless pit. [67]

CHAPTER 8

SETH—HIS SACRIFICE ACCEPTED—REBELLION IN THE HEAVENS—THE GATHERING OF THE PATRIARCHS IN THE VALLEY OF ADAM-ONDI-AHMAN—SACRIFICES OFFERED THERE.

The next eminent personage that appears is Seth. Concerning him, it is said in the Old Testament:

"And Adam knew his wife again, and she bare a son, and called his name Seth: For God, said she, hath appointed me another seed instead of Abel, whom Cain slew." (Genesis 4:25.)

There is a principle developed here pertaining to the economy of God with the human family. Abel held a representative position, as also did Cain, and that position, it would seem, associated Abel with what may be denominated the chosen seed. Cain slew Abel; but that the purposes relating to the perpetuation of that seed might stand, and the plan of God not be frustrated by the adversary, He gave to Adam Seth, who inherited the priesthood and promises of his martyred brother; in this substantiating a principle that Paul refers to, when he writes, "That the purpose of God, according to election, might stand, not of works, but of him that calleth." (Romans 9:11.) Yet, although Seth was one of the leading characters spoken of in the Scripture, and one to whom and through whom the promises were made, and who actually stood in the place of or represented his brother, Abel, yet there is nothing said in the ordinary translation pertaining to his offering sacrifices; we therefore again refer to the Pearl of Great Price. It is there stated that "Adam glorified the name of God, for he said, God hath appointed me another seed instead of Abel, whom Cain slew. And God revealed himself unto Seth, and he rebelled not, but offered an acceptable sacrifice like unto his brother Abel." (Moses 6:2-3.) [68]

Seth, we are here told, rebelled not, but offered an acceptable sacrifice, thus carrying out the same idea of the atonement of the Only Begotten. In this connection we must remember that there had been a rebellion in heaven, and many of the angels, they "which kept not their first estate," (Jude 1:6) were cast out. Lucifer was the leader of these rebellious ones who were then cast down to the earth. He had rebelled against God, his Father, and it would seem, from revelations that we shall hereafter draw attention to, that his rebellion had its origin in his rejection of the counsel given to him by his Father pertaining to the salvation and exaltation of mankind. When man was placed upon the earth, Lucifer, or Satan, still manifested the same animus and spirit; and through his influence he operated upon Cain, for Cain listened to his wiles, and being controlled by him, he also rebelled against his father and his God. Thus the rebellion in the heavens was transmitted to a rebellion on the earth, and all who became subject to this influence placed themselves in a state of enmity and antagonism to God, and one of the first results exhibited was covetousness and murder, even the murder by Cain of his brother Abel. Thus we find the first man slain (Abel) was one holding the holy Priesthood, and the same vindictive spirit manifested against the servants of God of all later ages, gave the martyr Stephen good reason to ask his persecutors,

"Which of the prophets have not your fathers persecuted? and they have slain them which showed before of the coming of the Just One; of whom ye have been now the betrayers and murderers." (Acts 7:52.)

Although there is nothing said in the Book of Genesis in relation to sacrifices offered up by Enos, who was the son of Seth, nor by his descendants, Canaan, Mahalaleel, Jared, Enoch and Methuselah, all of whom held the High Priesthood, and were consequently prophets of the Lord, yet it is quite reasonable to suppose that they, being of the promised seed through whom the Messiah was to come, did offer up sacrifices as com[69]memorative of that great promised event. Further, in relation to this subject, we are informed in the Book of Doctrine and Covenants that "three years previous to the death of Adam, he called Seth, Enos, Cainan, Mahalaleel, Jared-Enoch and

Methuselah [the persons mentioned above,] who were all High Priests, with the residue of his posterity who were righteous, into the valley of Adam-ondi-Ahman, and there bestowed upon them his last blessing. And the Lord appeared unto them, and they rose up and blessed Adam, and called him Michael, the Prince, the Archangel. And the Lord administered comfort unto Adam, and said unto him, I have set thee to be at the head—a multitude of nations shall come of thee, and thou art a prince over them for ever. And Adam stood up in the midst of the congregation, and notwithstanding he was bowed down with age, being full of the Holy Ghost, predicted whatsoever should befall his posterity unto the latest generation. These things were all written in the Book of Enoch, and are to be testified of in due time." (D&C 107:53-57.)

Although, in the above, there is nothing directly said about the offering of sacrifices, yet, as this was a usual ceremony, and it belonged to the Priesthood and to the promised seed to offer sacrifices, it would be reasonable to suppose that Adam did then and there officiate in that rite; indeed, it was stated by the Prophet Joseph Smith, in our hearing while standing on an elevated piece of ground or plateau near Adam-ondi-Ahman[1] (Davis Co., Missouri), where there were a number of rocks piled together, that the valley before us was the valley of Adam-ondi-Ahman; or in other words, the valley where God talked with Adam, and [70] where he gathered his righteous posterity, as recorded in the above revelation, and that this pile of stones was an altar built by him when he offered up sacrifices, as we understand, on that occasion. If Adam then offered up sacrifices in the presence of these prominent men, he being the President of these High Priests, he would officiate for them as well as for himself; while it is quite reasonable to believe that they assisted in the offerings made upon that altar. Regarding this the Saints sing:

This earth was once a garden place,
With all her glories common,
And men did live a holy race,

---

[1] "Revelation to Joseph, the Seer, given near Wight's Ferry, at a place called Spring Hill, Davis County, Missouri, May 29th, 1838, wherein Spring Hill is named by the Lord, Adam-ondi-Ahman, Because, said he, it is the place where Adam shall come to visit his people, or the Ancient of days shall sit, as spoken of by Daniel the Prophet." (D&C 116.)

And worship Jesus face to face,
In Adam-ondi-Ahman.
We read that Enoch walk'd with God,
Above the power of mammon,
While Zion spread herself abroad,
And Saints and angels sung aloud,
In Adam-ondi-Ahman.
Her land was good and greatly blest,
Beyond old Israel's Canaan;
Her fame was known from east to west,
Her peace was great, and pure the rest
Of Adam-ondi-Ahman.
Hosannah to such days to come—
The Savior's second coming,
When all the earth in glorious bloom,
Affords the Saints a holy home,
Like Adam-ondi-Ahman. [71]

CHAPTER 9

Enoch, his Life and Translation—References to Him by Paul and Jude—Copious Extracts from His Prophecy—The Prophet Joseph Smith on Enoch and the Doctrine of Translation—The Office of Translated Saints—Enoch's Future Work—Translation and Resurrection—Christ the Creator—Summary of the Results of Enoch's Faith in the Saving Blood of Christ.

We next come to Enoch, who presents a very important figure among the antediluvians, and of whom there are some very marvelous things related. The Bible record of him is as follows:

"And Jared lived an hundred, sixty and two years, and he begat Enoch. . . . And Enoch lived sixty and five years, and begat Methuselah: and Enoch walked with God after he begat Methuselah three hundred years, and begat sons and daughters; and all the days of Enoch were three hundred, sixty and five years; and Enoch walked with God, and he was not; for God took him." (Genesis 5:18, 21-24.)

This is certainly a very meager history of so great a personage, and to supply the deficiency we must have recourse to other testimonies: one important fact, however, is here stated, that "he walked with God;" another is, that "God took him." There was evidently a book written by this Patriarch, which is called the Book of Enoch, for Jude says;

"And Enoch also, the seventh from Adam, prophesied of these, saying, Behold, the Lord cometh with ten thousand of his saints, to execute judgment upon all, and to convince all that are ungodly among them of all their ungodly deeds which they have ungodly committed, and of all their hard speeches which ungodly sinners have spoken against him." (Jude 1:14-15.)

From the above it would seem that not only had Enoch written a book, but that Jude had access to it; [72] or if not had had a communication or revelation from Enoch, as referred to by Joseph Smith, hereafter, for we discover that he had a knowledge of the Son of God, the Messiah. It is true, the Only Begotten, as He is spoken of elsewhere, is not here mentioned, but only the Lord is referred to; yet the circumstances connected therewith are indicative of it being that personage; for Paul expresses the same sentiment in regard to the second coming of the Messiah, and says:

"And to you, who are troubled, rest with us, when the Lord Jesus shall be revealed from heaven with his mighty angles, in flaming fire taking vengeance on them that know not God, and that obey not the gospel of our Lord Jesus Christ: who shall be punished with everlasting destruction from the presence of the Lord, and from the glory of his power; when he shall come to be glorified in his saints, and to be admired in all them that believe (because our testimony among you was believed) in that day." (2 Thessalonians 1:7-10.)

Moreover, Jesus Himself makes the following remarks concerning the same subject:

"When the Son of man shall come in his glory, and all the holy angels with him, then shall he sit upon the throne of his glory: and before him shall be gathered all nations: and he shall separate them one from another, as a shepherd divideth his sheep from the goats." (Matthew 25:31-32.)

Thus showing that it was the same personage that was referred to by Enoch.

Paul, in his epistle to the Hebrews, writes:

"By faith Enoch was translated, that he should not see death; and was not found, because God had translated him; for before his translation he had this testimony, that he pleased God." (Hebrews 11:5.)

These declarations are very strongly corroborated by the following extracts from a revelation given to the Prophet Joseph Smith, relating to the prophecy of Enoch, and published in the Pearl of Great Price:

"And from that time forth Enoch began to pro[73]phesy, saying unto the people, That, as I was journeying, and stood in the place

Mahujah, and cried unto the Lord, there came a voice out of heaven, saying, Turn ye, and get ye upon the Mount Simeon. And it came to pass that I turned and went up on the mount; and as I stood upon the mount, I beheld the heavens open, and I was clothed upon with glory, and I saw the Lord; and he stood before my face, and he talked with me, even as a man talketh one with another, face to face; and he said unto me, Look, and I will show unto thee the world the world for the space of many generations.... And the Lord said unto me, Go forth to this people and say unto them, Repent, lest I come out and smite them with a curse, and they die. And he gave unto me a commandment that I should baptize in the name of the Father, and of the Son, who is full of grace and truth, and the Holy Ghost, which beareth record of the Father and the Son. And it came to pass that Enoch continued to call upon all the people, save it were the people of Cainan, to repent; and so great was the faith of Enoch, that he led the people of God, and their enemies came to battle against them; and he spake the word of the Lord, and the earth trembled, and the mountains fled, even according to his command; and the rivers of water were turned out of their course; and the lions was heard out of the wilderness; and all nations feared greatly.... And there went forth a curse upon all the people who fought against God; and from that time forth there were wars and bloodshed among them; but the Lord came and dwelt with his people, and they dwelt with his people, and they dwelt in righteousness. And the fear of the Lord was upon all nations, so great was the glory of the Lord, which was upon his people.... And it came to pass that Enoch talked with the Lord; and he said unto the Lord, Surely, Zion shall dwell in safety for ever. But the Lord said unto Enoch, Zion have I blessed, but the residue of the people have I cursed. And it came to pass that the Lord showed [74] unto Enoch all the inhabitants of the earth; and he beheld, and lo, Zion, in process of time, was taken up into heaven! And the Lord said unto Enoch, Behold mine abode for ever." (Moses 7:2-4, 10-13, 15-17, 20-21.)

The Prophet Joseph Smith, when speaking of Enoch and his people and the doctrine of translation, said;

"If Cain had fulfilled the law of righteousness as did Enoch, he would have walked with God all the days of his life, and never failed of a blessing. Genesis 5: 22: 'And Enoch walked with God after he begat Methuselah three hundred years, and begat sons and daughters; and all the days of Enoch walked with God and he was not, for God took him.' Now this Enoch God reserved unto Himself, that he should not die at that time, and appointed unto him a ministry unto terrestrial bodies, of whom there has been but little revealed. He is reserved also unto the Presidency of a dispensation, and more shall be said of him and terrestrial bodies in another treatise. He is a ministering angel, to minister to those who shall be heirs of salvation, and appeared unto Jude as Abel did unto Paul: therefore Jude spoke of him, 14th and 15th verses: 'And Enoch, the seventh from Adam, revealed these sayings: Behold, the Lord cometh with ten thousand of his Saints.'

"Paul was also acquainted with this character, and received instructions from him: Hebrews 11:5: 'By faith Enoch was translated, that he should not see death, and was not found, because God had translated him; for before his translation he had this testimony, that he pleased God; but without faith it is impossible to please him, for he that cometh to God must believe that he is, and that he is a revealer to those who diligently seek him.'

"Now the doctrine of translation is a power which belongs to this Priesthood. There are many things which belong to the powers of the Priesthood and the Keys thereof, that have been kept hid from before the foun[75]dation of the world; they are hid from the wise and prudent, to be revealed in the last times.

"Many may have supposed that the doctrine of translation was a doctrine of translation was a doctrine whereby men were taken immediately into the presence of God, and into an eternal fulness, but this is a mistaken idea. Their place of habitation is that of the terrestrial order, and a place prepared for such characters He held in reserve to be ministering angels unto many planets, and who as yet have not entered into so great a fulness as those who are resurrected from the dead. See Hebrews 11, part of 35th verse, 'Others were tortured, not accepting deliverance, that they might obtain a better resurrection.'

"Now it is evident that there was a better resurrection, or else God would not have revealed it unto Paul. Wherein then can it be said a better resurrection? This distinction is made between the doctrine of the actual resurrection and translation: translation obtains deliverance from the tortures and sufferings of the body, but their existence will prolong as to the labors and toils of the ministry, before they can enter into so great a rest and glory.

"On the other hand, those who were tortured, not accepting deliverance, received an immediate rest from their labors. See Revelations, 14:13: 'And I heard a voice from heaven, saying, Blessed are the dead who die in the Lord, for from henceforth they do rest from their works do follow them.'

"They rest from their labors for a long time, and yet their work is held in reserve for them, that they are permitted to do the same works after they receive a resurrection for their bodies." (History of Joseph Smith, Deseret News, Vol. 4, No. 30; or Teachings of the Prophet Joseph Smith, 169-171.)

"He [President Joseph Smith] explained the difference between an angel and a ministering spirit; the one a resurrected or translated body, with its spirit, ministering to embodied spirits; the other a disembodied spirit, visiting or ministering to disembodied spirits. Jesus Christ became a ministering spirit (while his body was [76] lying in the sepulchre) to the spirits in prison, to fulfil an important part of his mission, without which he could not have perfected his work, nor entered into his rest. After his resurrection he appeared as an angel to his disciples, &c. Translated bodies cannot enter into rest until they have undergone a change equivalent to death. Translated bodies are designed for future missions.

"The angel that appeared to John on the Isle of Patmos was a translated or resurrected body. Jesus Christ went in body, after his resurrection, to minister to translated and resurrected bodies. There has been a chain of authority and power from Adam down to the present time." (History of Joseph Smith, Deseret News, Vol. 5, No. 11; or Teachings of the Prophet Joseph Smith, 191.)

It would appear that the translated residents of Enoch's city are under the direction of Jesus, who is the Creator of worlds; and that He, holding the keys of the government of other worlds, could, in His administrations to them, select the translated people of Enoch's Zion, if He thought the medium of the Holy Priesthood to act as ambassadors, teachers, or messengers to those worlds over which Jesus holds the authority. We read in the Times and Seasons:

"Truly Jesus Christ created the worlds, and is Lord of Lords, and, as the Psalmist said, 'judges among the Gods.' Then Moses might have said with propriety, he is the 'living God,' and Christ, speaking of the flesh, could say, I am the Son of Man; and Peter, enlightened by the Holy Ghost, Thou art the Son of the living God, meaning our Father in Heaven, and who, with Jesus Christ His first begotten Son, and the Holy Ghost, are one in power, one in dominion, and one in glory, constituting the First Presidency of this system and this eternity. But they are as much three distinct persons as the sun, moon and earth are three different bodies.

"And again, the 'twelve kingdoms' which are under [77] the above-mentioned Presidency of the Father. Son and Holy Ghost, are governed by the same rules, and destined to the same honor. For, 'Behold, I will liken these kingdoms unto a man having a field, and he sent forth his servants into the field, to dig in the field; and he said unto the first, Go ye and labor in the field, and in the first hour I will come unto you, and ye shall behold the joy of my countenance: and he said unto the second, Go ye also into the field, and in the second hour I will visit you with the joy of my countenance; and also unto the third, saying, I will visit you; and unto the fourth, and so on unto the twelfth.' (D&C 88:51-55.)"

It is further stated in this section: "Therefore, unto this parable will I liken all these kingdoms, and the inhabitants thereof; every kingdom in its hour, and in its time, and in its season; even according to the decree which God hath made." (v. 61.)

That is, each kingdom, or planet, and the inhabitants thereof, were blessed with the visits and presence of their Creator, in their several times and seasons.

It is recorded that to Jesus has been given all power in heaven and in earth, and from the foregoing quotations He evidently had power which He used to commission the citizens of the Zion of Enoch to go to other worlds on missions. In an extract from the teachings of the Prophet Joseph (elsewhere inserted) it is written:

"Elijah was the last prophet that held the keys of this Priesthood, and who will, before the last dispensation, restore the authority and deliver the keys of this Priesthood, in order that all the ordinances may be attended to in righteousness. It is true that the Savior had authority and power to bestow this blessing; but the sons of Levi were too prejudiced." (History of Joseph Smith, Deseret News, Vol 4, No. 30; or Teachings of the Prophet Joseph Smith, 172.)

The Mediation and Atonement

Here Jesus paid deference to the Priesthood, who held keys relating to the ministration of its powers and [78] blessings, but it is not unreasonable to suppose, when other worlds are concerned, over whom also He holds the keys of salvation, that these considerations would not necessarily interpose, and that He would send or commission members of the translated Priesthood of Enoch's Zion amongst terrestrial worlds whithersoever it pleased Him, in the interests of the peoples thus situated.

We now resume our extracts from the prophecy of Enoch;

"And Enoch beheld angels descending out of heaven, bearing testimony of the Father and of the Son; and the Holy Ghost fell on many, and they were caught up by the power of heaven into Zion. . . .

"And it came to pass that Enoch looked; and from Noah, he beheld all the families of the earth; and he cried unto the Lord, saying, When shall the day of the Lord come? When shall the blood of the Righteous be shed, that all they that mourn may be sanctified, and have eternal life? And the Lord said, It shall be in the meridian of time, in the days of wickedness and vengeance. And behold, Enoch saw the day of the coming of the Son of Man, even in the flesh; and his soul rejoiced, saying, The Righteous is lifted up, and the Lamb is slain from the foundation of the world; and through faith I am in the bosom of the Father, and behold, Zion is with me! . . . .

"Enoch continued his cry unto the Lord, saying, I ask thee, O Lord, in the name of thine Only Begotten, even Jesus Christ, that thou wilt have mercy upon Noah and his seed, that the earth might never more be covered by the floods? And the Lord could not withhold; and he covenanted with Enoch, and sware unto him with an oath, that he would stay the floods; that he would call upon the children of Noah; and he sent forth an unalterable decree, that a remnant of his seed should always be found among all nations, while the earth should stand; and the Lord said, Blessed is he through whose seed Messiah shall come; for he saith, I [79] am Messiah, the King of Zion, the Rock of Heaven, which is broad as eternity; and whoso cometh in at the gate and climbeth up by me, shall never fall. . . .

"And the Lord said unto Enoch, Look; and he looked and beheld the Son of Man lifted up on the cross, after the manner of men; and he heard a loud voice; and the heavens were veiled; and all the creations of God mourned; and the earth groaned; and the rocks were rent; and the Saints arose, and were crowned at the right hand of the Son of Man, with crowns of glory; and as many of the spirits as were in prison came forth, and stood on the right hand of God; and the remainder were reserved in chains of darkness until the judgment of the great day. . . .

"And it came to pass that Enoch saw the day of the coming of the Son of Man, in the last days, to dwell on the earth in righteousness for the space of a thousand years. . . .

"And the Lord showed Enoch all things, even unto the end of the world; and he saw the day of the righteous, the hour of their redemption, and received a fulness of joy; and all the days of Zion, in the days of Enoch, were three hundred and sixty-five years; and Enoch and all his people walked with God, and he dwelt in the midst of Zion; and it came to pass that Zion was not, for God received it up into his own bosom; and from thence went forth the saying, Zion is fled." (Moses 7:27, 45-47, 50-53, 55-57, 65, 67-69.)

From the foregoing extracts we learn amongst other truths, all based upon Enoch's faith in the atoning blood of the Lamb slain from before the foundation of the world, the following:

That Enoch was clothed with glory and saw the Lord, who talked with Him as one man talks with another, even face to face.

That the Lord commanded Enoch to preach repentance; and to baptize in the name of the Father, and the Son, which is full of grace and truth, and the Holy Spirit, which bears record of the Father and the Son. [80]

That so great was the faith of Enoch that he led the people of God, overthrew their enemies, and at his word the earth trembled, whilst the mountains, rivers and seas obeyed his command.

That through this faith Enoch saw the days of the coming of the Son of Man in the flesh, and by it he obtained a covenant from the Lord that after Noah's day He would never again cover the earth by a flood, and obtained an unalterable decree that a remnant of his seed should always be found among all nations while the earth should stand.

That the Lord showed Enoch the world and its future history for the space of many generations, even unto the end of the world.

That so great was the faith and righteousness of Enoch and his people, that the Lord came down and dwelt with them, and in process of time Enoch's City, Zion, was taken up into heaven, and many, through the testimony of the Father and the Son, were afterwards caught up by the powers of Heaven into Zion.

And, further, that while Enoch, through the favor of the Almighty, not only had a mission to preach the Gospel and to gather the people, but that he was also empowered to have the people that he had thus gathered, and taught and instructed in the laws of life, and the city in which they dwelt, translated and taken into the latter times, while the threatened calamities should overtake the world. But he also further obtained a promise that the future peopling of the earth should come through his seed; thus making him one of the great agencies to administer salvation in the heavens and upon the earth. [81]

CHAPTER 10

Noah—His Sacrifice—God's Covenant with Him—Melchizedek—His Priesthood—Its Powers—Instances thereof Recorded in the Bible, in the Book of Mormon and in Latter-days—All Power of the Priesthood the Result of Faith in Christ and Impossible without the Atonement—The Power of the Priesthood the Power of God—The Glory of God in the Immortality of Man—Christ the Word, the Creator.

After the waters of the flood had subsided, we are told, Noah and his family came forth out of the ark:

"And Noah built an altar unto the Lord, and took of every clean beast and of every clean fowl, and offered burnt offerings on the altar. And the Lord smelled a sweet savour: and the Lord said in his heart, I will not again curse the ground any more for man's sake; for the imagination of man's heart is evil from his youth: neither will I again smite any more every thing living, as I have done. While the earth remaineth, seed-time and harvest, and cold and heat, and summer and winter, and day and night, shall not cease." (Genesis 8:20-22.)

The details of this act are given us somewhat differently in the inspired translation: it is there written:

"And Noah built an altar unto the Lord, and took of every clean beast, and of every clean fowl, and offered burnt offerings on the altar; and gave thanks unto the Lord, and rejoiced in his heart. And the Lord spake unto Noah, and he blessed him. And Noah smelt a sweet savour, and he said in his heart, I will call on the name of the Lord, that he will not again curse the ground any more for man's sake, for the imagination of man's heart is evil from his youth; and that he will not smite any more every thing living, as he hath done, while the earth remaineth; and that seed time and harvest, and cold and heat, and summer and [82] winter, and day and night may not cease with man." (JST Genesis 9:4-7.)

Thus, we discover that the first act after the destruction of the world by a flood was a recognition of the great expiatory principle of the atonement, which was to be made by the Only Begotten Son of God, as revealed by the angel to Adam. And as God recognized Adam's and Abel's offerings, so He also recognized that of Noah: and as a result, the Patriarch obtained great promises, in which the people of all ages, then to come, would be interested. For "God spake unto Noah, and to his sons with him, saying, And I, behold, I will establish my covenant with you, which I made unto your father Enoch, concerning your seed after you. And it shall come to pass, that every living creature that is with you, of the fowl, and of the cattle, and of the beast of the earth that is with you, which shall go out of the ark, shall not altogether perish: neither shall all flesh be cut off any more by the waters of a flood; neither shall there any more be a flood to destroy the earth. And I will establish my covenant with you, which I made unto Enoch, concerning the remnants of your posterity. And God made a covenant with Noah, and said, This shall be the token of the covenant I make between me and you, and for every living creature with you, for perpetual generations, I will set my bow in the cloud, and it shall be for a token of a covenant between me and the earth. And it shall come to pass, when I bring a cloud over the earth, that the bow shall be seen in the cloud; and I will remember my covenant, which I have made between me and you, for every living creature of all flesh. And the waters shall no more become a flood to destroy all flesh. And the bow shall be in the cloud; and I will look upon it, that I may remember the everlasting covenant, which I made unto thy father Enoch; that, when men should keep all my commandments, Zion should again come on the earth, the city of Enoch, which I have caught up unto myself. And this is mine everlasting covenant, [83] that when thy posterity shall embrace the truth, and look upward, then shall Zion look downward, and all the heavens shall shake with gladness, and the earth shall tremble with joy; and the general assembly of the Church of the First-born shall come down out of heaven and possess the earth, and shall have place until the end come. And this is mine everlasting covenant, which I made with thy father Enoch. And the bow shall be in the cloud, and I will establish my covenant unto thee, which I have made between me and thee, for every living creature of all flesh that shall be upon the earth." (JST Genesis 9:15-24.)

We will now turn to Melchizedek, of whom it is written in King James' translation:

"And Melchizedek, king of Salem, brought forth bread and wine: and he was the priest of the most high God. And he blessed him, and said, Blessed be Abram of the most high God, possessor of heaven and earth: and blessed be the most high God, which hath delivered thine enemies into thy hand. And he gave him tithes of all." (Geneses 14:18-20.)

This passage is given with greater completeness in the inspired translation, where it appears as follows: "And Melchizedek, King of Salem, brought forth bread and wine; and he brake bread and blessed it; and he blessed the wine, he being the priest of the Most High God; and he gave to Abram, and he blessed him, and said, Blessed Abram, thou art a man of the Most High God, possessor of heaven and of earth; and blessed is the name of the Most High God, which hath delivered thine enemies into thine hand. And Abram gave him tithes of all he had taken." (JST Genesis 14:17-20.)

In this action of Melchizedek, in administering the bread and wine, by virtue of his priestly office, is there not a representation of the body and blood of our Lord and Savior Jesus Christ, as also indicated by the Messiah Himself when He partook of the passover with His disciples? For Melchizedek was a great High Priest, of the same order and like Priesthood as was held by the [84] Son of God. So great, indeed, that "before his day it was called the Holy Priesthood, after the order of the Son of God; but out of respect or reverence to the name of the Supreme Being, to avoid the too frequent repetition of his name, they, the church, in ancient days, called that Priesthood after Melchizedek, or the Melchizedek Priesthood." (D&C 107:3-4.)

Paul, also, in reasoning on this subject in his epistle to the Hebrews, chapter 7, writes:

"For this Melchizedek, king of Salem, priest of the most high God, who met Abraham returning from the slaughter of the kings, and blessed him; to whom also Abraham gave a tenth part of all; first being by interpretation King of righteousness, and after that also King of Salem, which is, King of peace; without father, without mother, without descent, having neither beginning of days, nor end of life; but made like unto the Son of God; abideth a priest continually. Now consider how great this man was, unto whom even the patriarch Abraham gave the tenth of the spoils. And verily they that are of the sons of Levi, who receive the office of the priesthood, have a commandment to take tithes of the people according to the law, that is, of their brethren, though they come out of the loins of Abraham: but he whose descent is not counted from them received tithes of Abraham, and blessed him that had the promises. And without all contradiction the less is blessed of the better." (v. 1-7.)

To make the matter still plainer we transcribe the third verse from the inspired translation:

"For this Melchizedek was ordained a priest after the order of the Son of God, which order was without father, without mother, without descent, having neither beginning of days nor end of life. And all those who are ordained unto this priesthood are made like unto the Son of God, abiding a priest continually." (JST Hebrews 7:3.)

In Genesis, inspired translation, chapter 14, it is also stated regarding Melchizedek: [85]

"Thus, having been approved of God, he was ordained an high priest after the order of the covenant which God made with Enoch, it being after the order of the Son of God; which order came, not by man, nor the will of man; neither by father, nor mother; neither by beginning of days, nor end of years; but of God. And it was delivered unto men by the calling of his own voice, according to his own will, unto as many as believed on his name. For God having sworn unto Enoch and unto his seed with an oath by himself, that every one being ordained after this order and calling should have power, by faith, to break mountains, to divide the seas, to dry up waters, to turn them out of their course, to put at defiance the armies of nations, to divide the earth, to break every band, to stand in the presence of God; to do all things according to his will, according to his command, subdue principalities and powers; and this by the will of the Son of God, which was from before the foundation of the world. And men having this faith, coming up unto this order of God, were translated and taken up into heaven. And now, Melchizedek was a priest of this order;

therefore he obtained peace in Salem, and was called the Prince of peace, and his people wrought righteousness, and obtained heaven, and sought for the city of Enoch which God had before taken; separating it from the earth, having reserved it unto the latter-days, or the end of the world, and hath said, and sworn with an oath, that the heavens and the earth should come together; and the sons of God should be tried so as by fire. And this Melchizedek, having thus established righteousness, was called the king of heaven by his people, or, in other words, the King of peace." (v. 27-36.)

From the above it would seem that this people possessed the power of Translation, and that they "obtained heaven, and sought for the city of Enoch which God had before taken," (v. 34) or which was before translated.

The principle of power also over the varied creations of God, above spoken of, pertaining to the Holy Priesthood [86] after the order of the Son of God, has, by faith, been manifested to the world in the lives and actions of numbers of the servants of the Most High. The power of Enoch, wherein he caused the earth to tremble, whilst mountains fled at his command, and rivers were turned out of their course, has already been referred to. By this power, exercised in mighty faith, Melchizedek stopped the mouths of lions and quenched the violence of fire (JST Genesis 14:26); by it the waters of the Red Sea were divided by Moses, and the children of Israel passed through dry shod (Exodus 14:21); by it Elijah (2 Kings 2:7-8) and Elisha (2 Kings 2:14) smote the waters of the Jordan and crossed on dry land; by it Daniel escaped the ferocity of the lions (Daniel 6:16-23), and the three Hebrew children were delivered from the fiery furnace. (Daniel 3:19-27.)

By this same power in the Messianic dispensation the Apostles were delivered from bonds and imprisonment; by it Paul shook off the viper that had fastened upon his hand (Acts 28:3-6); by it Philip (Acts 8:39) was caught away by the Spirit of the Lord after he had baptized the Ethiopean eunuch; by it John was preserved when he was cast into a cauldron of boiling oil, that it did not hurt him; by it the dead were raised, the lepers cleansed, the sick healed, devils cast out, and other mighty works performed by Jesus and His disciples; and by it Christ broke the bands of death and became the resurrection and the life, the first fruits of them that slept, the conqueror of death, the Savior of the

The Mediation and Atonement 87

world and Redeemer of mankind.

Again, on this continent, one of the Nephite Prophets, Jacob, the son of Lehi, records: "We truly can command in the name of Jesus, and the very trees obey us, or the mountains, or the waves of the sea." (Jacob 4:6.) By faith the brother of Jared, who held this power, said unto the mountain Zerin, Remove; and it was removed (Ether 12:30); by it Alma and Amulek caused the walls [87] of the prison in Ammonihah to tumble to the ground (Alma 14:26-29); by it Nephi and Lehi wrought the surpassing change upon the Lamanites that they were baptized with fire and the Holy Ghost (Helaman 5:43-49); by it Ammon and his brethren wrought so great a miracle in the conversion of the Lamanites (Alma 17-27); and by it also the disciples of Jesus who tarried amongst the Nephites showed forth the power spoken of in the following passage:

"Therefore they did exercise power and authority over the disciples of Jesus who did tarry with them, and they did cast them into prison: but by the power of the word of God, which was in them, the prisons were rent in twain, and they went forth doing mighty miracles among them. Nevertheless, and notwithstanding all these miracles, the people did harden their hearts, and did seek to kill them, even as the Jews at Jerusalem sought to kill Jesus, according to his word; and they did cast them into furnaces of fire, and they came forth receiving no harm; and they also cast them into dens of wild beasts, and they did play with the wild beasts even as a child with a lamb; and they did come forth from among them, receiving no harm." (4 Nephi 1:30-33.)

This same power has also been abundantly manifested in these latter days in the midst of the Saints of God, in deliverances from evil, in escapes from enemies, in the quelling of mobs, in the stilling of the angry waves of the sea, in the healing of the sick, in the casting out of unclean spirits, and in many other miraculous manifestations of the power and goodness of God, and of the authority with which He has invested His servants who are endowed and clothed upon with the Priesthood, which is endless and after the order of the Son of God.

Thus, through the atonement of Jesus, and the salvation and redemption brought about by that atonement [88] these wonderful manifestations and deliverances have been accomplished by faith in God; and the Priesthood being after the order of the Son of God, and proceeding from Him, through the atonement, those who held this

Priesthood possessed, according to their faith, the above mentioned powers; and without that atonement this power never could have existed, for men without that sacrifice could not have been brought into that relationship to God, by which they would have the right, the power and authority to act in His name, or to be His representatives to fallen humanity.

In fact, the power manifested by the Priesthood is simply the power of God, for He is the head of the Priesthood, with Jesus as our President and great High Priest; and it is upon this principle that all the works of God have been accomplished, whether on the earth or in the heavens; and any manifestation of power through the Priesthood on the earth is simply a delegated power from the Priesthood in the heavens, and the more the Priesthood on the earth becomes assimilated with and subject to the Priesthood in the heavens the more of this power shall we possess. Hence Paul, in speaking on this subject, says:

"Through faith we understand that the worlds were framed by the word of God, so that things which are seen were not made of things which do appear." (Hebrews 11:3.)

The work of God and the glory of God is to bring to pass the immortality and eternal life of man; as it is written: "For this is my work and my glory, to bring to pass the immortality and eternal life of man." (Moses 1:39.) The creation of man and the multiplication of man was one thing, the immortality and eternal life of man and his exaltation is another thing; and in the organization of the world, and in the calculations of the Almighty pertaining to this immortality and eternal life, it would seem that it was decreed that the Only Begotten Son was provided for the purpose of accomplishing this object; and hence Christ was the [89] Lamb slain, according to the eternal purposes of God, before the foundation of the world.

In relation to the creation of the worlds, as above referred to by Paul, John, in the commencement of his Gospel, somewhat after the manner of a preface or introduction, writes: "In the beginning was the Word, and the Word was with God, and the Word was God. The same was in the beginning with God, All things were made by him; and without him was not anything made that was made. In him was life; and the life was the light of men. And the light shineth in darkness; and the darkness comprehended it not." (John 1:1-5.) Or to give the passage, in the wording of the inspired translation: "In the beginning was the Gospel preached through the Son. And the Gospel was the word, and the word was with the Son, and the Son was with God, and the Son was of God. The same was in the beginning with God. All things were made by him; and without him was not anything made which was made. In him was the Gospel, and the Gospel was the life, and the life was the light of men; and the light shineth in the world, and the world perceiveth it not." (JST John 1:1-5.) From the testimony of John, as given in the Book of Doctrine and Covenants, we also extract the following:

"And he bore record, saying, I saw his glory that he was in the beginning before the world was; therefore in the beginning the Word was, for he was the Word, even the messenger of salvation, the light and the Redeemer of the world; the Spirit of truth, who came into the world, because the world was made by him, and in him was the life of men and the light of men. The worlds were made by him: men were made by him: all things were made by him, and through him, and of him. And I, John, bear record that I beheld his glory, as the glory of the Only Begotten of the Father, full of grace and truth, even the Spirit of truth, which came and dwelt in the flesh, and dwelt among us." (D&C 93:7-11.)

Paul, likewise, in his Epistles, more than once [90] directs attention to this great truth. In writing to the Colossians he says:

"For by him were all things created, that are in heaven, and that are in earth, visible and invisible, whether they be thrones, or dominions, or principalities, or powers: all things were created by him, and for him: and he is before all things, and by him all things consist." (Colossians 1:16-17.)

And to the Hebrews he writes, that God "hath in these last days spoken unto us by his Son, whom he hath appointed heir of all things, by whom also he made the worlds; who being the brightness of his glory, and the express image of his person, and upholding all things by the word of his power, when he had by himself purged our sins, sat down on the right hand of the Majesty on high. (Hebrews 1:2-3.)

God revealed these things unto Moses; but his words in relation thereto are among the precious things that have been taken from the Scriptures by the iniquity of man; amongst those restored to us by modern revelation are the following words of God to that Patriarch with regard to the creation:

"And by the word of my power have I created them, which is mine Only Begotten Son, who is full of grace and truth. And worlds without number have I created; and I also created them for mine own purpose; and by the Son I created them which is mine Only Begotten. And the first man of all men have I called Adam, which is many. But only an account of this earth, and the inhabitants thereof, give I unto you. For behold, there are many worlds which have passed away by the word of my power. And there are many also which now stand, and numberless are they unto man, but all things are numbered unto me, for they are mine and I know them." (Moses 1:32-35.) [91]

CHAPTER 11

ABRAHAM'S RECORD CONCERNING THE CREATION—THE COUNCIL IN HEAVEN—
THE FATHER'S PLAN, THE SON'S ACCEPTANCE, SATAN'S REBELLION—THE AGENCY
OF MAN—SUGGESTIONS REGARDING SATAN'S PLAN TO SAVE ALL MANKIND.

The Lord also revealed to Abraham many great and glorious principles and truths relating to the creation. We extract the following from the fragment of the writings of that Patriarch, which has been graciously restored to us by the Lord in these days:

"And the Gods prepared the earth to bring forth the living creature after his kind, cattle and creeping things, and beasts of the earth after their kind; and it was so, as they had said. And the Gods organized the earth to bring forth the beasts after their kind, the cattle after their kind, and everything that creepeth upon the earth after their kind; and the Gods saw they would obey. And the Gods took counsel among themselves and said, Let us go down and form man in our image, after our likeness; and we will give them dominion over the fish of the sea, and over the fowl of the air, and over the cattle, and over all the earth, and over every creeping thing that creepeth upon the earth. So the Gods went down to organize man in their own image, in the image of the Gods to form they him, male and female, to form they them; and the Gods said, We will bless them. And the Gods said, We will cause them to be fruitful, and multiply, and replenish the earth, and subdue it, and to have dominion over the fish of the sea, and over the fowl of the air, and over every living thing that moveth upon the earth. And the Gods said, Behold, we will give them every herb bearing seed that shall come upon the face of all the earth, and every tree which shall have fruit upon [92] it, yea, the fruit of the tree yielding seed to them we will give it; it shall be for their meat; and to every beast of the earth, and to every fowl of the air, and to every thing that creepeth upon the earth, behold, we will give them life, and also we will give to them every green herb for meat, and all these things shall be thus organized. And the Gods said, We will do every thing that we have said, and organize them; and behold, they shall be very obedient. And it came to pass that it was from evening until morning they called night; and it came to pass that it was from morning until evening that they called day; and they numbered the sixth time.

"And thus we will finish the heavens and the earth, and all the hosts of them. And the Gods said among themselves, On the seventh time we will end our work which we have counseled; and we will rest on the seventh time from all our work which we have counseled. And the Gods concluded upon the seventh time, because that on the seventh time they would rest from all their works which they (the Gods) counseled among themselves to form, and sanctified it. And thus were their decisions at the time that they counseled among themselves to form the heavens and the earth.

"And the Gods came down and formed these the generations of the heavens and of the earth, when they were formed in the day that the Gods formed the earth and the heavens, according to all that which they had said concerning every plant of the field before it was in the earth, and every herb of the field before it grew; for the Gods had not caused it to rain upon the earth when they counseled to do them, and had not formed a man to till the ground; but there went up a mist from the earth, and watered the whole face of the ground. And the Gods formed man from the dust of the ground, and took his spirit (that is, the man's spirit,) and put it into him, and breathed into his nostrils the breath of life, and man became a living soul." (Abraham 4:24-31, 5:1-7.)

Although this matter of the Council or Conference [93] is not so fully exhibited in the Old Testament Scriptures as in this revelation to Abraham, yet it is definitely stated in the Book of Genesis that God said, "Let *us* make man in *our* image, after *our* likeness;" (Genesis 1:26) and again, after Adam had taken of the forbidden fruit the Lord said, "Behold, the man has become as one of *us*;" (*Ibid.* 3:22) and the inference is direct that in all that related to the work of the creation of the world, there was a consultation; and though God spake as it is recorded in the Bible, yet it is evident He counseled with others. The Scriptures tell us there are "Gods many and Lords many. But to us there is but one God, the Father." (1 Corinthians 8:5.) And for this reason, though there were others engaged in the creation of the worlds, it is given to us in the Bible in the shape that it is; for the fulness of these truths is only revealed to highly favored persons for certain reasons known to God; as we are told in the Scriptures: "The secret of the Lord is with them that fear him; and he will show them his covenant." (Psalms 25:14.)

It is consistent to believe that at this Council in the heavens the plan that should be adopted in relation to the sons of God who were then spirits, and had not yet obtained tabernacles, was duly considered. For, in view of the creation of the world and the placing of men upon it, whereby it would be possible for them to obtain tabernacles, and in those tabernacles obey laws of life, and with them again be exalted among the Gods, we are told, that at that time, "the morning stars sang together, and all the sons of God shouted for joy." (Job 38:7.) The question then arose, how, and upon what principle, should the salvation, exaltation and eternal glory of God's sons be brought about? It is evident that at that Council certain plans had been proposed and discussed, and that after a full discussion of those principles, and the declaration of the Father's will pertaining to His design, Lucifer came before the Father, with a plan of his own, saying, "Behold I, send me, I will be thy Son, and I will redeem all mankind, that one [94] soul shall not be lost, and surely I will do it; wherefore, give me thine honor." (Moses 4:1.) But Jesus, on hearing this statement made by Lucifer, said, "Father, thy will be done, and the glory be thine forever." (v. 2.) From these remarks made by the well beloved Son, we should naturally infer that in the discussion of this subject the Father had made known His will and developed His plan and design pertaining to these matters, and all that His well beloved Son wanted to do was to carry out the will of His Father, as it would appear had been before expressed. He also wished the glory to be given to His Father, who, as God the Father, and the originator and designer of the plan, had a right to all the honor and glory. But Lucifer wanted to introduce to plan contrary to the will of his Father, and then wanted His honor, and said: "I will save every soul of man, wherefore give me thine honor." (See v. 1.) He wanted to go contrary to the will of his Father, and presumptuously sought to deprive man of his free agency, thus making him a serf, and placing him in a position in which it was impossible for him to obtain that exaltation which God designed should be man's, through obedience to the law which He had suggested; and again, Lucifer wanted the honor and power of his Father, to enable him to carry out principles which were contrary to the Father's wish.

And further, in regard to agency; if man had not had his agency, or if he had been deprived of his agency, he could not have been tempted of the devil, or of any other power; for if the will of God prevailed, and was carried out without man's action or agency, it would have been impossible for him to have done anything wrong, for he would have been deprived of the power of doing that wrong. This was the position that Satan desired to place, not only the spirits in the heavens, but also mankind upon the earth. And Satan said, "Surely I will save every one of them, wherefore, give me thine honor." But God's plan was different from this, and, as stated above, had been decided upon in the Councils of heaven; and the Father had made a decree as to how these things should be done; and that both the inhabitants of heaven and the inhabitants of earth should have their free agency. It was against this that Lucifer rebelled; and he could not have rebelled against a plan or commandment that had not been given; for rebellion signifies a violation of law, command, or authority; and he was cast out of heaven because of this rebellion. This rebellion could not have existed without a free agency; for without a free agency they would all have been compelled to do the will of the Father. But having the free agency, they used it; and Lucifer and a third part of the angels were cast out because they rebelled and used this agency in opposition to their heavenly Father. And not only because they rebelled, but because, as stated, "they sought to destroy the agency of man;" (See v. 3) and their agency would have been used in opposition to the interests, happiness and eternal exaltation of mankind, which were proposed to be accomplished through the atonement and redemption provided by Jesus Christ. In accordance with this we find the following statements in the revelations given to the Prophet Joseph Smith:

"Behold, the devil was before Adam, for he rebelled against me, saying, Give me thine honor, which is my power: and also a third part of the hosts of heaven turned he away from me because of their agency; and they were thrust down, and thus came the devil and his angels. And, behold, there is a place prepared for them from the beginning, which place is hell: and it must needs be that the devil should tempt the children of men, or they could not be agents unto themselves, for if they never should have bitter, they could not know the sweet." (D&C 29:36-39.)

And again. "And this we saw also, and bear record, that an angel of God who was in authority in the presence of God, who rebelled against the Only Begotten Son, whom the Father loved, and who was in the bosom of the Father—was thrust down from the presence of God and the Son, and was called Perdition, for the heavens wept over him—he was Lucifer, a son of the morning. And we beheld, and lo, he is fallen! is fallen! even a son of the morning. And while we were yet in the Spirit, the Lord commanded us that we should write the vision, for we beheld Satan, that old serpent—even the devil—who rebelled against God, and sought to take the kingdom of our God and his Christ." (D&C 76:25-28.)

The Father accepted the offer of His well beloved Son, and proceeded to carry out the decision of the Council, and, as we are informed in the Bible (inspired translation), God said to His Only Begotten, "Let us make man in our image, after our likeness, and it was so." (JST Genesis 1:27.)

There are other questions mixed up with this rebellion besides those above referred to, and those questions are directly connected with the atonement. In the event of man having his free will and being subject to the power of temptation, the weakness of the flesh, the allurements of the world, and the powers of darkness, it was known that he must necessarily fall, and being fallen, it would be impossible for him to redeem himself, and that, according to an eternal law of justice, it would require an infinite, explatory atonement to redeem man, to save him from the effects and ruin of the Fall, and to place him in a condition where he could again be reinstated in the favor of God, according to the eternal laws of justice and mercy; and find his way back to the presence of the Father. Satan (it is possible) being opposed to the will of his Father, wished to avoid the responsibilities of this position, and rather than assume the consequences of the acceptance of the plan of the Father, he would deprive man of his free agency, and render it impossible for him to obtain that exaltation which God designed. It would further seem probable that he refused to take the position of redeemer, and assume all the consequences associated therewith, but he did propose, as stated before, to take another [97] plan and deprive man of his agency, and he probably intended to make men atone for their own acts by an act of coercion, and the shedding of their own blood as an atonement for their sins; therefore, he says, "I will redeem all mankind, that one soul shall not be lost; and surely I will do it; wherefore, give me thine honor." (Moses 4:1.) His plan, however, was rejected as contrary to the counsel of God, his Father. The well beloved Son then addressed the Father, and instead of proposing to carry out any plan of his own, knowing what His Father's will was, said, "Thy will be done;" (v. 2) "I will carry out thy plans and thy designs, and, as man will fall, I will offer myself as an atonement according to thy will, O God. Neither do I wish the honor, but thine be the glory;" and a covenant was entered into between Him and His Father, in which He agreed to atone for the sins of the world; and He thus, as stated, became the Lamb slain from before the foundation of the world. In this connection it is related by Abraham:

"And there stood one among them that was like unto God, and he said unto those who were with him, We will go down, for there is space there, and we will take of these materials, and we will make an earth whereon these may dwell; and we will prove them herewith, to see if they will do all things whatsoever the Lord their God shall command them; and they who keep their first estate, shall be added upon; and they who keep not their first estate, shall not have glory in the same kingdom with those who keep their first estate; and they who keep their second estate, shall have glory added upon their heads for ever and ever." (Abraham 3:24-26.)

And hence, as Jesus Himself said, "Thus it is written and thus it behooved Christ to suffer, and to rise from the dead the third day; and that repentance and remission of sins should be preached in his name among all nations, beginning at Jerusalem." (Luke 24:46-47.)

We will now give in full the quotation from the Pearl of Great Price with regard to the above matter, and also add a short recapitulation. [98]

"And I, the Lord God, spake unto Moses, saying, That Satan, whom thou hast commanded in the name of mine Only Begotten, is the same which was from the beginning, and he came before me, saying, Behold I, send me, I will be thy son, and I will redeem all mankind, that one soul shall not be lost, and surely I will do it; wherefore give me thine honor. But, behold, my Beloved Son, which was my Beloved and Chosen from the beginning, said unto me, Father, thy will be done, and the glory be thine for ever. Wherefore, because that Satan rebelled against me, and sought to destroy the agency of man, which I, the Lord God, had given him, and also, that I should give unto him mine own power, by the power of mine Only Begotten I caused that he should be cast down, and he became Satan, yea, even the Devil, the father of all lies, to deceive, and to blind men, and to lead them captive at his will, even as many as would not hearken unto my voice." (Moses 4:1-4.)

From the above we gather: First, that the proposition of Lucifer was an act of rebellion "against me"—God. (v. 3.)

Second, that God had already decreed that man should have his free agency, and this agency had been given to him by the Lord, as it is said, "which I, the Lord God, had given him." (v. 3.)

Third, that Lucifer coveted and asked for a power which was the prerogative of the Almighty and alone belonged to God; and which He called "mine own power." (v. 3.)

Fourth, that for this rebellion Lucifer was cast out and became Satan.

Fifth, that the power by which he was cast out, was by a certain power or Priesthood which had been conferred by God on His Only Begotten; for he said, "By the power of mine Only Begotten I caused that he should be cast down." (v. 3.)

Sixth, that being cast down and becoming Satan, "even the devil, the father of lies," his office was to deceive and to blind men; as it is stated, "to deceive, and to blind men, and to lead them captive at his will, even as many as would not hearken unto my voice." (v. 4.) [99]

CHAPTER 12

ABRAHAM, ISAAC AND JACOB—SACRIFICES OFFERED BY THEM—ABRAHAM AND THE GOSPEL COVENANT—EXTRACTS FROM THE BOOK OF ABRAHAM AND THE WRITINGS OF PAUL.

We will now return to Abraham, who is denominated the Father of the Faithful, and who, as we have before seen, was a contemporary of Melchizedek. The testimony in the Bible is direct and explicit that Abraham fulfilled the law requiring the offering of sacrifices, and furthermore was in possession of the principles of the Gospel and understood the saving value of the atonement.

In the historical narrative of the Book of Genesis, we have numerous testimonies that Abraham offered up sacrifices, in connection with his worship of the Almighty. For instance, it is written:

"And Abram passed through the land unto the place of Sichem, unto the plain of Moreh. And the Canaanite was then in the land. And the Lord appeared unto Abram, and said, Unto thy seed will I give this land; and there builded he an altar unto the Lord, who appeared unto him. And he removed from thence unto a mountain on the east of Beth-el, and pitched his tent, having Beth-el on the west, and Hai on the east: and there he builded an altar unto the Lord, and called upon the name of the Lord." (Genesis 12:6-8.)

In the next chapter we are told that Abraham "went on his journeys from the south even to Beth-el, unto the place where his tent had been at the beginning, between Beth-el and Hai; unto the place of the altar, which he had made there at the first: and there Abram called on the name of the Lord." (Genesis 13:3-4.)

And afterwards he removed his "tent, and came and dwelt in the plain of Mamre, which is in Hebron, and built there an altar unto the Lord." (Genesis 13:18.) [100]

The Book of Abraham gives some further details on these matters. The Patriarch therein states:

"Now I, Abraham, built an altar in the land of Jershon, and made an offering unto the Lord, and prayed that the famine might be turned away from my father's house, that they might not perish; and then we passed from Jershon through the land, unto the place of Sechem. It was situated in the plains of Moreh, and we had already come into the borders of the land of the Canaanites, and I offered sacrifice there in the plains of Moreh, and called on the Lord devoutly, because we had already come into the land of this idolatrous nation. And the Lord appeared unto me in answer to my prayers, and said unto me, Unto thy seed will I give this land. And I, Abraham, arose from the place of the altar which I had built unto the Lord, and removed from thence unto a mountain on the east of Bethel, and pitched my tent there, Bethel on the west, and Hai on the east: and there I built another altar unto the Lord, and called again upon the name of the Lord." (Genesis 2:17-20.)

Although full details are not given of the mode of sacrifice in those ancient times, nor of all the creatures that were acceptable unto the Lord, in the performance of this rite, yet the narrative of the contemplated sacrifice of Isaac by his father is indicative of the principle being well understood. We are told that the young man said: "My Father: and he said, Here am I, my son. And he said, Behold the fire and the wood, but where is the lamb for a burnt-offering? And Abraham said, My son, God will provide himself a lamb for a burnt-offering." (Genesis 22:7-8.)

It is evident from other scriptures that Abraham offered up these sacrifices in token of the great expiatory sacrifice of the Son of God. Indeed the Redeemer himself told the Jews, "Your father Abraham rejoiced to see my day: and he saw it, and was glad." (John 8:56.)

In confirmation of this statement we read in the inspired translation of the Book of Genesis that the Lord [101] said to Abraham, in relation to his possession of the land of Canaan. "Though thou wast dead, yet am I not able to give it thee? And if thou shalt die, yet thou shalt possess it, for the day cometh that the Son of Man shall live; but how can he live if he be not dead? He must first be quickened. And it came to pass, that Abram looked forth and saw the days of the Son of Man, and was glad, and his soul found rest, and he believed in the Lord; and the Lord counted it unto him for righteousness." (JST Genesis 15:10-12.)

Again, Paul, in writing to the Galatians, states: "And the scripture, foreseeing that God would justify the heathen through faith, preached before the gospel unto Abraham, saying, In thee shall all nations be blessed. So then they which be of faith are blessed with faithful Abraham." (Galatians 3:8-9.)

This promise is corroborated by the statements of Peter to the Jews:

"Ye are the children of the prophets, and of the covenant which God made with our fathers, saying unto Abraham, And in thy seed shall all the kindreds of the earth be blessed. Unto you first, God, having raised up his Son Jesus, sent him to bless you, in turning away every one of you from his iniquities." (Acts 3:25-26.)

The record of this covenant is to be found in the Book of Genesis, as follows:

"Now the Lord had said unto Abram, Get thee out of thy country, and from thy kindred, and from thy father's house, unto a land that I will show thee; and I will make of thee a great nation; and I will bless thee, and make thy name great; and I will bless them that bless thee, and curse him that curseth thee, and in thee shall all families of the earth be blessed." (Genesis 12:1-3; see also Genesis 18:18; 22:18.)

It will be noticed in the above quotation from the Book of Genesis, that no reference is made to the preaching of the Gospel to Abraham in connection with these great promises as spoken of by Paul. This de[102]ficiency is supplied by the Book of Abraham, wherein the covenant between God and His faithful servant is given at greater length in that covenant we find the following:

"My name is Jehovah, and I will make of thee a great nation and I will bless thee above measure, and make thy name great among all nations, and thou shalt be a blessing unto thy seed after thee, that in their hands they shall bear this ministry and priesthood unto all nations, and I will bless them through thy name; for as many as receive this Gospel shall be called after thy name, and shall be accounted thy seed, and shall rise up and bless thee, as their father; and I will bless them that bless thee, and curse them that curse thee; and in thee (that is, in thy priesthood) and in thy seed, (that is, thy priesthood,) for I give unto thee a promise that this right shall continue in thee, and in thy seed after thee (that is to say, the literal seed, or the seed of the body,) shall all the families of the earth be blessed, even with the blessings of the Gospel, which are the blessings of salvation, even of life eternal." (Abraham 2:8, 9-11.)

Of the personal history of Isaac we have but a very meagre account in the Bible; however, sufficient is said to inform us that he, like his father, offered up sacrifices, that his offering was acceptable to God, and that He renewed with him the covenant previously made with Abraham. Of Isaac it is written: "And he went up from thence to Beer-sheba. And the Lord appeared unto him the same night, and said, I am the God of Abraham thy father: fear not, for I am with thee, and will bless thee, and multiply thy seed for my servant Abraham's sake. And he builded an altar there, and called upon the name of the Lord." (Genesis 26:23-25.)

Jacob followed in the footsteps of his father. He worshipped the true and living God, and had the blessings of his fathers confirmed on him. Regarding sacrifices we are informed that, after his sudden departure [103] from Laban and their later somewhat stormy interview, "Jacob offered sacrifice upon the mount" (Genesis 31:52); and again, shortly after, by command of the Lord, he journeyed to Bethel, "and he built there an altar and called the place El-beth-el," or the House of God. (Genesis 35:7.)

CHAPTER 13

Sacrifices in the Days of Moses—The Institution of the Passover and the Exodus—The Symbolism of the Paschal Lamb—The Covenant of the Atonement between Christ and His Father—The Redeemed—Tokens of Covenants—The Rainbow—The Name of Jesus the Only Name—The Levites.

In regard to the offering of sacrifices, it is very evident that in the days of Moses the children of Israel were quite familiar with this rite, as also were the Egyptians. For one great request which Moses and Aaron made of Pharaoh, King of Egypt, was, "Let us go, we pray thee, three days' journey into the desert, and sacrifice unto the Lord our God;" (Exodus 5:3) and as a reason why they should thus go into the wilderness it was urged by them, when the Egyptian monarch said, "Go ye, sacrifice to your God in the land," (*Ibid.* 8:25) that "it is not meet so to do; for we shall sacrifice the abomination of the Egyptians to the Lord our God: lo, shall we sacrifice the abomination of the Egyptians before their eyes, and will they not stone us? We will go three days' journey into the wilderness, and sacrifice to the Lord our God, as he shall command us." (v. 26-27.)

It is further stated, that after a time, when all [104] other judgments had failed to bring about the desired effect with Pharaoh, that "Moses said, Thus saith the Lord, About midnight will I go out into the midst of Egypt: and all the first-born in the land of Egypt shall die, from the first-born of Pharaoh that sitteth upon his throne, even unto the first-born of the maid-servant that is behind the mill; and all the first-born of beasts. And there shall be a great cry throughout all the land of Egypt, such as there was none like it, nor shall be like it any more. But against any of the children of Israel shall not a dog move his tongue, against man or beast: that ye may know how that the Lord doth put a difference between the Egyptians and Israel." (Exodus 11:4-7.)

The next chapter gives the history of the fulfilment of this threatened judgment and the results that flowed therefrom. It is recorded:

"And the Lord spake unto Moses and Aaron in the land of Egypt, saying, This month shall be unto you the beginning of months; it shall be the first month of the year to you. Speak ye unto all the congregation of Israel, saying, In the tenth day of this month they shall take to them every man a lamb according to the house of their fathers, a lamb for an house: and if the household be too little for the lamb, let him and his neighbor next unto his house take it according to the number of the souls: every man according to his eating shall make your count for the lamb. Your lamb shall be without blemish, a male of the first year: ye shall take it out from the sheep or from the goats: and ye shall keep it up until the fourteenth day of the same month: and the whole assembly of the congregation of Israel shall kill it in the evening. And they shall take of the blood, and strike it on the two side-posts, and on the upper door-post of the houses, wherein they shall eat it. And they shall eat the flesh in that night, roast with fire, and unleavened bread; and with bitter herbs they shall eat it." (Exodus 12:1-8.)

"And thus shall ye eat it; with your loins girded your shoes on your feet, and your staff in your hand: [105] and ye shall eat it in haste; it is the Lord's passover. For I will pass through the land of Egypt this night, and will smite all the first-born in the land of Egypt, both man and beast: and against all the gods of Egypt I will execute judgment: I am the Lord. And the blood shall be to you for a token upon the houses where ye are: and when I see the blood, I will pass over you, and the plague shall not be upon you to destroy you, when I smite the land of Egypt. And this day shall be unto you for a memorial; and ye shall keep it a feast to the Lord throughout your generations: ye shall keep it a feast by an ordinance for ever." (Exodus 12:11-14.)

"Then Moses called for all the Elders of Israel, and said unto them,

Draw out, and take you a lamb, according to your families, and kill the passover. And ye shall take a bunch of hyssop, and dip it in the blood that is in the basin, and strike the lintel and the two side-posts with the blood that is in the basin: and none of you shall go out at the door of his house until the morning. For the Lord will pass through to smite the Egyptians; and when he seeth the blood upon the lintel, and on the two side-posts, the Lord will pass over the door, and will not suffer the destroyer to come in unto your houses to smite you. And ye shall observe this thing for an ordinance to thee and to thy sons for ever." (Exodus 12:21-24.)

"And the children of Israel went away, and did as the Lord had commanded Moses and Aaron, so did they. And it came to pass, that at midnight the Lord smote all the first-born in the land of Egypt, from the first-born of Pharaoh that sat on his throne, unto the first-born of the captive that was in the dungeon; and all the first-born of cattle. And Pharaoh rose up in the night, he, and all his servants, and all the Egyptians; and there was a great cry in Egypt: for there was not a house where there was not one dead. And he called for Moses and Aaron by night, and said, Rise up, and get you forth from among my people, both ye [106] and the children of Israel: and go, serve the Lord, as ye have said. Also take your flocks and your herds, as ye have said, and be gone: and bless me also. And the Egyptians were urgent upon the people, that they might send them out of the land in haste; for they said, We be all dead men." (Exodus 12:28-33.)

It is further said: "And it shall be when thy son asketh thee in time to come, saying, What is this? that thou shalt say unto him, By strength of hand the Lord brought us out from Egypt, from the house of bondage; and it came to pass, when Pharaoh would hardly let us go, that the Lord slew all the first-born in the land of Egypt, both the first-born of man, and the first-born of beasts; therefore I sacrifice to the Lord all that openeth the matrix, being males; but all the first-born of my children I redeem." (Exodus 13:14-15.)

From the above quotations, amongst other important matters, it appears, that when the destroying angel passed by the houses of the children of Israel he found the blood of a lamb sprinkled on the door post; which was a type of the blood of Christ, the Lamb of God. The angel who was the executor of justice could not touch those who were protected by that sacred symbol; because that prefigured the sacrifice of the Son of God, which was provided at the beginning of creation for the redemption of the human family, and which was strictly in accordance with provisions then made by the Almighty for that purpose—"the Lamb slain from before the foundation of the world" (Revelation 13:8; See also Moses 7:47.)—and accepted in full as an atonement for the transgressions of mankind, according to the requirements of eternal justice and agreed to by the Savior and His Father. A proposition is made to meet the requirements of justice, which proposal is accepted by the contracting parties, all these contracting parties being satisfied with the arrangement thus made. Hence it is said by one of the prophets: "Then he is gracious unto him, and saith, Deliver him from going down to the pit: I have found a ransom." (Job 33:24.) [107]

And further: "Therefore the redeemed of the Lord shall return, and come with singing unto Zion; and everlasting joy shall be upon their head: they shall obtain gladness and joy; and sorrow and mourning shall flee away." (Isaiah 51:11.)

Who are the redeemed, except those who have accepted the terms of the ransom thus provided? The ransom being provided and accepted, the requirements of justice are met, for those contracts are provided and sanctioned by the highest contracting parties that can be found in the heavens, and the strongest, most indubitable and infinite assurances are given for the fulfilment of that contract, and until the contract is fulfilled the sacrifices are offered as a token and remembrance of the engagements and covenants entered into. God gave a token to Noah, of a rainbow, which should be a sign between Him and mankind that He would nevermore destroy the earth by water; He accepted these sacrifices as a token of the covenant that the Messiah should come to take away sin by the sacrifice of Himself, and thus fulfil the covenant, pertaining to this matter, made before the world was.

And again there was another token, which was given to Adam by an angel. This holy messenger said to our great father, "Thou shalt do all that thou doest in the name of the Son. And thou shalt repent, and call upon God, in the name of the Son for evermore." (Moses 5:8.) For, as expressed in the New Testament, "there is none other name under heaven given among men, whereby we must be saved." (Acts 4:12.) Or, to quote from the Book of Mormon, "There shall be no other name given, nor any other way nor means whereby salvation can come unto the children of men, only in and through the name of Christ, the Lord Omnipotent." (Mosiah 3:17.) And furthermore, that name, or token, will continue to be given until the Scripture is fulfilled which saith: "Wherefore God also hath highly exalted him, and given him a name which is above every name: that at the name of Jesus every [108] knee shall bow, of things in heaven, and things in earth, and things under the earth; and that every tongue should confess that Jesus Christ is Lord, to the glory of God the Father." (Philpians 2:9-11.)

Again, the Lord, through the sprinkling of the blood of a lamb on the door-posts of the Israelites, having saved the lives of all the first-born of Israel, made a claim upon them for their services in His cause. It is written:

"And I, behold, I have taken the Levites from among the children of Israel instead of all the first-born that openeth the matrix among the children of Israel; therefore the Levites shall be mine; because all the first-born are mine; for on the day that I smote all the first-born in the land of Egypt I hallowed unto me all the first-born in Israel, both man and beast; mine they shall be: I am the Lord." (Numbers 3:12-13.)

But the first-born of the Egyptians, for whom no lamb as a token of the propitiation was offered, were destroyed. It was through the propitiation and atonement alone that the Israelites were saved, and, under the circumstances they must have perished with the Egyptians, who were doomed, had it not been for the contemplated atonement and propitiation of Christ, of which this was a figure.

Hence the Lord claimed those that He saved as righteously belonging to Him, and claiming them as His He demanded their services; but afterwards, as shown in the above quotation, He accepted the tribe of Levi in lieu of the first-born of Israel; and as there were more of the first-born than there were of the Levites, the balance had to be redeemed with money, which was given to Aaron, as the great High Priest and representative of the Aaronic Priesthood, he being also a Levite. (See Numbers 3:50-51.) [109]

CHAPTER 14

HISTORY OF SACRIFICES AND THE LAW OF MOSES AMONG THE NEPHITES—
REFERENCES TO THE BOOKS OF NEPHI, JACOB, MOSIAH AND ALMA—THE
TESTIMONY OF JESUS REGARDING THE LAW OF MOSES.

From the Bible we turn to the Book of Mormon, with a view to discover to what extent the law of sacrifice, as a type of the offering up of the promised Messiah, was observed among that branch of the house of Israel which God planted on this continent. In perusing the pages of this sacred record, we shall find several important facts and ideas, in connection with this subject, presented very prominently by the ancient Nephite historians: among them—

First, that the law of Moses, with all its rites, ordinances, and sacrifices, was strictly observed by the faithful Nephites from the time of their arrival on the promised land, until it was fulfilled in Christ, and by his command ceased to be observed.

Second, that when the Nephites brought any of the Lamanites to the knowledge and worship of the true God, they taught them to observe this law.

Third, that those who apostatized from the Nephites, as a general thing, ceased to observe this law.

Fourth, that the true import of the law of Moses, and of its ceremonies and sacrifices, as typical of the atonement yet to be made by our Lord and Savior, was thoroughly taught by the Priesthood among that people, and very generally understood by them.

Fifth, that associated with the observance of this law, there were continued admonitions given that salvation was in Christ and not in the law, which was but the shadow and type of that of which he was the prototype and reality.

Sixth, that temples were erected of the same pattern [110] as that of Solomon at Jerusalem, evidently for the reason that they were to be used for the same purposes.

Seventh, that the Gospel was preached in connection with the law, and churches were established and organized according to the Gospel requirements, and that the higher Priesthood, although not fully organized in all its parts, ministered to the Nephites as well as the lesser.

Eighth, it appears indubitable from the two records, the Bible and the Book of Mormon, that the intent and true meaning of the law of Moses, of its sacrifices, etc., were far better understood and comprehended by the Nephites than by the Jews. But in this connection, it must not be forgotten, that a great many most plain and precious things, as the Book of Mormon states, have been taken from the Bible, through the ignorance of uninspired translators or the design and cunning of wicked men.

As might naturally be expected, we find that Lehi, like his forefathers of the Mosaic age, offered sacrifices to the Lord during his journeyings in the wilderness. These sacrifices were occasions of thanksgiving and praise to God. As examples, we note the occasion of the safe return of Lehi's sons from Jerusalem with the records, when, we are told by Nephi, their parents "did rejoice exceedingly, and did offer sacrifice and burnt offerings unto the Lord; and they gave thanks unto the God of Israel. And after they had given thanks unto the God of Israel, my father, Lehi, took the records which were engraven upon the plates of brass, and he did search them from the beginning. (1 Nephi 5:9-10.)

Another occasion was when Nephi and his brethren again returned from the Holy City, bringing with them Ishmael and his family. Of this Nephi writes: "After I and my brethren, and all the house of Ishmael, had come down unto the tent of my father, they did give thanks unto the Lord their God; and they did offer sacrifice and burnt offerings unto him." (1 Nephi 7:22.)

After the arrival of the colony on the promised [111] land and the death of Lehi, his sons and their families divided into two communities, or nationalities; the one righteous and Godfearing, the other rebellious and debased. Owing to the contentious and quarrelsome disposition of the latter, who recognized Laman, Lehi's eldest son, as their head, the portion who sought to serve the Lord, for the sake of peace and security moved some distance to the northward. Nephi was their leader, and of them he records:

"And all those who were with me, did take upon them to call themselves the people of Nephi. And we did observe to keep the judgments, and the statutes, and the commandments of the Lord in all things, according to the law of Moses. And the Lord was with us: and we did prosper exceedingly." (2 Nephi 5:9-11.)

One of the first things that the Nephites did on their arrival at their new home was to build a temple. They could not keep the judgments, the commandments, and the statutes of the Lord in all things, according to the law of Moses, unless they did so; and necessarily it was fashioned after the one at Jerusalem, for it was to be used for the same purposes; in it the same ordinances were to be performed, the same sacrifices were to be offered. Nephi writes:

"And I, Nephi, did build a temple: and I did construct it after the manner of the temple of Solomon, save it were not built of so many precious things; for they were not to be found upon the land; wherefore, it could not be built like unto Solomon's temple. But the manner of the construction was like unto the temple of Solomon; and the workmanship thereof was exceeding fine." (2 Nephi 5:16.)

Thus the fulfilling of the Divine commandments was provided for; a place was erected where the law of Moses could be carried out, and the sacrifices be offered which formed so important a part of that code.

The Nephites were not left by their Priesthood in ignorance of the intent and symbolism of these ceremo[112]nies. They were not unmeaning, burdensome, spiritless performances to them. Nephi and his successors were particularly careful in explaining that these ordinances, like all other rites of the Church of God, had their value in their association with or being directly typical of the great, infinite sacrifice of atonement to be offered up by the Lamb of God in His own person. Nephi informs us:

"Behold, my soul delighteth in proving unto my people the truth of the coming of Christ: for, for this end hath the law of Moses been given; and all things which have been given of God from the beginning of the world, unto man, are the typifying of him." (2 Nephi 11:4.)

And a little later he writes:

"And notwithstanding we believe in Christ, we keep the law of Moses, and look forward with steadfastness unto Christ, until the law shall be fulfilled; for, for this end was the law given; wherefore the law hath become dead unto us, and we are made alive in Christ, because of our faith; yet we keep the law because of the commandments; and we talk of Christ, we rejoice in Christ, we preach of Christ, we prophesy of Christ, and we write according to our prophecies, that our children may know to what source they may look for a remission of their sins. Wherefore, we speak concerning the law, that our children may know the deadness of the law; and they, by knowing the deadness of the law, may look forward to the life which is in Christ, and know for what end the law was given. And after the law is fulfilled in Christ, that they need not harden their hearts against him, when the law ought to be done away." (2 Nephi 25:24-27.)

Which agrees with the statement of Paul: "Wherefore the law was our schoolmaster, to bring us unto Christ, that we might be justified by faith." (Galatians 3:24.)

So firm a foundation having been laid for the faith of the Nephite people, we find that in every period of their history they retained their reverence for the law [113] of Moses, though disputations sometimes arose, by reason of iniquity, with regard to its symbolism or its saving quality. The apostates, who separated themselves from the Church, occasionally fell into the grievous error ef exalting the law above the Gospel, and, whilst maintaining its divine origin, they ignored its typical value and denied that it was a preparatory system leading to a higher, holier and more perfect law; they refused to recognize it as a schoolmaster to bring them to Christ. The first of these apostacies occurred in the days of Jacob, the brother of Nephi. With regard to the people in general, he writes:

"Behold, they believed in Christ and worshipped the Father in his name, and also we worship the Father in his name. And for this intent we keep the law of Moses, it pointing our souls to him; and for this cause it is sanctified unto us for righteousness, even as it was accounted unto Abraham in the wilderness, to be obedient unto the commandments of God in offering up his son Isaac, which is a similitude of God and his only begotten Son." (Jacob 4:5.)

The Mediation and Atonement 111

But while the majority of the Nephites fully recognized these saving truths, there arose a man named Sherem, who disputed and denied that the law pointed the souls of men to Christ, as the great Propitiator for sin and the Redeemer of the world.

This Sherem declared unto the people that there should be no Christ, and his flatteries and sophistries led away many people. Of him and his doings Jacob writes:

"And it came to pass that he came unto me; and on this wise did he speak unto me, saying: Brother Jacob, I have sought much opportunity that I might speak unto you: for I have heard and also know, that thou goest about much, preaching that which you call the gospel, or the doctrine of Christ; and ye have led away much of this people, that they pervert the right way of God, and keep not the law of Moses, which is the right way: and convert the law of Moses into the [114] worship of a being, which ye say shall come many hundred years hence. And now behold, I, Sherem, declare unto you, that this is blasphemy; for no man knoweth of such things; for he cannot tell of things to come. And after this manner did Sherem contend against me. But behold, the Lord God poured in his Spirit into my soul, insomuch that I did confound him in all his words. And I said unto him, Deniest thou the Christ who should come? And he said, If there should be a Christ, I would not deny him; but I know that there is no Christ, neither has been, nor ever will be. And I said unto him, Believest thou the scriptures? And he said, Yea. And I said unto him, Then ye do not understand them; for they truly testify of Christ. Behold, I say unto you, that none of the prophets have written, nor prophesied, save they have spoken concerning this Christ. And this is not all: it has been made manifest unto me, for I have heard and seen; and it also has been made manifest unto me by the power of the Holy Ghost; wherefore, I know, if there should be no atonement made, all mankind must be lost." (Jacob 7:6-12.)

Somewhat similar was the argument that took place between the martyr Abinadi and the apostate priests of the iniquitous Noah, king of the land of Lehi-Nephi. They officiated in the Temple, observed the outward forms of the Mosaic law, but revelled in licentiousness, covetousness, gluttony and all manner of iniquity. To them was Abinadi sent to warn them and their king of the results of their mutual wrong doing. In the account of this mission of Abinadi we read that he said:

"Ye have not applied your hearts to understanding; therefore, ye have not been wise. Therefore, What teach ye this people? And they said, We teach the law of Moses. And again he said unto them, If ye teach the law of Moses why do ye not keep it? Why do ye set your hearts upon riches? Why do ye commit whoredoms and spend your strength with harlots, yea, and cause this people to commit sin, that the Lord has [115] cause to send me to prophesy against this people, yea, even a great evil against this people? Know ye not that I speak the truth? Yea, ye know that I speak the truth; and you ought to tremble before God. And it shall come to pass that ye shall be smitten for your iniquities: for ye have said that ye teach the law of Moses. And what know ye concerning the law of Moses? Does salvation come by the law of Moses? What say ye? And they answered and said, that salvation did come by the law of Moses. But now Abinadi said unto them, I know if ye keep the commandments of God ye shall be saved; yea, if ye keep the commandments which the Lord delivered unto Moses in the mount of Sinai." (Mosiah 12:27-33.)

He then rehearsed to them the commandments; after which he again inquired:

"Have ye taught this people that they should observe to do all these things? for to keep these commandments? I say unto you nay; for if ye had, the Lord would not have caused me to come forth and to prophesy evil concerning this people. And now ye have said that salvation cometh by the law of Moses. I say unto you that it is expedient that ye should keep the law of Moses as yet; but I say unto you, that the time shall come when it shall no more be expedient to keep the law of Moses. And moreover, I say unto you, that salvation doth not come by the law alone; and were it not for the atonement which God himself shall make for the sins and iniquities of his people, that they must unavoidably perish, notwithstanding the law of Moses. And now I say unto you, that it was expedient that there should be a law given to the children of Israel, yea, even a very strict law; for they were a stiff-necked people; quick to do iniquity, and slow to remember the Lord their God; therefore there was a law given them, yea, a law of performances and of ordinances, a law which they were to observe strictly, from day to day, to keep them in remembrance of God, and their duty towards him. But behold, I say unto [116] you, that all these things were types of things to come. And now, did they understand the law? I say unto you, Nay, they did not all understand the law; and this because of the hardness of their hearts; for they understood not that there could not any man be saved, except it were through the redemption of God. For behold, did not Moses prophesy unto them concerning the coming of the Messiah, and that God should redeem his people, yea, and even all the prophets who have prophesied ever since the world began? Have they not spoken more or less concerning these things?" (Mosiah 13:25-33.)

At this time the righteous Nephites in the land of Zarahemla were keeping the law of Moses strictly, so far as its outward ordinances were concerned, and understandingly with regard to its symbolism and similitudes. When the obedient Nephites were led out of the land of Nephi by Mosiah, they found in the land, afterwards called Zarahemla, a people who proved to be a branch of the house of Israel, but who, owing to the fact that they had no records nor scriptures, had corrupted their language, failed to observe the law of Moses, and had so far fallen that they actually denied the existence of God. Mosiah and the Nephites amalgamated with this people, taught them their language, instructed them in the worship of God and built a temple in that land, which indeed they made their permanent home. Mosiah had a son called Benjamin, who ruled in righteousness all the days of his long life. Shortly before his death he instructed his son Mosiah to gather the people to the temple, that he might give them a charge and nominate his successor. It is written:

"After Mosiah had done as his father had commanded him, and had made a proclamation throughout all the land, that the people gathered themselves together throughout all the land, that they might go up to the temple to hear the words which king Benjamin should speak unto them And there were a great number, even so many that they did not number them; for they had multi[117]plied exceedingly, and waxed great in the land. And they also took of the firstlings of their flocks, that they might offer sacrifice and burnt offerings, according to the law of Moses." (Mosiah 2:1-3.)

Here we observe that the law in relation to sacrifices and burnt offerings was still faithfully observed, although nearly five hundred years had passed since Lehi left Jerusalem; for the colony which he led started on their eventful journey six hundred years before the birth of

Christ, whilst this gathering took place one hundred and twenty-five years before that same most important appearing.

During the days that the Judges ruled the Nephites the righteous portion of that people continued to observe the requirements of this law. We will simply give two quotations from the Book of Alma on this point, though the references are numerous. The first is:

"Yea, and they did keep the law of Moses; for it was expedient that they should keep the law of Moses as yet, for it was not all fulfilled. But notwithstanding the law of Moses, they did look forward to the coming of Christ, considering that the law of Moses was a type of his coming, and believing that they must keep those outward performances, until the time that he should be revealed unto them. Now they did not suppose that salvation came by the law of Moses; but the law of Moses did serve to strengthen their faith in Christ; and thus they did retain a hope through faith, unto eternal salvation, relying upon the spirit of prophecy, which spake of those things to come." (Alma 25:15-16.)

With this the words of Paul, when speaking on this subject, precisely agree: "But before faith came, we were kept under the law, shut up unto the faith, which should afterwards be revealed. Wherefore the law was our schoolmaster to bring us unto Christ, that we might be justified by faith." (Galatians 3:23-24.)

The second quotation is:

"Therefore it is expedient that there should be a great and last sacrifice; and then shall there be, or it [118] is expedient that there should be, a stop to the shedding of blood; then shall the law of Moses be fulfilled; yea, it shall be all fulfilled; every jot and tittle, and none shall have passed away. And behold, this is the whole meaning of the law; every whit pointing to that great and last sacrifice; and that great and last sacrifice will be the Son of God: yea, infinite and eternal." (Alma 34:13-14.)

But some of those who apostatized from the Nephites and organized churches of their own ceased to keep this law. Such a sect were the Zoramites, of whom it is written:

"Now the Zoramites were dissenters from the Nephites; therefore they had the word of God preached unto them. But they had fallen into great errors, for they would not observe to keep the commandments of God, and his statutes, according to the law of

THE MEDIATION AND ATONEMENT 115

Moses; neither would they observe the performances of the church, to continue in prayer and supplication to God daily, that they might not enter into temptation; yea, in fine, they did pervert the ways of the Lord in very many instances." (Alma 31:8-11.)

Shortly after the appearance of the signs that betokened the birth of the Savior at Bethlehem, there arose a few among the Nephites who endeavored "to prove by the Scriptures that it was no more expedient to observe the law of Moses. Now in this thing they did err, having not understood the Scriptures. But it came to pass that they soon became converted, and were convinced of the error which they were in, for it was made known unto them that the law was not yet fulfilled." (3 Nephi 1:24-25.)

After His resurrection, Jesus, in His ministrations in the midst of the Nephites, perceiving that they wondered regarding the fulfilment of the law of Moses, said unto the listening multitude, "Behold, I say unto you that the law is fulfilled that was given unto Moses. Behold, I am he that gave the law, and I am he who covenanted with my people Israel; therefore the law in [119] me is fulfilled, for I have come to fulfil the law; therefore it hath an end. Behold, I do not destroy the prophets, for as many as have not been fulfilled in me, verily I say unto you, shall all be fulfilled. And because I said unto you that old things hath passed away, I do not destroy that which hath been spoken concerning things which are to come. For behold, the covenant which I have made with my people is not all fulfilled; but the law which was given unto Moses hath an end in me." (3 Nephi 15:4-8.)

CHAPTER 15

The Offering of Sacrifice in the Times of the Restitution of all Things—
Teachings of the Prophet Joseph Smith thereof—The Sons of Levi—
Malachi's Prophecy—The Dispensation of the Fulness of Times.

It would appear that, when everything shall have been accomplished pertaining or relating to the sacrifice and atonement of the Son of God, in the time of the restitution of all things the sons of Levi will offer up an acceptable offering unto the Lord; what this offering will be does not distinctly appear. There are many things associated with the final salvation of man, and the working out and accomplishment of the purposes of God in relation to the human family, which lie yet in the future: the peculiar position which the children will occupy, also the position of the heathen who have died without law, and of those who have been translated, and who it would appear have a specified labor to perform associated with their mission to the terrestrial worlds; the letting loose of Satan after [120] the thousand years, and many other things which it is not permitted for us at the present time to comprehend in full. These will all be revealed in the due time of the Lord. The Prophet Joseph makes the following statement with regard to the offerings above referred to:

"Thus we behold the keys of this Priesthood consisted in obtaining the voice of Jehovah, that He talked with him [Noah] in a familiar and friendly manner, that He continued to him the keys, the covenants, the power and the glory with which He blessed Adam at the beginning; and the offering of sacrifice, which also shall be continued at the last time; for all the ordinances and duties that ever have been required by the Priesthood, under the directions and commandments of the Almighty, in any of the dispensations, shall all be had in the last dispensation; therefore all things had under the authority of the Priesthood at any former period, shall be had again, bringing to pass the restoration spoken of by the mouth of all the holy Prophets; then shall the sons of Levi offer an acceptable sacrifice to the Lord. See Malachi, 3:3: 'And he shall sit as a refiner and purifier of silver, and he shall purify the sons of Levi, and purge them as gold and silver, that they may offer unto the Lord.' It will be necessary here to make a few observations on the doctrine set forth in the above quotation, as it is generally supposed that sacrifice was entirely done away when the Great Sacrifice was offered up, and that there will be no necessity for the ordinance of sacrifice in future; but those who assert this are certainly not acquainted with the duties, privileges, and authority of the Priesthood, or with the Prophets. The offering of sacrifice has ever been connected with and forms a part of the duties of the Priesthood. It began with the Priesthood, and will be continued until after the coming of Christ, from generation to generation. We frequently have mention made of the offering of sacrifice by the servants of the Most High in ancient days, prior to the law of Moses; which ordinances will be continued when the Priesthood is [121] restored with all its authority, power and blessings. Elijah was the last Prophet that held the keys of this Priesthood, and who will, before the last dispensation, restore the authority and deliver the keys of this Priesthood, in order that all the ordinances may be attended to in righteousness. It is true that the Savior had authority and power to bestow this blessing, but the sons of Levi were too prejudiced. 'And I will send Elijah the Prophet before the great and terrible day of the Lord,' etc., etc. Why send Elijah? Because he holds the keys of the authority to administer in all the ordinances of the Priesthood, and without the authority is given, the ordinances could not be administered in righteousness. It is a very prevalent opinion that the sacrifices which were offered were entirely consumed. This was not the case; if you read Leviticus, second chapter, second and third verses, you will observe that the priest took a part as a memorial and offered it up before the Lord, while the remainder was kept for the maintenance of the priests, so that the offerings and sacrifices are not all consumed upon the altar, but the blood is sprinkled, and the fat and certain other portions are consumed. These sacrifices, as well as every ordinance belonging to the Priesthood, will, when the Temple of the Lord shall be built, and the sons of Levi be purified, be fully restored and attended to in all their powers, ramifications and blessings. This ever did and will exist when the powers of the Melchizedek Priesthood are sufficiently manifest, else how can the restitution of all things spoken of by all the holy Prophets be brought to pass? It is not to be understood that the law of Moses will be established again with all its rites and variety of ceremonies. This has never been spoken of by the Prophets, but those things which existed prior to Moses' day, namely, sacrifice, will be continued. It may be asked by some, What necessity for sacrifice, since the Great Sacrifice was offered? In answer to which, If repentance, baptism and faith existed prior to the days of Christ, what necessity for them since that [122] time? The Priesthood has descended in a regular line from father to son, through their succeeding generations. See Book of Doctrine and Covenants." (History of Joseph Smith, Deseret News, Vol. 4, No. 30; or Teachings of the Prophet Joseph Smith, 171-173.)

The remarks of President Joseph Smith are very plain and explicit, and are a strong confirmation of the passage he himself refers to, pertaining to the times of the restitution of all things; which will embrace all systems, doctrines, ordinances, dispensations, and Priesthoods connected with the Church and Kingdom of God. That there will be a full manifestation of all these things, relating to the various times and dispensations, is assured; yet, as Joseph Smith has very properly said, the details of those rituals and observances cannot now be fully defined. But as ancient Israel preserved in the Ark of the Covenant memorials of God's power, goodness and mercy, manifested during the exodus from Egypt, in the two tables of stone and the pot of manna; and of the recognition of the Aaronic Priesthood in Aaron's rod that budded; and as the sword of Laban, the sacred plates already revealed, as well as numerous others yet to be made manifest, and a Urim and Thummim were preserved on this continent; so will there be an exhibition an evidence, a memorial, and an actual manifestation of matters pertaining to laws, ordinances, ceremonies and dispensations, from the commencement of the world to the present time, preserved and manifested in the dispensation that the Lord in His loving kindness has now inaugurated. This will be in accordance with the eternal plans and purposes of God, and with the rights, ceremonies and ordinances belonging to the Priesthoods of God in the different ages, pertaining to the organization of this world, the proposed mediation and atonement of the Son of God, the manifestations and developments of the Melchizedek Priesthood, as the Prophet Joseph has referred to, as well relating to sacrifices in early days as in other matters, the introduction of the Aaronic Priesthood, together with the Ark and the Tabernacle, which we [123] are told were made after the patterns shown unto Moses in the mount—patterns which existed in the heavens; the eternal existence, authority and power of both Priesthoods as connected with God and administering in time and eternity; the attempts of Satan to overthrow the dynasty, power and authority of Jehovah and his complete failure and discomfiture; exhibiting in a panorama all the leading, prominent details of the creation, atonement, redemption, salvation and exaltation of the world and man, the organization of a new heaven and a new earth, and all the purposes of God, His plans and ordinances, manifested through the Priesthood from the first inception of the organization of the world to the final consummation, purification and exaltation of the world and its inhabitants, according to the foreknowledge and determinate counsel of the Almighty.

For as these memorials of the atonement were used by the ancient Patriarchs and Prophets to manifest to God their faith in the plan of redemption and in the coming Redeemer; so will these great types be again introduced as exhibiting the sacrifice of the great antitype, Jesus, the Mediator of the New Covenant, and as a perpetual recognition of the eternal salvation and exaltation wrought out by Him for the human family by the sacrifice of Himself. (See also 3 Nephi 15:4-8, previously quoted.) [124]

CHAPTER 16

BRIEF RETROSPECT OF THE HISTORY OF SACRIFICE AND ITS SYMBOLISM—THE PASSOVER AND THE LORD'S SUPPER—CHRIST'S RELATION TO BOTH THESE ORDINANCES—THE LAST SUPPER.

As before stated, these sacrifices, which were offered up from the days of Adam until the time of our Savior's advent, were typical of the great expiatory sacrifice which He was to make by the sacrifice of Himself. They were so many types, shadows and forms of which He was the great prototype—the substance, the reality prefigured and foreshadowed by the other sacrifices which had been offered up from the beginning.

When the law was given by Moses, all the forms pertaining to the sacrificial ceremonies were revealed in detail, and the instructions in relation thereto were not simply of a general nature, but they entered into minute particulars in relation to all things connected with those who officiated, the form and pattern of the sacred utensils and of the vestments of the Priesthood, the creatures to be sacrificed, the order of the proceedings, and indeed of all matters associated with the observance of these rites. Almost the whole of the book of Leviticus, and considerable of the book of Numbers, is occupied with these instructions and kindred matters. This Mosaic law, with all its duties, observances, ceremonies and sacrifices, continued in force until Christ's death.

The time having come when the great atonement should be made by the offering up of Himself, Christ told Peter and John to go and prepare a place where He might, according to His custom, eat the

Passover with His disciples. Eat what with His disciples? The Passover. Was it the Passover, or the Sacrament of the Lord's Supper? The Lord, in Egypt, passed by, or passed over the houses of the Israelites whose door posts had [125] been sprinkled with the blood of the lamb sacrificed for that purpose; and the Israelites were commanded to observe this Passover in all their generations. Jesus, in compliance with this command, directed that a place be made ready where He might eat the Passover with His Apostles; for He, the great prototype, was going to offer up Himself as a lamb without spot or blemish; not only for the Israelites, but for all nations, for every people, and kindred, and tongue under the face of the whole heavens: "For God so loved the world, that he gave his only begotten Son, that whosoever believeth in him should not perish, but have everlasting life. For God sent not his Son into the world to condemn the world; but that the world through him might be saved." (John 3:16-17.)

But previous to the offering up of Himself, as the great expiatory sacrifice, having fulfilled the law and made it honorable, and having introduced the Gospel, He met with His disciples, as already noticed, to eat the Passover. He then told them, "With desire I have desired to eat this passover with you before I suffer." (Luke 22:15.) To eat what with you? The Passover. To eat what with you? The Sacrament of the Lord's Supper. Thus He eat both, for the two ceremonies centered in Him, He was the embodiment of both, He was the Being provided before the foundation of the earth, and prophecied of by men of God throughout all the preceding ages; and also on account of whom the sacrifices were offered up by all the servants of the Lord, from the fall of Adam to that time; and all the various atonements heretofore offered pointed to Him, for whom they were all made and in whom they all centered. On the other hand. He it was who introduced the more perfect law, and offering Himself once for all, an infinite atonement, He through this sacrifice, accomplished that which was designed by the Almighty before the world was, and of which the blood of bullocks, of goats and of lambs was merely the shadow.

In view of what was almost immediately to take place, He instituted the sacrament of the Lord's Supper [126] in commemoration of this great crowning act of redemption. When at the table, "He took bread, and gave thanks, and brake it, and gave unto them, saying, This is my body which is given for you: this do in remembrance of me;"

(*Ibid.* 22:19) afterwards, "He took the cup, and gave thanks, and gave it to them saying, Drink ye all of it; for this is my blood of the new testament which is shed for many for the remission of sins." (Matthew 26:27-28.)

In reality, this act of the atonement was the fulfilment of the sacrifices, of the prophecying, of the Passover, and of all the leading, prominent acts of the Patriarchs and Prophets relating thereto; and having performed this, the past and the future both centered in Him. Did these worthies offer sacrifices? They prefigured His appearing and atonement. Did they prophecy? It was of Him, for the testimony of Jesus is the spirit of prophecy. Did they keep the Passover? He Himself was the great expiatory offering. Were the people called upon afterwards to commemorate this event? They did it in remembrance of Him, as a great memorial among all of His disciples in all nations, throughout all time; of the sacrifice of His broken body and spilt blood; the antitype of the sacrificial lamb slain at the time of the Passover; of Him; as being the Mediator, the Messiah, the Christ, the Alpha and Omega, the Beginning and the End: the Son of the living God.

As from the commencement of the world to the time when the Passover was instituted, sacrifices had been offered as a memorial or type of the sacrifice of the Son of God; so from the time of the Passover until that time when He came to offer up Himself, these sacrifices and types and shadows had been carefully observed by Prophets and Patriarchs; according to the command given to Moses and other followers of the Lord. So also did He Himself fulfil this requirement, and kept the Passover as did others; and now we, after the great sacrifice has been offered, partake of the Sacrament of the Lord's Supper in remembrance thereof. Thus this act was the great connecting link between the [127] past and the future; thus He fulfilled the law, met the demands of justice, and obeyed the requirements of His Heavenly Father, although laboring under the weight of the sins of the world, and the terrible expiation which He had to make, when, sweating great drops of blood, He cried: "Father, if it be possible let this cup pass from me; nevertheless not my will but thine be done," (See Matthew 26:39 and Luke 22:42.) and when expiring in agony upon the cross He cried, "It is finished," (John 19:30) and gave up the ghost.

During this ever memorable supper, the Savior said unto His disciples, "But I say unto you, I will not drink henceforth of the fruit of the vine, until that day when I drink it new with you in my Father's kingdom." (Matthew 26:29; Mark 14:25.) He was the Lamb proposed to be slain from before the foundation of the world; He was the Lamb spoken of by the Prophets in the different ages, and for which sacrifices were made; in Him was now fulfilled everything that prefigured His approach, and that was prophesied of Him pertaining to the atonement. He also was to burst the barriers of the tomb, become the first fruits of those that slept, and introduce the resurrection, and indeed to be the Resurrection and the Life. He was also to ascend to the heavens, resurrect His Saints, and after resurrecting them, drink of the fruit of the vine with them in His Father's kingdom. Every knee should yet bow to Him, and every tongue confess that He was the Christ to the glory of God the Father. Every nation, kindred, and tongue should bow to His sceptre, and the earth through Him be filled with the knowledge of God, as the waters cover the sea, the earth be redeemed and become celestial, a new heaven and a new earth be instituted, wherein dwelleth righteousness, and the redemption and resurrection of the living and the dead, according to the eternal plan of Jehovah, should be brought about through His mediation and atonement. [128]

CHAPTER 17

THE ATONEMENT AND THE RESURRECTION—ADAM AND CHRIST—WHY A LAW WAS GIVEN UNTO ADAM—THE RESULTS OF DISOBEDIENCE TO THAT LAW—TESTIMONY OF OUR FIRST PARENTS—"ADAM FELL THAT MAN MIGHT BE"—THE FALL A NECESSARY PART OF THE PLAN OF SALVATION—GOD'S PLAN A MERCIFUL PLAN—THE PLAN OF LUCIFER—MAN'S FREE AGENCY—THE CHAIN COMPLETE.

In the economy of God and the plan proposed by the Almighty, it was provided that man was to be placed under a law apparently simple in itself, yet the test of that law was fraught with the gravest consequences. The observance of that law would secure eternal life, and the penalty for the violation of that law was death. For, we are told, in Adam all die, and hence the declaration, "It is appointed for man once to die." (Hebrews 9:27.) There is another principle associated with this, which is, that the atonement provided a means and plan whereby death could be overcome, and the resurrection of the body from death be brought about, for it is written, "As in Adam all die, even so in Christ shall all be made alive." (1 Corinthians 15:22.) But without this atonement the resurrection of the body could not be brought about; hence Jesus, when on earth, proclaimed, "I am the Resurrection and the Life," (John 11:25) and He Himself "was the first fruits of them that slept." (1 Corinthians 15:20.)

Men could not have been tested without a law. The penalty for the violation of that law was death. If the law had not been broken, man would have lived; but would man thus living have been capable of perpetuating his species, and of thus fulfilling the designs of God in preparing tabernacles for the spirits which had been created in the

THE MEDIATION AND ATONEMENT

spirit world? And further, could they have had the need of a mediator, who was to act as a propitiation for the violation of this law, which it would appear from the circumstances was destined to be broken; or [129] could the eternal increase and perpetuity of man have been continued, and his high exaltation to the Godhead been accomplished, without the propitiatory atonement and sacrifice of the Son of God?

Jesus said, "Thus it is written, and thus it behooved Christ to suffer." (Luke 24:46.) Could it have behooved Christ to suffer if man had not sinned, and was it not part of the eternal plan of God that man should violate that law, that an atonement might be provided and had, and by this means man be purified and perfected, through the struggles and trials incident to his coming in contact with the powers of darkness, and, through the mediation and atonement of Jesus Christ, and his own obedience to the requirements of the law associated therewith, be raised to a higher state of existence than it would have been possible for him to have obtained without the transgression of that law?

These points are made exceedingly plain in the Pearl of Great Price. It is there stated:

"And Adam called upon the name of the Lord, and Eve also, his wife; and they heard the voice of the Lord from the way towards the garden of Eden, speaking unto them, and they saw him not; for they were shut out from his presence. And he gave unto them commandments, that they should worship the Lord their God, and should offer the firstlings of their flocks, for an offering unto the Lord. And Adam was obedient unto the commandments of the Lord. And after many days an angel of the Lord appeared unto Adam, saying, Why dost thou offer sacrifices unto the Lord? And Adam said unto him, I know not, save the Lord commanded me. And then the angel spake, saying, This thing is a similitude of the sacrifice of the Only Begotten of the Father, which is full of grace and truth. Wherefore, thou shalt do all that thou doest in the name of the Son, and thou shalt repent and call upon God in the name of the Son for evermore. And in that day the Holy Ghost fell upon Adam, which beareth record of the Father and the Son, saying, I am the Only [130] Begotten of the Father from the beginning, henceforth and for ever, that as thou hast fallen thou mayest be redeemed; and all mankind, even as many as will. And in that day Adam blessed God and was filled, and began to prophesy concerning all the families of the earth, saying, Blessed be the name of God, for because of my transgression my eyes are opened, and in this life I shall have joy, and again in the flesh I shall see God. And Eve, his wife, heard all these things and was glad, saying, Were it not for our transgression we never should have had seed, and never should have known good and evil, and the joy of our redemption, and the eternal life which God giveth unto all the obedient. And Adam and Eve blessed the name of God; and they made all things known unto their sons and their daughters." (Moses 4:4-12.)

Thus we find: Firstly. That Adam and Eve both considered that they had gained, instead of suffered loss, through their disobedience to that law; for they made the statement, that if it had not been for their transgression they never would "have known good and evil." (v. 11.) And again, they would have been incapable of increase; and without that increase the designs of God in relation to the formation of the earth and man could not have been accomplished; for one great object of the creation of the world was the propagation of the human species, that bodies might be prepared for those spirits who already existed, and who, when they saw the earth formed, shouted for joy.

Secondly. By pursuing the course they did, through the atonement, they would see God as they had done before; and furthermore, they would be capable of exaltation, which was made possible only through their fall, and the atonement of Jesus Christ; and also, they might have the comforting influence of the Spirit of God, and His guidance and direction here, as well as eternal lives and exaltations in the world to come.

Paul, in his Epistle to the Romans, also writes very directly upon these truths; he says: [131]

"Nevertheless, death reigned from Adam to Moses, even over them that had not sinned after the similitude of Adam's transgression, who is the figure of him that was to come. But not as the offence, so also is the free gift. For if, through the offence of one many be dead, much more the grace of God, and the gift by grace, which is by one man, Jesus Christ, hath abounded unto many. And not as it was by one that sinned, so is the gift; for the judgment was by one to condemnation, but the free gift is of many offences unto justification. For if by one man's offence death reigned by one; much more they which receive abundance of grace and of the gift of righteousness shall

THE MEDIATION AND ATONEMENT 127

reign in life by one Jesus Christ. Therefore, as by the offence of one judgment came upon all men to condemnation; even so by the righteousness of one the free gift came upon all men unto justification of life. For as by one man's disobedience many were made sinners, so by the obedience of one shall many be made righteous. Moreover, the law entered, that the offence might abound. But where sin abounded, grace did much more abound: that as sin hath reigned unto death, even so might grace reign through righteousness unto eternal life, by Jesus Christ our Lord." (Romans 5:14-21.)

Whilst in the Book of Mormon Lehi teaches:

"And now, behold, if Adam had not transgressed, he would not have fallen; but he would have remained in the garden of Eden. And all things which were created, must have remained in the same state which they were, after they were created; and they must have remained for ever, and had no end. And they would have had no children; wherefore, they would have remained in a state of innocence, having no joy, for they knew no misery; doing no good, for they knew no sin. But behold, all things have been done in the wisdom of Him who knoweth all things. Adam fell that men might be; and men are, that they might have joy. And the Messiah cometh in the fulness of time, that he may redeem the children of men from the fall. And because that they [132] are redeemed from the fall, they have become free for ever, knowing good from evil; to act for themselves, and not to be acted upon, save it be by the punishment of the law at the great and last day, according to the commandments which God hath given. Wherefore, men are free according to the flesh; and all things are given them which are expedient unto man. And they are free to choose liberty and eternal life, through the great mediation of all men, or to choose captivity and death, according to the captivity and power of the devil; for he seeketh that all men might be miserable, like unto himself." (2 Nephi 2:22-27.)

In the same book it is written:

"Yea, I know that ye know, that in the body he shall show himself unto those at Jerusalem, from whence we came; for it is expedient that it should be among them; for it behooveth the great Creator that he suffereth himself to become subject unto man in the flesh, and die for all men, that all men might become subject unto him. For as death hath passed upon all men, to fulfil the merciful plan of the great Creator, there must needs be a power of resurrection, and the resurrection must needs come unto man by reason of the fall; and the fall came by reason of transgression; and because man became fallen, they were cut off from the presence of the Lord. Wherefore it must needs be an infinite atonement. Save it should be an infinite atonement, this corruption could not put on incorruption. Wherefore, the first judgment which came upon man must needs have remained to an endless duration. And if so, this flesh must have laid down to rot and to crumble to its mother earth, to rise no more. O the wisdom of God! his mercy and grace! For behold, if the flesh should rise no more, our spirits must become subject to that angel who fell from before the presence of the eternal God, and became the devil, to rise no more." (2 Nephi 9:5-8.)

There is a principle developed in the above quotation to the effect that death was "passed upon all men to [133] fulfil the *merciful plan of the great Creator;*" (v. 6) and furthermore, that the resurrection came "by reason of the fall." (v. 6.) For if man had not sinned. there would have been no death, and if Jesus had not atoned for the sin, there would have been no resurrection Hence these things are spoken of as being according to the merciful plan of God. This corruption could not have put on incorruption, and this mortality could not have put on immortality; for, as we have elsewhere shown, man by reason of any thing that he himself could do or accomplish, could only exalt himself to the dignity and capability of man and therefore it needed the atonement of a God, before man, through the adoption, could be exalted to the Godhead.

Again, if the body could not have been resurrected, it would have had to "crumble to its mother earth," (v. 7) and remain in that condition without the capability of ascending to the Godhead: and furthermore, not only would our bodies have lost their entity, their life and power, but the spirit also would have been placed in a state of subjection "to that angel who fell from before the presence of the eternal God, and became the devil," (v. 8) without a capability or even hope of life, salvation and exaltation, and would have been deprived of all free agency and power, and subject to the influences, dominion and eternal destruction of Lucifer, the enemy of man and of God. Hence, on this ground, and because of the terrible effects which would have resulted to humanity from the proposed plan to deprive man of his free agency, and in seeking to do away with the atonement, Lucifer was cast out of heaven, as were also those associated with him in the same diabolical plans and purposes.

The testimony of the Book of Doctrine and Covenants is in full accord with the revelations in the ancient scriptures. In it we are instructed that God "created man, male and female, after his own image and in his own likeness created he them, and gave unto them commandments that they should love and serve him, the [134] only living and true God, and that he should be the only being whom they should worship. But by the transgression of these holy laws, man became sensual and devilish, and became fallen man. Wherefore the Almighty God gave his Only Begotten Son, as it is written in those scriptures which have been given of him. He suffered temptations, but gave no heed unto them; he was crucified, died, and rose again the third day; and ascended into heaven, to sit down on the right hand of the Father, to reign with almighty power according to the will of the Father." (D&C 20:18-24.)

Again, we read from the same source:

"Behold, I gave unto him that he should be an agent unto himself: and I gave unto him commandment, but no temporal commandment gave I unto him, for my commandments are spiritual, they are not natural nor temporal, neither carnal nor sensual." (D&C 29:35.)

"Wherefore, it came to pass that the devil tempted Adam, and he partook the forbidden fruit and transgressed the commandment, wherein he became subject to the will of the devil, because he yielded unto temptation. Wherefore, I the Lord God caused that he should be cast out from the garden of Eden, from my presence, because of his transgression, wherein he became spiritually dead, which is the first death, even that same death, which is the last death, which is spiritual, which shall be pronounced upon the wicked when I shall say, Depart, ye cursed. But, behold. I say unto you, that I the Lord God gave unto Adam and to his seed that they should not die as to the temporal death, until I the Lord God should send forth angels to declare unto them repentance and redemption, through faith on the name of mine Only Begotten Son. And thus did I, the Lord God, appoint unto man the days of his probation; that by his natural death he might be raised in immortality unto eternal life, even as many as would believe." (D&C 29:40-43.) [135]

In accordance with this we find it written in the Pearl of Great Price, that the Lord did send an angel to Adam (as elsewhere quoted) who taught unto him the Gospel.

Thus it would appear that if any of the links of this great chain had been broken, it would have interfered with the comprehensive plan of the Almighty pertaining to the salvation and eternal exaltation of those spirits who were His sons and for whom principally the world was made; that they through submission to the requirements of the eternal principle and law governing these matters might possess bodies and these bodies united with the spirits might become living souls, and being the sons of God, and made in the image of God, they, through the atonement might be exalted by obedience to the law of the Gospel; to the Godhead.

CHAPTER 18

Christ, as the Son of God—A Comparison between His Position Glory, etc., and Those of other Sons of God—His Recognition by the Father—Christ called the Very Eternal Father.

It may here be asked. What difference is there between the Son of God, as the Son of God, the Redeemer, and those who believe in Him and partake of the blessings of the Gospel?

One thing, as we read, is that the Father gave Him power to have life in Himself: "For as the Father hath life in himself, so hath he given to the Son to have life in himself;" (John 5:26) and further, He had power, when all mankind had lost their life, to restore life [136] to them again; and hence He is the Resurrection and the Life, which power no other man possesses.

Another distinction is, that having this life in Himself, He had power, as He said, to lay down His life and to take it up again, which power was also given Him by the Father. This is also a power which no other being associated with this earth possesses.

Again, He is the brightness of His Father's glory and the express image of His person. Also, He doeth what He seeth the Father do, while we only do that which we are permitted and empowered to do by Him.

He is the Elect, the Chosen, and one of the Presidency in the heavens, and in Him dwells all the fulness of the Godhead bodily, which could not be said of us in any of these particulars.

Another thing is, that all power is given to Him in heaven and upon earth, which no earthly being could say.

It is also stated that Lucifer was before Adam; so was Jesus. And Adam, as well as all other believers, was commanded to do all that he did in the name of the Son, and to call upon God in His name for ever more; which honor was not applicable to any earthly being.

He, in the nearness of His relationship to the Father, seems to occupy a position that no other person occupies. He is spoken of as His well beloved Son, as the Only Begotten of the Father—does not this mean the only begotten after the flesh? If He was the first born and obedient to the laws of His Father, did He not inherit the position by right to be the representative of God, the Savior and Redeemer of the world? And was it not His peculiar right and privilege as the firstborn, the legitimate heir of God, the Eternal Father, to step forth, accomplish and carry out the designs of His Heavenly Father pertaining to the redemption, salvation and exaltation of man? And being Himself without sin (which no other mortal was), He took the position of Savior and Redeemer, which by right belonged [137] to Him as the first born. And does it not seem that in having a body specially prepared, and being the offspring of God, both in body and spirit, He stood preeminently in the position of the Son of God, or in the place of God, and was God, and was thus the fit and only personage capable of making an infinite atonement? Hence we read:

"Wherefore, when he cometh into the world, he saith, Sacrifice and offering thou wouldst not, but a body hast thou prepared me: in burnt offerings and sacrifices for sin thou hast had no pleasure. Then said I, Lo, I come (in the volume of the book it is written of me) to do thy will, O God. Above, when he said, Sacrifice and offering and burnt-offerings and offering for sin thou wouldst not, neither hadst pleasure therein; which are offered by the law; then said he, Lo, I come to do thy will, O God He taketh away the first, that he may establish the second." (Hebrews 10:5-9.)

We are told, in the Pearl of Great Price, that when Satan proposed a plan of his own, promising to redeem every soul of man, but wherein the free agency of man would be destroyed, and said, "Wherefore give me thine honor," (Moses 4:1) the Only Begotten said, "Father, thy will be done, and the glory be thine for ever" (v. 2) "I am prepared to carry out thy plan." The Apostle above quoted states, "A body hast thou prepared me . . . Then said I, Lo, I come to do thy will, O Lord." (Hebrews 10:5, 7.) Hence from the above we learn that though others might be the sons of God through Him, yet it needed His body, His fulfilment of the law, the sacrifice or offering up of that body in the atonement, before any of these others, who were also sons of God by birth in the spirit world, could attain to the position of sons of God as He was; and that only through His mediation and atonement. So that in Him, and of Him, and through Him, through the principle of adoption, could we alone obtain that position which is spoken of by John: "Beloved, now are we the sons of God; and it doth not yet appear what we shall be: but we know [138] that when he shall appear we shall be like him, for we shall see him as he is." (1 John 3:2.) Thus His atonement made it possible for us to obtain an exaltation, which we could not have possessed without it.

"His name shall be called Immanuel," (See Matthew 1:23; Isaiah 7:14) which being interpreted is, God with us. Hence He is not only called the Son of God, the First Begotten of the Father, the Well Beloved, the Head, and Ruler, and Dictator of all things, Jehovah, the I Am, the Alpha and Omega, but He is also called the Very Eternal Father. Does not this mean that in Him were the attributes and power of the Very Eternal Father? For the angel to Adam said that all things should be done in His name. A voice was heard from the heavens, when Jesus was baptized by John the Baptist, saying, "This is my beloved Son, in whom I am well pleased," (Matthew 3:17) and when the Father and the Son appeared together to the Prophet Joseph Smith they were exactly alike in form, in appearance, in glory; and the Father said, pointing to His Son. "This is my beloved Son; hear Him."(Joseph Smith-History 1:17.) There the Father had His apparent tabernacle, and the Son had His apparent tabernacle; but the Son was the agency through which the Father would communicate to man; as it is elsewhere said, "Wherefore, thou shalt do all that thou doest in the name of the Son. And thou shalt repent, and shalt call upon God, in the name of the Son, for evermore." (Moses 5:8.) [139]

CHAPTER 19

MAN AS MAN - HIS EXCELLENCY AND HIS LIMITATIONS—SALVATION AND ETERNAL PROGRESSION IMPOSSIBLE WITHOUT THE ATONEMENT—IN CHRIST ONLY CAN ALL BE MADE ALIVE.

Man, as man, can only make use of the powers which are possessed by man. Made, indeed, as represented in the Scriptures, in the image of God, as monarch of the universe he stands erect on the earth in the likeness of his Great Creator; beautifully constructed in all his parts, with a body possessing all the functions necessary for the wants of humanity; standing, not only by right, but by adaptability, beauty, symmetry and glory, at the head of all creation; possessing also mental powers and the capacity of reflecting upon the past, with capabilities to reason upon cause and effect, and by the inductive powers of his mind, through the inspiration of the Almighty, to comprehend the magnificent laws of nature as exhibited in the works of creation; with the capacity also of using the elements and forces of nature, and of adapting them to his own special benefit; and by his powers penetrating into the deep, ascending into the heavens, rushing with mighty velocity across the earth, making use of the separate or combined forces of nature with which he is surrounded and subjugating them to his will; as, likewise, by his intelligence, he has dominion over the fishes of the sea, over the fowls of the air, and over the cattle. He can girdle the earth with the electric fluid and convey his thoughts to any land or zone: by the same subtle influence he can talk with his fellows, and be heard when hundreds of miles apart. He can apply the forces of earth, air, fire and water to make them subservient to his will, and stands proudly erect as the head of all creation and the representative of God upon the earth. [140] But while he occupies this exalted position, and is in the image of God, yet he possesses simply, as a man, only the powers which belong to man; and is subject to weakness, infirmity, disease and death. And when he dies, without some superior aid pertaining to the future, that noble structure lies silent and helpless, its organs, that heretofore were active, lively and energetic, are now dormant, inactive and powerless. And what of the mind, that before went back into eternity and reached forward into eternity? And what of its powers? Or what of that spirit, which, with its Godlike energies, its prescience and power, could grasp infinity? What of it, and where is it? The Scriptures say that the body returns to the dust and the spirit returns to God who gave it. But what of its powers as made known to us, what of the hereafter? The philosophy of the world tells us that the spirit dies with the body, and like it is dissipated in surrounding nature, but as an entirety no longer exists; and all the power the being ever had was to propagate its own species and to impart the powers of the body and the mind to its posterity. Such philosophers can comprehend nothing pertaining to the future—no glory, no exaltation, no eternal progression, only as developed by a succession of manhood. If, then, there is a spirit in man which reaches into futurity, that would grasp eternal progress, eternal enjoyments, and eternal exaltations; then those glories, those exaltations, those capabilities and those powers must be the gift of some superior being, power, or authority to that which exists in man; for the foregoing is a brief exhibition of the powers and capabilities of humanity. It is of this gift that we now speak. It is of a principle that emanates from God, that originates with a superior intelligence, whose plans, and powers, and capabilities are exalted above those of mortal man, as the heavens are above the earth, or as the majestic works of the Great Creator throughout the infinitude of space are superior to the puny efforts of the children of mortality. It is for the exaltation of man to this state [141] of superior intelligence and Godhead that the mediation and atonement of Jesus Christ is instituted; and that noble being, man, made in the image of God, is rendered capable not only of being a son of man, but also a son of God, through adoption, and is rendered capable of becoming a God, possessing the power, the majesty, the exaltation ad the position of a God. As it is written,

"Beloved, now are we the sons of God; and it doth not yet appear what we shall be: but we know that, when he shall appear, we shall be like him; for we shall see him as he is." (1 John 3:2.)

As a man through the powers of his body he could attain to the dignity and completeness of manhood, but could go no further; as a man he is born, as a man he lives, and as a man he dies; but through the essence and power of the Godhead, which is in him, which descended to him as the gift of God from his heavenly Father, he is capable of rising from the contracted limits of manhood to the dignity of a God, and thus through the atonement of Jesus Christ and the adoption he is capable of eternal exaltation, eternal lives and eternal progression. But this transition from his manhood to the Godhead can alone be made through a power which is superior to man—an infinite power, an eternal power, even the power of the Godhead: for as in Adam all die, so in Christ *only* can all be made alive. Through Him mankind are brought into communion and communication with God; through His atonement they are enabled, as He was, to vanquish death; through that atonement and the power of the Priesthood associated therewith, they become heirs of God and joint heirs with Jesus Christ, and inheritors of thrones, powers, principalities and dommions in the eternal worlds. And instead of being subject to death, when that last enemy shall be destroyed, and death be swallowed up in victory, through that atonement they can become the fathers and mothers of lives, and be capable of perpetual and eternal progression. [142]

CHAPTER 20

Christ to be Subject to Man—His Descent Below all Things—Man's Condition had there been no Atonement—The Sons of God—Man's Inability to Save Himself—Christ's Glory before the World Was—Necessity for an Infinite Atonement—The Father and Son have Life in Themselves.

Again we will return to the quotation from the Book of Mormon. Satan, as we have remarked before, wanted to deprive man of his agency, for if man had his agency, it would seem that necessarily the Lord would be subject to him; as is stated, "For it behooveth the Great Creator that he suffereth himself to become subject unto man in the flesh, and die for all men, that all men might become subject unto him." (2 Nephi 9:5.)

The Lord being thus subjected to man, He would be placed in the lowest position to which it was possible for Him to descend; because of the weakness, the corruption and the fallibility of human nature. But if man had his free agency, this necessarily would be the result, and hence, as it is said, Jesus descended below all things that He might be raised above all things; and hence also, while Satan's calculation was to deprive man of his free agency, and to prevent himself or the Only Begotten from being subject to this humiliation and infamy, the Lord's plan was to give man his free agency, provide a redeemer, and suffer that redeemer to endure all the results incidental to such a position, and thus, by offering himself as a substitute and conquering death, hell and the grave, he would ultimately subjugate all things unto himself; and at the same time make it possible for man to obtain an exaltation that he never could have had without his agency. It is said, as already stated, "For behold, if the flesh should [143] rise no more, our spirits must become subject to that angel who fell from before the presence of the eternal God, and became the devil, to rise no more;" (v. 8) and hence the plan of Satan it appears would have frustrated the designs of the Almighty, and have deprived man of that exaltation and glory which his Heavenly Father contemplated. It is further written:

"And our spirits must have become like unto him, and we become devils, angels to a devil, to be shut out from the presence of our God, and to remain with the father of lies; in misery, like unto himself; yea, to that being who beguiled our first parents; who transformeth himself nigh unto an angel of light, and stirreth up the children of men unto secret combinations of murder, and all manner of secret works of darkness. O how great the goodness of our God, who prepareth a way for our escape from the grasp of this awful monster; yea, that monster, death and hell, which I call the death of the body, and also the death of the spirit. And because of the way of deliverance of our God, the Holy One of Israel, this death, of which I have spoken, which is the temporal, shall deliver up its dead; which death is the grave. And this death of which I have spoken, which is the spiritual death, shall deliver up its dead; which spiritual death is hell; wherefore, death and hell must deliver up their dead, and hell must deliver up its captive spirits, and the grave must deliver up its captive bodies, and the bodies and the spirits of men will be restored one to the other; and it is by the power of the resurrection of the Holy One of Israel. O how great the plan of our God! For on the other hand, the paradise of God must deliver up the spirits of the righteous, and the grave deliver up the body of the righteous; and the spirit and the body is restored to itself again, and all men become incorruptible and immortal, and they are living souls, having a perfect knowledge like unto us in the flesh save it be that our knowledge shall be perfect; wherefore, we shall have a perfect knowledge of all our guilt; [144] and our uncleanness, and our nakedness; and the righteous shall have a perfect knowledge of their enjoyment, and their righteousness, being clothed with purity, yea, even with the robe of righteousness. And it shall come to pass, that when all men shall have passed from this first death unto life, insomuch as they have become immortal, they must appear before the judgment seat of the Holy One of Israel; and then cometh the judgment, and then must they be judged according to the holy judgment of God. And assuredly, as the Lord liveth, for the Lord God hath spoken it, and it is his eternal word, which cannot pass away, that they who are righteous, shall be righteous still, and they who are filthy, shall be filthy still; wherefore, they who are filthy, are the devil and his angels; and they shall go away into everlasting fire, prepared for them; and their torment is as a lake of fire and brimstone, whose flame ascendeth up for ever and ever, and has no end. O the greatness and the justice of our God! For he executeth all his words, and they have gone forth out of his mouth, and his law must be fulfilled." (2 Nephi 9:9-17.)

In the economy of God pertaining to the salvation of the human family, we are told in the Scriptures that it was necessary that Christ should descend below all things, that He might be raised above all things; as stated above, He had to "become subject to man in the flesh" (v. 5.) It was further necessary that He should descend below all things, in order that He might raise others above all things; for if He could not raise Himself and be exalted through those principles brought about by the atonement, He could not raise others; He could not do for others what He could not do for Himself, and hence it was necessary for him to descend below all things that He might be raised above all things; and it was necessary that those whom He proposed to save should also descend below all things, that by and through the same power that He obtained His exaltation, they also, through His atonement, expiation and intercession, might [145] be raised to the same power with Him; and, as He was the Son of God, that they might also be the adopted sons of God; hence John says:

"Beloved, now are we the sons of God; and it doth not yet appear what we shall be: but we know that, when he shall appear, we shall be like him; for we shall see him as he is." (1 John 3:2.)

And by this power we shall overcome and sit down on His throne, as Jesus overcame and sat down upon the throne of His Father.

We are told in the foregoing quotation from the Book of Mormon that the atonement must needs be infinite. Why did it need an infinite atonement? For the simple reason that a stream can never rise higher than its fountain; and man having assumed a fleshly body and become of the earth earthy, and through the violation of a law having cut himself off from his association with his Father, and become subject to death; in this condition, as the mortal life of man was short, and in and of himself he could have no hope of benefitting himself, or redeeming himself from his fallen condition, or of bringing himself back to the presence of his Father, some superior agency was needed to elevate him above his low and degraded position. This superior agency was the Son of God, who had not, as man had, violated a law of His Father, but was yet one with His Father, possessing His glory, His power, His authority, His dominion. As He, Himself, prayed:

"And now, O Father, glorify thou me with thine own self, with the glory which I had with thee before the world was." (John 17:5.)

A man, as a man, could arrive at all the dignity that a man was capable of obtaining or receiving; but it needed a God to raise him to the dignity of a God. For this cause it is written, "Now are we the sons of God; and it doth not yet appear what we shall be: but we know that when he shall appear we shall be like him." (1 John 3:2.) And how and why like Him? Because, through the instrumentality of the atonement and the [146] adoption, it is made possible for us to become of the family of God, and joint heirs with Jesus Christ; and that as He, the potential instrument, through the oneness that existed between Him and His Father, by reason of obedience to divine law, overcame death, hell and the grave, and sat down upon His Father's throne, so shall we be able to sit down with Him, even upon His throne. Thus, as it is taught in the Book of Mormon, it must needs be that there be an infinite atonement; and hence of Him, and by Him, and through Him are all things; and through Him do we obtain every blessing, power, right, immunity, salvation and exaltation. He is our God, our Redeemer, our Savior, to whom, with the Father and the Holy Spirit, be eternal and everlasting praises worlds without end.

Again, Jesus testifies of Himself:

"Verily, verily, I say unto you, The hour is coming, and now is, when the dead shall hear the voice of the Son of God: and they that hear shall live. For as the Father hath life in himself, so hath he given to the Son to have life in himself; and hath given him authority to execute judgment also, because he is the Son of man. Marvel not at this: for the hour is coming, in the which all that are in the graves shall hear his voice, and shall come forth; they that have done good, unto the resurrection of life; and they that have done evil, unto the resurrection of damnation." (John 5:25-29.)

It would seem from the above that the Son hath life inherent in Himself, even as the Father hath life in Himself, He having received this power from the Father. Also, that He had power in Himself, as elsewhere stated, to lay down this body, and also to take it up again; and in this respect He differed from others. While man dies and lays down his body, he has not power under any circumstance to raise it again, only through the power of Jesus and His intercession and atonement; for the Redeemer has proclaimed Himself to be the Resurrection and the Life; and it is by [147] this resurrective power which He possesses, as the gift of God through obedience to the will of the Father, that the dead shall hear the voice of God and shall live. Hence He not only becomes the first fruits of those that slept, having conquered death Himself and triumphed over it, but He also becomes the means of the resurrection of all men from the dead. Hence He says:

"Therefore doth my Father love me, because I lay down my life, that I might take it again. No man taketh it from me, but I lay it down of myself. I have power to lay it down, and I have power to take it again. This commandment have I received of my Father." (John 10:17-18.)

Thus, when He says He has power to lay down His life and power to take it up again, He speaks of a power never before exhibited among men upon this earth; and which power, indeed, does not belong to man in and of himself. [148]

CHAPTER 21

The Relation of the Atonement to Little Children—Jesus Assumes the Responsibility of Man's Transgression, and Bears the Weight of his Sins and Sufferings—The Inferior Creatures and Sacrifice—The Terrors and Agonies of Christ's Passion and Death—The Tribulations, Earthquakes, etc., when He gave up the Ghost—Universal Nature Trembles—The Prophecies of Zenos and Enoch— The Testimony of the Centurion—Heirship, and the Descent of Blessings and Curses.

The Redeemer Himself, when tabernacling in the flesh, said to His disciples on the Eastern Continent, "Suffer little children to come unto me, and forbid them not: for of such is the kingdom of God. Verily I say unto you, Whosoever shall not receive the kingdom of God as a little child shall in no wise enter therein." (Luke 18:16-17.) And after His crucifixion and resurrection He repeated this same admonition to His Nephite disciples: "And again I say unto you, Ye must repent, and be baptized in my name and become as a little child, or ye can in no wise inherit the kingdom of God." (3 Nephi 11:38.)

Without Adam's transgression those children could not have existed; through the atonement they are placed in a state of salvation without any act of their own. These would embrace, according to the opinion of statisticians, more than one-half of the human family, who can attribute their salvation only to the mediation and atonement of the Savior. Thus, as stated elsewhere, in some mysterious, incomprehensible way, Jesus assumed the responsibility which naturally would have devolved upon Adam; but which could only be accomplished through the mediation of Himself, and by taking upon

Himself their sorrows, assuming their responsibilities, and bearing their transgressions or sins. In a manner to us incomprehensible and inexplicable, he bore [149] the weight of the sins of the whole world; not only of Adam, but of his posterity; and in doing that, opened the kingdom of heaven, not only to all believers and all who obeyed the law of God, but to more than one-half of the human family who die before they come to years of maturity, as well as to the heathen, who, having died without law, will, through His mediation, be resurrected without law, and be judged without law, and thus participate, according to their capacity, works and worth, in the blessings of His atonement.

Again, there is another phase of this subject that must not be forgotten. From the commencement of the offering of sacrifices the inferior creature had to suffer for the superior. Although it had taken no part in the act of disobedience, yet was its blood shed and its life sacrificed, thus prefiguring the atonement of the Son of God, which should eventually take place. The creature indeed was made subject to vanity not willingly, but by reason of Him who hath subjected the same in hope. Millions of such offerings were made, and hecatombs of these expiatory sacrifices were offered in view of the great event that would be consummated when Jesus should offer up Himself. With man this was simply the obedience to a command and a given law, and with him might be considered simply a pecuniary sacrifice: with the animals it was a sacrifice of life. But what is the reason for all this suffering and bloodshed, and sacrifice? We are told that "without shedding of blood is no remission" of sins. (Hebrews 9:22.) This is beyond our comprehension. Jesus had to take away sin by the sacrifice of Himself, the just for the unjust, but, previous to this grand sacrifice, these animals had to have their blood shed as types, until the great antitype should offer up Himself once for all. And as He in His own person bore the sins of all, and atoned for them by the sacrifice of Himself, so there came upon Him the weight and agony of ages and generations the indescribable agony consequent upon this great sacrificial atonement wherein He bore the sins of the world, and suffered in [150] His own person the consequences of an eternal law of God broken by man. Hence His profound grief, His indescribable anguish, His overpowering torture, all experienced in the submission to the eternal fiat of Jehovah and the requirements of an inexorable law.

The suffering of the Son of God was not simply the suffering of personal death; for in assuming the position that He did in making an atonement for the sins of the world He bore the weight, the responsibility, and the burden of the sins of all men, which, to us, is incomprehensible. As stated, "the Lord, your Redeemer, suffered death in the flesh; wherefore he suffereth the pains of all men;" (D&C 18:11) and Isaiah says: "Surely he hath borne our griefs and carried our sorrows," (Isaiah 53:4) also, "The Lord hath laid on him the iniquity of us all," (v. 6) and again, "He hath poured out his soul unto death, and he was numbered with the transgressors; and he bare the sins of many;" (v. 12) or, as it is written in the Second Book of Nephi: "For behold, he suffereth the pains of all men; yea, the pains of every living creature, both men, women and children, who belong to the family of Adam;" (2 Nephi 9:21) whilst in Mosiah it is declared: "He shall suffer temptations, and pain of body, hunger, thirst and fatigue, even more than man can suffer, except it be unto death; for behold, blood cometh from every pore, so great shall be his anguish for the wickedness and abominations of his people." (Mosiah 3:7.)

Groaning beneath this concentrated load, this intense, incomprehensible pressure, this terrible exaction of Divine justice, from which feeble humanity shrank, and through the agony thus experienced sweating great drops of blood, He was led to exclaim, "Father, if it be possible, let this cup pass from me." (Matthew 26:39.) He had wrestled with the superincumbent load in the wilderness, He had struggled against the powers of darkness that had been let loose upon him there; placed below all things, His mind surcharged with agony and pain, lonely and apparently helpless and forsaken, in his agony the blood oozed from His pores. Thus rejected by His own, attacked by the [151] powers of darkness, and seemingly forsaken by His God, on the cross He bowed beneath the accumulated load, and cried out in anguish, "My God, my God, why hast thou forsaken me!" (Matthew 27:46; Mark 15:34.) When death approached to relieve Him from His horrible position, a ray of hope appeared through the abyss of darkness with which He had been surrounded, and in a spasm of relief, seeing the bright future beyond, He said, "It is finished! Father, into thy hands I commend my spirit." (See John 19:30 and Luke 23:46.) As a God, He descended below all things, and made Himself

THE MEDIATION AND ATONEMENT

subject to man in man's fallen condition; as a man, He grappled with all the circumstances incident to His sufferings in the world. Anointed, indeed, with the oil of gladness above His fellows, He struggled with and overcame the powers of men and devils, of earth and hell combined; and aided by this superior power of the Godhead, He vanquished death, hell and the grave, and arose triumphant as the Son of God, the very eternal Father, the Messiah, the Prince of peace, the Redeemer, the Savior of the world; having finished and completed the work pertaining to the atonement, which His Father had given Him to do as the Son of God and the Son of man. As the Son of Man, He endured all that it was possible for flesh and blood to endure; as the Son of God He triumphed over all, and forever ascended to the right hand of God, to further carry out the designs of Jehovah pertaining to the world and to the human family.

And again, not only did His agony affect the mind and body of Jesus, causing Him to sweat great drops of blood, but by reason of some principle, to us unfathomable, His suffering affected universal nature.

"World upon world, eternal things,
 Hang on thy anguish, King of kings."

When he gave up the ghost, the solid rocks were riven, the foundations of the earth trembled, earthquakes shook the continents and rent the isles of the sea, a deep darkness overspread the sky, the mighty waters overflowed their accustomed bounds, huge mountains sank and valleys rose, the handiwork of feeble [152] men was overthrown, their cities were engulphed or consumed by the vivid shafts of lightning, and all material things were convulsed with the throes of seeming dissolution. Thus was brought to pass that which was spoken by the prophet Zenos: "The rocks of the earth must rend; and because of the groanings of the earth, many of the kings of the isles of the sea shall be wrought upon by the Spirit of God to exclaim, The God of nature suffers." (1 Nephi 19:12.) And it is recorded, that so confessed the Centurion, and they that were with him watching the body of Jesus. For when they witnessed the earthquake, and the other things that were done, they feared greatly, saying, "Truly this was the Son of God." (Matthew 27:54.) So also was fulfilled that which is written in the prophecy of Enoch:

"And the Lord said unto Enoch, Look; and he looked and beheld the Son of Man lifted up on the cross, after the manner of men; and he heard a loud voice; and the heavens were veiled; and all the creations of God mourned; and the earth groaned; and the rocks were rent; and the Saints arose, and were crowned at the right hand of the Son of Man, with crowns of glory; and as many of the spirits as were in prison came forth, and stood on the right hand of God; and the remainder were reserved in chains of darkness until the judgment of the great day." (Moses 7:55-57.)

Thus, such was the torturing pressure of this intense, this indescribable agony, that it burst forth abroad beyond the confines of His body, convulsed all nature and spread throughout all space.

The statement previously quoted, "The Lord hath laid on him the iniquity of us all," (Isaiah 53:6) could only be in reference to the transgression of our first parent, who, acting as the progenitor and head of the human family, assumed a responsibility not only for himself, but for all of his seed; for the whole of the human family not having then been born, could not be responsible, personally, for acts that transpired before they had an existence on the earth. But as children inherit blessings [153] from their fathers, so it would also seem that they must inherit curses, or share in their calamities. The Lord, in speaking to the children of Israel, said He would visit "the iniquity of the fathers upon the children unto the third and fourth generation of them that hate"(Exodus 20:5) him; and furthermore "a bastard shall not enter into the congregation of the Lord, even to his tenth generation." (Deuteronomy 23:2.) This ostracism or punishment could be for no personal act of their own, for they had no part in the sin of their parents; any more than Adam's progeny had in the original sin or transgression. But it seems to be a principle admitted, that if they share the blessings accruing to their father for righteous acts, they must also share the condemnation for acts that are unrighteous. Hence comes in the atonement of the Messiah, which amply covers all of these acts, and more than that, for as Paul says: "But not as the offence, so also is the free gift. For if through the offence of one many be dead, much more the grace of God, and the gift by grace, which is by one man, Jesus Christ; hath abounded unto many." (Romans 5:15.) Hence we say, as above, the atonement covered more, apparently, than the transgression; for Adam, without the transgression, would have had no increase. That transgression opened the way for the increase, as stated by Eve, "Were it not for our transgression, we never should have had seed, and never should have known good and evil, and the joy of our redemption, and the eternal life which God giveth unto all the obedient." (Moses 5:11.) That being the case, all children born among any people, not having arrived at the years of accountability, are saved through the atonement of Jesus Christ, as stated by Moroni:

"Little children cannot repent; wherefore it is awful wickedness to deny the pure mercies of God unto them, for they are all alive in him because of his mercy. And he that saith, that little children need baptism, denieth the mercies of Christ, and setteth at naught the atonement of him and the power of his redemption. Wo unto such, for they are in danger of death, hell, and [154] endless torment. I speak it boldly, God hath commanded me. Listen unto them and give heed, or they stand against you at the judgment seat of Christ. For behold, that all little children are alive in Christ, and also all they that are without the law. For the power of redemption cometh on all they that have no law; wherefore, he that is not condemned, or he that is under no condemnation, cannot repent; and unto such baptism availeth nothing. But it is mockery before God, denying the mercies of Christ, and the power of his Holy Spirit, and putting trust in dead works." (Moroni 8:19-23.)

CHAPTER 22

The Operations of the Priesthood in the Heavens and upon the Earth, in Time and Eternity—The Heirs of the Celestial Kingdom—Those who Die without Law—The Judges of the Earth—Priests and Kings—Christ the King of Kings—Condition of Patriarch Joseph Smith, Apostle David Patten and Others—Moses and Elias—The Visits of Angels and their Testimonies—Peter, James and John—The Angel in the Book of Revelation.

There is something peculiarly interesting in the contemplation of events associated with the future destiny of mankind. Among other things it will be seen that there is a very close connection or affinity between the operations of the Priesthood in the heavens and the Priesthood upon earth. In examining this subject we find it written:

"The Lord redeemeth none such that rebel against him and die in their sins; yea, even all those that have perished in their sins ever since the world began, [155] that have wilfully rebelled against God, that have known the commandments of God, and would not keep them; these are they that have no part in the first resurrection." (Mosiah 15:26.)

But on the other hand it is promised that those who would have received the Gospel if they had had the opportunity shall yet have that privilege. The Prophet Joseph Smith records in his history: "Thus came the voice of the Lord unto me, saying, All those who have died without a knowledge of this Gospel, who would have received it if they had been permitted to tarry, shall be heirs of the celestial kingdom of God; also all that shall die henceforth without a knowledge of it, who would have received it with all their hearts, shall be heirs of that kingdom, for I, the Lord, will judge all men according to their works, according to the desire of their hearts." (Deseret News, Vol. 2, No. 22; or D&C 137:7-9.)

With this agree the words of the Apostle Paul, that those who have died without law shall be judged without law; whilst the Lord further reveals to the Prophet Joseph that "that which is governed by law is also preserved by law, and perfected and sanctified by the same. That which breaketh a law, and abideth not by law, but seeketh to become a law unto itself, and willeth to abide in sin, and altogether abideth in sin, cannot be sanctified by law, neither by mercy, justice, nor judgment. Therefore they must remain filthy still." (D&C 88:34-35.)

With this teaching is associated a grand principle connected with the everlasting Priesthood, which administers in time and in eternity. When we reflect upon the statement of creatures being judged without law, the question arises as to who are to be their judges. We may here state that Christ is called the judge of the quick and the dead, the judge of all the earth. We further read that the Twelve Apostles who ministered in Jerusalem "shall sit upon twelve thrones, judging the twelve tribes of Israel." (Matthew 19:28.) Also the following:

"And again, verily, verily, I say unto you, and it [156] hath gone forth in a firm decree, by the will of the Father, that mine apostles, the Twelve who were with me in my ministry at Jerusalem, shall stand at my right hand at the day of my coming in a pillar of fire, being clothed with robes of righteousness, with crowns upon their heads, in glory even as I am, to judge the whole house of Israel, even as many as have loved me and kept my commandments. and none else." (D&C 29:12.)

And Nephi writes in the Book of Mormon:

"And the angel spake unto me, saying, Behold the twelve disciples of the Lamb, who are chosen to minister unto thy seed. And he said unto me, Thou rememberest the twelve apostles of the Lamb? Behold, they are they who shall judge the twelve tribes of Israel; wherefore, the twelve ministers of thy seed shall be judged of them; for ye are of the house of Israel. And these twelve ministers, whom thou beholdest, shall judge thy seed. And, behold they are righteous for ever; for because of their faith in the Lamb of God, their garments are made white in his blood." (1 Nephi 12:8-10.)

This exhibits a principle of adjudication or judgment in the hands, firstly, of the Great High Priest and King, Jesus of Nazareth, the Son of God; secondly, in the hands of the Twelve Apostles on the continent of Asia, bestowed by Jesus Himself; thirdly, in the Twelve Disciples on this continent, to their peoples, who it appears are under the presidency of the Twelve Apostles who ministered at Jerusalem; which presidency is also exhibited by Peter, James and John, the acknowledged presidency of the Twelve Apostles; they, holding this Priesthood first on the earth, and then in the heavens, being the legitimate custodians of the keys of the Priesthood, came and bestowed it upon Joseph Smith and Oliver Cowdery. It is also further stated that the Saints shall judge the world. Thus Christ is at the head, His Apostles and disciples seem to take the next prominent part; then comes the action of the Saints, or other [157] branches of the Priesthood, who it is stated shall judge the world. This combined Priesthood, it would appear, will hold the destiny of the human family in their hands and adjudicate in all matters pertaining to their affairs; and it would seem to be quite reasonable, if the Twelve Apostles in Jerusalem are to be the judges of the Twelve Tribes, and the Twelve Disciples on this continent are to be the judges of the descendants of Nephi, then that the brother of Jared and Jared should be the judges of the Jaredites, their descendants; and, further, that the First Presidency and Twelve who have officiated in our age, should operate in regard to mankind in this dispensation, and also in regard to all matters connected with them, whether they relate to the past, present, or future, as the aforementioned have done in regard to their several peoples; and that the Patriarchs, the Presidents, the Twelve, the High Priests, the Seventies, the Elders, the Bishops, Priests, Teachers and Deacons should hold their several places behind the veil, and officiate according to their calling and standing in that Priesthood. In fact, the Priesthood is called an everlasting Priesthood; it ministers in time and in eternity. Moses speaks of the Levitical Priesthood as an everlasting Priesthood. (Exodus 40:15.) Paul refers to the Melchizedek Priesthood as being "without father, without mother, without descent, having neither beginning of days, nor end of life." (Hebrews 8:3.) Whilst the Prophet Joseph Smith states that this "Priesthood continueth in the Church of God in all generations, and is without beginning of days or end of years." (D&C 74:17.)

This being the case, it necessarily follows that those holding the Priesthood on the earth continue in the exercise of the Priesthood in the heavens, their operations being changed from this to another state of existence; and when the dead, small and great, shall be judged, while God stands at the head, and Jesus is the great High Priest of our profession, all those who have ever lived who are worthy will stand in their proper [158] positions, according to their callings, Priesthood, ordinations or quorums. It is written that they without us can not be made perfect, and that we without them can not be made perfect. (See Hebrews 11:40; D&C 128:15-18.) We have commenced to build temples, and to administer in them according to the decrees, purposes and foreknowledge of God. When we have got through with our personal affairs connected with our individual families and interests, so far as we can legitimately trace them, then it becomes a question as to the position of those that are behind the veil of whom we have no personal knowledge. Does it not seem consistent that to the ancient as well as the modern Patriarchs, Prophets, Presidents, Apostles, Seventies, High Priests, Elders, Bishops and others would be committed the manipulation and judgment of those who are behind the veil; and with whom we, at present, have nothing to do? And if temples are to be built here and ordinances performed in them in the interest of those who have died without law, and in the adjudication of all these matters, that the Priesthood behind the veil, to whom is committed the judgment of these things, should communicate with the Priesthood upon the earth, that they may be administered for by proxy in the temples erected by us, and those who shall follow after us; that all things may be done according to equity, law, and justice, and that none but those worthy to receive those great blessings and high exaltations can participate in the same; being thus sanctioned by the Priesthood in heaven and the Priesthood upon the earth? Hence, while they are saviors, preach to the spirits in prison and judge the dead, we build temples and administer for them upon the earth, and thus become, as it is written, "saviors upon Mount Zion;" (See Obadiah 1:21) operating and co-operating with the Priesthood behind the veil, in the interest, happiness, salvation and exaltation of the human family. Thus shall we also become legitimately and by right, through the atonement and adoption, Kings and Priests—Priests to administer in the holy ordinances [159] pertaining to the endowments and exaltations; and Kings, under Christ, who is King of Kings and Lord of Lords, to rule and govern, according to the eternal laws of justice and equity, those who are thus redeemed and exalted.

In corroboration of these ideas is the statement, in the Book of Doctrine and Covenants, that Father Joseph Smith, who was the first Patriarch to the Church in this dispensation, is now at the right hand of Abraham, who was also a presiding Patriarch. The passage reads:

"That I may receive him unto myself, even as I did . . . my aged servant, Joseph Smith, sen., who sitteth with Abraham at his right hand, and blessed and holy is he, for he is mine." (D&C 124:19.)

It is also stated of David Patten, one of the Twelve Apostles, who was slain by the mobbers in Missouri, that "David Patten I have taken unto myself; behold, his Priesthood no man taketh from him; but, verily I say unto you, another may be appointed unto the same calling." (D&C 124:130.)

The same is said of Seymour Brunson, one of the High Council, and of Edward Partridge, the first Bishop of the Church, both of whom were dead:

"Seymour Brunson I have taken unto myself, no man taketh his Priesthood, but another may be appointed unto the same Priesthood in his stead." (D&C 124:132.) "That when he shall finish his work, that I may receive him unto myself, even as I did my servant David Patten, who is with me at this time, and also my servant Edward Partridge." (v. 19.)

We read that Moses and Elias came to administer to Jesus, on the Mount, while Peter, James and John were with him. Who were this Moses and this Elias? Moses was a great Prophet, appointed by the Lord to deliver Israel from Egyptian bondage, and lead them to the promised land; and he held the keys of the gathering dispensation, which keys he afterwards conferred upon [160] Joseph Smith in the Kirtland Temple. Who was Elias? Elijah; which name in the old Scriptures is made synonymous with Elias; and who held, according to the testimony of Joseph Smith as elsewhere stated, the keys of the Priesthood. These men, who held those keys and officiated upon the earth, having left the earth, now come, associated with Jesus, to administer to Peter, James and John, and confer upon them the Priesthood which they hold; and these three ancient Apostles conferred the Priesthood upon Joseph Smith and Oliver Cowdery in this dispensation. This principle is very clearly illustrated in the following quotation from the Book of Doctrine and Covenants, Section 128, verses 20, 21:

"And again, what do we hear? Glad tidings from Cumorah! Moroni, an angel from heaven, declaring the fulfilment of the prophets—the book to be revealed. A voice of the Lord in the wilderness of Fayette, Seneca County, declaring the three witnesses to bear record of the book. The voice of Michael on the banks of the Susquehanna, detecting the devil when he appeared as an angel of light. The voice of Peter, James and John in the wilderness between Harmony, Susquehanna county, and Colesville, Broome county, on the Susquehanna river, declaring themselves as possessing the keys of the kingdom, and of the dispensation of the fulness of times.

"And again, the voice of God in the chamber of old Father Whitmer, in Fayette, Seneca County, and at sundry times and in divers places through all the travels and tribulations of this Church of Jesus Christ of Latter-day Saints. And the voice of Michael, the archangel: the voice of Gabriel, and of Raphael, and of divers angels, from Michael or Adam, down to the present time, all declaring their dispensation, their rights, their keys, their honors, their majesty and glory, and the power of their Priesthood; giving line upon line, precept upon precept; here a little and there a little—giving us consolation by holding forth that which is to come, confirming our hope." [161]

Hence their Priesthood was everlasting, it administered in time and in eternity. In consonance with the same idea is a remark made by a mighty angel, to be found in the Revelation received by St. John on the Isle of Patmos. After this angel had communicated to John many great and important events yet to transpire, the Apostle was so overawed by his presence that he fell at his feet to worship him; whereas the angel said, "See that thou do it not; I am thy fellow servant, and of thy brethren that have kept the testimony of Jesus: worship God; for the testimony of Jesus is the spirit of prophecy." (Revelation 19:10.) In other words, he had held the holy Priesthood on the earth and had officiated therein; he had been subjected to all the obloquy, contumely and reproach which the Prophets of God generally suffered. But now the scene was changed; he was officiating in another sphere, and was revealing unto the Apostle John, who had a peculiar mission on the earth, some of the great and important truths or events that should be developed in the accomplishment of the purposes of God. All of these men, having held the everlasting Priesthood on earth, still retain the power and authority conferred upon them, and stand forth as prominent examples of the perpetuity of the everlasting Priesthood, administering on the earth or in the heavens, as the purposes of God and the fulfilment of their duties render necessary, or the circumstances require. [162]

CHAPTER 23

The Laws of God Unchangeable, Universal and Eternal—Examples and Definitions—Evolutionists—Kingdoms and Light—Christ the Creator. etc.—Deviations from General Laws—Every Kingdom has a Law Given

There is an inexorable law of God that requires from His professed followers the principles of virtue, honor, truth, integrity, righteousness, justice, judgment and mercy, as exhibited in the following Scriptures:

"Justice and judgment are the habitation of thy throne: mercy and truth shall go before thy face." (Psalms 84:14.)

"Thou lovest righteousness, and hatest wickedness: therefore God, thy God, hath anointed thee with the oil of gladness above thy fellows." (Psalms 45:7.)

"Lord, who shall abide in thy tabernacle? who shall dwell in thy holy hill? He that walketh uprightly, and worketh righteousness, and speaketh the truth in his heart. He that backbiteth not with his tongue, nor doeth evil to his neighbor, nor taketh up a reproach against his neighbor. In whose eyes a vile person is contemned; but he honoreth them that fear the Lord. He that sweareth to his own hurt, and changeth not. He that putteth not out his money to usury, nor taketh reward against the innocent. He that doeth these things shall never be moved." (Psalms 15:1-5.)

"Who shall ascend into the hill of the Lord? or who shall stand in his holy place? He that hath clean hands, and a pure heart; who hath not lifted up his soul unto vanity, nor sworn deceitfully. He shall receive the blessing from the Lord, and righteousness from the God of his salvation." (Psalms 24:3-5.)

"Who among us shall dwell with the devouring fire? who among us shall dwell with everlasting burn[163]ings? He that walketh righteously, and speaketh uprightly; he that despiseth the gain of oppressions, that shaketh his hands from holding of bribes, that stoppeth his ears from hearing of blood, and shutteth his eyes from seeing evil. He shall dwell on high; his place of defence shall be the munitions of rocks: bread shall be given him; his waters shall be sure." (Isaiah 33:14-16.)

There are eternal, unchangeable laws associated with God, and with all His plans, His works and ways, the requirements of which must be met; nor can they be evaded or changed, except on certain principles provided for and contained in the laws themselves. When man had transgressed, an atonement had to be made commensurate with the act, and fully adequate to meet the inexorable demands of justice; so that, as stated, justice might be satisfied, which, if it had not been, the law pertaining to this matter could not have been carried out, and must necessarily have been violated.

All the works of God connected with the world which we inhabit, and with all other worlds, are strictly governed by law. So accurate are the movements of the heavenly bodies that even with our limited knowledge we can compute, after the departure of most of these bodies, the time of their return to a minute. The sun rises and sets with great regularity, and we can tell to a moment, by calculating the revolution of the earth, at what time it will make its appearance in the morning and disappear in the evening; the same rule applies to the moon, the whole of the solar system, and to all bodies that can be reached by our instruments. There is perfect regularity, exactitude and order associated with all worlds; a departure from which would produce incalculable evil and irretrievable destruction and ruin. With regard to the matter of which the earth is composed, it is also governed by strict, unchangeable laws; matter possessing the same properties under the same conditions, in all parts of the world. The various grasses, herbs, plants, shrubs, flowers, minerals, metals, waters, [164] fluids or gases, when under the same conditions, are subject to or governed by unchangeable laws; and by those laws chemists or scientists are enabled to apply tests to demonstrate the properties of the various elements in nature, which they find are always immutable, and the same degree of accuracy applies to the laws and various formations of crystallization, under the same circumstances. The animal and vegetable creations are governed by certain laws, and are composed of certain elements peculiar to themselves. This applies to man, to the beasts, fowls, fish and creeping things, to the insects and to all animated nature; each one possessing its own distinctive features, each requiring a specific sustenance, each having an organism and faculties governed by prescribed laws to perpetuate its own kind. So accurate is the formation of the various living creatures that an intelligent student of nature can tell by any particular bone of the skeleton of an animal to what class or order it belongs.

These principles do not change, as represented by evolutionists of the Darwinian school, but the primitive organisms of all living beings exist in the same form as when they first received their impress from their Maker. There are, indeed, some very slight exceptions, as for instance, the ass may mix with the mare and produce the mule; but there it ends, the violation of the laws of procreation receives a check, and its operations can go no further. Similar compounds may possibly be made by experimentalists in the vegetable and mineral kingdoms, but the original elements remain the same. Yet this is not the normal, but an abnormal condition with them, as with animals, birds, etc.; and if we take man, he is said to have been made in the image of God, for the simple reason that he is a son of God; and being His son, he is, of course, His offspring, an emanation from God, in whose likeness, we are told, he is made. He did not originate from a chaotic mass of matter, moving or inert, but came forth possessing, in an embryotic state, all the faculties and powers of a God. And when he shall be [165] perfected, and have progressed to maturity, he will be like his Father—a God; being indeed His offspring. As the horse, the ox, the sheep, and every living creature, including man, propagates its own species and perpetuates its own kind, so does God perpetuate His.

There are different organisms possessing different qualities, from which the same results are uniformly obtained. The body of a sheep produces wool, that of a goat produces hair, the flesh of certain kinds of fish produces scales, the flesh of birds produces feathers, and by the coverings of the various kinds of animals, birds and fishes, may their originals be known. It is true that some of these coverings may be slightly changed by a removal of the creature from the arctic to the torrid zone, or vice versa; wool may assume a nearer approach to hair in length and texture, or hair may become more woolly, but these modifications are slight, and this covering of the animal is predisposed to return to its original qualities when the creature is replaced in his natural habitat. Paul, in speaking on the resurrection, refers to the different qualities of flesh as follows:

"But God giveth it a body as it hath pleased him, and to every seed his own body. All flesh is not the same flesh; but there is one kind of flesh of men, another flesh of beasts, another of fishes, and another of birds." (1 Corinthians 15:38-39.)

These different qualities seem to be inherent in the several species, as much so as the properties of silver, gold, copper, iron and other minerals are inherent in the matter in which they are contained, whilst herbs, according to their kind, possess their specific properties, or as the leading properties of earth, air, and water, are distinct from one another; and hence, on physiological grounds, this principle being admitted, and it cannot be controverted, it would be impossible to take the tissues of the lower, or, indeed, of any order of fishes, and make of them an ox, a bird, or a man; as impossible as it would be to take iron and make it [166] into gold, silver, or copper, or to produce other changes in the laws which govern any kind of matter. And when the resurrection and exaltation of man shall be consummated, although more pure, refined and glorious, yet will he still be in the same image, and have the same likeness, without variation or change in any of his parts or faculties, except the substitution of spirit for blood.

This principle of exactitude in all the works of God represents the principles that dwell in God Himself. He is called in Scripture the I AM, in other words, I AM THAT I AM, because of those inherent principles, which are also eternal and unchangeable; for where those principles exist, He exists; and when speaking of the worlds by which are surrounded, it is said, "Behold, all these are kingdoms, and any man who hath seen any, or the least of these, hath seen God moving in his majesty and power." (D&C 88:47.)

And again it is written:

"He comprehendeth all things, and all things are before him, and all things are round about him: and he is above all things, and in all things, and is through all things, and is round about all things; and all things are by him, and of him, even God, for ever and ever. And again, verily I say unto you, he hath given a law unto all things, by which they move in their times and their seasons." (*Ibid.* 41-42.)

And again, in the same revelation, we read:

"As also he is in the sun, and the light of the sun, and the power thereof by which it was made. As also he is in the moon, and is the light of the moon, and the power thereof by which it was made. As also the light of the stars, and the power thereof by which they were made. And the earth also, and the power thereof; even the earth upon which you stand. And the light which now shineth, which giveth you light, is through him who enlighteneth your eyes, which is the same light that quickeneth your understandings; which light pro[167]ceedeth forth from the presence of God to fill the immensity of space. The light which is in all things; which giveth life to all things: which is the law by which all things are governed: even the power of God who sitteth upon his throne, who is in the bosom of eternity, who is in the midst of all things." (*Ibid.* 7-13.)

The world was made by Him, and without Him was not anything made that was made, and, therefore, having made all things He has given to all things a law; and hence those laws which we have briefly alluded to, are the productions of His comprehensive, intelligent, and infinite mind: He is the Alpha and Omega, the Beginning and the End, the Fountain of all life, of all light, of all truth, of all intelligence, of all existence. He is also the sustainer of all life and all light in all created beings; in Him all animal life of every form has its being.

There are some apparent deviations from general laws. But these apparent deviations are merely appendages to the great general law, in order that creation may be perfect in all its parts. For instance, there is a general law of what is termed gravitation which causes bodies to fall to the earth from a given height, with the same velocity according to their specific gravity. But there are other local laws which disturb the normal conditions, so far as they extend, of what may be termed the general law. As, for example, the magnet, in its limited sphere, is more powerful than the general law of gravity, it attracting certain matter to itself in opposition to the general law, while the magnet itself is subject to the general law. There is also another principle, called capillary attraction, which causes water and other fluids to ascend in the earth, in tubes, etc. Take away these local agencies and everything resumes its normal condition. A bird, through the use of its wings, possesses the power of locomotion through the air; let that bird, however, lose its mechanism and power by being maimed or killed, and it is governed by the [168] same law of gravitation and drops to the earth. Balloons will ascend and carry a specified weight with them to great altitudes, but this is owing to a modification of one part of the law of gravitation; which causes denser bodies to cling with greater tenacity to the earth, and the gas that enters the balloons is more rarified than the atmosphere immediately contiguous to the earth; which dense atmosphere forces the lighter gases to their proper place, causing them to bound upwards; this being done and the equilibrium obtained, if the gas is permitted to escape, the materials of which the balloon is composed, together with its occupants, are precipitated, according to the general laws of gravitation, to the earth.

God is unchangeable, so are also his laws, in all their forms, and in all their applications, and being Himself the essence of law, the giver of law, the sustainer of law, all of those laws are eternal in all their operations, in all bodies and matter, and throughout all space. It would be impossible for Him to violate law, because in so doing He would strike at His own dignity, power, principles, glory, exaltation and existence.

The book of Doctrine and Covenants states:

"And again, verily I say unto you, that which is governed by law is also preserved by law, and perfected and sanctified by the same. That which breaketh a law, and abideth not by law, but seeketh to become a law unto itself, and willeth to abide in sin, and altogether abideth in sin, cannot be sanctified by law, neither by mercy, justice, nor judgment. Therefore they must remain filthy still. All kingdoms have a law given: and there are many kingdoms; for there is no space in the which there is no kingdom; and there is no kingdom in which there is no space, either a greater or a lesser kingdom. And unto every kingdom is given a law; and unto every law there are certain bounds also and conditions. All beings who abide not in those conditions are not justified; for intelligence cleaveth unto intelligence: wisdom receiveth wisdom; truth embraceth [169] truth; virtue loveth virtue; light cleaveth unto light; mercy hath compassion on mercy, and claimeth her own; justice continueth its course, and claimeth its own; judgment goeth before the face of him who sitteth upon the throne,

THE MEDIATION AND ATONEMENT 161

and governeth and executeth all things." (D&C 88:34-40.)

Hence, the law of atonement had to be met as well as all other laws, for God could not be God without fulfilling it.

Jesus said, "If it be possible, let this cup pass." (Matthew 26:39.) But it was not possible; for to have done so would have been a violation of the law, and he had to take it. The atonement must be made, a God must be sacrificed. No power can resist a law of God. It is omnipresent, omnipotent, exists everywhere, in all things, through all things and round about all things. We read:

"O the greatness of the mercy of our God, the Holy One of Israel! For he delivereth his saints from that awful monster the devil, and death, and hell, and that lake of fire and brimstone, which is endless torment. O how great the holiness of our God! For he knoweth all things, and there is not any thing, save he knows it. And he cometh into the world that he may save all men, if they will hearken unto his voice; for behold, he suffereth the pains of all men; yea, the pains of every living creature, both men, women, and children, who belong to the family of Adam. And he suffereth this, that the resurrection might pass upon all men, that all might stand before him at the great and judgment day. And he commandeth all men that and judgment day. And he commandeth all men that they must repent, and be baptized in his name, having perfect faith in the Holy One of Israel, or they cannot be saved in the Kingdom of God. And if they will not repent and believe in his name, and be baptized in his name, and endure to the end, they must be damned; for the Lord God, the Holy One of Israel, has spoken it; Wherefore he has given a law; and where there is no law given, there is no punishment; and where there is [170] no punishment, there is no condemnation; and where there is no condemnation, the mercies of the Holy One of Israel have claim upon them, because of the atonement; for they are delivered by the power of him; for the atonement satisfieth the demands of his justice upon all those who have not the law given to them, that they are delivered from that awful monster, death and hell, and the devil, and the lake of fire and brimstone, which is endless torment; and they are restored to that God who gave them breath, which is the Holy One of Israel. But wo unto him that has the law given; yea, that has all the commandments of God like unto us, and that transgresseth them, and that wasteth the days of his probation, for awful is his state." (2 Nephi

9:19-27.)

CHAPTER 24

The Results of the Atonement—The Debt Paid—Justice and Mercy—
Extracts from the Teachings of Alma and Others.

From the facts in the case and the testimony presented in the Scriptures it becomes evident that through the great atonement, the expiatory sacrifice of the Son of God, it is made possible that man can be redeemed, restored, resurrected and exalted to the elevated position designed for him in the creation as a Son of God: that eternal justice and law required the penalty to be paid by man himself, or by the atonement of the Son of God: that Jesus offered Himself as the great expiatory sacrifice; that this offering being in accordance with the demands or requirements of the law, was accepted by the [171] great Lawgiver; that it was prefigured by sacrifices, and ultimately fulfilled by Himself according to the eternal covenant. "He was wounded (as prophesied of) for our transgressions, he was bruised for our iniquities, the chastisement of our peace was upon him, and with his stripes we are healed." (Isaiah 53:5.)

The Savior thus becomes master of the situation—the debt is paid, the redemption made, the covenant fulfilled, justice satisfied, the will of God done, and all power is now given into the hands of the Son of God—the power of the resurrection, the power of the redemption, the power of salvation, the power to enact laws for the carrying out and accomplishment of this design. Hence life and immortality are brought to light, the Gospel is introduced. and He becomes the author of eternal life and exaltation, He is the Redeemer, the Resurrector, the

Savior of man and the world; and He has appointed the law of the Gospel as the medium which must be complied with in this world or the next, as He complied with His Father's law; hence "he that believeth shall be saved, and he that believeth not shall be damned" (See Mark 16:16.)

The plan, the arrangement, the agreement, the covenant was made, entered into and accepted before the foundation of the world; it was prefigured by sacrifices, and was carried out and consummated on the cross.

Hence being the mediator between God and man, He becomes by right the dictator and director on earth and in heaven for the living and for the dead, for the past, the present and the future, pertaining to man as associated with this earth or the heavens, in time of eternity, the Captain of our salvation, the Apostle and High-Priest of our profession, the Lord and Giver of life.

Is justice dishonored? No; it is satisfied, the debt is paid. Is righteousness departed from? No; this is a righteous act. All requirements are met. Is judgment violated? No; its demands are fulfilled. Is mercy triumphant? No; she simply claims her own Justice, [172] judgment, mercy and truth all harmonize as the attributes of Deity. "Justice and truth have met together, righteousness and peace have kissed each other." (See Psalms 85:10.) Justice and judgment triumph as well as mercy and peace; all the attributes of Deity harmonize in this great, grand, momentous, just, equitable, merciful and meritorious act.

The Book of Mormon is very explicit on these principles. We read therein:

"And behold, I say unto you, this is not all: For O how beautiful upon the mountains are the feet of him that bringeth good tidings, that is the founder of peace: yea, even the Lord, who has redeemed his people: yea, him who has granted salvation unto his people: For were it not for the redemption which he hath made for his people, which was prepared from the foundation of the world; I say unto you, were it not for this, all mankind must have perished. But behold, the bands of death shall be broken, and the Son reigneth, and hath power over the dead; therefore, he bringeth to pass the resurrection of the dead. And there cometh a resurrection, even a first resurrection; yea even a resurrection of those that have been, and who are, and who shall be, even until the resurrection of Christ: for so shall he be called. And now, the resurrection of all the prophets, and all those that have believed in their words, or all those that have kept the commandments of God, shall come forth in the first resurrection; therefore, they are the first resurrection. They are raised to dwell with God who has redeemed them: thus they have eternal life through Christ, who has broken the bands of death. And these are those who have part in the first resurrection; and these are they that have died before Christ came, in their ignorance, not having salvation declared unto them. And thus the Lord bringeth about the restoration of these; and they have a part in the first resurrection, or have eternal life, being redeemed by the Lord. And little children also have eternal life. But behold, and fear, and tremble before [173] God; for ye ought to tremble: for the Lord redeemeth none such that rebel against him. and die in their sins; yea, even all those that have perished in their sins ever since the world began, that have wilfully rebelled against God, that have known the commandments of God, and would not keep them; these are they that have no part in the first resurrection. Therefore had ye not ought to tremble? For salvation cometh to none such; for the Lord hath redeemed none such; yea, neither can the Lord redeem such; for he cannot deny himself; for he cannot deny justice when it has its claim." (Mosiah 15:18-27.)

The next is a portion of a sermon of the Prophet Amulek, the companion of Alma, to the Zoramites:

"My brother has called upon the words of Zenos, that redemption cometh through the Son of God, and also upon the words of Zenoch; and also he has appealed unto Moses, to prove that these things are true. And now behold, I will testify unto you of myself that these things are true. Behold, I say unto you, that I do know that Christ shall come among the children of men, to take upon him the transgressions of his people, and that he shall atone for the sins of the world; for the Lord God hath spoken it; for it is expedient that an atonement should be made; for according to the great plan of the eternal God, there must be an atonement made, or else all mankind must unavoidably perish; yea, all are hardened; yea, all are fallen and are lost, and must perish, except it be through the atonement which it is expedient should be made; for it is expedient that there should be a great and last sacrifice; yea, not a sacrifice of man, neither of beast, neither of any manner of fowl; for it shall not be a human sacrifice; but it must be an infinite and eternal sacrifice. Now there is not any man that can sacrifice his own blood, which will atone for the sins of another. Now if a man murdereth, behold will our law, which is just, take the life of his brother? I say unto you nay. But the law requireth the life of him who hath mur[174]dered; therefore there can be nothing which is short of an infinite atonement, which will suffice for the sins of the world: therefore it is expedient that there should be a great and last sacrifice; and then shall there be, or it is expedient there should be a stop to the shedding of blood; then shall the law of Moses be fulfilled; yea, it shall be all fulfilled; every jot and tittle; and none shall have passed away. And behold, this is the whole meaning of the law: every whit pointing to that great and last sacrifice; and that great and last sacrifice will be the Son of God: yea, infinite and eternal; and thus he shall bring salvation to all those who shall believe on his name; this being the intent of this last sacrifice, to bring about the bowels of mercy, which overpowereth justice, and bringeth about means unto men that they may have faith unto repentance. And thus mercy can satisfy the demands of justice, and encircles them in the arms of safety, while he that exercises no faith unto repentance, is exposed to the whole law of the demands of justice; therefore only unto him that has faith unto repentance, is brought about the great and eternal plan of redemption. Therefore may God grant unto you, my brethren, that ye may begin to exercise your faith unto repentance, that ye begin to call upon his holy name, that he would have mercy upon you." (Alma 34:7-17.)

And again, to quote from the commandments of Alma to his son Corianton:

"And now, my son, I perceive there is somewhat more which doth worry your mind, which ye cannot understand, which is concerning the justice of God, in the punishment of the sinner; for ye do try to suppose that it is injustice that the sinner should be consigned to a state of misery. Now, behold, my son, I will explain this thing unto thee: for behold, after the Lord God sent our first parents forth from the Garden of Eden, to till the ground, from whence they were taken; yea, he drew out the man, and he placed at the east and of the Garden of Eden, Cherubim, and a flaming sword [175] which turned every way, to keep the tree of life. Now we see that the man had become as

God, knowing good and evil; and lest he should put forth his hand, and take also of the tree of life, and eat and live for ever, the Lord God placed Cherubim and the flaming sword, that he should not partake of the fruit; and thus we see, that there was a time granted unto man to repent, yea, a probationary time, a time to repent and serve God. For behold, if Adam had put forth his hand immediately, and partook of the tree of life, he would have lived for ever, according to the word of God, having no space for repentance; yea, and also the word of God would have been void, and the great plan of salvation would have been frustrated. But behold, it was appointed unto man to die; therefore as they were cut off from the tree of life they should be cut off from the face of the earth, and man become lost for ever; yea, they became fallen man. And now we see by this, that our parents were cut off, both temporally and spiritually, from the presence of the Lord; and thus we see they became subjects to follow after their own will. Now behold, it was not expedient that man should be reclaimed from this temporal death, for that would destroy the great plan of happiness; therefore, as the soul could never die, and the fall had brought upon all mankind a spiritual death as well as a temporal; that is, they were cut off from the presence of the Lord; it was expedient that mankind should be reclaimed from this spiritual death; therefore, as they had become carnal, sensual, and devilish by nature, this probationary state became a state for them to prepare; it became a preparatory state. And now remember, my son, if it were not for the plan of redemption, (laying it aside,) as soon as they were dead, their souls were miserable, being cut off from the presence of the Lord. And now there was no means to reclaim men from this fallen state which man had brought upon himself, because of his own disobedience; therefore, according to justice, the plan of redemption could not be brought about, only on [176] conditions of repentance of men in this probationary state; yea, this preparatory state; for except it were for these conditions, mercy could not take effect except it should destroy the work of justice. Now the work of justice could not be destroyed; if so, God would cease to be God. And thus we see that all mankind were fallen, and they were in the grasp of justice; yea, the justice of God, which consigned them for ever to be cut off from his presence. And now the plan of mercy could not be brought about, except an atonement should be made; therefore God himself atoneth for the sins of the world, to bring about the plan of mercy, to appease the demands of justice, that God might be a perfect, just God, and a merciful God also. Now repentance could not come unto men, except there were a punishment, which also was eternal as the life of the soul should be, affixed opposite to the plan of happiness, which was as eternal also as the life of the soul. Now, how could a man repent, except he should sin? How could he sin, if there was no law? How could there be a law, save there was a punishment? Now there was a punishment affixed, and a just law given, which brought remorse of conscience unto man. Now if there was no law given if a man murdered he should die, would he be afraid he would die if he should murder? And also, if there was no law given against sin, men would not be afraid to sn. And if there was no law given if men sinned, what could justice do, or mercy either; for they would have no claim upon the creature? But there is a law given, and a punishment affixed, and a repentance granted; which repentance, mercy claimeth; otherwise, justice claimeth the creature, and executeth the law, and the law inflicteth the punishment: if not so, the works of justice would be destroyed, and God would cease to be God. But God ceaseth not to be God, and mercy claimeth the penitent, and mercy cometh because of the atonement; and the atonement bringeth to pass the resurrection of the dead; and the resurrection of the dead bringeth back men into the presence of [177] God; and thus they are restored into his presence, to be judged according to their works; according to the law and justice; for behold, justice exerciseth all his demands. and also mercy claimeth all which is her own; and thus, none but the truly penitent are saved. What! do ye suppose that mercy can rob justice? I say unto you, nay; not one whit. If so, God would cease to be God. And thus God bringeth about his great and eternal purposes, which were prepared from the foundation of the world. And thus cometh about the salvation and the redemption of men, and also their destruction and misery." (Alma 42:1-26.)

In the first place, according to justice men could not have been redeemed from temporal death, except through the atonement of Jesus Christ; and in the second place, they could not be redeemed from spiritual death, only through obedience to His law.

CHAPTER 25

The Resurrection—The Universality of the Atonement—The Promises to those who Overcome—The Gospel—Its First Principles—Faith, Repentance, Baptism and the Gift of the Holy Ghost—Its Antiquity—It is Preached in Various Dispensations, from Adam until the Present—The Final Triumph of the Saints.

The great pre-requisites having been fulfilled, it now becomes our duty to enquire what next had to be done to consummate the great object obtainable through the fulfillment of this law, or what was accomplished by the atonement. [178]

First, the Resurrection. The penalty of the broken law in Adam's day was death; and death is passed upon all. The word of the Lord was, "In the day that thou eatest thereof thou shalt surely die." (Genesis 2:17.) The atonement made by Jesus Christ brought about the resurrection from the dead, and restored life. And hence Jesus said: "I am the Resurrection and the Life; he that believeth in me, though he were dead, yet shall he live;" (John 11:25) and Jesus Himself became the first fruits of those who slept.

The next question that arises is, how far does this principle extend and to whom is it applicable? It extends to all the human family; to all men of every nation: as it is written:

"For, if by one man's offence death reigneth by one; much more they which receive abundance of grace, and of the gift of righteousness, shall reign in life by one, Jesus Christ. Therefore, as by the offence of one judgment came upon all men to condemnation, even so by the righteousness of one the free gift came upon all men unto justification of life." (Romans 5:17-18.)

This will not all take place at once. "But every man in his own order: Christ, the first fruits; afterward they that are Christ's at his coming." (1 Corinthians 15:23.) "But the rest of the dead lived not again until the thousand years were finished." (Revelation 20:5.)

Hence what was lost in Adam was restored in Jesus Christ, so far as all men are concerned in all ages, with some very slight exceptions arising from an abuse of privileges. Transgression of the law brought death upon all the posterity of Adam, the restoration through the atonement restored all the human family to life. "For since by man came death, by man came also the resurrection of the dead. For as in Adam all die, even so in Christ shall all be made alive." (1 Corinthians 15:21-22.) So that whatever was lost by Adam, was restored by Jesus Christ.

The penalty of the transgression of the law was the death of the body. The atonement made by Jesus [179] Christ resulted in the resurrection of the human body. Its scope embraced all peoples, nations and tongues.

"For all my Lord was crucified,
 For all, for all my Savior died."

This is one part of the restoration. This is the restoration of the body. The next question for us to examine is, How, and in what manner are men benefitted by the atonement and by the resurrection? In this, that the atonement having restored man to his former position before the Lord, it has placed him in a position and made it possible for him to obtain that exaltation and glory which it would have been impossible for him to have received without it; even to become a son of God by adoption; and being a son then an heir of God, and a joint heir with Jesus Christ; and that, as Christ overcame, He has made it possible, and has placed it within the power of believers in Him, also to overcome; and as He is authorized to inherit His Father's glory which He had with Him before the world was, with His resurrected body, so through the adoption, may we overcome and sit down with Him upon His throne, as He has overcome and has sat down upon His Father's throne. And as he has said, "I and the Father are one," (John 10:30) so are the obedient saints one with Him, as He is one with the Father, even as He prayed:

"That they all may be one; as thou, Father, art in me, and I in thee, that they also may be one in us; that the world may believe that thou hast sent me. And the glory which thou gavest me, I have given them; that they may be one, even as we are one; I in them, and thou in me, that they may be made perfect in one; and that the world may know that thou hast sent me, and hast loved them as thou hast loved me." (John 17:21-23.)

Being the sons of God through the atonement and adoption, and through faith in Jesus Christ, they rise to the dignity and glory of the Godhead, even to be Gods; as it is promised: [180]

"Him that overcometh, will I make a pillar in the temple of my God, and he shall go no more out: and I will write upon him the name of my God, and the name of the city of my God, which is new Jerusalem, which cometh down out of heaven from my God: and I will write upon him my new name. (Revelation 3:12.)

Again, "To him that overcometh will I grant to sit with me in my throne, even as I also overcame, and am set down with my Father in his throne." (*Ibid.* 3:21.)

Yet again, "He that overcometh shall inherit all things; and I will be his God, and he shall be my son." (*Ibid.* 21:7.)

Hence, through His atonement, believers in Christ, and those who obey His law, partake of His glory and exaltation, and are inheritors of the Godhead; whilst those who do not obey His law although resurrected cannot inherit this exaltation; they are raised from the dead, but cannot inherit a celestial glory without being obedient to a celestial law, and thus we come again to a scripture quoted before. Jesus said, "Thus it is written, and thus it behooved Christ to suffer, and to rise from the dead the third day: and that repentance and remission of sins should be preached in his name among all nations, beginning at Jerusalem." (Luke 24:46-47.)

Having noticed the great blessings, privileges, powers and exaltations that are placed within the reach of man, through the atonement of Jesus Christ, it next becomes our duty to enquire what is required of man to place him in possession of them.

That the world might be benefitted through the redemption brought about by Jesus Christ, He called and ordained twelve Apostles, and commanded them to go forth into all the world, and preach the Gospel to every creature, saying, "He that believeth and is baptized shall be saved; but he that believeth not shall be damned,"

(Mark 16:16) or condemned. Thus placing it within the reach of every man to obtain the glory and exaltation referred to above, and leaving all men without excuse [181] who would not obey the law and be subject to the conditions imposed. The penalty of Adam's sin having been removed through the atonement, it now became the privilege of all men, in all nations, to partake of the salvation provided by the great Mediator.

And this provision applies not only to the living, but also to the dead, so that all men who have existed in all ages, who do exist now, or who will exist while the earth shall stand, may be placed upon the same footing, and that all men may have the privilege, living or dead, of accepting the conditions of the great plan of redemption provided by the Father, through the Son, before the world was; and that the justice and mercy of God may be applied to every being, living or dead, that ever has existed, that does now exist, or that ever will exist.

The conditions required of the human family to enable them to obtain the high exaltation which the atonement makes it possible for them to receive, are: First, Faith in God as our Father and the great Supreme Ruler of the universe; in whose hands are the destinies of the human family; in whom we live and move and have our being. And in His Son Jesus Christ, as the Lamb slain from before the foundation of the world, as the great Mediator and great propitiatory sacrifice provided by the Father before the creation, and consummated by the offering of Himself upon the cross. For "God so loved the world, that he gave his only begotten Son, that whosoever believeth in him should not perish, but have everlasting life." (John 3:16.) Or, to use the words of the Nephite King Benjamin:

"Believe in God; believe that he is, and that he created all things, both in heaven and in earth; believe that he has all wisdom, and all power, both in heaven and in earth; believe that man doth not comprehend all the things which the Lord can comprehend." (Mosiah 4:9.)

Or as Paul writes; "He that cometh to God must believe that he is, and that he is a rewarder of them that diligently seek him." (Hebrews 11:6.) [182]

The second principle of the Gospel of salvation, is repentance. It is a sincere and godly sorrow for and a forsaking of sin, combined with full purpose of heart to keep God's commandments. As is written by the Prophet Isaiah: "Let the wicked forsake his way, and the unrighteous man his thoughts; and let him return unto the Lord, and he will have mercy upon him; and to our God, for he will abundantly pardon." (Isaiah 55:7.) And to quote from the Book of Mormon:

"And again: Believe that ye must repent of your sins and forsake them, and humble yourselves before God; and ask in sincerity of heart that he would forgive you; and now, if you believe all these things, see that ye do them." (Mosiah 4:10.)

Thirdly, Baptism for the remission of sins, of our personal transgressions, which, through this means, provided by divine mercy, are, by reason of the atonement, blotted out. To use the words of Paul: "Therefore we are buried with him by baptism into death: that like as Christ was raised up from the dead by the glory of the Father, even so we also should walk in newness of life. For if we have been planted together in the likeness of his death, we shall be also in the likeness of his resurrection." (Romans 6:4-5.)

Next, the reception of the Holy Ghost through the laying on of hands of those who have received the Holy Priesthood, and are duly authorized, ordained, and empowered to impart this blessing: Thus Peter preached on the day of Pentecost:

"Repent, and be baptized every one of you in the name of Jesus Christ, for the remission of sins, and ye shall receive the gift of the Holy Ghost. For the promise is unto you, and to your children, and to all that are afar off, even as many as the Lord our God shall call." (Acts 2:38-39.)

These are the introductory or first principles of the everlasting, unchangeable Gospel of our Lord and Savior Jesus Christ, that is and has been the same to all men, amongst all nations, in all ages, whenever, or wherever [183] it has been taught by the authority of heaven. Hence we read: It was "preached from the beginning, being declared by holy angels, sent from the presence of God, and by his own voice, and by the gift of the Holy Ghost. And thus all things were confirmed unto Adam, by an holy ordinance, and the Gospel preached, and a decree sent forth, that it should be in the world, until the end thereof." (Moses 5:58-59.)

And in that day "the Lord God called upon men by the Holy Ghost everywhere, and commanded them that they should repent; and as many as believed in the Son, and repented of their sins, should be saved; and as many as believed not and repented not, should be damned; and the words went forth out of the mouth of God in a firm decree; wherefore they must be fulfilled." (v. 14-15.)

This same Gospel was preached to Seth, and to all the antediluvian Patriarchs, and they ministered under its authority. By its power, as we have already shown, Enoch and his people were translated. Of Noah it is written: "And the Lord ordained Noah after his own order, and commanded him that he should go forth and declare his gospel unto the children of men, even as it was given unto Enoch." (Moses 8:19.) And further, to quote from the testimony of Noah before the flood: "And it came to pass that Noah continued his preaching unto the people, saying, Hearken, and give heed unto my words; believe and repent of your sins, and be baptized in the name of Jesus Christ, the Son of God, even as our fathers did, and ye shall receive the Holy Ghost, that ye may have all things made manifest; and if ye do not this, the floods will come in upon you." (v. 23-24.)

From this we learn that the principles of the Gospel in the first ages of the world were identical with those taught in our day.

The Gospel and the Holy Priesthood continued from Noah to Abraham. "Abraham received the priesthood from Melchizedek, who received it through the lineage of his fathers, even till Noah." (D&C 84:14.) [184] As Paul writes, "And the Scripture, foreseeing that God would justify the heathen through faith, preached before the Gospel unto Abraham, saying, 'In thee shall all nations be blessed;'" (Galatians 3:8) whilst Jesus declared, "Abraham saw my day and was glad." (See John 8:56.) The knowledge and practice of the Gospel were perpetuated through Isaac, Jacob, Joseph and other Patriarchs, until the age of Moses, who, it is said, esteemed "the reproach of Christ greater riches than the treasures in Egypt;" (Hebrews 11:26) and of the Israelites, of whom he was the great lawgiver, Paul writes:

"Moreover, brethren, I would not that ye should be ignorant how that all our fathers were under the cloud, and all passed through the sea; and were all baptized unto Moses in the cloud and in the sea; and did all eat the same spiritual meat; and did all drink the same spiritual drink: (For they drank of that spiritual Rock that followed them: and that Rock was Christ.) But with many of them God was not pleased: for they were overthrown in the wilderness." (1 Corinthians 10:1-5.)

The further history of the Gospel in its relation to the house of

Israel is briefly told in the following paragraphs from the Book of Doctrine and Covenants:

"Now this Moses plainly taught to the children of Israel in the wilderness, and sought diligently to sanctify his people that they might behold the face of God; but they hardened their hearts and could not endure his presence, therefore the Lord in his wrath (for his anger was kindled against them) swore that they should not enter into his rest while in the wilderness, which rest is the fulness of his glory. Therefore he took Moses out of their midst, and the Holy Priesthood also; and the lesser priesthood continued, which priesthood holdeth the key of the ministering of angels and the preparatory gospel; which gospel is the gospel of repentance and of baptism, and the remission of sins, and the law of carnal commandments, which the Lord in his wrath caused to continue with the house of Aaron among the children of Israel until John, whom [185] God raised up, being filled with the Holy Ghost from his mother's womb; for he was baptized while he was yet in his childhood, and was ordained by the angel of God at the time he was eight days old unto this power, to overthrow the kingdom of the Jews, and to make straight the way of the Lord before the face of his people, to prepare them for the coming of the Lord, in whose hand is given all power." (D&C 84:23-28.)

It was this same Gospel that the crucified Redeemer commanded His disciples to preach, when "he said unto them, Go ye into all the world, and preach the gospel to every creature. He that believeth and is baptized, shall be saved; but he that believeth not shall be damned. And these signs shall follow them that believe: In my name shall they cast out devils; they shall speak with new tongues; they shall take up serpents; and if they drink any deadly thing, it shall not hurt them; they shall lay hands on the sick, and they shall recover." (Mark 16:15-18.)

And Mark testifies: "They went forth, and preached every where, the Lord working with them, and confirming the word with signs following." (v. 20.)

Hence we find on the day of Pentecost, Peter, the senior of the Apostles, in answer to the cry of the believing multitude, "Men and brethren, what shall we do?" replying in the words already quoted: "Repent and be baptized, every one of you, in the name of Jesus Christ, for the remission of sins; and ye shall receive the gift of the Holy Ghost. For the promise is unto you and your children, and to all that are afar off, even as many as the Lord our God shall call." (Acts 2:37-39.)

Again, it was this same everlasting, unalterable, unchangeable Gospel whose restoration to the earth John, the Apostle, spoke of as follows:

"And I saw another angel fly in the midst of heaven, having the everlasting gospel to preach unto them that dwell on the earth, and to every nation, and [186] kindred, and tongue, and people, saying with a loud voice, Fear God and give glory to him; for the hour of his judgment is come: and worship him that made heaven, and earth, and the sea, and the fountains of waters." (Revelation 14:6-7.)

From the Bible, we turn to the Book of Mormon, and in its pages discover that the same Gospel which Jesus directed His disciples to go into all the world and preach, was preached on this continent, from the earliest ages. The Jaredites became acquainted with it through the revelations given to the brother of Jared; in one of which Jesus said unto him:

"Behold, I am he who was prepared from the foundation of the world to redeem my people. Behold, I am Jesus Christ. I am the Father and the Son. In me shall all mankind have light and that eternally, even they who shall believe on my name; and they shall become my sons and my daughters." (Ether 3:14.)

"And he ministered unto him, even as he ministered unto the Nephites." (Ether 3:18.)

The principles of this Gospel were very fully understood by the Nephites before the advent of the Messiah. We quote from a sermon of the younger Alma. He says:

"Now if it had not been for the plan of redemption, which was laid from the foundation of the world, there could have been no resurrection of the dead; but there was a plan of redemption laid, which shall bring to pass the resurrection of the dead, of which has been spoken. And now behold, if it were possible that our first parents could have went forth and partaken of the tree of life, they would have been for ever miserable, having no preparatory state; and thus the plan of redemption would have been frustrated, and the word of God would have been void, taking none effect. But behold, it was not so; but it was appointed unto man that they must die; and after death they must come to judgment; even that same judgment of which we have spoken, which is the end. And after God had appointed [187] that these things should come unto man, behold, then he saw that it was expedient that man should know concerning the things whereof he had appointed unto them; therefore he sent angels to converse with them, who caused men to behold of his glory." (Alma 12:25-29.)

It will be seen from this, in the first place, that, as we have before stated, God's plan in relation to man was that he should fall, and having fallen and obtained a knowledge of good and evil, (which knowledge he could not have obtained without placing himself in that position,) then it became necessary that he should know concerning the atonement and redemption which should be brought about through the mediation of Jesus Christ; and hence the angel communicated, as before related, this knowledge to Adam, and Alma's testimony on this continent is found to agree precisely with the testimony given in the Pearl of Great Price, pertaining to the revelation of God's will through an angel to Adam. We again quote from the same discourse:

"And they began from that time forth to call on his name; therefore God conversed with men, and made known unto them the plan of redemption, which had been prepared from the foundation of the world; and this he made known unto them according to their faith and repentance, and their holy works; wherefore he gave commandments unto men, they having first transgressed the first commandments as to things which were temporal, and becoming as Gods, knowing good from evil, placing themselves in a state to act, or being placed in a state to act according to their wills and pleasures, whether to do evil or to do good; therefore God gave unto them commandments, after having made known unto them the plan of redemption, that they should not do evil, the penalty thereof being a second death, which was an everlasting death as to things pertaining unto righteousness; for on such the plan of redemption could have no power, for the works of justice could not be destroyed, according to the supreme goodness of [188] God. But God did call on men, in the name of his Son, (this being the plan of redemption which was laid,) saying, If ye will repent, and harden not your hearts, then will I have mercy upon you, through mine only begotten Son; therefore, whosoever repenteth, and hardeneth not his heart, he shall have claim on mercy through mine only begotten Son, unto a remission of his sins; and these shall enter into my rest. And whosoever will harden his heart, and will do iniquity, behold, I swear in my wrath that he shall not enter into my rest." (Alma 12:30-35.)

When Jesus Himself appeared to the Nephites, He preached the same identical principles that He had previously taught to the Jews, adding occasionally further truths, because of the greater faith of the first named people; "And he did expound all things, even from the beginning even until the time he should come in his glory." (3 Nephi 26:3.) Amongst other things He said: "Whosoever will hearken unto my words and repenteth, and is baptized, the same shall be saved. Search the prophets, for many there be that testify of these things." (3 Nephi 23:5.)

And it is this same Gospel, attended by the same power and spirit, blessed by the same inspiration, and led by the same Priesthood, that is now being preached to all the world for a witness. Through its principles, and by its power the Kingdom of God will be established, righteousness spread, evil overcome, and Satan be vanquished; by it Zion and the New Jerusalem will be built up, Enoch and his city be received, the work of the Millennium be done, the renovation of the earth accomplished, and all God's glorious will be fulfilled, until the vision becomes a reality which Daniel saw and wrote:

"Behold, one like the Son of man came with the clouds of heaven, and came to the Ancient of days, and they brought him near before him. And there was given him dominion, and glory, and a kingdom, that all people, nations, and languages should serve him; his [189] dominion is an everlasting dominion, which shall not pass away. and his kingdom, that which shall not be destroyed. . . . And the kingdom and dominion, and the greatness of the kingdom under the whole heaven, shall be given to the people of the saints of the Most High, whose kingdom is an everlasting kingdom, and all dominions shall serve and obey him." (Daniel 7:13-14, 27.) [190]

APPENDIX

The Ideas of a General Atonement and Redemption, Entertained by Ancient Heathen Nations, Derived Originally from the Teachings of Earlier Servants of God.

The following are some natural deductions drawn from the theories entertained by men and recorded in history, which tend to establish rather than to overturn the principles which are so clearly demonstrated in the foregoing pages, exhibiting and showing that the atonement was a great plan of the Almighty for the salvation, redemption and exaltation of the human family; and that the pretenders in the various ages had drawn whatever of truth they possessed, from a knowledge of those principles taught by the Priesthood from the earliest periods of recorded time; instead of Christianity being indebted, as some late writers would allege, to the turbid systems of heathen mythology and to pagan ceremonials.

We believe in the foregoing pages it has been clearly demonstrated to all Latter-day Saints, that the prophecy and promise of the coming of the Son of God was fully understood in every dispensation of God's providence from the earliest period of the world's history, down through the succeeding ages, everywhere and at all times when the Church of God existed on the earth. Furthermore, that the doctrine of the atonement, as understood by us, was understood in like manner by the ancient servants of the Lord, and that it was the central principle of their faith, the foundation of their hope for eternal felicity and salvation, and their only trust for the resurrection of their bodies and life everlasting in the presence of the Father. Again [191] that the ancient Patriarchs, Seers, Prophets, High Priests and others, were almost as intimately acquainted with the earthly life and ministry of the Savior, by and through the gift of prophecy and the spirit of revelation, as we are by the perusal of His history, given to us in the sacred Scriptures. These worthies of olden time knew where He would be born and the names that would be given to Him; that His mother would be called Mary, and be virgin of the tribe of Judah and house of David. Herod's massacre of the Innocents, and the flight of the holy family into Egypt, were not hidden from them. They spake of Christ's baptism by John in Jordan, and of the Divine approval that would follow; they prophesied of His ministry, rejoiced in His wonderful works of power and deeds of charity and love; they understood that He should be betrayed for thirty pieces of silver; they mourned at the vision of His sufferings and death, and rejoiced at his triumph and resurrection. Even the minor details of the soldiers parting His raiment among them, His death between two malefactors, and His burial in the rich man's tomb were revealed; and still further, His descent into Hades, His preaching to the spirits in prison, His visits to the Nephites and His ultimate ascension to the Father, were all comprehended. They knew that He would triumph over death, hell and the grave, be crowned with glory at the right hand of the Majesty on high, and that all power would be given to Him in heaven and on earth. These and many more details were understood, prophesied of, talked about and rejoiced in by the Priesthood and Saints from the days of Adam to the hour that they began to be fulfilled by His advent and incarnation.

It is needless for us to go backward to the days before the flood to learn to what extent these truths were understood by the antediluvian races; for all the accounts that we have of those peoples come down to us through the channel of the Holy Priesthood, and all the records, books, traditions, etc., of those early inhabi[192]tants of our globe were brought to the children of the renovated earth through one family, that of Noah; and that Patriarch, by right of universal fatherhood to the new generations, ruled them as High Priest, Patriarch and King, as one to whom the living God revealed His mind and will, through whom the keys, rights and powers of the everlasting Priesthood were continued upon the earth, and with whom special covenants were made by the Almighty and the bow set in the clouds as an everlasting token of their perpetuity and unchangeableness.

It will be perceived that in the first days after the flood there was but one religion, and that was the worship of the true God under the ministration and guidance of His duly authorized servants. Further, that the belief of the first inhabitants of the postdiluvian age was not only the true one, but it was accompanied by the power and authority of the Holy Priesthood, which received revelations direct from the Almighty. Thus the young world, like the old, was opened with a dispensation of God's mercy, and the posterity of Noah were not left to grope in the dark for light and truth, any more than had been the immediate descendants of our great original father. The effects of thus repeopling the earth under the direct and immediate guidance of Jehovah, through His duly appointed servants, have been felt through all succeeding generations; for men, as they scattered over the earth, took with them the seeds of Divine truth, and though, frequently, in after ages, they disfigured it with false and base theories of their own, introduced all manner of corruptions into their forms of worship, established orders of uninspired and unauthorized priesthood, and replaced the worship of the true God by idolatry, yet the fact of the existence of God the universal Father was not entirely forgotten, nor was the doctrine of the atonement ever utterly obliterated from the minds of men. So strong and so universal a hold had this principle in the varied religions of antiquity, that its very strength has been used as an argu[193]ment against the doctrine; and it has been vigorously asserted that the Gospel taught by the Savior was of pagan origin, and that He was simply a reformer who took the most excellent wisdom of past ages and framed it into a code of morals and system of religious faith to suit His own ideas and accomplish His own purposes, however noble those purposes might have been.

The earliest departures from the straight and narrow path to the lives that are eternal, appear to have been made in Chaldea and Egypt. In the former land, Nimrod was one of the first leaders in apostacy and wickedness. (See Josephus' Antiquities, Book 1, Chap. 4.) These evils so rapidly spread, that as early as the days of Melchizedec and Abraham, the worship of false deities and idols seems to have become almost universal; and even those who did not worship graven images, the starry hosts of heaven, or the forces of nature, had so far perverted the principles of the Gospel, that they taught numerous soul destroying errors, totally inconsistent with the plan devised by heaven. In Egypt the apostacy began, and an unauthorized priesthood was established as early as the days of the grandson of Ham. The origin of this defection is explained in the Book of Abraham, as follows:

"Now the first government of Egypt was established by Pharaoh, the eldest son of Egyptus, the daughter of Ham, and it was after the manner of the government of Ham, which was Patriarchal. Pharaoh being a righteous man, established his kingdom and judged his people wisely and justly all his days, seeking earnestly to imitate that order established by the fathers in the first generations, in the days of the first Patriarchal reign, even in the reign of Adam, and also of Noah, his father, who blessed him with the blessings of the earth, and with the blessings of wisdom, but cursed him as pertaining to the Priesthood.

"Now, Pharaoh being of that lineage by which he could not have the right of Priesthood, notwithstanding [194] the Pharaohs would fain claim it from Noah, through Ham." (Abraham 1:25-27.)

As the idolatries of Chaldea and Egypt gave marked tone and color to the mythologies of the dominant races of antiquity on the eastern hemisphere, we shall not trace the growth and development of the religions of Persia, Greece, Rome, etc., through their various branches and ramifications. Such an effort would require a volume; but we shall confine ourselves simply to a brief consideration of the doctrine of the atonement, as understood by the ancient Gentile nations; referring only to such other theories and ideas as have naturally a bearing on that doctrine.

As a starting point we believe we may state with assurance of its truth that the expectation of the coming of a Son of God, a Messiah, in the flesh was universal with all the leading nations that flourished in the ages previous to the advent of the Redeemer. This is true of the people of Egypt, Babylon, Arabia, Persia, Hindostan, Greece and Rome; as also of the races that inhabited the American continent. And so strong in certain cases had this idea grown that by gradual stages it became changed into the belief that that expected Son of God had already come, and such a being was reverenced and worshiped under various names. In Greece and Rome this idea became so prevalent that nearly every very eminent man was thought to be a son of one of the gods; and evil designing men sometimes personated these deities on purpose to seduce the virtuous of the other sex, whose chastity they could overcome in no other way than by falsely declaring themselves to be the god for whom such women had particular reverence and esteem. (See Josephus' Antiquities, Book 18, Chapter 3.) Whilst on the other hand young women who found themselves mothers without husbands would cunningly declare that their children were the offspring of a god; or, to use the words of the historian Grote, when speaking of Greece, "the furtive pregnancy of young [195] women, often by a god, is one of the most frequently recurring incidents in the legendary narratives of the country." To such an extent did this excess run, that at a later period a decree was issued subjecting to a very severe penalty any woman who should pretend that her child was of divine parentage. One writer states: "Many are the cases noted in history of young maidens claiming a paternity for their male offspring by a god. In Greece it became so common that the reigning king issued an edict, decreeing the death of all young women who should offer such an insult to Deity as to lay to him the charge of begetting their children." Whilst on this point Mr. Draper writes: "Immaculate conceptions and celestial descents were so currently received in those days, that whoever had greatly distinguished himself in the affairs of men was thought to be of supernatural lineage. Even in Rome, centuries later, no one could with safety have denied that that city owed its founder. Romulus, to an accidental meeting of the god Mars with the virgin Rhea Sylyia as she went with her pitcher for water to the spring. The Egyptian disciples of Plato would have looked with anger on those who rejected the legend that Perictione, the mother of the great philosopher, a pure virgin, had suffered an immaculate conception through the influences of Apollo, and that the god had declared to Ariston, to whom she was betrothed, the parentage of the child. When Alexander issued his letters, orders and decrees, styling himself 'King Alexander, the son of Jupiter Ammon,' they came to the inhabitants of Egypt and Syria with an authority that now can hardly be realized. The freethinking Greeks, however, put on such a supernatural pedigree its proper value Olympias [Alexander's mother], who, of course, better than all others knew the facts of the case, used jestingly to say, that 'she wished Alexander would cease from incessantly embroiling her with Jupiter's wife.'" (Draper's Conflict between Religion and Science.)

Returning to Egypt where, as before stated, a priesthood,

disowned of God, had been set up, we are in[196]formed (See Osborn's "Religions of the World") that those who were initiated into the inner mysteries of its mythology, were taught that God created all things at the first, by His first born, who was the author and giver of all knowledge in heaven and on earth, being at the same time the wisdom and the word of God. The incarnation and earthly life of this important being constituted the grand mystery of their entire religious system. So great was their faith in the advent of this Holy One, that they had chambers prepared in their temples for His nativity.

The priesthood of the Egyptians, though entirely without Divine authority, taught many great truths which they had received from Noah, through Ham and Pharaoh, and it took generations before these Gospel truths were so entirely overlaid and corrupted by false hood and pagan innovations, that they became undiscernable to all but the initiated. It is an important fact, holding good of other ancient civilizations as well as that of Egypt, that the farther we trace back their religious beliefs and mythologies, the purer does the creed become, the nearer it approaches to heavenly truth. and the stronger and more evident are the traces of Gospel teachings. This fact alone is sufficient to prove that paganism had its origin in the revelations of heaven, from which, in its various diverse branches, it had turned and strayed, and by gradual growth, had become the vile, inconsistent, degrading and loathsome system which is abhorred by all pure minded, honorable and intelligent people. Had the various forms of ancient dominant pagan worship been radically and entirely different, with only those features in common that could reasonably be attributed to accident or the inter-communication of races, the inference would be strong that they had different origins; but when, as is the case, there is a strong family likeness, and that likeness grows stronger the further it is traced back, and continually points to a common parentage, and that parent[197]age is the truth as taught by the early patriarchs and inspired servants of heaven, our conclusions must necessarily be that these correct and God-given teachings were the source from whence the whole sprang, and the differences in development arose from the varied incidents in the history, and the peculiar surroundings of the various races that gave a local hue and tinge to their forms of belief. It is also noteworthy that the fundamental principles of the everlasting plan devised by infinite wisdom, and which were the most widely taught and accepted, are those which prevailed the most extensively in pagan creeds, and which longest retained their hold in the faith of the different races. (See Writings of Hitzig, Hyde, Faber, Goodsir, Higgins, Osborn, Levy, etc.) Amongst these ideas or principles we will mention a few that were so general that they might almost be called universal:

1st. The belief in one great father God.

2d. The expectation of the coming of His Son to dwell in the flesh and redeem mankind.

3d. The belief in a resurrection, and in future rewards and punishments for acts done in this life.

4th. The observance of the rite of sacrifice.

5th. The doctrine of repentance, and in certain cases the ordinance of baptism.

We ask, when it is proved that all these principles were taught by the duly appointed servants of God in the earliest ages, where else but from them could the ancient Gentile races have obtained their knowledge thereof?

Men have been ever prone to apostacy; our fallen nature is at enmity with a godly life, sometimes in one way, sometimes in another, Satan led men from the right path and under the influences of a false or diabolic inspiration many errors were introduced; as well as through the natural corrupt ambition of men who sought to obtain power over their fellows by promulgating new theories in the name of God and under the auspices of religion. The "ologies" of to-day would have [198] been impossible in the days of Pharaoh and Nimrod. The style of apostacy was necessarily fashioned by the condition of men's minds, their advance in civilization, and their understanding of physical laws. In the rudimentary condition of the nations who scattered at Babel, the easiest thing for them to do was to worship their dead ancestors and the heavenly orbs. In due course naturally followed the framing of idols, which at first only represented the being or thing worshiped, but which were afterwards regarded as gods themselves, and as such reverenced. The idea of God's anger at men's sins, associated with the law of sacrifice, led mankind to believe that the more precious and beloved was the offering to him who offered it, the more acceptable would it be to heaven. As a result, men soon began to offer up their sons and their daughters to appease the wrath of their gods. Abraham informs us:

"Now, at this time it was the custom of the priest of Pharaoh, the king of Egypt, to offer up upon the altar which was built in the land of Chaldea, for the offering unto these strange gods, men, women and children. And it came to pass that the priest made an offering unto the god of Pharaoh, and also unto the god of Shagreel, even after the manner of the Egyptians. Now the god of Shagreel was the Sun. Even the thank-offering of a child did the priest of Pharaoh offer upon the altar which stood by the hill called Potiphar's Hill, at the head of the plain of Olishem. Now, this priest had offered upon this altar three virgins at one time, who were the daughters of Onitah, one of the royal descent directly from the loins of Ham. These virgins were offered up because of their virtue; they would not bow down to worship gods of wood or of stone, therefore they were killed upon this altar, and it was done after the manner of the Egyptians." (Abraham 1:8-11.)

This practice of offering human sacrifices had become very general on the eastern continent in Abraham's day. [199]

One peculiar phase of false doctrine with regard to the atonement had grown strong in the days of this Patriarch. It was "that the blood of the righteous Abel was shed for sins." (JST Genesis 17:7.) This was a very natural mental outgrowth among people who believed in the consequences of the fall of Adam and had been taught the necessity of a redeemer. It was a very easy thing to fall into the error that as Adam had transgressed, so his immediate son atoned by his blood for his father's act. And in the spread of this incorrect idea of Abel's atonement amongst the early peoples, may be found the origin of the many diversified legends of a sacrificed redeemer. This theory was taught at a day so early in the world's history, that it spread with the migrating races in every direction, so that traces of it can be found from Hindostan to Spain, from the Baltic to Ethiopia. Of course, every people in their own language had their peculiar name for this savior, and each race claimed him as theirs, as Abel certainly belonged as much to one as the other, having no posterity; and by degrees they wove many fanciful and mythical legends round his life and death, varying according to the tastes, imaginative power and environment of the different races. This, to a very great extent, explains that enigma to Christians, who believe that Gospel truths were first taught by Jesus when in the flesh, how the knowledge of the principle of the atonement and the tradition of a Savior was so wide spread throughout the world before His actual coming.

There is another way by which the knowledge of these truths was taught. We refer to the extended preaching of such worthies as Melchizedec, Abraham, Jethro, Job, Jeremiah, Jonah and others; and above all to that of the Apostles after the Redeemer's death. Dispensation succeeded dispensation, as age succeeded age; time and time again the people apostatized, but each time some little remnant of divine truth remained [200] with them. Jesus Christ was preached by name soon after the creation, as Cyrus was named by divine revelation about two hundred years before his birth. Thus, in some languages, we have accounts of great men of God or gods, as the case may be, whose acts are said to have been, in a greater or less degree, the counterpart of those of the Messiah when He tabernacled in the flesh; and whose names bear a most remarkable likeness to that of the Son of God. Hence we have Cheesna or Chrishna of Hindostan, and Hesus of the Druids, both of which names bear a marked similarity to those of the Redeemer; the first to Christ, the second to Jesus. It appears altogether probable that the histories of these men are simply the shadowy traditions of the Savior, the faint recollection of the teachings of inspired men, which were localized to suit sectional vanity or pride of race; or that some ancient teacher of their own peoples has been clothed with the attributes and works of Christ, and during the lapse of ages the acts and deeds of the two lives have been intermingled in one, until at this day a rightful separation is impossible. This habit of mixing and mingling the great deeds of several distinct persons, and forming therefrom one grand, if not altogether harmonious whole, is one well understood by those who have studied the traditions of mankind; it is not peculiar to any age or race, and even in our day we often find a certain anecdote, whether real or imaginary, told of various celebrities, some of whom may be yet living, while others are among the recent dead. The effects of this habit, when continued through long ages, amongst semi-civilized or barbarous nations, went far to fashion the history of their gods, and often to manufacture deities out of altogether imaginary personages.

Modern revelation has restored another most important key to unlock the mystery of the almost universal knowledge of the

Redeemer and of the plan of the atonement. It is found in the statement that Jesus, after his resurrection, visited at least the inhabitants of [201] two distinct portions of the earth, which could not have been reached through the ministry of His Jewish Apostles. These two peoples were the Nephites on this land, and the Ten Tribes in their distant northern home. The knowledge that the Mexicans, and other aboriginal races of America had, at the time of their discovery by the Spaniards, of the life of the Savior, was so exact, that the Catholics suggested two theories (both incorrect, however) to solve the mystery. One was that the devil had invented an imitation gospel to delude the Indians; the other, that the Apostle Thomas had visited America and taught its people the plan of salvation.

The story of the life of the Mexican divinity, Quetzalcoatl, closely resembles that of the Savior; so closely, indeed, that we can come to no other conclusion than that Quetzalcoatl and Christ are the same being. But the history of the former has been handed down to us through an impure Lamanitish source, which has sadly disfigured and perverted the original incidents and teachings of the Savior's life and ministry. Regarding this god, Humboldt writes: "How truly surprising is it to find that the Mexicans, who seem to have been unacquainted with the doctrine of the migration of the soul and the Metempsychosis *should have believed in the incarnation of the only Son of the supreme God, Tomaeateuctli.* For Mexican mythology, speaking of no other Son of God, except Quetzalcoatl, who was born of Chimelman, the virgin of Tula (without man), by His breath alone, by which may be signified his word or will, when it was announced to Chimelman, by the celestial messenger, whom He dispatched to inform her that she should conceive a son, it must be presumed this was Quetzalcoatl, who was the only son. Other authors might be adduced to show that the Mexicans believe that this Quetzalcoatl was both God and man; that He had previously to His incarnation existed from eternity, and that He had been the Creator both of the world and man; and that He had descended to reform the world by endurance, [202] and being king of Tula, was crucified for the sins of mankind, etc., as is plainly declared in the tradition of Yucatan, and mysteriously represented in the Mexican paintings."

The following brief extracts relating to Quetzalcoatl, are from Lord Kingsborough's "Antiquities of Mexico." Speaking of a certain plate, he observes: "Quetzalcoatl is there painted in the attitude of a person crucified, with the impression of nails in his hands and feet, but not actually upon the cross." Again: "The seventy-third plate of the Borgain MS. is the most remarkable of all, for Quetzalcoatl is not only represented there as crucified upon a cross of Greek form, but his burial and descent into hell are also depicted in a very curious manner." In another place he observes: "The Mexicans believe that Quetzalcoatl took human nature upon him, partaking of all the infirmities of man, and was not exempt from sorrow, pain or death, which he suffered *voluntarily to atone for the sins of man*."

Rosales, in his history, when speaking of the people of the extreme southern portion of America, states: "They had heard their fathers say, a wonderful man had come to that country . . . who performed many miracles, cured the sick with water, caused it to rain that their crops of grain might grow, kindled fire at a breath, healing the sick and giving sight to the blind; and that he spoke with as much propriety and elegance in the language of their country as if he had always resided in it, addressing them in words very sweet and new to them, telling them that the Creator of the universe resided in the highest place of heaven, and that many men and women, resplendent as the sun, dwelt with him."

Thus we see that in the traditions with regard to this especial God, we have an almost complete life of the Savior, from the announcement of His birth to His virgin mother by an angel, to His resurrection from the grave. Had we space, other extracts could be given, showing that there were many details, not above [203] mentioned, ascribed to Quetzalcoatl, that relate to incidents in the life of Christ. The Book of Mormon alone explains the mystery. The account there given of Christ's ministrations amongst the forefathers of these peoples makes the whole thing plain. We understand, through that record, how and by what means they obtained this great knowledge, and can also readily perceive how the unworthy descendants of those whom the Savior visited, gradually added much childish rubbish to the original facts; making their story, like almost all other mythology, an unseemly compound of heavenly truth and puerile fable. But, in view of these facts, when all things are considered, it is almost a wonder that so much of the truth was retained to the days when America became known to Europeans.

We find, in the mythology of the Northmen, certain traditions that lead us to imagine that it is possible that the visit of the Savior to the Ten Tribes was by some means communicated to them. But this is simply a conjecture. However, it is asserted that they claimed that Woden, one of their principal deities, was a descendant of King David, a very curious circumstance, that it is difficult to explain, only on the supposition of Christ's visit, and that Woden, with them, occupied the place that Quetzalcoatl did with the Mexicans.

There is yet another source from which the ancients obtained their ideas of the life and mission of the Son of God. It is to be found in the translation of Enoch and his city. The fact of Enoch's translation was generally known by the people who lived immediately after the flood. It had occurred so short a time before, that it was almost a matter of personal recollection with the sons of Noah. They must also have been acquainted with the fact that others were caught up by the power of heaven into Zion, and it would appear strongly probable that Melchizedec and many of his people were also translated. Revelation does not state this in so many words, but the inference to be drawn from what is said, points clearly in that direction. The fact of these trans[204]lations, the frequent visits of angels to men holding the Priesthood, and the manifestation of God's power over the elements of nature made manifest through His servants, laid a foundation for many of the fables of ancient mythology; some of which, if we were to change the names and localities to those of Bible history, would not be as far from the truth as many suppose. This era of inter-communication with the holy beings of the other world was easily magnified and distorted into the Golden Age when gods dwelt with men, associated with much of earth life, and were swayed by passions very much as were their mortal companions. And, as before remarked, the simplicity of these traditions was greatly changed as the ages rolled around, until they were completely overlaid and hidden by abominable and monstrous fables, invented, taught and used by the priests and their associates for their own sinister and unholy purposes.

From the whole of these statements, we gather that while men, who have written in relation to the various gods, or virgins who have, each in her turn, conceived and borne a god or a messiah, would argue that the accounts of the birth, ministry, death, resurrection, etc., of the Savior, were simply a backing up and resuscitating of some of the old legends of heathen mythology which had been in existence in ages long antecedent to His advent, and that, therefore, the account of the life and works of the Redeemer was simply an act of priestcraft, to introduce another messiah, and another establishment of religion in the interests of the projectors, and that Christianity was simply a copy of the old paganisms that had exhibited themselves in the forms above referred to, whereas the reverse is clearly demonstrated in the foregoing chapters on the atonement. The fact is clearly proved, instead of Christianity deriving its existence and facts from the ideas and practices of heathen mythologists, and from the various false systems that had been introduced by apostacy, unrecognized pretensions and fraud, that those very systems themselves [205] were obtained from the true Priesthood, and founded on its teachings from the earliest ages to the advent of our Lord and Savior Jesus Christ; that those holy principles were taught to Adam, and by him to his posterity; that Enoch, Noah, Abraham, and the various Prophets had all borne testimony of this grand and important event, wherein the interest and happiness of the whole world were concerned, pertaining to time and to eternity. The Gospel is a system, great, grand and comprehensive, commencing in eternity, extending through all time, and then reaching into the eternities to come; and the ideas with regard to these disjointed materials, that are gathered together from the turbid waters of heathen mythology, are so much clap trap and nonsense, calculated only to deceive the unwary, superstitious and ignorant, and are as far below those great and eternal principles of heavenly truth which permeate through all time, penetrate into the heavens, and are interwoven with all the interests, happiness and exaltation of man, as the earth is below the heavens above. The object of placing this statement before our brethren, is to prove and demonstrate, what was stated in the commencement, that these truths should "grow together unto the confounding of false doctrines, and laying down of contentions." (2 Nephi 3:12.)

THE
GOVERNMENT OF GOD

BY

JOHN TAYLOR,

ONE OF THE TWELVE APOSTLES OF THE CHURCH OF JESUS CHRIST
OF LATTER-DAY SAINTS.

"O LET THE NATIONS BE GLAD AND SING FOR JOY: FOR THOU SHALT
JUDGE THE PEOPLE RIGHTEOUSLY, AND GOVERN THE NATIONS UPON
EARTH." (Psalm 67:4.)

LIVERPOOL
LONDON

1852

CONTENTS

PREFACE.. 197

CHAPTER 1: The Wisdom, Order, And Harmony of The Government of God. 199

CHAPTER 2: The Government of Man. 205

CHAPTER 3: On The Incompetency of The Means Made Use of By Man To Regenerate The World. 214

CHAPTER 4: What Is Man? What Is His Destiny And Relationship To God?.. 226

CHAPTER 5: The Object of Man's Existence on the Earth; And His Relationship Thereto. 231

CHAPTER 6: Man's Accountability to God. 246

CHAPTER 7: The Lord's Course in the Moral Government of the World.. 254

CHAPTER 8: Whose Right is it to Govern the World? Who has Governed It?. 257

CHAPTER 9: Will Man Always be Permitted to Usurp Authority

over Men and the Works of God. 268

CHAPTER 10: Will God's Kingdom Be A Literal or A Spiritual Kingdom?. 282

CHAPTER 11: The Establishment of the Kingdom of God Upon the Earth. 288

CHAPTER 12: The Effects of the Establishment of Christ's Kingdom or the Reign of God Upon the Earth. . . . 305

PREFACE

It was Elder Taylor's intention to superintend the publishing of "THE GOVERNMENT OF GOD" in person, previous to his departure for Great Salt Lake City last spring; but the numerous cares attending the French and German Missions, of which he was President; the translation of the Book of Mormon into the French and German language; the establishment of the *L'Etoile du Déséret* at Paris, and *Zions Banier* at Hamburg; together with a multitude of other business connected with the welfare of the Kingdom of God, rendered it impossible.

The manuscript was therefore handed to me by Elder Taylor, with a request to superintend the printing of the work, which I have done to the best of my ability.

Considering the disadvantage arising from the Author's absence during the reading of the proofs, I believe it is as correctly rendered as was possible from a manuscript copy.

The Work is now before the Public, and form one portion at least it will meet with a cordial reception, treating as it does upon the theme most dear to their hearts—the Reign of Righteousness and Peace.

From other portions it will meet with varied reception, but will nevertheless lead the minds of all the contemplate the glory of that time when the Messiah, even Jesus, shall come with all his holy angels, and sit upon the throne of his glory, and govern all nations upon earth.

JAMES LINFORH
Liverpool, *August,* 1852.

CHAPTER 1

The Wisdom, Order, and Harmony of the Government of God

The Kingdom of God, is the government of God, on the earth, or in the heavens. The earth, and all the planetary systems, are governed by the Lord; they are upheld by his power, and are sustained, directed, and controlled by his will. We are told, that "by him were all things created that are in heaven, and that are in earth, visible and invisible, whether they be thrones, or dominions, or principalities, or powers; all things were created by him, and for him: and he is before all things, and by him all things consist."[1] (Colossians 1:16-17.) If all things, visible and invisible, are made by and for him, he governs and sustains all worlds to us known, together with the earth on which we live. If he governs them, they are under his dominion, subject to his laws, and controlled by his will and power.

If the planets move beautifully, and harmoniously in their several spheres, that beauty and harmony are the result of the intelligence and wisdom that exist in his mind. If on this earth we have day and night, summer and winter, seed time and harvest, with the various changes of the seasons; this regularity, beauty, order, and harmony, are the effects of the wisdom of God. [2]

There are two kinds of rule on the earth; one with which man has

---

[1] I wish here to be understood, that at present I am writing to believers in the Bible. I may hereafter give my reasons for this faith; at the present I refer to the Scriptures without this.

nothing directly to do, another in which he is intimately concerned. The first of these applies to the works of God alone, and His government and control of those works; the second, to the moral government, wherein man is made an agent. There is a very striking difference between the two, and the comparison is certainly not creditable to man; and however he may feel disposed to vaunt himself of his intelligence, when he reflects he will feel like Job did when he said, "I abhor myself, and repent in dust and ashes." (Job 42:6.)

In God's government there is perfect order, harmony, beauty, magnificence, and grandeur; in the government of man, confusion, disorder, instability, misery, discord, and death. In the first, the most consummate wisdom and power are manifested; in the second, ignorance, imbecility, and weakness. The first displays the comprehension, light, glory, benificence, and intelligence of God; the second, the folly, littleness, darkness, and incompetency of man. The contemplation of the first elevates the mind, expands the capacity, produces grateful reflections, and fills the mind with wonder, admiration, and enlivening hopes; the contemplation of the second produces doubt, distrust, and uncertainty, and fills the mind with gloomy apprehensions. In a word, the one is the work of God, and the other that of man.

In order to present the subject in a clear light, I shall briefly point out some of the leading features of the two governments.

The first, then, is that over which God has the sole control, such as the heavens and the earth, for "He governs in the heavens above, and in the earth beneath." It may be well here to say a few words on His moral government, in the heavens. All we can learn of that is very imperfectly set forth in the Scriptures. It would seem, however, that all was perfect order, for "He spake, and said, Let there be light, and there was light; and He divided the light from the darkness." (See Genesis 1:3-4.) "He spake, and the waters were gathered together, and the dry land appeared." (*Ibid.* 1:9-10.) And in the creation of the fish, the fowls, the beasts, the creeping things, and man, it was done in the councils of God. The word was, Let us do this, and it was done. It would seem, then, that that government is perfect in its operations, for all the mandates of God are carried out with the greatest exactitude and perfection. God spake, chaos heard, and the world was formed. [3]

We find also that transgression is punished; when Satan rebelled he was cast out of heaven, and with him those who sinned.

Here, then, in these things consummate wisdom was manifested, and power to carry it out.

The plan of redemption was also made thousands of years ago. Jesus is spoken of by the prophets as being "The Lamb slain from before the creation of the world." (See Revelation 13:8; Moses 7:47.) The future destiny of this earth is also spoken of by prophecy; the binding of Satan; the destruction, and redemption of the world; its celestial destiny; its becoming as a sea of glass; the descent of the new Jerusalem from heaven; the destruction of iniquity by a power exercised in the heavens, associated with one on the earth; and a time is spoken of where John says—"Every creature which is in heaven, and on the earth, and under the earth, and such as are in the sea, and all that are in them, heard I saying, Blessing, and honor, and glory, and power, be unto Him that sitteth upon the throne, and unto the Lamb for ever and ever." (Revelation 5:13.) But I shall let this pass for the present, and content myself with saying on this subject, that in the councils of God, in the eternal world, all these things were understood: for if He gave prophets wisdom to testify of these things, they obtained their knowledge from Him, and He could not impart what He did not know; but "known unto God are all his works, from the beginning of the world." (Acts 15:18.) God, then, has a moral government in the heavens, and it is the developement of that government that is manifested in the works of creation; as Paul says, "The invisible things of Him from the creation of the world are clearly seen, being understood by the things that are made, even his eternal power and Godhead." (Romans 1:20.)

But when we speak of the heavens, we mean also the planetary system; for the world, and other worlds are governed by principles independent of man. The power that causes this earth to roll on its axis, and regulates the planets in their diurnal and annual motions, is beyond man's control. Their revolutions and spheres are fixed by nature's God, and they are so beautifully arranged, and nicely balanced, that an astronomer can calculate the return of a planet scorces of years beforehand, with the greatest precision and accuracy. And who can contemplate, without admiration, those stupendous worlds, rolling through the immensity of space at such an amazing velocity, [4] moving regularly in their given spheres without coming into collision, and reflect that they have done so for thousands of years. Our earth has its day and night, summer and winter, and seed time and harvest. Well may the poet say that they—

"Proclaim for ever, as they shine,
The hand that made us is divine."

And here let me remark how different is this to the works of man. We see, then, the power of God manifested in their preservation and guidance; but when we reflect a little further, that while our planetary system rolls in perfect order round the sun, there are other systems which perform their revolutions round their suns; and the whole of these, our system with its centre, and other systems with their centres, roll round another grand centre: and the whole of those, and innumerable others, equally as great, stupendous, and magnificent, roll round another more great, glorious, and resplendent, till numbers, magnificence, and glory, drown the thought, we are led to exclaim with the prophet, "O the depth of the riches both of the wisdom and knowledge of God! how unsearchable are His judgments, and His ways past finding out!" (Romans 11:33.) Without referring again to the motions of our earth, and the beautiful regularity and precision of the whole of this elegant machinery, we will turn our attention a little to the works of creation as found on the earth. The make, construction, and adaptation of each for its proper sphere, are the work of God; and they are all controlled by His wisdom and power, independent of man. In the conformation of the birds, the beasts, the fishes, the reptiles, the grains, herbs, plants, and trees, we see a striking exemplification of this fact. No matter which way we turn our attention, the same order and intelligence are displayed. The fish in their organization are peculiarly adapted to their proper element; the birds and beasts to theirs; the amphibious animals to theirs. The nicely organized machinery of their bodies; their bones, muscles, skins, feathers, scales, or hair; the formation of their bodies, their manner of living, together with the nature of their food, and their particular adaptation to the various elements and climates which they occupy, are all so many marked evidences of skill, forethought, intelligence and power. We will here notice a few examples. [5] Plunge bird, beast, or man, into the water, and let them remain there, and they will soon die; take a fish out of the water, and death ensues; yet all are happy, and move with perfect enjoyment in their proper spheres. Elevate a man, beast, or fish, into the air, and let them fall, and they will be bruised to death; but the bird, with its wings, light bones, and fragile body, is peculiarly adapted to the ariel element in which it moves, and is perfectly at home; while the brute creation and men feel as much so on the earth. Again, their habits, food, coatings, or coverings, digestive powers, and the organization of their systems, are all peculiarly adapted to their several situations. The same principle is developed in their arrangement and position on the earth. Those that inhabit a southern climate are peculiarly adapted to that situation; while those that inhabit a northern are equally fitted for theirs.

Take the reindeer and polar bear to the torrid zone, and they would be out of their proper latitude, and would probably die. Remove the elephant, lion, or tiger, to Iceland or Greenland, and leave them to their own resources, and they would inevitably perish.

We will notice for a moment the construction of their systems. Each one is possessed with muscular strength, or agility, according to its position, wants, or dangers, and there is a beauty, a symmetry, and a perfection about all God's works, which baffle and defy human intelligence to copy. An artist is considered talented if he can make, after years of toil, a striking likeness of any of those things, either on canvas, or in marble. But when he has done, it is only a dead outline; remove a little paint, or tear the canvas, and its beauty is destroyed; break the arm of a statue, and we see nothing but a mutilated stone. But take a man, for example, and remove the skin, there is still order and beauty; remove the flesh, there is still workmanship and skill, and the bones, the flesh, the muscles, the arteries and veins, and the nerves, and the lungs, not to forget the exquisite fineness of the sensitive organs, manifesting a skill, a forethought, a wisdom, and a power, as much above that of man as the heavens are above the earth.

We see the power, wisdom, and government of God, displayed in the amazing strength of some of the largest of the brute creation; as also in the fineness and delicacy, of the arrangement of the smaller. And while we admire the stupendous power of the elephant, we are [6] equally struck with the fineness, delicacy, and beauty of some of the smaller insects. The prescience, and intelligence of God, are as much manifested in arranging the bones, muscles, arteries, and digestive organs of the smallest animaculæ, as in the construction of the horse, rhinoceros, elephant, or whale. I might touch upon the organization of plants, herbs, trees, and fruits; their various compositions, modes of nourishment, manner of propagating their kind, &c.; but enough has already been said upon this subject. It is one that no one will dispute upon; Jew and Gentile, black and white, Christian and Heathen, philosopher and fool, all have one faith on this subject.

I have briefly touched upon it for the purpose of presenting in a clear light the imbecility and weakness of man; for wherever we turn our attention, we see power, wisdom, prescience, order, forethought, beauty, grandeur and magnificence.

These are the works of God, and shew His skill, workmanship, glory, and intelligence. They reflect His divine power, and shew in unmistakeable characters the wisdom of his government, and the order that prevails in that part of creation over which He has the sole and unlimited control.

We can perceive very clearly that what God has done, is rightly done. It is not governed by instability and disorder, but continues from eternity to eternity to bear the impress of Jehovah. [7]

CHAPTER 2

THE GOVERNMENT OF MAN

We will now turn our attention a little to the government of man, and see how that will compare with the foregoing, for man stands at the head of this beautiful creation; he is endued with intelligence and capacity for improvement; he is placed as a moral agent, and has the materials put into his hands to work with, the works of his Father as a pattern, the conduct of many of the inferior creation as an example—and might make the earth a garden, a paradise, a place of uninterrupted happiness and felicity, a heaven below. And if God had not delegated this moral agency and power to man, and thus given him the privilege, in part, of being the arbiter of his own destiny, such it would have been to this day, like the Eden from which he was ejected because of his transgression. For he had everything placed within his power, and was made lord of the creation. The beasts, birds, fish, and fowl, were placed under his control; the earth yielded plenty for his wants, and abounded in fruits, grain, herbs, flowers and trees, both to satisfy his hunger, and to please the sight, taste, and smell. The fields waved with plenty, and produced a perennial harvest. The fruits teemed forth in all their luscious varieties to satisfy his most capacious desires. The flowers, in all their gaiety, beauty, and richness, delighted the eye; while their rich fragrance filled the air with odoriferous perfumes. The feathered tribes, with all their gorgeous plumage and variety of song, both pleased the eye, and enchanted and charmed the ear. The horse, the cow, and other animals, were there to promote his happiness, supply his wants, and make him comfortable and happy. All were under his control, to contribute to his happiness [8] and comfort, supply his most extended desires, and to add to his enjoyment; but with all these privileges what is his situation?

With celestial blessings within his reach, he has plunged down to the very verge of hell, and is found in a state of poverty, confusion, and distress. He found the earth an Eden—a paradise; he has filled it with misery and woe, and has made it comparatively a howling wilderness. And let us not blame Adam alone for this state of things; for after his ejection from Paradise, the earth was sufficiently fertile to satisfy all the desires of man with moderate industry, and is at the present day, if it were not for the confusion that exists, and if men were properly situated, and its resources developed. But more of this anon.

At present we will examine some of these evils, and then point out their cause, and the remedy.

We find the world split up and divided into different nations, having different interests, and different objects; with their religious and political views as dissimilar as light and darkness, all the time jealous of each other, and watching each other as so many thieves; and that man at the present day (and it has been the case for ages), is considered the greatest statesman, who, with legislation or diplomacy, can make the most advantageous arrangement with, or coerce by circumstances, other nations into measures that would be for the benefit of the nation with which he is associated. No matter how injurious it might be to the nation or nations concerned, the measure that would yield his nation an advantage, might plunge another in irremediable misery, while there is no one to act as father and parent of the whole, and God is lost sight of. What is it that the private ambition of man has not done to satisfy his craving desires for the acquisition of territory and wealth, and what is falsely called *honor* and *fame?*

Those private, jarring interests have kept the world in one continual ferment and commotion from the commencement until the present time; and the history of the world is a history of the rise and fall of nations—of wars, commotions, and bloodshed—of nations depopulated, and cities laid waste. Carnage, destruction, and death, have stalked through the earth, exhibiting their horrible forms in all their cadaverous shapes, as though they were the only rightful possessors. Deadly jealousy, fiendish hate, mortal combat, and dying groans, have [9] filled the earth, and our bulwarks, our chronicles, our histories, all bear testimony to this; and even our most splendid paintings, engravings, and statuary, are living memorials of bloodshed, carnage, and destruction. Instead of men being honoured who have sought to promote the happiness, peace, and wellbeing of the human family, and greatness concentrating in that, those have been generally esteemed the most who produced the most misery and distress, and were wholesale robbers, ravagers, and murderers.

And from whence come these things? Let the apostle James answer: "From whence come wars and fightings among you? Come. they not hence, even of your lusts that war in your members? Ye lust, and have not—ye kill, and desire to have, and cannot obtain: ye fight and war, yet ye have not, because ye ask not. Ye ask, and receive not, because ye ask amiss, that ye may consume it upon your lusts." (James 4:1-3.) Here is evidently a lack of that consummate wisdom, that moral and physical control, that parental power which balances the universe, and directs the various planets. For let the same recklessness, selfishness, individuality, and nationality there be manifested, and we should see the wildest confusion.

Man has come in contact with man, morally, physically, religiously, and nationally, from the foundation of the earth. If God's works had done so, what tumult and ruin there would have been in the immensity of space! Instead of the order that now prevails, man would have been sometimes frozen to death, and at other times burned up; one or two seasons of irregularity, even in climate, would depopulate the earth. But what if the planets, irrespective of the power by which they are controlled, were to rush wildly through space, and, with their mighty impetus dash against each other? What fearful consequences would ensue. There would be "system on system wrecked, and world on world." What terrible destruction and ruin! We have read of earthquakes destroying countries, of wars depopulating nations—of volcanoes overwhelming cities, and of empires in ruin; but what would the yawning earthquake, the bellowing volcano, the clang of arms, or a nation's distress, be in comparison to a scene like this? System would be shattered with system; planet madly rush on planet; worlds, with their inhabitants, would be destroyed, and creations crumble into ruins. There would be truly a [10] war of planets, "a wreck of matter and a crash of worlds." (Joseph Addison, "Cato," Act 5, Scene 1.) These, indeed, would be fearful results, and shew plainly the distinction between the beautiful order of God's work, and the confusion and disorder of man's. God's work is perfect—man's imperfect. The one is the government of God, and the other that of man.

We notice the same mismanagement in the arrangement of cities and nations. We have large cities containing immense numbers of human beings, pent up, as it were in one great prison-house, inhaling a fœtid, unwholesome atmosphere, impregnated with a thousand deadly poisons; millions of whom, in damp cellars, lonely garrets, and pent up corners, drag out a miserable existence, and their wan faces, haggard countenances, and looks, tell but too plainly the tale of their misery and wretchedness. A degenerate, sickly, puny race tread in their steps, inheriting their fathers' misery and distress.

If we notice the situation of the nations of Europe at the present time, we see the land burthened with an overplus population, and groaning beneath its inhabitants, while the greatest industry, perseverance, economy, and care, do not suffice to provide for the craving wants of nature. And so fearfully does this prevail in many parts, that parents are afraid to fulfil the first great law of God, "Be fruitful and multiply, and replenish the earth;" (Genesis 1:28) and by desperate circumstances are almost forced to the unnatural wish of not propagating their species; while, corrupted with a correspondent depravity with that which reigns among nations, they are found using suicidal measures to prevent an otherwise numerous progeny from increasing their father's misery, and inheriting his misfortunes. And yet, while this is the case, there are immense districts of rich soil, covering millions of square miles, inhabited only by a few untutored savages, or the wild beast of the forest; and such is the infatuation of man that in many districts of country, which were once the seats of the most powerful empires, and where flourished the mightiest nations, there is nothing but desolation and wildness. Such are Nineveh and Babylon, on the Asiatic Continent; and Otolum, and many others discovered by Stephens and Catherwood, in Central America; and recently discovered ruins—unequalled in the old world—a little above the head of the California Gulf. Not only their cities, but their lands are desolate, deserted, and forsaken, and the same evils that once existed [11] there are transferred to another soil, all bespeaking plainly that we want a great, governing, ruling principle to regulate the affairs of the world, and assist poor, feeble, erring humanity.

Again, if we examine some of the details of these evils, we shall see more clearly the importance and necessity of a change. Nearly one-third, speaking in general terms, of the inhabitants of the earth are engaged in a calling that would be entirely useless if the world were set right.

If men and nations, instead of being governed by their unruly passions, covetous desires, and ambitious motives, were governed by the pure principles of philanthropy, virtue, purity, justice, and honor, and were under the guidance of a fatherly and intelligent head, directed by that wisdom which governs the universe, and regulates the motions of the planetary systems, there would be no need of so many armies, navies, and police regulations, which are now necessary for the protection of those several nations from the aggressions of each other, and internal factions. Let any one examine the position of Europe alone, and he will find this statement abundantly verified. Look at the armies and navies of France and England; and the confusion of Germany, also of Austria, Turkey, Russia and Spain, not to mention many of the smaller nations, and let their armies, their navies, and police be gathered together, and what an abundant host of persons there would be. They would be sufficient to make one of the largest nations in the world! And what are they doing? To use the mildest term, watching each other, as a person would watch a thief for fear of being imposed upon, and robbed, or killed; but generally strolling around as the world's banditti, robbing, plundering, and committing aggressions upon each other; and if they have peace, acquiring it by the sword; and if prevented from aggression and war, it is generally, not that they are governed by just, or virtuous principles, but because they are afraid that aggression might lead to combinations against them which would result in their overthrow and ruin.

In the city of Paris alone, at the present time, and its immediate environs, there are one hundred thousand soldiers, besides police to a very great number, not to mention the vast number of custom-house officers and others. Suppose we add to these their families, where they have any, and where they have not, notice the vast amount of [12] prostitution, misery, degradation, and infamy, that such an unnatural state of things produces. I give the above as an example of the whole, but here the navies are not included. I say again, What are these all doing? They do not raise corn to supply the wants of men, nor are they occupied in any useful avocation; but they *must* live, and their wants *must* be supplied by the products of the labour of others. There has to be an immense amount of legislation for the accomplishment of this thing, and instead of having one government of righteousness and the world obeying, we have scores of governments, all having to be sustained in regal pomp, to be equal to their neighbouring nations; and all this magnificence and national pride having to be supported by the labour of the people. Again, all these legislatures have to provide immense hosts of men, in the shape of custom-house, excise, and police officers, to carry out their designs, all of whom, and their families, help to increase the burden, till it becomes insupportable. That, together with the unnatural state of society, before referred to, in regard to the situation of the inhabitants of cities and the nations, plunges millions of the human family into a state of hopeless destitution, misery, and ruin, for they are groaning under all these hopeless burdens without having sufficient land to till to meet their demands, and as natural means fail they are obliged to have recourse to those that are unnatural. Hence, in England a great majority of the inhabitants are made slaves of, virtually to supply the wants of the greatest part of the world, and are forced to be their labourers. Thousands of them are immured in immense factories, little less than prisons, groaning under a wearisome, sickening, unhealthy labour; deprived of free, wholesome air; weak and emaciated, not having a sufficiency of the necessaries of life. Thousands more from morning till night are immured in pits, shut out from the light of day, the carol of the birds, and the beauty of nature, sickly and weak, in many instances for want of food; and yet, in the midst of their wretchedness, gloom, and misery, you will sometimes hear them trying to sing in their dungeons and prison-houses, in broken, dying accents,

"Britons never shall be slaves."

I will here give, as one example, an iron works that I visited lately [13] in Wales. One of the proprietors informed me that they employed fifteen thousand persons, and paid them £5,000 per week. Most of these people laboured under ground, in the pits, digging for iron ore and coal; the remainder were employed principally about the furnaces, in rolling the iron, &c., at heavy, laborious, fatiguing work. And who were they toiling for? Principally for the Americans and Russians, at that time, to furnish them with railroad iron. And what did they get for their labour? The riches of those countries? No. £5,000 a week among about fifteen thousand persons. I suppose, however, a number of these were boys and girls. The average wages of men was from ten to twelve shillings per week. And this is their pay for that labour; and yet the masters are not to be blamed, that I can learn, for they are forced by competition to this state of things, and by the unnatural, artificial state of society. If they did not do this their workmen must be out of employ, and ten times worse off, if that were possible, than they are now. In the State of Pennsylvania, in America, where the railroads run through coal and iron mines both, they leave them untouched, and come to England for iron to make the rails of, that they cannot afford to make at home, because of higher wages, and an *outlet* to society, which prevents them from being coerced into bondage. If the world was right, the labour would be done there, and not here, and the labour of carriage saved.

The situation of the peasantry and workmen in France, Germany, Prussia, Austria, and Russia, and in fact I may say of Europe generally, is worse even than that of the same class in England; and wherever we turn our attention, we see nothing but poverty, distress, misery, and confusion; for if men do not copy after the good and virtuous, they generally do after the evil. When nations and rulers set the pattern, they generally find plenty to follow their example; hence covetousness, fraud, rapine, bloodshed, and murder, prevail to an alarming extent. If a nation is covetous, an individual thinks he may be also; if a nation commits a fraud, it sanctions his acts in a small way; and if a nation engages in wholesale robbery, an individual does not see the impropriety of doing it in retail; if a strong nation oppresses a weak one, he does not see why he may not have the same privilege; corruption follows corruption, and fraud treads on the heels of fraud, and all those noble, honourable, virtuous, principles that ought to [14] govern men are lost sight of, and chicanery and deception ride rampant through the world. The welfare, happiness, exaltation, and glory of man, are sacrificed at the shrine of ambition, pride, covetousness and lasciviousness. By these means nations are overthrown, kingdoms destroyed, communities broken up, families rendered miserable, and individuals ruined. I might enter into a detail of the crimes, abominations, lusts, and corruptions that exist in many of our large cities, but I shall leave this subject, and conclude with the remarks of the prophet Isaiah, who gazed in prophetic vision on this scene: "Behold, the Lord maketh the earth empty, and maketh it waste, and turneth it upside down, and scattereth abroad the inhabitants thereof. . . . The earth also is defiled under the inhabitants thereof, because they have transgressed the laws changed the ordinances, and broken the everlasting covenant. Therefore hath the curse devoured the earth, and they that dwell therein are desolate." (Isaiah 24:1, 5-6.)

Iniquity of every description goes hand in hand; vice, in all its sickening and disgusting forms, revels in the palace, in the city, in the cottage; depravity, corruption, debauchery, and abominations abound, and man, that once stood proudly erect in the image of his Maker, pure, virtuous, holy, and noble, is vitiated, weak, immoral, and degraded; and the earth, which was once a garden, not only brings forth briars and thorns, but is actually "defiled under the inhabitants thereof." (v. 5.)

Those great national evils of which I have spoken are things which at present seem to be out of the reach of human agency, legislation, or control. They are diseases that have been generating for centuries; that have entered into the vitals of all institutions, religious and political; that have prostrated the powers and energies of all bodies politic, and left the world to groan under them, for they are evils that exist in church and state, at home and abroad; among Jew and Gentile, Christian, Pagan, and Mahomedan; king, prince, courtier, and peasant; like the deadly simoon, they have paralyzed the energies, broken the spirits, damped the enterprize, corrupted the morals, and crushed the hopes of the world.

Thousands of men would desire to do good, if they only knew how; but they see not the foundation and extent of the evil, and long-[15]established opinions, customs and doctrines, blind their eyes, and damp their energies. And if a few should see the evil, and try a remedy, what are a few in opposition to the views, power, influence, and corruption of the world?

No power on this side of heaven can correct the evil. It is a world that is degenerated, and it requires a God to put it right.

CHAPTER 3

On The Incompetency of the Means Made Use of By Man to Regenerate the World

I purpose in this Chapter to shew the incompetency of the means made use of by man for the accomplishment of the purposes of God—the establishment of His Kingdom, or Millennial reign.

Now, if it is the kingdom of God, that is to be established, it must be introduced by God. He must not only be the originator of it, but the controller also, and any means short of these must fail of the object designed.

The great evils that now exist in the world are the consequences of man's departure from God. This has introduced this degeneracy and imbecility, and nothing but a retracing of his steps, and a return to God can bring about a restitution.

God gave to man a moral agency, as head of the world, under himself. Man has usurped the sole authority, and taken upon himself to reign and rule without God. The natural consequence is, that we have inherited all the evils of which I have spoken, and nothing but the wisdom, goodness, power, and compassion of God, can deliver us [16] therefrom, restore the earth to its pristine excellence, and put man again in possession of those blessings which he has forfeited by his transgression. Emperors, kings, princes, potentates, statesmen, philosophers, and churches, have tried for ages to bring this state of things about; but they have all signally failed, not having derived their wisdom from the proper source. And all human means made use of at the present time to ameliorate the condition of the world must fail, as all human means have always done.

There are some who suppose that the influence of Christianity, as it is now preached and administered, will bring about a Millennial reign of peace. We will briefly examine the subject.

First, we will take the Greek and Catholic Churches as they have existed for ages—without an examination of their doctrines, whether right or wrong—for they form two of the largest branches of the Christian Church. They have, more or less, governed a great portion of Europe at different times; and what is the situation of the people and nations where they have held sway? We have noticed the effects, and already briefly touched upon the evils that prevail in those countries; and if Greece and Russia, or any other country where the Greek Church has held sway, be a fair specimen of the influence of that church, we have very little prospect, if that religion were more widely diffused or extended, that the results would be more beneficial, for if it has failed in a few nations to ameliorate their condition, it would necessarily fail to benefit the earth if extended over it. Nor do we turn with any better prospect to the Catholic religion. Of what benefit has it been to nations where it has prevailed the most? Has there been less war, less animosity, less butchery, less evil of any kind under its empire? It cannot be said that it has been crippled in its progress or its operations. It has held full sway in Spain, Rome, and a great portion of Italy, in France and Mexico for generations, not to mention many smaller states. Has it augmented the happiness of those nations of the world? I need not here refer to the history of the Waldenses, and Albigenses, and Huguenots, to that of the Crusades, wherein so many Christian kings engaged; nor to the unhappy differences, the wars and commotions, the bloodshed and carnage, that have existed among these people, for their history is well known. And the present position of both the Greek and Roman churches, [17] presents a spectacle that is anything but encouraging to lead us to hope, that if the world were under their influence, a Millennial reign of peace and righteousness would ensue.

And let not any one say that these churches have not had a fair opportunity to develop themselves, for their religion prevailed and was cherished in those nations. They have held universal sway, at different times, for generations. The kings, councils and legislatures, have been Catholic or Greek. In Rome, the Pope has ruled supreme, and also for some time in Lombardy, Ravenna, and other States. In Greece, the Patriarch of Constantinople, and in Russia, the Emperor, is head of the church.

But, methinks I hear the Protestants say, we fully accord with you thus far, but we have placed Christianity on another footing. Let us examine this subject for a moment.

The question would naturally follow, What have the reformations of Calvin, Luther, and other reformers, done for the world? We may notice that Denmark, Sweden, Prussia, with a great part of Germany, Holland, and Switzerland, as also England and the United States, are Protestant. What can we say of them? That they are a part of the disorganized world, and have manifested the same unhappy dispositions as other portions. Reform has not altered their dispositions or circumstances. We see among them the same ambitious, grasping, reckless disposition manifested, and consequently the same wars, bloodshed, poverty, misery, and distress; and millions of human beings have been sacrificed to their pride, ambition, and avarice, and thirst for national fame and glory.

The Reformation of the Church of England is anything but creditable to that church. I refer to Henry VIII, and the vacillating course taken by some of its early reformers; and its persecution of those who were opposed to it in religious faith.

I might here refer to the religious intolerance of Calvin of Geneva, and Knox of Scotland, and other reformers; but, as these are mere individual affairs, I pass over them. If we look at Christian nations as a whole, we see a picture that is truly lamentable, a miserable portrait of poor, degenerated, fallen humanity. We see Christian nations arrayed against Christian nations in battle, with the Christian ministers of each Christian nation calling upon the Christian's God to give [18] them each the victory over their enemies! Christians! and worshippers of the same God!!

Hence, Christian England has been arrayed against Christian France; Christian Russia against Christian Prussia; Christian Spain against Christian Holland; Christian Austria against Christian Hungary; Christian England against Christian United States; and Christian United States against Christian Mexico. Not to mention the innumerable aggressions and conquests of some of the larger nations, not only upon their Christian brethren, but against other nations of the earth.

Before those several nations have engaged in their wars, their ministers have presented their several prayers before the same God; and if He had been as infatuated as they, and listened to their prayers, they would long ago have been destroyed, and the Christian world depopulated. After their prayers they have met in deadly strife; foe has rushed against foe with mortal energy, and the clarion of war, the clang of arms, and the cannon's roar have been followed by dying groans, shattered limbs, carnage, blood, and death; and unutterable misery and distress, desolate hearths, lonely widows, and fatherless children. And yet these are all Christian nations, Christian brethren, worshippers of the same God. Christianity has prevailed more or less for eighteen hundred years. If it should still continue and overspread the world in its present form, what would it accomplish? The world's redemption and regeneration? No, verily. Its most staunch supporters, and most strenuous advocates would say, *No*. For like causes always produce like effects: and if it has failed to regenerate the nations where it has had full sway for generations, it must necessarily fail to regenerate the world. If it has failed in a small thing, how can it accomplish a large one?

There are some of the Evangelical Churches, and modern reformers who will tell me that the above is not Christianity; only a form, not the spirit and life. But it is national Christianity; and it is the nations—the world and its redemption—that we are speaking of. But, lest they should think me unfair in making this application, I will briefly examine their position. Which of the sects or parties is it that is good, evangelical, and pure? The Church of England, Methodists, Presbyterians, Independents, Baptists, Universalists, or [19] which of the hundreds of sects that flood Christendom? For they do not agree; there exists as much unhappy difference among them as there does among the nations. They have not power, of course, to act nationally; but, as individual sects, there is as much virulence, discord, division, and strife among them as among any other people. There is sect against sect; party against party; polemical essay against polemical essay; discussion after discussion; and hard words, bitter feelings, angry disputes, wrangling, hatred, and malice, prevail to an alarming extent: and it is enough, in many instances, for a member even of a family to be of a different religious persuasion, no matter how honest, to cause his expulsion from the family.

In fact, if we look at Christianity, as exhibited among the evangelical societies of England, and the United States, where Protestantism bears rule unchecked, what do we see? Nothing but a game at hazard, where a thousand opinions distract the people, each clamoring for his own peculiar form of worship, and, like the Athenians, clinging with tenacity to their own favorite god, no matter how absurd or ridiculous his pretensions. I would remark, however, both to Catholic and Protestant, that there is much good associated with both their systems, in the teaching of morality, virtue, faith in God, and our Lord Jesus Christ; that there are thousands of sincere, honest, good, and virtuous people among them, as also among the nations; that these evils have been the growth of ages. "The fathers have eaten sour grapes, and the children's teeth have been set on edge." (Jeremiah 31:29.)

It is unnecessary here to say anything of missionary societies, tract societies, and evangelical societies; for if the fountain is impure, the stream must be impure; if the tree is bad, the fruit will be bad also. It is certainly a praiseworthy object to spread the Bible, and all useful information, and to do good as far as we can; but to talk of this evangelizing the world, is folly.

We will now turn our attention for a short time to another society, which has been formed lately in Europe, called a "Peace Society," and which has lately held several congresses in London, Berlin, and elsewhere, with representatives from many of the European nations, and the United States. Their object is, to ameliorate the condition of the world, and bring about universal peace; but, with all deference to their feelings, and fervent desires that such a happy event might [20] be consummated, I must beg leave to differ from them in their views. Peace is a desirable thing; it is the gift of God, and the greatest gift that God can bestow upon mortals. What is more desirable than peace? Peace in nations, peace in cities, peace in families. Like the soft murmuring zephyr, its soothing influence calms the brow of care, dries the eye of sorrow, and chases trouble from the bosom; and let it be universally experienced, and it would drive sorrow from the world, and make this earth a paradise. But peace is the gift of God. Jesus said to his disciples, "Peace I leave with you; my peace I give unto you, not as the world giveth give I unto you." (John 14:27.) Moral suasion is always good, and the most happy that man can employ; but without the interposition of God, it will be useless.

The nations of the world have corrupted themselves before God, and we are not in a position to be governed by those principles without regeneration. If they were pure, and living in the fear of God, it would be another thing; but the world at the present time is not made of the proper materials to submit to a congressional interposition, of a kind similar to the one now established. The materials will not combine, and no power, short of the power of God, can accomplish it. We have got into the feet and toes of Daniel's national image; they are composed of iron and clay, which will not mix; there is no chemical affinity between the bodies. As it has been in generations past, the strong nations feel independent, and capable of taking care of their own affairs; and if the weak unite, it is to protect themselves against the strong. The principles of aggression and protection still rule as strong in the human bosom as ever they did. The world is as belligerent now as it ever was, and as full of commotion and uncertainty.

The dispositions of the nations, of kings, rulers, and people, are the same. The late revolutions in Europe, and present uncertain state of political affairs, are an evident proof of this. The political atmosphere of the European nations is full of combustion, and only needs igniting to set the whole in one common blaze. Talk of peace ! there is war in the councils and cabinets, uncertainty and distrust with emperors, kings, presidents, and princes; war in the churches, clubs, cabals, and parties that now distract the world. It is whispered in the midnight caucus, and proclaimed in open day. The [22] same spirit enters into the social circle, and breaks up families: father is arrayed against son, and son against father; mother against daughter, and daughter against mother; and brother against brother: it presides triumphant at the assemblies of the "Peace Society," and spreads confusion, discord, and division there. A moral, deadly, evil has infused itself throughout the world, and it needs a more powerful restorative than the one proposed to ameliorate its condition. If the root of the evil be not eradicated, in vain we regulate the branches; if the fountain be impure, in vain we strive to purify the streams. The means used are not adequate to the end designed, and in spite of all those weak, puny efforts, the world will continue in its present sickly state, unless a more powerful antidote be applied.

Another principle has many advocates on the Continent of Europe at the present time; a principle of Socialism. Like everything else, it is possessed of different phases, and has been advocated in its various branches by Fourier, Robert Owen, Cabet, Pierre Leroux, and Proudhon, in Europe, and Fanny Wright in America. The leading object of many of these people is to have a community of goods and property. Some of them discard Christianity altogether, and others leave every one to do as they please; others attach a little importance to it. I would briefly remark on the first of those, that if scepticism is to be the basis of the happiness of man, we shall be in a poor situation to improve the world. It is practical infidelity that has placed the world in its present position; how far the unblushing profession of it will lead to restoration and happiness, I must leave my readers to judge. It is our departure from God, that has brought upon us all our misery. It is not a very reasonable way to alleviate it by confirming mankind in scepticism. I am aware that there is much in the world to induce doubt, and uncertainty on religious affairs, and religious professors have much to answer for; but there is a very material difference between the religion of God, and our Lord Jesus Christ, and that of those who profess His name.

As regards Communism, in the abstract, or on the voluntary principle, we will examine that briefly. Pick out a number of men in Paris, London, Berlin, or any other city, associated with all the evils and corruptions of those cities, and organize them into a community. Will the mere removal of them from one place to another make them better? [22] Certainly not. If they were corrupt before, they will be after their removal; and if they were unhappy before, they will be after. This temporary change will not make a difference; for men in possession of different religious, and political, and moral views, never can be united in harmony. The difficulties that exist in the world on a large scale, would exist there in miniature; and though prudence, forbearance, and policy, in smaller circles, might operate for a time, the evils would still exist; and though they might smoulder and be pent up, like a volcano, they would only rage with greater fury when they did burst out.

I have conversed with some who seem to think that all that is necessary to promote the happiness of man, is, that he have sufficient to eat and drink, and that through this means it would be obtained. I grant that the comforts and happiness of men are in a great measure augmented by these things; but to place them as the root and foundation, is wrong. In the present situation of Europe, where so much squalid poverty, wretchedness, and distress abound, it is not to be wondered at that such feelings should obtain. But, if we cast our eyes abroad in the world, we shall find that unhappiness is not always associated with the poor: it revels in the church and state; among kings, potentates, princes, and rulers: it follows the haunts of the libertine and profligate, and gnaws in many instances the conscience of the minister: it rides with lords and ladies in their carriages and chariots, and revels in splendid saloons and in banquet halls. Many a pleasant countenance covers an aching heart, and many a gorgeous costume hides the deadly worm; jealousy, disappointed ambition, blasted hopes, cold neglect, and conjugal infidelity, produce many a miserable heart; and rage, envy, malice, and murder, lurk in many instances under the cover of pomp, splendor, competency, or magnificence; not to mention the care, anxiety, and trouble of officers of state in these troublous times. If the poor knew the situation of many of those in different circumstances, they would not envy their situations.

Again, if we notice the position of some of the southern and western States of America. They have abundance to eat and to drink, their lands bring forth bountifully. But does this make them happy? Verily, no. The same false state of society exists there; men are awfully under the influence of their depraved passions; men are frequently put [23] to death by what is called "Lynch law," without judge or jury. The pistol, the bowie knife, the rifle, and the dirk, are in frequent requisition, and misery and unhappiness prevail.

In Mexico, where they possess one of the richest countries in the world, a salubrious climate, a rich soil, abounding also with the most valuable mineral resources, yet the people are unhappy. Guerillas plunder the traveller, their streets are crowded with beggars; its men are without courage or energy, and the country is left a prey to any nation, who has covetousness or power to oppress it. The Scriptures say, that "Man shall not live by bread alone, but by every word that proceedeth from the mouth of God;" (Matthew 4:4) and as they do not exist in this way, another Scripture tells the story in plain terms, for it says, "Where there is no vision the people perish." (Proverbs 29:18.)

There is also another political party, who desire, through the influence of legislation and coercion, to level the world. To say the least, it is a species of robbery; to some it may appear an honorable one, but, nevertheless, it is robbery. What right has any private man to take by force the property of another? The laws of all nations would punish such a man as a thief. Would thousands of men engaged in the same business make it more honorable? Certainly not. And if a nation were to do it, would a nation's act sanctify a wrong deed? No; the Algerine pirates, or Arabian hordes, were never considered honorable, on account of their numbers; and a nation, or nations, engaging in this would only augment the banditti, but could never sanctify the deed. I shall not, here, enter into the various manners of obtaining wealth; but would merely state, that any unjust acquisition of it ought to be punished by law. Wealth is generally the representation of labour, industry, and talent. If one man is industrious, enterprising, diligent, careful, and saves property, and his children follow in his steps, and accumulate wealth; and another man is careless, prodigal, and lazy, and his children inherit his poverty, I cannot conceive upon what principles of justice, the children of the idle and profligate have a right to put their hands into the pockets of those who are diligent and careful, and rob them of their purse. Let this principle exist, and all energy and enterprise would be crushed. Men would be afraid of again accumulating, lest they should again be robbed. Industry and talent would have no stimulant, and confusion [24] and ruin would inevitably follow. Again, if you took men's property without their consent, the natural consequence would be that they would seek to retake it the first opportunity; and this state of things would only deluge the world in blood. So that let any of these measures be carried out, even according to the most sanguine hopes of the parties, they would not only bring distress upon others, but also upon themselves; certainly they would not bring about the peace of the world.

One thing more upon this subject, and I have done. In Europe, there has been of late years a great mania for revolutions—a strong desire to establish republican governments; but let me remark here, that the form of government will not materially affect the position of the people, nor add to the resources of a country. If a country is rich and prosperous under a monarchy, it will be so under a republic, and *vice versa*. If poor under one, it will be under another. If nations think proper to change their form of government, they of course have a right to do so; but to think that this will ameliorate their condition, and produce happiness, is altogether a mistake. Happiness and peace are the gifts of God, and come from Him. Every kind of government has its good and evil properties. Rome was unhappy under a kingly government, and also under a republican form. Carthage as a republic was no more happy than many of its monarchial contemporaries; nor was Corinth, Holland, or Venice; and republican Genoa has not manifested anything very much in favor of these principles. France was unhappy under her emperor, she was unhappy under her kings, and is unhappy as a republic. America is perhaps some little exception to this; but the difference lies not so much in her government, as in the extent of her country, the richness of her soil, and abundance of her resources; for, as I have already mentioned, "Lynch law" prevails to an alarming extent in the south and west. In the state of New York, in the east, there are mobs painted as Indians resisting the officers of the law, and doing it with impunity; and it is a matter of doubt whether persons having paid for property, shall own it, or be dispossessed by their tenants, not in law, for the constitution and laws are good, but in practice defective, through popular clamor and violence. I refer to the estates of Van Ranseller and others; and, in the west, to [25] Joseph and Hyrum Smith, who were murdered in Carthage jail, without any redress, although their murderers were known to the officers of state; and to the inhabitants of a city, ten thousand in number, together with twenty thousand others, principally farmers, labourers, and mechanics, occupying a country about ten miles wide, and thirty long, most of which was well cultivated and owned by the occupants,—who were all forced by continual harassing by lawless mobs, to leave a country in which they could not be protected, and seek an asylum in a far off desert home, there being no power in the government to give redress.

    It is altogether an infatuation to think that a change in government will mend the circumstances, or increase the resources, when the whole world is groaning under corruption. If there are twenty men who have twenty pounds of bread to divide amongst them, it matters but little whether it is divided by three, ten, or the whole, it will not increase the amount. I grant, however, that there are flagrant abuses, of which we have mentioned some, associated with all kinds of governments, and many things to be complained of justly; but they arise from the wickedness of man, and the corrupt and artificial state of society. Do away with one set of rulers, and you have only the same materials to make another of; and if ever so honestly disposed, they are surrounded with such a train of circumstances, over which they have no control, that they cannot mend them.

There is frequently much excitement on this subject; and many people ignorant of these things, are led to suppose that their resources will be increased, and their circumstances bettered; but when they find, after much contention, struggling, and bloodshed, that it does not rain bread, cheese, and clothing; that it is only a change of men, papers, and parchment, chagrin and disappointment naturally follow. There is much that is good, and much that is bad in all governments; and I am not seeking here to portray a perfect government, but to show some of the evils associated with them, and the utter incompetency of all the plans of men to restore a perfect government; and as all their plans have failed, so they will fail, for it is the work of God, and not of man. The moral agency of man without God, has had its full development; his weakness, wickedness, and corruption, have placed the world where it is: he can see as in a glass his [26] incompetency, and folly, and nothing but the power of God can restore it.

It is not to be wondered at, that those various plans should exist, for the world is in a horrible situation. Jesus prophesied of it, and said, there should be upon the earth "distress of nations, perplexity, men's hearts failing them, for fear, and for looking after those things which are coming upon the earth," (Luke 21:25-26.) Men see these things, and their hearts fear; confusion, disorder, misery, blood, and ruin, seem to stare them in the face; and in the absence of something great, noble, and magnificent, suited to the exigency of the case, they try the foregoing remedies, as a sailor, in the absence of a boat, would cling with tenacity to any floating piece of wreck, to save him from a watery grave.

Neither can men be blamed for trying to do good; it is certainly a laudable object; and with all the selfishness, ambition, and pride, associated with the foregoing, it must be admitted that there is much uprightness, sincerity, and honest zeal.

There are very many philanthropists who would gladly ameliorate the condition of men, and of the world, if they knew how. But the means employed are not commensurate with the end; every grade of society is vitiated and corrupt. "The whole head is sick, and the whole heart faint." (Isaiah 1:5.) Our systems, our policy, our legislation, our education, and philosophy, are all wrong, neither can we be particularly blamed, for these evils have been the growth of ages. Our fathers have left God, his guidance, control, and support, and we have been left to ourselves; and our present position is a manifest proof of our incompetency to govern; and our past failures make it evident, that any future effort, with the same means, would be as useless. The world is diseased, and it requires a world's remedy. [27]

CHAPTER 4

WHAT IS MAN? WHAT IS HIS DESTINY AND RELATIONSHIP TO GOD?

Having shewn in the foregoing chapters, that the rule of God is perfect where he governs alone, that the rule of man is imperfect, and has introduced confusion and misery, and that the plans of men are not competent to restore the world to happiness, and the fulfilment of the object for which it was created; it now devolves upon us to investigate the way that this thing can, and will be accomplished; for there is a time spoken of in the Scriptures, when there will be a reign of righteousness.

First, then, we will enquire who and what is man? and what is his destiny, and what his relationship to God? For before we can define government correctly, it will be necessary to find out the nature of the being that has to be governed.

What, then, is man? Is he a being temporal and earthly alone, and when he dies, does he sink into forgetfulness? Is he annihilated? or has he a spirit as well as a body? If the first be the case, he alone has a right to regulate his own affairs, to frame his own government, and to pursue that course which to him seems good; if not, the case is different. I do not here wish to enter into a philosophical disquisition on the subject, but, as I am writing at present to believers in the Bible, I shall confine myself more to that. I will state, that man is an eternal being, composed of body and spirit: his spirit existed before he came here; his body exists with the spirit in time, and after death the spirit exists without the body. In the resurrection, both body and spirit will finally be reunited; and it requires both body and spirit to make a perfect man, whether in time, or eternity. [28]

I know there are those who suppose that the spirit of man comes into existence with his body, and that intelligence and spirit are organized with the body; but we read, that when God made man, he made him of the dust of the earth; he made him in his own likeness. Man was then a lifeless body; He afterwards "breathed into him the breath of life, and man became a living soul." (See Genesis 2:7.)

Before that spirit was given, he was dead, lifeless; and when that spirit is taken away, he is again lifeless; and let not any one say that the body is perfect without the spirit; for the moment the spirit leaves the body, no matter how perfect its organization may be, the man is inanimate, and destitute of intelligence and feeling: "it is the spirit that gives life."(See 2 Corinthians 3:6.) Hence, we find that when Jarius's daughter was dead, his servant came and told him, saying, "Thy daughter is dead, trouble not the master;" but when she was restored, it is said "her spirit *came again*, and she arose straightway." (Luke 8:49, 55.) When her spirit was absent, the body was dead; when it returned, the body lived. "Moses spake unto the Lord, and said, let the Lord, the God of *the spirits of all flesh*, set a man over the congregation." (Numbers 27:16.) Again, the Lord in speaking to Jeremiah, said, "Before I formed thee in the belly, I knew thee," (Jeremiah 1:5) I would ask, What part of Jeremiah did he know? It could not be his body, for it was not in existence; but he knew his spirit, for "he was the father of his spirit." The Lord speaks to Job and says, "Where wast thou when I laid the foundations of the earth? declare if thou hast understanding, who hath laid the measures thereof, if thou knowest? or who hath stretched the line upon it. Whereupon are the foundations thereof fastened? or who laid the corner stone thereof? when the morning stars sung together, and all the sons of God shouted for joy?" (Job 38:4-7.) Again, John says, "They that dwell on the earth, shall wonder, whose names were not written in the book of life from the foundation of the world." (Revelation 17:8.)

This spirit proceeds forth from God, and is eternal; hence Solomon says, in speaking of death, "Then shall the dust return to the earth as it was, and the spirit unto God who gave it." (Ecclesiastes 12:7.) That the spirit is eternal, is very evident, from the Scriptures; Jesus prayed to his father, and said, "O Father, glorify thou me, with thine own self, with the glory which I had, *the world was.*" (John 17:5.) [29] Here Jesus speaks of an existence before he came here, of a glory he had with his Father before the world was. Christ, then, existed before he came here and took a body. Again Jesus says, "I have manifested thy name unto the men which thou gavest me out of the world: thine they were, and thou gavest them me." (John 17:6.)

Let us see what the Apostle Paul says on the subject: "Blessed be the God and Father of our Lord Jesus Christ, who hath blessed us with all spiritual blessings, in heavenly places, in Christ; according as he hath chosen us in him, before the foundation of the world." (Ephesians 1:3-4.) Christ, then, existed with his Father before the world was, and the Saints existed in, or with him. What part? their bodies? no, their spirits. Again, man exists after he leaves here. It is unnecessary to say anything about the life of the spirit, after the death of the body, or of the resurrection, as the subjects are so generally known and believed. Paul says, "If in this life only, we have hope in Christ, we are of all men most miserable. But now is Christ risen from the dead, and become the first fruits of them that slept. For since by man came death, by man came also the resurrection of the dead. . . . The trumpet shall sound, and the dead shall be raised incorruptible, and we shall be changed; for this corruptible must put on incorruption, and this mortal must put on immortality, then shall be brought to pass the saying that is written, Death is swallowed up in victory." (1 Corinthians 15:19-21, 52-54.)

If man, then, is an eternal being, came from God, exists here for a short time, and will return, it is necessary that he know something about God, and his government. For he has to do with him not only in time, but in eternity, and whatever man may be disposed to do, or however he may vaunt himself of his own abilities, there are some things he has no control over. He came into the world without his agency, he will have to leave it, whether he desires it or not; and he will also have to appear in another world. He is destined, if he improves his opportunities, to higher and greater blessings and glory than are associated with this earth in its present state: and hence the necessity of the guidance of a superior power, and intelligence, that he may not act the part of a fool here, and jeopardize his eternal interests; but that his intelligence may be commensurate with his position; that his actions here may have a bearing upon his future destiny; that he may [30] not sink into the slough of iniquity and degradation, and contaminate himself with corruption; that he may stand pure, virtuous, intelligent, and honourable, as a son of God, and seek for, and be guided and governed by his Father's counsels. Having said so much on this subject, we will continue our investigation still further, and enquire next, What is our relationship to God? In answering this, I would briefly remark, that the position that we stand in to him, is that of a son. Adam is the father of our bodies, and God is the father of our spirits. I know that some are in the habit of looking upon God, as a monster only to be dreaded, known only in the earthquake, the tempest, the thunder, and the storm, and that there is something gloomy and dismal attached to his service. If there is, it is the appendage of man, and not of God. Is there anything gloomy in the works that God has made? Turn where we will, we see harmony, loveliness, cheerfulness, and beauty.

The blessings of providence were made for man, and his enjoyment; he is placed as head of creation. For him the earth teems with the richest profusion; the golden grain, the luscious fruit, the choicest vines; for him, the herbs, and flowers, bedeck the earth, shed their odoriferous perfumes, and display their gorgeous beauty; for him, the proud horse yields his back, the cow gives her milk, and the bee its honey; for him, the sheep yields its fleece, the cotton-tree its down, and the worm its silk. For him, the shrub and vine bloom and blossom, and nature clothes herself in her richest attire; the rippling stream, the pure fountain, the crystal river flow for him, all nature spreads her richest charms, and invites him to partake of her joyousness, beauty, and innocence, and to worship her God.

Talk about melancholy, in the fear of God, and in his service! It is the corruption of the world, that has made men unhappy; and the corruption of religion that has made it gloomy: these are the miseries entailed by men, not the blessings of God. Talk about gloom! is there gloom in the warbling of the birds, in the prancing of the horse, in the playfulness of the lamb, or kid; in the beauty of flowers, in any of Nature's gifts, or rich attire, or in God, that made them, or in his service?

There are others, again, who would place the Lord at an immense distance, and render our approach to him almost impossible; but this [31] is a superstitious idea, for our Father listens to the cries of his children, numbers the hairs of their heads; and the Scriptures say, "a sparrow cannot fall to the ground, without his notice." (See Matthew 10:29.) He speaks to his elect, and says, "He that toucheth you, toucheth the apple of his eye." (Zechariah 2:8.) He is our Father; and hence the Scriptures tell us to pray, "Our Father, who art in heaven." (Matthew 6:9.) Paul says, "We have had fathers of our flesh, which corrected us, and we gave them reverence; shall we not much rather be in subjection unto the Father of spirits, and live?" (Hebrews 12:9.) We have, then, both a temporal and a spiritual Father; and hence his solicitude for our welfare, and his desire for our happiness. Says Jesus, "If a son ask bread, will he for bread give him a stone? or if he ask a fish, will he give him a serpent. If ye, then, being evil, know how to give good gifts unto your children, how much more shall your Father which is in heaven, give good things to them that ask him." (See Matthew 7:9-11.)

What a delightful reflection for his servants, to draw nigh to their Father, as to an endearing parent, and ask for blessings, as a son would ask for bread, and be confident of receiving. Hence the faithful in the Apostles' days received a spirit, whereby they could say, "Abba, Father," (See Romans 8:14-16) or Father, Father. What an endearing relationship! And if the world could comprehend, how gladly would they throw themselves upon his guardianship, seek his wisdom and government, and claim a father's benediction; but Satan has blinded the eyes of the world, and they know not the things which make for their peace. [32]

CHAPTER 5

The Object of Man's Existence on the Earth; And His Relationship Thereto

We next enquire, What is the object and design of man's existence on the earth; and what is his relationship thereto? for all this magnificent world, with its creation, life, beauty, symmetry, order, and grandeur, could not be without design; and as God existed before man, there must have been some object in man's creation, and in his appearance on the earth. As I have before stated, man existed before he came here, in a spiritual substance, but had not a body; when I speak of a body, I mean an earthly one, for I consider the spirit is substance, but more elastic, subtle, and refined than the fleshy body; that in the union of the spirit and flesh, there is more perfection than in the spirit alone. The body is not perfect without the spirit, nor the spirit without the body; it takes the two to make a perfect man, for the spirit requires a tabernacle, to give it power to develope itself and to exalt it in the scale of intelligence, both in time and eternity. One of the greatest curses inflicted on Satan and his followers, when they were cast out of heaven, was, that they should have no body. Hence, when he appeared before the Lord, and was asked from whence he came, he answered, "From going to and fro in the earth, and from walking up and down in it." (Job 1:7, 2:2.) For this reason he is denominated "The Prince of the power of the air, the Spirit that now worketh in the children of disobedience." (Ephesians 2:2.) Hence he exerts an invisible agency over the spirits of men, darkens their minds, and uses his infernal power to confound, corrupt, destroy and envelope the world in confusion, misery, and distress; and, although deprived personally of operating with a body, he uses his influence [33] over the spirits of those who have bodies, to resist goodness, virtue, purity, intelligence, and the fear of God; and consequently, the happiness of man; and poor erring humanity is made the dupe of his wiles. The Apostle says, "The God of this world hath blinded the minds of them which believe not, lest the light of the glorious gospel of Christ who is the image of God, should shine unto them." (2 Corinthians 4:4.) But not content with the ravages he has made, the spoliation, misery, and distress, not having a tabernacle of his own, he has frequently sought to occupy that of man, in order that he might yet possess greater power, and more fully accomplish the devastation. We read, that in our Saviour's days, there were persons possessed with devils, who were tormented by them; and Jesus and his disciples cast them out. Mary Magdalene was dispossessed of seven. A legion had entered one man, and when commanded to leave, rather than have no bodies, they desired permission to enter those of swine, which they did, and the swine were destroyed. Man's body to him, then, is of great importance, and if he only knew and appreciated his privileges, he might live above the temptation of Satan, the influence of corruption, subdue his lusts, overcome the world, and triumph, and enjoy the blessings of God, in time and in eternity.

The object of man's taking a body is, that through the redemption of Jesus Christ, both soul and body may be exalted in the eternal world, when the earth shall be celestial, and to obtain a higher exaltation than he would be capable of doing without a body. For when man was first made, he was made "a little lower than the angels;" (Hebrews 2:7) but through the atonement and resurrection of Jesus Christ, he is placed in a position to obtain an exaltation higher than that of angels. Says the Apostle, "Know ye not that we shall judge angels?" (1 Corinthians 6:3.) "Jesus descended below all things, that he might be raised above all things." He took upon him a body, that he might die as a man, and "that through death, he might destroy him that had the power of death, that is, the Devil." (Hebrews 2:14.) Having conquered Death, then, in his own dominions, burst the barriers of the tomb, and ascended with his body triumphant to the right hand of God, he has accomplished a purpose which God had decreed from before the foundation of the world, "and opened the kingdom of heaven to all believers." Hence man, through obedience [34] to the Gospel, is placed in a position to be an adopted son of God, and have a legitimate right to his Father's blessings, and to possess the gift of the Holy Ghost. And the Apostle says, that "If the spirit of him that raised up Jesus from the dead, dwell in you, he that raised up Christ from the dead shall also quicken your mortal bodies by his Spirit that dwelleth in you." (Romans 8:11.) Thus, as Jesus vanquished death, so may we; as he overcame, so may we; and, if faithful, sit with him upon his throne, as he has overcome, and sat down upon his Father's throne. (Revelation 3:21.) Thus, man will not only be raised from degradation, but will also be exalted to a seat among the intelligences which surround the throne of God. This is one great object of our coming here and taking bodies.

Another object that we came here for, and took bodies, was to propagate our species. For if it is for our benefit to come here, it is also for the benefit of others. Hence the first commandment given to man was, "Be fruitful and multiply, and replenish the earth, and subdue it." (Genesis 1:28.) And as man is an eternal being, and all his actions have a relevancy to eternity, it is necessary that he understand his position well, and thus fulfil the measure of his creation. For as he, and his offspring are destined to live eternally, he is not only responsible for his own acts, but in a great measure for those of his children, in framing their minds, regulating their morals, setting them a correct example, and teaching them correct principles; but more especially in preserving the *purity* of his own body. And why? Because, if he abuses his body, and corrupts himself, he not only injures himself, but his partner and associates, and entails misery incalculable upon his posterity, who are doomed to inherit the father's misery; and this is not only associated with time, but with eternity. Hence the Lord has given laws regulating marriage and chastity of the strictest kind, and entailed the severest punishment upon those, who, in different ages have abused this sacred ordinance. For example, the curse of Sodom and Gomorrah: and the terrible judgments pronounced against those who should corrupt and defile their bodies, let any one read Deuteronomy 22:13-30. And Paul says, "Know ye not that ye are the temple of God, and that the Spirit of God dwelleth in you? If any man defile the temple of God, him shall God destroy." (1 Corinthians 3:16-17.) Whoremongers and adulterers shall not enter into the [35] kingdom of heaven. (1 Corinthians 6:9-10; and Hebrews 13:4.) And why? Because man being made a free agent over his own body, that he might exalt himself and posterity, both in time and in eternity, if he abuses that power, he not only affects himself, but unborn bodies and spirits, corrupting the world, and opening the flood gates of vice, immorality, and estrangement from God. Hence the children of Israel were told not to marry with the surrounding nations, lest their seed should be corrupted, and the people turned to idolatry, which would lead to the forgetfulness of God, to an ignorance of his purposes and designs, and cause them to lose sight of the object of their creation, and corrupt themselves; and to the introduction of every other evil, as a natural consequence. But where the order of God is carried out, it places things in a lovely position.

What is more amiable and pleasant than those pure, innocent, endearing affections which God has placed in the hearts of the man and woman, who are united together in lawful matrimony? With a love and confidence pure as the love of God, because it springs from him, and is his gift; with bodies chaste, and virtuous; and an offspring, lovely, healthy, innocent, and uncontaminated; confiding in each other, they live together in the fear of God, enjoying nature's gifts uncorrupted and undefiled as the driven snow, or the crystal stream. But how would this enjoyment be enhanced, if they understood their destiny; could unravel the designs of God, and contemplate an eternal union, in another state of existence; a connexion with their offspring, commenced here to endure for ever, and all their ties, relationships, and affections strengthened! A mother feels great delight in beholding her child, and gazing on its lovely infant form. How would her bosom swell with ecstacy at the contemplation of that child being with her for ever! And if we only understood our position, this was the object for which we came into the world. And the object of the kingdom of God is, to re-establish all those holy principles.

Chastity and purity are things of the greatest importance to the world. Hence the Prophet says, "Because the Lord hath been witness between thee and the wife of thy youth, against whom thou hast dealt treacherously; yet is she thy companion, and the wife of thy covenant. And did not he make one? Yet had he the residue [36] of the Spirit. And wherefore one? that he might *seek a godly seed*. Therefore take heed to your spirit, and let none deal treacherously against the wife of his youth." (Malachi 2:14-15.) Here, then, the object of purity is pointed out clearly; and what is it? that God might preserve a godly seed. St. Paul says, "What? know ye not that he who is joined to an harlot is one body? for two, saith he, shall be one flesh. . . . Flee fornication. Every sin that a man doeth is without the body; but he that committeth fornication, sinneth against his own body. What? know ye not that your body is the temple of the Holy Ghost which is in you, which ye have of God, and ye are not your own." (1 Corinthians 6:16-20.) And in the next chapter he speaks of the same things which Malachi does concerning a pure seed. "For the unbelieving husband is sanctified by the wife, and the unbelieving wife is sanctified by the husband, else were your children unclean; *but now are they holy*." (1 Corinthians 7:14.)

The legislators of all civilized nations have seen the necessity of sustaining these things, and consequently have passed, generally, very rigid laws for the protection of female virtue, and the support of the marriage contract. Hence Acts have been passed and enforced, disinheriting those who were not born in wedlock. This, in some instances, has produced a salutary effect. Ministers of the various churches have also used their influence, in a great measure, in support of virtuous principles. These have had their effect in assisting to stem the torrent of iniquity. But as the nations themselves have forsaken God, how can they expect to stop this crying evil; for the very legislators who pass these laws are in many instances guilty themselves; and when kings, princes, and rulers, corrupt themselves, how can they expect the people to be pure? for no matter how rigid law may be, corrupt persons will always find means to evade it. And, indeed, so far have these abominations gone, that it seems to be an admitted fact, that these things cannot be controlled; and, although there are laws relative to matrimonial alliances, yet there are some nations, called Christian, who actually give licence for prostitution, and all the degradation and misery associated with it. Nor are these things connected with the lower ranks of life only; wantonness and voluptuousness go hand in hand, and revel unchecked in courts, among the nobles and kings of the earth. The statesman, the politician, and the [37] merchant, the mechanic and the labourer, have all corrupted themselves. The world is full of adultery, intrigues, fornication, and abominations. Let any one go to the masked balls in the principal theatres in Paris, and he will see thousands of people of both sexes, impudently, shamelessly, and unblushingly, manifesting their lewd dispositions. Indeed, debauch and wantonness bear full sway, not to speak of the dens of abomination that exist elsewhere. London abounds with unfortunate beings, led on by example, seduction, and misery, to their fallen, degraded condition. The same thing exists throughout England, France, the United States, and all nations. Hence millions of youth corrupt themselves, engender the most loathsome diseases, and curse their posterity with their sin, who, in their turn, rise up and tread in the corrupt steps of their fathers. Not to say anything of the thousands of lovely beings whom God designed for companions of man in time and in eternity, and for raising up a pure offspring, who are corrupted, degraded, polluted, fallen, poor, miserable wretches; outcasts of society, insulted, oppressed, despised, and abused; dragging out a miserable existence; led on from one degree of degradation to another, till death, as a friend, closes their wretched career, and yet without hope. Thus, man that was made pure, in the image of his Maker, that could stand proudly erect as the representative of God, pure, and uncontaminated, is debased, fallen, corrupt, diseased, and sunk below the brute creation; a creature of lust and passion, and a slave to his unbridled appetites. I write plainly on this subject; and I do it because it is a curse to the world, and God will have a reckoning with the nations for these things. In vain, then, men legislate on these matters: the nations have corrupted themselves, and these things are beyond their control. Men must be governed by higher, and purer motives than merely human enactments. If the world understood its true position, and the eternal consequences to them and their seed, they would feel different. They would feel that they were eternal beings; that they were responsible to God, both for their bodies and spirits. Nothing but a knowledge of man's fall and true position, and the developement of the kingdom of God, can restore him to his proper state, restore the order and economy of God, and place man again in his natural position on the earth. [38]

Having spoken of man as an eternal being, we will now examine what relation he has to this earth; for it is the government of God that we wish to keep your minds upon. This earth is man's eternal inheritance, where he will exist after the resurrection, for it is destined to be purified and become celestial. I know that this position is considered strange by many, because it is generally supposed that we are going to heaven; that heaven is the final destination of the righteous; and that when we leave this world, we never return. Hence Wesley says—

"Beyond the bounds of time and space,
Look forward to that heavenly place,
The Saints' secure abode;"

And this is an opinion generally believed by the Christian world.

We shall therefore commence by enquiring, Where is heaven? Can any one point out its location? I would remark, that it is a word of almost unlimited signification; nevertheless we will investigate the matter a little. We read, that in the beginning "God created the heavens and the earth;" (Genesis 1:1.) and furthermore, that he called the "firmament heaven." (v. 8.) From the above we learn, that the heavens were created by the Lord, and that the heavens were created at, or about the same time as the earth, and that the firmament is called heaven. We are further told concerning the firmament, that "God separated the waters that were below the firmament, from those that were above the firmament." (See v. 7.) Hence, when God destroyed the world with a flood, "He opened the windows of heaven;" (Genesis 7:11.) when the rain ceased, he "shut the windows of heaven." (See Genesis 8:2.) Now, a word on this firmament; Where is it? "And God said, Let the waters bring forth abundantly the moving creature that hath life, and fowl that may fly above the earth in the open firmament of heaven." (*Ibid.* 1:20.) We find out, then, from the foregoing, that the firmament is called heaven, viz., the heaven associated with this earth; and that the firmament is the place where the birds fly, and the rain falls from heaven; and the scriptures say, that Jesus will come in the clouds of heaven. (Matthew 24:30; Mark 13:26.) But there are other heavens: for God created this heaven, and this earth; and his throne existed before this world rolled into existence, or the morning stars sang together for joy; for "Heaven is God's throne, and the earth is his footstool." (See Isaiah 66:1.) Solomon [39] says, "The heaven of heavens cannot contain thee." (1 Kings 8:27.) This heaven is veiled from mortal vision; spirits abound, but we cannot see them; and angels hover there, but to us are invisible, and can only be known or seen by the revelation of God. Hence Paul says, he "was caught up into the *third* heaven." (2

Corinthians 12:2.) Stephen "saw the heavens opened, and Jesus sitting on the right hand of God." (See Acts 7:56.) Where this revelation exists, there exists without the removal of the body a perfect knowledge of things as they are known to God, so far as they are revealed. Thus, when John was on the Isle of Patmos, he says, "I was in the spirit on the Lord's day, and heard behind me a great voice, as of a trumpet, Saying, I am Alpha and Omega, the first and the last, and What thou seest write in a book." (Revelation 1:10-11.) Then commenced the revelation. It was the same also with Stephen. From this we gather, that there is a veil that obscures the heavens from our sight; but when that veil is removed, and our vision is enlightened by the spirit of God, then we can gaze upon the glories of the eternal world, and heaven is opened for our view.

When persons are taken from the earth, and hid from our view, it is said they are gone to heaven. Hence it is said, that Elijah went by a whirlwind into heaven, (2 Kings 2:11.) And it is also said of Jesus that "while he blessed them he was parted from them, and carried up into heaven." (Luke 24:51.) But it is the destination of the Saints that we have to do with; and on this I would remark, that there are many glories, and man will be judged according to his deeds. "There is one glory of the sun, and another glory of the moon, and another glory of the stars; for as one star differeth from another star in glory, so also is the resurrection." (2 Corinthians 15:41-42.)

It would not comport with my object at the present time to enter into the whole of the details of this subject. I would briefly remark, however, inasmuch as I am now talking of man's body, that there is a place called "Paradise," to which the spirits of the dead go, awaiting the resurrection, and their reunion with the body. This was an old doctrine of the Jews. Paul, too, "was caught up into paradise and heard unspeakable words." (2 Corinthians 12:4.) John says, "to him that overcometh will I grant to eat of the tree of life, which is in the midst of the paradise of God." (Revelation 2:7.) This Paradise, however, is not the place for resurrected bodies, but for departed spirits: for Jesus said to the thief on the cross, "To day shalt thou be with me in Paradise." (Luke [40] 23:43.) Two days after this, and after the resurrection of his body, Mary was looking for the Lord, and he appeared to her: he said to her "Touch me not, for I am not yet ascended to my Father; but go to my brethren, and say unto them, I ascend unto my Father and your Father; and to my God, and your God." (John 20:17.) We learn here, then, that Jesus went to Paradise, with the thief on the cross, in spirit; but that he had not been with his body to his Father.

We will now speak of heaven, as a place of reward for the righteous. Daniel, in speaking of the resurrection, says, "Many of them that sleep in the dust of the earth shall awake; some to everlasting life, and some to shame and everlasting contempt." (Daniel 12:2.) Jesus says, those who have forsaken all and followed him, "shall inherit everlasting life." (Matthew 19:29.)

There is also a Book of Life spoken of. Paul speaks of some whose names were written therein. (Philippians 4:3.) John also refers to the same things: he says "He that overcometh, the same shall be clothed in white raiment; and I will not blot out his name out of the Book of Life." (Revelation 3:5.) Again, John 1n speaking of the New Jerusalem, says, There shall not enter into it anything that worketh abomination, or maketh a lie; but they which are written in the Lamb's Book of Life. (Revelation 21:27.) From this it would appear, that those who obey all the commandments of God, and have their names written in the Lamb's Book of Life, shall finally enter into the New Jerusalem. Jesus again says, "To him that overcometh will I grant to sit with me in my throne, even as I also overcame, and am sat down with my Father in his throne." (Revelation 3:21.) This, then, is the heaven, as far as I can conceive, that people expect to go to.

We will now try to find out its location. Above we have noticed that the saints are to have everlasting life, that they are to be with Jesus, and also in the New Jerusalem. We have now to enquire, Where Jesus's kingdom will be, and Where will be the place of the New Jerusalem. Daniel says, "I saw in the night visions, and behold one like the son of man came with the clouds of heaven, and came to the Ancient of Days, and they brought him near before him. And there was given him dominion, and glory, and a kingdom, that all people, nations, and languages, should serve him: his dominion is an everlasting dominion, which shall not pass away, and his kingdom that [41] which shall not be destroyed." (Daniel 7:13-14.) Here, then, we find Jesus coming to establish a kingdom. Where is that kingdom? The Scriptures say, that all nations, languages, and tongues shall serve and obey him. Where do those nations, languages, and tongues exist? The answer is, on the earth. We will next enquire, Where the saints will be. Daniel says, in the 27th verse, "And the kingdom, and dominion, and the greatness of the kingdom under the *whole heaven* shall be given to the people of the saints of the Most High." Here, then, we find Jesus reigning under the whole heaven with his saints, and all nations, dominions, and powers, serving him. I noticed above, that those who overcame would be with Jesus, and with him have everlasting life. Zechariah speaks of a time when there will be a great assemblage of people against Jerusalem; after God's ancient people, the Jews, shall have been gathered there, and the Lord himself shall come forth to their defense. He says, "Then shall the Lord go forth, and fight against those nations, as when he fought in the day of battle. And his feet shall stand in that day upon the Mount of Olives, which is before Jerusalem on the east; and the Mount of Olives shall cleave in the midst thereof, toward the east and toward the west, and there shall be a very great valley; and half of the mountain shall remove toward the north, and half of it toward the south. And ye shall flee to the valley of the mountains; for the valley of the mountains shall reach unto Azal; yea, ye shall flee, like as ye fled from before the earthquake in the days of Uzziah, king of Judah: and the Lord my God shall come and all the saints with thee. And the Lord shall be king *over all the earth:* in that day there shall be one Lord, and his name one." (Zechariah 14:3-5, 9.) Here we find that Jesus is to come, and *all his saints* are to come with him. And that the Lord is to be King over *all the earth*. The question again arises, Where will Jesus reign with his saints? the answer is, *upon the earth*. Again, we will refer to the revelations of John. He says, "I saw the souls of them that were beheaded for the witness of Jesus and for the word of God . . . and they lived and reigned with Christ a thousand years." (Revelation 20:4.) And if we wish to know *Where* they will reign, we will again let John speak: "For thou wast slain, and hast redeemed us to God by thy blood, out of every kindred, and tongue, and people, and nation. And hast made us unto our God kings and priests, and we shall reign *on the earth*." (Revelation [42] 5:9-10.) It is not necessary to quote more on this subject; it is so plain that he that runs may read. I know that there are those who will tell us that this is not the final destination of the saints. I would here remark, that a great many events will take place in regard to the renovation of the earth, which it would be foreign to my subject at the present time to detail. I would state, however, that when the earth shall have become pure, if people suppose that they will then inhabit a heaven, not on the earth, they are mistaken; for if we have the good fortune to have our names written in the Lamb's Book of Life, and to enter into the New Jerusalem, we shall in that very New Jerusalem have to descend to the earth. Methinks I hear persons saying, What! shall we not, then, stay in heaven? Yes—in heaven; but that heaven will be on the earth; for John says, "And I saw a new heaven and a new earth; for the first heaven and the first earth were past away (purified by fire and become celestial), and there was no more sea. And I John saw the holy city, New Jerusalem, coming down from God out of heaven, prepared as a bride adorned for her husband. And I heard a great voice out of heaven, saying, Behold the tabernacle of God is with men, and he will dwell with them, and they shall be his people, and God himself shall be with them, and be their God. And God shall wipe away all tears from their eyes; and there shall be no more death, neither sorrow, nor crying, neither shall there be any more pain; for the former things are passed away." (Revelation 21:1-4.) Here, then, we find man's final dwelling place is the earth; and for this purpose it was first created, and it never will fulfil the measure of its creation until this shall take place. Nor will man ever attain to the end for which he was created, till his spirit and his body are purified, and he takes his proper position on the earth.

The prophets of God, in every age, have looked forward to this time; and while many considered them to be fools, they were laying for themselves an eternal foundation: they looked with scorn upon the gaudy baubles that fascinated foolish and corrupt man: they could not yield to his chicanery and deception; but with the fear of God before their eyes, and a knowledge of the future, they stood proudly erect in a consciousness of their innocence and integrity; despised alike the praise and powers of men, endured afflictions, privations, and [43] death; wandered in sheep skins and goat skins, destitute, tormented, and afflicted, for "they looked for a city which hath foundations, whose builder and maker is God." (Hebrews 11:10.) Hence Job says, "I know that my Redeemer liveth, and that he shall stand at the latter day *upon the earth*; and though after my skin worms destroy this body, yet in my flesh shall I see God." (Job 19:25-26.) Man naturally clings to this earth; there seems to be something inherent in his nature that draws and binds his affections to the earth; hence he strives all that lays in his power to possess as much land as he can reasonably obtain; and not always honestly, but wars have been waged for the acquisition of territory, and the possessions of the earth. But what avails it all without God! So far from benefiting man, it is an injury, if obtained by fraud; for he has got to pass that test which none can avoid. And if circumstances here give him the power over his brother, when he leaves this world and appears before God, he goes to be judged for that very act of oppression; and the thing that he so anxiously desired to obtain in this world is his curse in the next. An honourable desire for property is not wrong; but no man can have a lasting claim unless it is given him of God. Lands, properties, possessions, and the blessings of this life, are of use only as they are sanctified, and have a bearing on the world to come. There have been hereditary laws established in England, and I believe in other countries, securing landed possessions to the eldest son, or heir. This has originated from the above feeling; and partly from the customs of the ancient Israelites, as recorded in the Scriptures; and families through this means seek to perpetuate their names. They may do this for a season; but if man rightly understood his true position, he would have a brighter object in view. The Scriptures tell us, "that every good and perfect gift comes from God;" (See James 1:17) that a man can receive nothing but what is given him from above. Men have conquered, and taken, bought and sold, the earth without God. But their possessions will perish with them; they may perpetuate them by law for a season to their descendants, but the Saints of God will finally inherit the earth for ever, in time, and in eternity. Abraham held his possessions on a very different footing from the above. The Lord appeared unto him, and made a covenant with him, and said, "And I will give unto thee, and to thy seed after thee, the land wherein thou [44] art a stranger. All the land of Canaan for an *everlasting possession.*" (Genesis 17:8.) This covenant was an eternal one; yet Abraham did not possess the land, for Stephen says, "he gave him none inheritance in it, no, not so much as to set his foot on." (Acts 7:5.) And Paul says, "By faith Abraham, when he was called to go out into a place which he should after receive for an inheritance, obeyed; and he went out, not knowing whither he went. By faith he sojourned in the land of promise, as in a strange country, dwelling in tabernacles with Isaac and Jacob, the heirs with him of the same promise; for he looked for a city which hath foundations, whose builder and maker is God." (Hebrews 11:8-10.) Here, then, we find land given to Abraham by promise, a land that he did not possess; but he will do so, "for he looked for a city which hath foundations, whose builder and maker is God." (v. 10.) He looked forward to the redemption of his seed, the establishment of the kingdom of God, and the inheritance of those blessings eternally. If any one doubts this, let them read the 31st chapter of Jeremiah, and the 36th to 39th chapters of Ezekiel; wherein it is stated that Israel is to be gathered to their own land, that it is to become as the Garden of Eden, and to be no more desolate. Ezekiel speaks of the resurrection of the dead, and the coming together of the bones, flesh, sinews, and skin, of a living army; of the uniting of the nations of Judah, and Israel, in one; and in consequence of the great development of the powers of God, the heathen would be filled with astonishment; and finally, that God's tabernacle should be planted in their midst for evermore. Then let them read from the 47th to the last chapter of Ezekiel; and they will find an account, not only of the restoration of the Jews, and ten tribes, but that the land is actually divided to them by inheritance, in their different tribes, according to the promise made thousands of years before to Abraham. In the 13th and 14th verses of the 47th chapter, he refers to this, and says, "Thus saith the Lord God, This shall be the border whereby ye shall inherit the land according to the twelve tribes of Israel: Joseph shall have two portions. And ye shall inherit it, one as well as another; concerning the which *I lifted up mine hand to give it unto your fathers;* and this land shall fall unto you for an inheritance." Thus we find that the promise unto Abraham concerning territory will be literally fulfilled. Again, I would refer my readers to the fourteenth chapter [45] of Zechariah. I would then turn their attention to the sealing of the twelve tribes mentioned in the seventh chapter of Revelations, where there are twelve thousand out of every tribe sealed; and then ask, Where are these to reign? The answer is, *on the earth;* together with those who have "washed their robes, and made them white in the blood of the Lamb, out of every nation, and kindred, and people, and tongue." (See v. 14.) Jesus says, "Abraham saw my day and was glad." (See John 8:6.) What! Was he glad to see his people scattered, dispersed, and peeled; Jerusalem trodden under foot, the Jewish nation, temple, and polity destroyed, and his seed cursed upon the face of the earth; or was it the second coming of Jesus, when they would be restored, Satan bound, the promises made to him, and to his seed fulfilled, and misery and sorrow done away; for according to the testimony of Paul, "all Israel shall be saved." (Romans 11:26.) Abraham's views concerning land and possessions were not the same as those entertained by men in our day; they were not only temporal, but eternal; and if the world was under the guidance of the same God as Abraham, they would be governed by the same principle; and anything short of this is transient, temporary, short lived, and does not accomplish the purpose of man's creation.

I cannot conclude this subject better than by giving a quotation from P. P. Pratt's "Voice of Warning." "By this time we begin to understand the words of the Saviour, 'Blessed are the meek, for they shall inherit the earth.' And also the song which John heard in heaven, which ended thus: 'We shall reign on the EARTH.' Reader, do not be startled: suppose you were to be caught up into heaven, there to stand with the redeemed of every nation, kindred, tongue, and people, and join them in singing, and to your astonishment, all heaven is filled with joy, while they tune the immortal lyre, in joyful anticipation of one day reigning on the earth; a planet now under the dominion of Satan, the abode of wretchedness and misery, from which your glad spirit had taken its flight, and as you supposed, an everlasting farewell. You might perhaps be startled for a moment, and enquire within yourself, Why have I never heard this theme sung among the churches on earth? Well, my friend, the answer would be, because you lived in a day when people did not understand the Scriptures. Abraham would tell you—you should have read the promise of God to him, Genesis 17:8, where God not only promised the [46] land of Canaan to his seed for an everlasting possession, but also to him. Then you should have read the testimony of Stephen, Acts 7:5, by which you would have ascertained that Abraham never had inherited the things promised, but was still expecting to rise from the dead, and be brought into the land of Canaan to inherit them. Yes, says Ezekiel, if you had read the 37th chapter of my Prophecies, you would have found a positive promise that God would open the graves of the whole house of Israel, who were dead, and gather up their dry bones, and put them together, each to its own proper place, and even clothe them again with flesh, sinews,

and skin, and put his spirit in them, and they should live; and then, instead of being caught up to heaven, they should be brought into the land of Canaan, which the Lord gave them, and they should inherit it. But, still astonished, you might turn to Job; and he, surprised to find one unacquainted with so plain a subject, would exclaim, did you never read my 19 chapter, from the 23rd to the 27th verses, where I declare, I wish my words were printed in a book, saying, that my Redeemer would stand on the earth in the latter day, and that I should see him in the flesh, for myself, and not another; though worms should destroy this body! Even David, the sweet singer of Israel, would call to your mind his 37th Psalm, where he repeatedly declares that the meek shall inherit the earth for ever, after the wicked are cut off from the face thereof. And last of all, to set the matter for ever at rest, the voice of the Saviour would mildly fall upon your ear in his Sermon on the Mount, declaring emphatically. 'Blessed are the meek, for they shall inherit the earth.' (Matthew 5:5.) To these things you would answer, I have read these passages, to be sure; but was always taught to believe that they did not mean so, therefore I never understood them until now. Let me go and tell the people what wonders have opened to my view, since my arrival in heaven, merely from having heard one short song. It is true, I have heard much of the glories of heaven described, while on earth, but never once thought of their rejoicing in anticipation of returning to the earth. Says the Saviour, 'They have Moses and the Prophets; if they will not believe them, neither would they believe, although one should rise from the dead.'"[2]
[47]

---

[2] Pages 48-50. Seventh Edition; Liverpool: F. D. Richards. This is an excellent work, and well worthy of any one's perusal.—J. T.

CHAPTER 6

Man's Accountability to God

This is a subject which it may be necessary for us to inquire into, in order that we may find out how far man is responsible. For if man be not a moral agent, he cannot be responsible for the present position of the world; and it would be unjust in God to punish him for acts that were not his, and for circumstances over which he had no control.

By a careful examination of the Scriptures, we shall find that man has had certain powers vested in his hands, which he holds subject to the control and guidance of the Lord; and that if he has acted without the counsel, guidance, or instruction of God, he has gone beyond the limits assigned him by the Lord, and is as much culpable as a minister plenipotentiary of any nation would be who should exceed the limits of his instructions; or a man holding a farm, or vineyard, by a certain lease, if he should disregard the conditions of that lease, and destroy the farm, or vineyard; for the earth is the Lord's, and man was put on it by the Lord. It is not man's possession, only as he holds it from God. Man's body was given him by God, and also his spirit, for the purpose heretofore mentioned. God had his object in view in the creation of the world and of man (which it is not necessary here to investigate); and if man is placed as an agent to act for the Lord, and also for himself, and then should neglect the Lord, he would certainly be held responsible to his Creator. That God had an object in view in regard to the creation of the world, is evident. Or, why was there a consultation in heaven about it? Why the beautiful regulation of sun, moon, and stars? Why the provision made for [48] the redemption of man before he came here? For Christ was "the Lamb slain from before the foundation of the world." (Revelation 13:8.) Why the arrangement of the resurrection? the New Jerusalem, and the reign of Jesus on the earth? Will any one say that all these things were done, and all nature organized in its present beauty, and order, without a design? It would be preposterous. If God has a design in those things, and man by his wilfulness, wickedness, corruption, and rebellion, should thwart the design of God, and yield himself to another influence, even that of Satan, will he not be held responsible? And whether God has a particular design or not, does not affect the question particularly; for the earth is the Lord's, and man also, and God has a perfect right to dictate what laws he pleases. That the Lord looks upon the world in this manner is evident from the words of our Saviour. "There was a certain householder which planted a vineyard, and hedged it round about, and digged a wine-press in it, and built a tower, and let it out to husbandmen, and went into a far country. And when the time of the fruit drew near, he sent his servants to the husbandmen, that they might receive the fruits of it. And the husbandmen took his servants, and beat one, and killed another, and stoned another. Again, he sent other servants more than the first; and they did unto them likewise. But last of all he sent unto them his son, saying, They will reverence my son. But when the husbandmen saw the son, they said among themselves, This is the heir; come, let us kill him, and let us seize on his inheritance. And they caught him, and cast him out of the vineyard, and slew him. When the Lord, therefore, of the vineyard cometh, what will he do unto those husbandmen? They say unto him, He will miserably destroy those wicked men, and will let out his vineyard unto other husbandmen, which shall render him the fruits in their seasons. Jesus saith unto them, Did ye never read in the Scriptures, The stone which the builders rejected, the same is become the head of the corner: this is the Lord's doing, and it is marvellous in our eyes? Therefore say I unto you, The kingdom of God shall be taken from you, and given to a nation bringing forth the fruits thereof. And whosoever shall fall on this stone shall be broken; but on whomsoever it shall fall, it will grind him to powder." (Matthew 21:33-44.) Here, then, the thing is clearly developed; man's agency; the abuse of that agency; [49] the punishment inflicted for that abuse, together with the awful consequences of resistance to the proper authority. "On whomsoever it shall fall, it shall grind him to powder." (v. 44.) God never gave man unlimited control of the affairs of this world; but always speaks of man as being under his guidance, inhabiting his territory, and responsible to him for his acts. The world is His vineyard, and man is the agent. Hence, when God made man, "God blessed him, and God said unto him, Be fruitful and multiply, and replenish the earth, and subdue it: and have dominion over the fish of the sea, and over the fowl of the air, and every living thing that moveth upon the earth." (See Genesis 1:28.) This, then, was man's dominion, *given him by the Lord*. And the word continues: "*And God gave them* every herb bearing seed, and every tree in which is the fruit of a tree." (See verse 29.) These things were given by God; but to show his power, and his right to be obeyed, and in order to test man, he forbid his eating of a certain tree; and when he did eat of it, and thus broke the commandment of God, he thrust him out of the garden, and decreed that he "should eat his bread by the sweat of his brow." (See Moses 5:1; Genesis 3:19.)

Again, God demanded worship and sacrifices, and when Cain and Abel offered them, he received one and rejected the other; and further, when Cain was wroth on account of his sacrifice not being accepted, the Lord said to him, "Why art thou wroth? and why is thy countenance fallen? If thou doest well, shalt thou not be accepted? and if thou doest not well, sin lieth at the door." (Genesis 4:5-7.) After the destruction of the world, which was in consequence of the people sinning against God, he blessed Noah, and spake to him, and gave him the same dominion which had been given before to Adam; and Noah offered sacrifices to him. The same recognition of the Almighty's power and authority was manifested by Abraham, Moses, the Children of Israel, and the Prophets; by Jesus also, and the primitive Christians. Man was left as a free agent with power to act, and vested with certain powers by his Father, and responsible to him for his acts, as a son, servant, or agent would be to his father, master, or employer. Perhaps it would be more correctly conveyed thus:—a man lets or rents a vineyard or farm, the man occupying it has a certain agency and discretionary power vested in his hands, but always subject to certain conditions imposed by the owner of the property. [50] Hence God made a covenant, with Noah, Abraham, the Children of Israel, and the primitive saints. The making of a covenant naturally implies two parties: in such cases, God is one, the people the other. If the people fulfil their covenant, the Lord is bound to fulfil his; but if man transgresses then the Lord is not bound to fulfil his engagement. For instance, in speaking to ancient Israel, he said, "And it shall come to pass if thou shalt hearken diligently unto the voice of the Lord thy God, to observe and to do all the commandments which I command thee this day, that the Lord thy God will set thee on high above all nations of the earth." (Deuteronomy 28:1.) He then describes what those blessings are; and further states, that if they do not observe his statutes they shall be cursed. The Lord set before them blessings and cursings; blessings if they obeyed, but cursings if they disobeyed. Man, then, acts as a moral agent, to improve upon the blessings which God puts within his power, or not, as he pleases; and it is the abuse of this moral agency, which has filled the world with misery and distress.[3]

Man has lost sight of the object of his creation, and his future destiny; and losing sight of his origin, his relationship to God, and his future destiny, he has fallen into the mazes of ignorance, superstition, and iniquity, and is groping in the dark, and knows not how to conduct himself in this world, or how to prepare for the world to come. For, instead of being governed by the Spirit, Wisdom, and Revelations of God, he is governed by the spirit of the Evil One, "the god of this world, who rules in the hearts of the children of disobedience." They have left God, and submitted themselves to his evil sway, and used that agency which God has given to them, not only in rejecting God, but in obeying Satan; and furthering his designs, which are in opposition to those of God, the happiness of mankind, and the salvation of the world. I know there are many who will ridicule this idea; but it is a thing which is plain in the Scriptures. The Apostle Paul says, "The god of this world hath blinded the minds of them which believe not, lest the light of the glorious Gospel of Christ, who is the image of God, should shine unto them." (2 Corinthians 4:4.) And if any man thinks he is wise, he has his moral agency and the world before him; and if he [51] can improve the situation of the world without God, he has ample opportunity to display his intelligence.

---

[3] This part of the subject is fully explained in the remarks on the Government of Man, chap. 2.

I would remark, further, that so far from Satan not exercising this power over man, he exercises it to such an extent, and he possesses such an unbounded influence over the human family, that God's purposes relative to man, and the earth, never can be carried out until Satan is bound, and cast into the bottomless pit. John says, "And I saw an angel come down from heaven, having the key of the bottomless pit, and a great chain in his hand. And he laid hold on the Dragon, that old serpent, which is the Devil, and Satan, and bound him a thousand years, and cast him into the bottomless pit, and shut him up, and set a seal upon him, that he should deceive the nations no more, till the thousand years should be fulfilled." (Revelation 20:1-3.) Here, then, he is described as *deceiving the nations*, and his power is curtailed for a season, that he shall not possess it. It is a difficult thing to persuade men that they are deceived; because that very power that deceives them, inflates the mind with self-sufficiency and assurance: but who, that looks abroad in the world, and sees the confusion, distress, and misery that abound, will say that man has acted wisely?

Man, then, is a moral agent, possessing the power to do good or to do evil; if he does well, he fulfils the measure of his creation, and secures his happiness in time and in eternity. If he does not well, and is involved in difficulties and misery, it is his own fault, and he may blame himself. There are many circumstances over which man individually has no control; but I am speaking more particularly of nations and the world, and man's moral agency associated with them: concerning individuals, the Lord will make his own arrangements. The Jews are cursed nationally, on account of their fathers' transgression, and cannot remove that curse, as a nation, until the time come. As individuals they can receive the Gospel as well as others. Their fathers committed grievous national offences against God for some length of time, and finally filled up the measure of their iniquity, in rejecting, and crucifying the Son of God. If they killed the prophets, and stoned those whom God sent, how could he treat with them? He could act no other way consistently than to "destroy those husbandmen, and give the vineyard to others." (Mark 12:9.) For if God be the [52] proprietor of the vineyard, and has a right to confer national blessings for obedience, he has also a right to visit them with national curses for disobedience. A nation rejecting God and his ordinances, and killing his prophets, and still professing to be his people, act hypocritically, and impose a great curse upon posterity. And if men will not acknowledge God, how can they expect him to acknowledge and bless them? Again. There are heathen nations enveloped in idolatry; and if millions of people came into the world in those places surrounded with idolatry and superstition, it would be unjust for them to be punished for what they did not know. Hence, if they have no law, they will be judged without law; and God in his own wisdom will regulate their affairs, for it is their misfortune, not their individual offence, that has placed them in their present position. If, however, we could trace their history, we should find, as with the Israelites, so with them. Their present darkness and misery originated in a departure from God; and as their fathers did not desire to retain God in their knowledge, he gave them up to their present darkness, confusion, and wretchedness. See Paul's remarks on this subject, Romans 1:21-25, 28. For nationally, the conduct of fathers has a great influence over their children, as well as in a family capacity. Hence the Jews will be blessed as a nation, in consequence of the promises made to Abraham, for as I have said before, these are eternal principles; man is an eternal being, and all his actions have a relevancy to eternity. The actions of fathers have a bearing and influence on their children, both as families and nations, in time and in eternity. And those great principles that God has his eye upon in relation to the nations, and to the world, will certainly be accomplished. Hence the stimulus to excite men to tread in the steps of Abraham, that like him they may obtain blessings for themselves and their posterity. And hence the choice of Abraham by the Lord. The Lord said, "I know him that he will command his children and his household after him, and they shall keep the way of the Lord." (Genesis 18:19.) And why did the Lord feel anxious about this? Because of his own purposes in relation to the earth, and because of his parental care of the bodies and spirits of man. For there are matters of great importance associated with these things, as before referred to; and the Lord has felt very anxious, for the perpetuation of correct prin[53]ciples. So strong were his feelings in relation to this matter, that he gave the following law to the children of Israel: "If thy brother, the son of thy mother, or thy son, or thy daughter, or the wife of thy bosom, or thy friend which is as thine own soul, entice thee secretly, saying, Let us go and serve other gods, which thou hast not known, thou, nor thy fathers; namely, of the gods of the people which are round about you, nigh unto thee, or far off from thee; from the one end of the earth even unto the other end of the earth; thou shalt not consent unto him, nor hearken unto him; neither shalt thine eye pity him, neither shalt thou spare, neither shalt thou conceal him; but thou shalt surely kill him; thine hand shall be first upon him, to put him to death, and afterwards the hand of all the people. And thou shalt stone him with stones, that he die, because he hath sought to thrust thee away from the Lord thy God, which brought thee out of the land of Egypt, from the house of bondage." (Deuteronomy 13:6-10.) Here, then, it is stated, that if brother, son, wife, or any one, wish to lead thee from God, thou shalt destroy them; and why? Because in forsaking God, they lose sight of their eternal existence, corrupt themselves, and entail misery on their posterity. Hence it was better to destroy a few individuals, than to entail misery on many. And hence the inhabitants of the old world and of the cities of Sodom and Gomorrah were destroyed, because it was better for them to die, and thus be deprived of their agency, which they abused, than entail so much misery on their posterity, and bring ruin upon millions of unborn persons. And having thus deprived them of their agency to act upon the earth, and punished them for their transgressions, Jesus went "and preached unto the spirits in prison; which sometime were disobedient, when once the long suffering of God waited in the days of Noah, while the ark was a preparing." (1 Peter 3:19-20.)

It is upon this principle that the world will be punished in the last days for their transgressions, because they have abused their agency, and broken the covenant that God made with them. They have yielded to the influence of Satan, perverted the designs of Jehovah, and brought upon themselves and posterity a curse, misery, and ruin. If any thing further is desired upon this subject, Isaiah has described it plainly, and has shewn the awful effects of an abuse of this moral agency and departure from God, and the breaking of this covenant. [54] To him I refer the reader as a conclusion on this subject. "Behold, the Lord maketh the earth empty, and maketh it waste, and turneth it upside down, and scattereth abroad the inhabitants thereof. And it shall be, as with the people, so with the priest; as with the servant, so with his master; as with the maid, so with her mistress; as with the buyer, so with the seller; as with the lender, so with the borrower; as with the taker of usury, so with the giver of usury to him. The land shall be utterly omptied, and utterly spoiled: for the Lord hath spoken this word. The earth mourneth and fadeth away, the world languisheth and fadeth away, the haughty people of the earth do languish. The earth also is defiled under the inhabitants thereof; because they have transgressed the laws, changed the ordinance, broken the everlasting covenant. Therefore hath the curse devoured the earth, and they that dwell therein are desolate: therefore the inhabitants of the earth are burned, and few men left." (24:1-6.)

CHAPTER 7

The Lord's Course in the Moral Government of the World

We will now enquire, What part the Lord has ever taken in the moral government of the world. In the last chapter I shewed that man has a moral agency; acting under the Lord, and is, consequently, responsible to him for his acts, as a moral agent. But does he leave him alone and unassisted to carry out his designs? No. Looking upon man as his son, he has from time to time offered his services and instructions, as a father. He has given revelations, instructing and warning his people. He has given promises to the obedient, and threatened the disobedient. He has instructed kings, rulers, and [55] prophets. He has also protected the righteous, and punished, by judgments, the wicked. He has promised to Abraham and others lands and possessions. He has held out promises of eternal life to the faithful; but has never coerced or forced the human mind. He destroyed the inhabitants of the old world because they had corrupted themselves. He did not govern their minds; they might forget God, "and every thought of their hearts be only evil, and that continually;" (See Genesis 6:5) but the earth was the Lord's, and he was the Father of our spirits; and although man had an agency to propagate his species, it was given him by God; and if he was so blind as to corrupt himself, and entail misery upon millions of unborn beings, the God of the universe, "the Father of Spirits," (Hebrews 12:9) had a right to prevent him. And if he was prostituting the use of those faculties given him by God, to the service of Satan, and abusing the liberty which his

Creator had so liberally given, although the Lord could not control the free action of his will, he could destroy his body, and thus prevent him from cursing posterity. Hence, if a man transgresses the laws of the land, he is considered a bad member of society, and is punished accordingly; sometimes imprisoned; sometimes banished; and sometimes put to death. Legislators assign as a reason for these things, that such persons are injurious to society; that if crime was not punished, the virtuous and good would be abused; the wicked would triumph; character, life, and property would be insecure; and anarchy, confusion, and desolation would inevitably ensue.

I would here ask, If man acts upon this principle, has not God a right to do so with the affairs of his government? Or should we arrogate to ourselves privileges that we will not allow the Lord to possess? Upon this principle the Devil and his angels were cast out of heaven. The devil having his agency, as well as man, came here, and sought to destroy the works of God; and succeeded so far as to obtain an influence over man's spirit, and bring his body into subjection to his agency; and if man was so ungrateful and corrupt as to yield to his influence, and obey his agency, God had as much right to punish him as he had the Devil; and as he cast the Devil and his angels out of heaven, he also cut man off from the earth, and thus punished the "spirits that were disobedient in the days of Noah." (See 1 Peter 3:19-20.) Satan, in heaven, had no power over those spirits; but when [56] they came to earth, he gained an ascendency over them, and not having a body himself, made use of their bodies to corrupt the world, and thus thwart the designs of Jehovah; they must therefore bear the consequences of their disobedience. And if I am asked by a sceptic why God destroyed so many human beings, I answer, this was God's government, they had transgressed his laws, were traitors to him, and he had a right to punish them, as I before stated, to prevent them from bringing ruin upon others, and perpetuating this misery of the human family, in time, and in eternity.

The Lord has given laws, and although he has not forced man to keep them, nor coerced his will, yet he has punished him for disobedience, as a father would a son. A father of a child can teach that child correct principles; but unless he controls or confines the body, he cannot force that child to observe them; he can punish him for disobedience, however, and thus exert a moral or physical influence over him. Our Father does the same. He punished the inhabitants of Sodom and Gomorrah, Babylon, Nineveh, Jerusalem, and many other cities, and will punish the world on the same principle.

Again: he has offered rewards, and given them to the faithful, such as Noah, Abraham, Isaac, and Jacob; he protected the Children of Israel, and blessed them with temporal and national prosperity, when they served him, and punished their enemies; and he would have extended his blessings to the world, if they would have been obedient to him. The Lord has used these influences; but never coerced the will. Hence Jesus said to the Jews, "How often *would I* have gathered you together as a hen gathereth her chickens under her wings, and *ye would* not." (See Matthew 23:37; Luke 13:34; see also 3 Nephi 10:4-6.) God would have benefitted them, but they would not be benefitted. Again, the Prophet says, "Because *I have called*, and ye *refused*, I have stretched out my hand, and no man regarded; but ye have set at nought all my counsel, and would none of my reproof: I also will laugh at your calamity; I will mock when your fear cometh." (Proverbs 1:24-26.) These things clearly prove that man is a free, moral agent, and that God never has controlled the human mind, and that, consequently, if man is found in a state of wretchedness, degradation, and ruin, he has himself to blame for it, and not the Lord. The Lord would have given him his counsel if he had sought it; for he *did* instruct men of God formerly, and gave [57] them laws, and ordinances; and he told his people that if they called upon him "in the day of trouble, he would hear them" (See Psalms 50:15); and James says, "If any of you lack wisdom, let him ask of God, who giveth to all men liberally, and upbraideth not, and it shall be given him." (1:5.) When the Children of Israel served God and obeyed him, they acknowledged his authority, and said, "The Lord is our judge; the Lord is our lawgiver; the Lord is our king; he will save us." (Isaiah 33:22.) If the Children of Israel had been obedient, and this principle had extended over the earth, we should have had the Kingdom of God established on the earth, and universal peace and happiness would have prevailed. But man's corruption and degeneracy have destroyed the world, and nothing but the wisdom, power, and blessings of God can restore it.

CHAPTER 8

WHOSE RIGHT IS IT TO GOVERN THE WORLD? WHO HAS GOVERNED IT?

Having traced out in the preceding chapters the nature of man, his destiny and parentage, spiritual and temporal; what his object is in being here; what his relation to this earth is; his moral agency; and shown that God has never controlled his actions; we will next enquire a little about the earth; whose right it is to govern it; and who has governed it.

It will not be necessary to say a great deal here about the earth, and its organization, for we have touched on this subject before, and it is one about which there should be no dispute among believers in the Bible. I will briefly state, that Paul says, "For by him were all [58] things created, that are in heaven, and that are in earth, visible and invisible, whether they be thrones, or dominions, or principalities, or powers: all things were created by him and for him." (Colossians 1:16.) This being the case, without further investigation, we will examine whose right it is to govern it. If the world be the Lord's, he certainly has a right to govern it; for we have already stated that man has no authority, except that which is delegated to him. He possesses a moral power to govern his actions, subject at all times to the law of God; but never is authorized to act independent of God; much less is he authorised to rule on the earth without the call and direction of the Lord; therefore, any rule or dominion over the earth, which is not given by the Lord, is surreptitiously obtained, and never will be sanctioned by him. I am aware that kings and queens are anointed, and set apart by their different ministers, according to the different forms and creeds of the several countries over which they reign. There are two things necessary, however, to make their authority legal, and to authorize them to act as God's representatives on the earth. The first is, that they should be called of God; and the second, that the persons by whom they are anointed are duly authorised to anoint them. First, then, it may be necessary to observe, that, if kings and queens are of God's selection, and are his representatives, they must themselves be appointed by him; for if not so, how can they be considered his representatives? The prophet Hosea complains, that "they have set up kings, but not by me; they have made princes, and I knew it not." (Hosea 8:4.) If they are sent by him, they must understand their office and calling, and the designs of the Lord concerning the people whom they govern, the same as a governor of a province, or a minister plenipotentiary, receives his credentials from the prince or court whom he serves. If, then, we examine the position of kings, and their relationship to their divine Sovereign, we shall find that there is only two ways for this calling to be legal. It must have been given, either by God, through revelation to the ancestors of the reigning kings, and handed down in an unbroken descent to the present time; or, otherwise, given by direct revelation, and they set apart by a prophet of the Lord God. But no nation, kingdom, or king in existence will acknowledge either of these ways. All the kingdoms that are now in existence were founded by the sword, with[59]out any respect to God. In relation to their anointing, the question would naturally arise, Who authorised the ministers to anoint those kings and queens? for if the persons officiating have not the authority thus to anoint, and set them apart, to execute God's law and reign over the nations, their anointing will avail them little: it will be merely the anointing of man without the direction and sanction of God.

Authority to anoint kings and queens, in order that they may be the anointed of the Lord, must be given in one of three ways. It must first, have been given by revelation to the primitive Christian Church, authorising them to administer in this ordinance, and empowering their successors to do it; secondly, by direct revelation; or, otherwise, it must have been transmitted from the ancient Jews, through a lineal descent. In regard to the first, we find no such record in the New Testament; neither Jesus, nor his Apostles, nor any of the seventies, nor elders, ever administered in this ordinance, or spoke of it as being associated with the powers of their ministry. Consequently, no power can come from there.[4] [60]

In regard to the second position, all Christendom deny present revelation; and thus from their own confession they have not obtained their authority from that source; and in regard to the third, if there was authority associated with the Jews to ordain kings, the Christians certainly could not claim a Jewish rite; for the Jewish nation and authority were all destroyed: "they were broken off because of unbelief." (Romans 11:17, 19-20.) The Christians obtained all their authority to officiate from Jesus Christ, and not from the Jews. Whichever way you look at it, there is no foundation for any such authority, and consequently the anointing is all a farce, for it does not originate with God.

But here let us enquire a little further, Does God set up Christian kings to fight against Christian kings? and Christian subjects to destroy Christian subjects? I know they call upon God; but what to do? In their wars they ask him to destroy one another. This patchwork dominion, and mongrel Christianity, although they may be quite feasible in the dark, yet they present a curious spectacle when brought

---

[4] I am aware that the Roman Catholic ministry will tell us, that they have traditionary authority to anoint kings, and to perform many ordinances that are not contained in the Scriptures. Without, however, arguing the point of their authority here, I would briefly remark, that in order for the administration to be legal, it is necessary that the kings themselves be called of God; that this call is requisite, as well as the anointing; and that, if they possessed all the power they claim, they have no more right to anoint a man to be king, who is not called by God, in one of the two mentioned ways, than any officer of state would be authorised to confer an office of trust or honor on any individual, the gift of which was vested in the king alone, if the king had never appointed the individual. All intelligent persons must see that either appointment is illegal, and consequently null and void. The following from a French History, is interesting, and needs no comment: it shows clearly the design of its usage first in France:—

"La cérémonie du sacre était-elle connue en France avant l'inauguration de Pepin?

"R. Non; elle n'avait jamais été employée: mais Pepin se servit de cette cérémonie empruntée des Juifs, inconnue jusqu' alors, pour imprimer à la royaute un caractére plus auguste; cette coutume s'est perpetuée depuis pour tous les Rois de France. Il commenca à régner, 752, A.D."

(*Nouvelle Histoire de France, par Louis Ardent, p. 47. Paris: chez Corbet, Libraire Quai des Augustins.*)

into the light of Truth.

It may be asked, Has not the Lord given authority to kings to reign? Yes; he has, to two kinds: to one, to accomplish certain purposes that he had in view relative to the nations; to the other, to rule over his people—these were legally called and anointed by him. Of the first kind, was Nebuchadnezzar; he had a kingdom and dominion given to him, so say the Scriptures, but certainly not to govern God's people, for he made, and caused to be worshipped, a large golden Image; and put Shadrach, Meschach, and Abednego into a furnace for not doing so. What, then, was his calling? First, it was to govern a wicked and idolatrous people; and secondly, to fulfil the will of God, in the punishment of his people. As the people over whom he ruled had given themselves up to idolatry, they had an idolatrous king given to them for their ruler, for the Lord, never having given up his right to govern the world, gives the people kings according to their deserts; and although he may not give them *legal authority as His representatives*, yet by his overruling Providence, he places wicked men in a position that they may have power over a wicked nation, both to trouble that nation and themselves. Such was the case with Pharaoh, king of Egypt; and also with Salmanaser, [61] king of Assyria, when he defied the God of Israel. Such was the case with some of the kings of Israel, in the rebellions of that people; and with Belshazzar, king of Babylon, who was eating and drinking with his wives and concubines in the palace at Babylon, when the handwriting was seen on the walls, "God hath numbered thy kingdom, and finished it. Thou art weighed in the balances and art found wanting." (Daniel 5:26-27.) Babylon was destroyed; and so fully have the purposes of God been accomplished in relation to that magnificent city, that the place where it then stood is now a desert. And such also will be the case with the nations and kings of the earth, in the last day, as spoken of by Zechariah. "Behold, the day of the Lord cometh. . . . For I will gather all nations against Jerusalem to battle. . . . then shall the Lord go forth and fight against those nations, as when he fought in the day of battle." (*Ibid.* 14:1-3; also read the 39th chapter of Ezekiel.) Here, then, is a slaughter the most terrible that could be conceived: the armies actually cover the land, and so dreadful is the slaughter, that they cannot bury the dead, so that their stench shall stop the noses of the passers by. The fowls of the air are commanded also to assemble, that they may eat the flesh of kings, captains, and mighty men; and yet those kings, princes, and rulers will, by the providence of God, be given to the people as a chastisement, that the Lord may punish both kings and people on account of their iniquities. Daniel clearly exemplifies this subject in the following words, in speaking of the judgments that should come upon Nebuchadnezzar. He states, that these judgments were "to the intent that the living may know that the Most High ruleth in the kingdom of men, and giveth it to whomsoever he will, and setteth up over it the basest of men." (*Ibid.* 4:17.) Another duty that wicked kings have to perform on the earth is, that of being used by the Almighty as a scourge or rod to punish nations that are corrupt. Hence when Israel had sinned against God, and the Lord determined to chastise them, he told them, through his prophets, that he would punish them by Nebuchadnezzar, King of Babylon. Accordingly, Nebuchadnezzar came against Jerusalem, and took the Children of Israel captive to Babylon, with the vessels of silver and gold belonging to the Temple. And God afterwards punished Babylon for its transgressions; Cyrus, king of Persia was raised up by the Lord to chastise it. [62]

But did either of these kings govern God's people? or were they ordained by the Lord? No, only as his sword to execute his judgments on the nations. Such, also, were Alexander, Cæsar, and others; and hence Paul tells the Christians in his day to submit themselves to kings and rulers. (Titus 3:1.) And why? These men were ordained for a certain purpose, and it was not for the Christians to set in order the affairs of God's kingdom, nor to regulate the world. The Lord would do that in his own time and way; it was for them to wait for the time "of the restitution of all things." (Acts 3:21.)

Another order of kings were those that were anointed to reign over God's people, the children of Israel. Such was Saul, who was anointed by Samuel; such also were David and Solomon, and many of the kings of Israel. Those kings that were anointed and acknowledged of the Lord were not only kings but priests. Hence, Saul, when he had sinned against God, and the Spirit of the Lord was withdrawn, "enquired of the Lord, and the Lord answered him not, neither by dreams, nor by Urim, nor by prophets." (1 Samuel 28:6.) David also acted as a priest, and could obtain knowledge or revelation from God also, for when Saul was rejected, and sought David's life, David called for the ephod, used by the priests: (see Exodus 28.) "And David said to Abiathar the priest, bring hither the ephod. Then said David, O Lord God of Israel, thy servant hath certainly heard that Saul seeketh to come to Keilah to destroy the city for my sake. Will the men of Keilah deliver me up into his hand? Will Saul come down, as thy servant hath heard, O Lord God of Israel? I beseech thee tell thy servant. And the Lord said, He will come down. Then said David, Will the men of Keilah deliver me and my men up into the hand of Saul? And the Lord said, They will deliver thee up." (1 Samuel 23:9-12.) Here we find David actually enquiring of God for direction, and obtaining information. The Lord had forsaken Saul, and would not answer him; but he would and did answer David: (see also the 23:2; and 30:8; and 2 Samuel 2:1; 5:19-25; 21:1; 1 Chronicles 14:10-14.) From the whole of the above we learn, that David took no step without enquiring of the Lord. Solomon also, acted as a priest as well as a king; and it is said of him, that Solomon loved the Lord, walking in the statutes of David his father. And the Lord gave him wisdom, and instructed [63] him in the affairs of his kingdom. When he prayed unto the Lord, and asked of him wisdom, God granted him the desire of his heart, and gave him with wisdom, riches and honor. "And Judah and Israel dwelt in safety, every man under his vine and fig tree, from Dan to Beersheba, all the days of Solomon;" (1 Kings 4:25) and when he had finished the temple, he offered his sacrifices, and acknowledged the God of Israel; and he prayed for the nation over which he ruled, not by proxy, but himself. "And Solomon stood before the altar of the Lord in the presence of all the congregation of Israel, and spread forth his hands towards heaven;" and then he uttered a prayer for himself, his people, and nation. (see 1 Kings 8:22.) And we read that afterwards the Lord appeared to him, and said unto him, "I have heard thy prayer and thy supplication, that thou hast made before me: I have hallowed this house, which thou hast built, to put my name there for ever; and mine eyes and mine heart shall be there perpetually. And if thou wilt walk before me, as David thy father walked, in integrity of heart, and in uprightness, to do according to all that I have commanded thee, and wilt keep my statutes and my judgments: then I will establish the throne of thy kingdom upon Israel for ever, as I promised to David thy father, saying, There shall not fail thee a man upon the throne of Israel. But if ye shall at all turn from following me, ye or your children, and will not keep my commandments and my statutes which I have set before you, but go and serve other gods, and worship them: then will I cut off Israel out of the land which I have given them; and this house, which I have hallowed for my name, will I cast out of my sight; and Israel shall be a proverb and a byword among all people: and at this house, which is high, every one that passeth by it shall be astonished, and shall hiss; and they shall say, Why hath the Lord done thus unto this land, and to this house? And they shall answer, Because they forsook the Lord their God, who brought forth their fathers out of the land of Egypt, and have taken hold upon other gods, and have worshipped them, and served them: therefore hath the Lord brought upon them all this evil." (1 Kings 9:3-9.)

Thus, then, these men, delegated and appointed of God, acted as his representatives on the earth. They received their kingdoms from him. They were anointed by prophets of God, who received the word [64] of the Lord concerning them, as in the case of Saul and David; and if they departed from God, he chastised, or removed them, as in the case of Saul and David, and of which the history of the Kings of Israel is a striking example, and faithful commentary. Those that were faithful among them sought to know the mind of God, and to carry out his designs. The greatest, most powerful, and prosperous rule that ever existed among them, as a nation, was that of Solomon, who asked, and obtained wisdom from God; and that wisdom as a necessary consequence brought honour, happiness, security, riches, magnificence, and power. Thus those kings that were righteous, who received their kingdoms from the Lord, went to war, or proclaimed peace by his directions; they were his representatives on the earth, and governed his people as the Lord's anointed. Yet even the monarchy of the House of Israel was not in strict accordance with the will of God; but originated in the rebellion and pride of the children of Israel, who, wishing to be like the nations around them, being dissatisfied with their judges, desired of the Lord a king. The following are their words, and the Lord's answer: "Then all the elders of Israel gathered themselves together, and came to Samuel unto Ramah, and said unto him, Behold thou art old, and thy sons walk not in thy ways: now make us a king to judge us like all the nations. But the thing displeased Samuel, when they said, Give us a king to judge us. And

Samuel prayed unto the Lord. And the Lord said unto Samuel, Hearken unto the voice of the people in all that they say unto thee; for they have not rejected thee, but they have rejected me, that I should not reign over them. According to all the works which they have done since the day that I brought them up out of Egypt even unto this day, wherewith they have forsaken me, and served other gods, so do they also unto thee. Now therefore hearken unto their voice: howbeit yet protest solemnly unto them, and shew them the manner of the king that shall reign over them. And Samuel told all the words of the Lord unto the people that asked of him a king. And he said, this will be the manner of the king that shall reign over you: he will take your sons, and appoint them for himself, for his chariots, and to be his horsemen; and some shall run before his chariots. And he will appoint him captains over thousands, and captains over fifties; and will set them to ear his [65] ground, and to reap his harvest, and to make his instruments of war, and instruments of his chariots. And he will take your daughters to be confectionaries, and to be cooks, and to be bakers. And he will take your fields, and your vineyards, and your oliveyards, even the best of them, and give them to his servants. And he will take the tenth of your seed, and of your vineyards, and give to his officers, and to his servants. And he will take your menservants, and your maidservants, and your goodliest young men, and your asses, and put them to his work. He will take the tenth of your sheep; and ye shall be his servants. And ye shall cry out in that day because of your king which ye shall have chosen you; and the Lord will not hear you in that day. Nevertheless the people refused to obey the voice of Samuel; and they said, Nay; but we will have a king over us; that we also may be like all the nations; and that our king may judge us, and go out before us, and fight our battles. And Samuel heard all the words of the people, and he rehearsed them in the ears of the Lord. And the Lord said to Samuel, Hearken unto their voice, and make them a king. And Samuel said unto the men of Israel, Go ye every man unto his city." (1 Samuel 8:4-22.)

We find that this thing was displeasing to the Lord; they resisted the counsel of God; but as they were the Lord's people, he listened to their requests, and gave according to their desires; he felt bound to fulfil his engagements, and, if they would not walk fully by the rule that he required, to give a government of their own asking, which, if not so good as the one he proposed, was nevertheless sanctioned by him; and that order once established, those kings set apart, and anointed by him, had a perfect right to look to him for his guidance, which they did, and inasmuch as they performed his will, as his representatives, were blessed of him. For kings could not be blamed for the order that existed, they did not originate the government; it was the people, all they could do was to rule according to the direction of the Lord. But this was not a perfect government. The Lord had his eye on something yet more glorious, something in which the salvation, and happiness of the world were concerned; a rule of righteousness, when, not only one nation, but the kingdoms and dominions of the whole earth, should be given to the Son of God; and when all nations, kindreds, people, and tongues should serve and obey him; and as the [66] earth belonged to him, and the people also, that he should govern them. Such will be the case as we shall hereafter show, and a system be introduced that will not only benefit one nation, but that will govern all nations, bless the whole of the human family, and exalt and happify the world. All these things that have existed, are merely temporary arrangements, adapted to the weakness, ignorance, and wickedness of the human family, in the times of darkness, and power of Satan. If the above is the case, in regard to the best of these governments, even that of the House of Israel, what is the situation of those who are governing, without even any pretensions to have received their government and authority from God! It may be asked, What is to be done in this state of things? how are they to be regulated? This is worthy of our attention, but as we shall devote some time to this hereafter, we will content ourselves with saying, this is God's work, and not man's. He has these things in his hands, and he must arrange them; confusion, revolt, rebellion, is not the way to bring these things about; for if the world is already evil, this will only make it worse. Besides, the kings and rulers of the present day are no more responsible than others; they did not make the nations as they are, they found them so; neither are they appointed to govern the world, nor do any of them profess it. According to their most extended calculation, their power would be confined to their own nations. Some of the kings and queens of the earth seem to be actuated by a desire to promote the happiness of the nations with which they are associated, and over which they rule. The Queen of England is almost universally beloved by her subjects, and that deservedly; she has been mild and pacific in her course, and her rule and dominion have been as near right as it is possible for a government to be under existing circumstances. If there are evils, she did not originate them, she found them so. She has kept her covenant that she made with the nation, and sought the welfare of her subjects, and they owe her fealty, and ought to render to her obedience. And as she, nor no monarch, is set to build up the kingdom of God, or establish universal rule, as a monarchy without authority from God, it is perhaps as good a form as could exist. The Emperor of Russia, with all his faults of government, nevertheless possesses many good traits; at any rate he seems to reverence the Lord. Some time ago, when the cholera broke out in St. Petersburgh, the [67] inhabitants supposed that their wells had been poisoned; a large number of people assembled for the purpose, as they thought, of finding out, and punishing the aggressors. The excitement was very great. The Emperor, hearing of the tumult, rushed into their midst and said, "My children, you are mistaken in supposing that the wells have been poisoned, and this is the cause of our affliction, this is a judgment that has come from God, let us fall down before him, and ask him to remove his scourge from our midst;" whereupon he fell upon his knees in the midst of the people, and prayed to the Lord to remove the plague from among them. He has a strong impression that God has a work for him to do on the earth; and in this he may be right. Although he is not delegated to establish the kingdom of God, he may nevertheless be appointed as Caesar, Nebuchadnezzar, and others, as a scourge to the nations, and so fulfil his destiny, for as we are on the eve of great events, and a fearful doom awaits the nations, some powerful means must be made use of, in this as well as in other ages, to bring these things about.

Some may remark on the foregoing, Does not Paul say, that "the powers that be, are ordained of God?" (Romans 13:1.) Yes, and so say I; but all powers that are ordained of God, do not rule for his glory, nor are they all associated with his government and kingdom. Nebuchadnezzar and Belshazzar were ordained of God, but they were both idolaters. Cyrus was ordained of God; but he was an heathen. God regulates his own affairs; and while the world is in a state of idolatry, apostasy, and rebellion, he, by his providence, overrules the affairs of the nation, as Daniel says, "to the intent that the living may know that the Most High ruleth in the kingdom of men, and giveth it to whomsoever he will, and setteth up over it the basest of men." (Daniel 4:17.) But others will say that Paul tells us "to be subject to the powers that be." (See Romans 13 and D&C 58:22.) So say I. God will establish his own government: the cavillings, rebellions, and contentions of men will not do it; and it is proper for well disposed persons to wait the Lord's time, to be peaceable and quiet, and to pray for kings, governors, and authorities. This was what Jeremiah taught the children of Israel to do, "And seek the peace of the city wherein I have caused you to be carried away captives, and pray unto the Lord for it, for in the peace thereof shall you have peace." (Jeremiah 29:7.) It is very evident, from what has been [68] shown, that there is no proper government nor rule upon the face of the earth; that there are no kings who are anointed, or legally appointed of God; and that, however much disposed any of them may feel to benefit the world, it is out of their power, it exceeds the limits of their jurisdiction, it requires a power, spirit, and intelligence, which they do not possess. We see, moreover, that tumults, commotions, rebellions, and resistance are not the way to do it. It requires more wisdom than that which emperors, kings, princes, or the wisest of men possess, to bring out of the wild chaos, the misery, and desolation that have overspread the world, that beautiful order, peace, and happiness portrayed by the prophets as the reign of the kingdom of God.

CHAPTER 9

WILL MAN ALWAYS BE PERMITTED TO USURP AUTHORITY OVER MEN, AND OVER THE WORKS OF GOD? WILL THE WORLD REMAIN FOR EVER UNDER A CURSE, AND GOD'S DESIGNS BE FRUSTRATED?

The above are grave questions, and will necessarily require examination, for they concern the earth and its inhabitants. Their true solution will affect man in time and in eternity. The world cannot remain as it is, for the following reasons:—

First. It would be unreasonable.

Secondly. It would be unjust.

Thirdly. It would be unscriptural.

Fourthly. It would frustrate the designs of God, in regard to the spirits of the righteous; the dead; the progression of the world, and its final exaltation; and also the exaltation of man. [69]

First.—It would be unreasonable for man to continue his usurped authority. If God is interested in the welfare of his creatures, he certainly never would permit, without some just cause, the destruction of his works, and the misery of his creatures; and we have fully demonstrated, that the world is full of abominations, and evils, and that those evils can only be removed by the interposition of the Lord; that the assumed authority of men, and the Devil, can only be checked by a superior power. God holds that power in his hands; he holds the life of the human family in his hands; and the world, notwithstanding its rebellion and iniquity, has to be sustained by him from day to day. Let him but withdraw his governing and controlling power from the earth, and it would wander wildly through space, unblest by the genial influences of the sun, or clash against some other system, involving all creation in ruin: let some slight variation take place in its diurnal motion, and the sea would leave its proper bounds, overflow the earth, and millions of the human family would perish. Let even some slight variation take place in the atmosphere, and the Lord withdraw the sanitory influences that preserve the earth in its present healthy state, and the murky atmosphere would contain contagion, and disease; the pestiferous air would spread desolation, and death; plague and pestilence would fill the earth; and millions of foetid loathsome beings would be living, and dying examples, of man's impotency and weakness. Even a small insect sent to destroy the grain, accompanied with the blight of the potatoes, such as has already been witnessed, would produce incalculable evil; let these things become more universal, and the death of the human family must ensue. Even so slight a thing as too much, or too little rain would produce uncalculated misery.

When we contemplate man as he is, a poor worm dependent upon God for his daily bread, and upon how many slight contingencies the brittle thread of life is continued, and that the least variation in the economy of God might, in numberless ways, involve the human family in ruin, and then notice his arrogance, pride, conceit, and rebellion; it seems to us mysterious that the mercy of God should be so long extended to him; and we can only account for it upon this principle, that God is too great, wise, powerful, and magnanimous to be moved to anger by the impotent ravings, the empty pride, the little meanness, the [70] swelling pusillanimity, and the utter helplessness, of the erratic, puerile, insignificant creature, man. He lets him wallow in his corruptions, gloat in his misery, and permits him to become a prey to Satan, for a season, that he may feel the greatness of his fall, the extent of his degeneracy, and the utter ruin that his own course, instigated by the powers of the adversary, has brought upon him; that he may afterwards learn to appreciate the mercies of God, see and understand the delusion, and be enabled eternally to appreciate the mercies and government of God, after having first atoned for his own acts and transgressions. For like a wayward and disobedient child, he will be glad on any conditions to find an asylum with his Father.

This state of things, then, is merely permitted for a season, to develope the designs and influences of Satan, and their effects; to develope the weakness of man, and his incompetency to rule and govern himself without God; to manifest the mercy of God, in bearing with man, in the midst of his rebellion; to show man his ingratitude, and the depth of his depravity, in order that he may appreciate more fully the mercy and long-suffering of God, and the purity and holiness that reign in the eternal world. Man has tasted the misery of sin and rebellion, and drunk of the cup of sorrow, in order that he may appreciate more fully the joy and happiness that spring from obedience to God, and his laws. But to think for a moment that man here will always be permitted to subvert the designs of God, and the world be for ever under the dominion of Satan, is the height of folly, and only developes more fully the pride, littleness, and emptiness of man. For notwithstanding man is a weak creature, in comparison to God, yet he has within him the germs of greatness and immortality. God is his Father, and though now wandering in darkness, sunk, degraded, and fallen, he is destined, in the purposes of God, to be great, dignified, and exalted; to occupy a glorious position in the eternal world, and to fulfil the object of his creation. Will this design be frustrated by the powers of darkness, or the influence of wicked and ungodly men? Verily, no. To suppose [71] such a thing, manifests the greatest absurdity, which can only be equaled by the weakness and ignorance from whence it springs. What! God, the author of the universe, and of all created good, suffer his plans to be frustrated by the powers of the Devil. Shall this beautiful world, and all its inhabitants, become a prey to Satan and his influences, and those celestial, pure, principles that exist in the eternal world, be for ever banished? Shall the earth still be defiled under the inhabitants thereof, when God is our Father? Shall iniquity, corruption, and depravity always spread their contaminating influences, and this earth, that ought to have been a paradise, be a desolate miserable wreck? Shall tyranny, oppression, and iniquity for ever rule? Shall the neck of the righteous always be under the feet of the ungodly? No, says every principle of reason, for the Almighty God is its maker. No, echoes the voice of all the prophets, there shall be a restitution of all things. No, say the Scriptures of all truth, "The earth shall become as the Garden of Eden," (see Ezekiel 36:35 and Joel 2:3) the wicked shall be rooted out of it; the time shall come when the Saints shall possess the kingdom, and the earth shall become as the garden of the Lord. No, responds the voice of all the dead Saints, we

died in the hope of better things, etc. No! say our later revelations—
"The Lord hath brought again Zion;
"The Lord hath redeemed his people, Israel,
"According to the election of grace,
"Which was brought to pass by the faith
"And covenants of their Fathers.
"The Lord hath redeemed his people,
"And Satan is bound, and time is no longer:
"The Lord hath gathered all things in one;
"The Lord hath brought down Zion from above;
"The Lord hath brought up Zion from beneath;
"The Earth hath travailed and brought forth her strength;
"And truth is established in her bowels:
"And the heavens have smiled upon her;
"And she is clothed with the glory of her God;
"For he stands in the midst of his people,
"Glory, and honor, and power, and might,
"Be ascribed to our God, for he is full of mercy, [72]
"Justice, grace, and truth, and peace,
"For ever, and ever. Amen." (D&C 84:99-102.)

It is therefore contrary to every principle of reason and intelligence to suppose such a thing.

Secondly.—It would be unjust: and "shall not the Judge of all the earth do right?" (Genesis 18:25.) But what right would there be in thus permitting Satan to usurp the dominion for ever? It would be giving in the first place to Satan that which belongs to God. This earth is not Satan's inheritance; it is the Lord Jesus Christ's, he is the rightful owner and proprietor. If Satan be indeed the God of this world, and rules in the hearts of the children of disobedience, he is only an usurper. It is not his rightful dominion, for all things were created by Christ, and for Christ, whether they be principalities, or powers, or thrones, or dominions, all these were created by him, and for him, and he only has a right to rule; but Satan has subverted the ways of God, deceived the human family, introduced misery, and confusion, and blighted this beautiful creation with his contaminating curse. As an usurper, it would be unjust to permit him to rule; it would be unjust to the government of God, for, if God has a right to rule, no other power can have that right, unless it is delegated, and if delegated, still the right is vested in the power that delegates.

It is therefore derogatory to God, for the world to be yielding obedience to another power. For while God, not the Devil, provides for, feeds, sustains, and beautifies the Universe, and nourishes the millions of people who inhabit the earth, with his beneficent hand and fatherly care;—for him to be neglected and despised, or forgotten, is the height of injustice, and the very climax of perverse ingratitude. But again, it would be unjust to the good and virtuous; this earth is properly the dwelling place, and rightful inheritance of the Saints. Inasmuch as it belongs to Jesus Christ, it also belongs to his servants and followers, for we are told, "The earth is the Lord's and the fulness thereof," (Psalms 24:1) and that, when things are in their proper place, "the Saints of the Most High shall take the kingdom, and possess the kingdom, and the greatness of the kingdom under the whole heaven, shall be given to the saints of the Most High." (Daniel 7:18, 27.) It is [73] therefore their rightful inheritance, and the usurpation before referred to, while it is unjust to God, is also as unjust to his Saints. Who can contemplate the position of the world, as it has existed, without being struck with this fact, Where has God ever had a people but they have been persecuted? The testimony of God has always been rejected, and his people trodden under foot. Paul tells us that they "were tempted, tried, sawn asunder, that they wandered about in sheep skins, and goat skins, being destitute, afflicted, and tormented." (Hebrews 11:37.) And to such an extent had this prevailed among the ancient Jews, that Stephen gravely asks the question, "Which of the prophets have not your fathers persecuted? and they have slain them, which shewed before, of the coming of the Just One, of whom ye have been now the betrayers and murderers." (Acts 7:52.) What did they do with Jesus! and what with his followers! We may here ask, Is it right, is it proper, is it just, for this state of things to continue? It is true that the saints have had a hope of joys to come, and this state of trial has been permitted for their ultimate good; but although this is the case, it does not make the thing the more just. "It must needs be," says Jesus, "that offences come, but woe to that man by whom the offence cometh. It were better for him that a millstone were hanged about his neck, and that he were drowned in the depth of the sea," than that he should offend one of those little ones. (Matthew 18:7, 6.) "They that touch you, touch the apple of mine eye." (Zechariah 2:8.) He has cried all along, "Touch not mine anointed, and do my prophets no harm." (1 Chronicles 16:22; Psalms 105:15.) The saints have suffered and endured, but they have done it in the hopes of a better resurrection; and as they have always looked upon this earth as their inheritance, to deprive them of this, would be to falsify the promises of God unto them, disappoint all their hopes, render inutile their sufferings and fidelity on the earth; and be to them an act, not only of temporary, but also of eternal injustice. For men of God in former days were just as much actuated by the prospect of a reward as a merchant, a warrior, a statesman, or any other person in search of wealth, honor, or fame. The only difference is, the one sought it in this life, the other in the life to come; the one looked for his reward here, the other expected it hereafter; the one had no hope concerning the future, the other had; the one was blinded by the God of this world, and knew not his position, or possessed not [74] a nobility of soul sufficient to make him brook the world, and the scorn of men, in search of a better inheritance; the other understood by revelation his relationship to God, the position of the world, and his high calling, and glorious hope; he sought the nearest way to eternal life, scorned to be captivated by the world's tinsel show, despised the short-lived pleasures offered by the god of this world, and possessed magnanimity of soul sufficient to lead him to acknowledge the God of the Universe, and to brook the scorn of empty fools, and ephemeral philosophers. If persecution's deadly shafts, and superstition's craven hate, were levelled against him, he dared to brook death in all its horrid forms, and live and die an honourable man, a true philosopher, a servant of God, and endure as seeing him who is invisible, in the hopes of a better resurrection. Deprive him of this hope, and you rob the just of his reward, dishonour God, and perpetuate misery and corruption in the world.

Thirdly.—As it would be unjust, so also it would be unscriptural. The Scriptures are full and clear on this subject; they represent Christ as being the rightful heir, and inheritor of this world; they represent him as having come once to atone for the sins of the world; but that he will afterwards come as its ruler, judge, and king; they represent him as the "Lord of the vineyard, the rightful heir" to the earth, and as having hitherto been dispossessed; but they again represent him as coming to claim his rights, to dispossess the usurpers; to take the authority, to rule, and reign, and to possess his own dominions. They represent the earth as labouring under a curse; but speak also of its deliverance therefrom; of its being blighted because of the transgression of man; but that it shall again yield its increase and become as the Garden of Eden. They represent the whole creation as groaning and travailing in pain, but that the creature also shall be delivered. That the Spirit of the Lord shall rest upon all flesh; that the wolf shall lie down with the lamb, the lion eat straw with the ox, and finally, every creature that is in the heavens, on the earth, or under the earth, shall be heard to say, glory and honor, and power, &c. That the law shall go forth from Zion, and the word of the Lord from Jerusalem. That Jerusalem shall become the throne of the Lord, and that the dead saints shall live, and reign with Christ, no longer deprived of their rightful inheritance; but as Jesus said when here, "Blessed are the meek, for they shall inherit the earth." (Matthew 5:5.) [75]

If, then, the Scriptures are not idle phantoms, if their visions, and prophecies were not mere phantasies, and written to deceive, we have as much right to look for these things as we have to believe in any event that has taken place; but lest any of my readers should be ignorant of the Scriptures relative to these subjects, I will give a few passages which are in themselves as clear and pointed, as any other portion of the word of God.

Concerning Christ being the rightful heir, it is written, "All things were created by him, and for him, and without him was not anything made that is made." (See John 1:3.) He is the "Mighty God, the everlasting Father," (Isaiah 9:6) &c. "For of him, and from him, and to him are all things." (See Romans 11:36.) "Thou sayest that I am a king, for this end was I born, etc." (See John 18:37.) "Then the Lord shall be king over all the earth." (See Zechariah 14:9.)

The Jews made a great mistake concerning the coming of Christ before; the Gentiles have made as great a mistake in regard to his second coming. The Jews expected him to come as a temporal deliverer alone, and overlooked his sufferings, trials, persecution, and death; the Gentiles having believed in his sufferings, have lost sight of his second coming; the promises of God made to the fathers; the redemption of the earth, and the kingdom of God. Both are wrong; both believed in part; neither in the whole. The Jews, in consequence of their unbelief, were cut off; but when Christ comes again, he will come in the way that their fathers looked for him, as a King, with power, and authority. The Gentiles having fallen into darkness, have lost sight of the great purposes of God, in regard to the redemption of man, and of the world; the restitution of all things, and the coming of Christ to reign. They have so far forgotten themselves, that they are actually fulfilling the prophecy of Peter: "There shall come in the last days scoffers, walking after their own lusts, and saying, Where is the promise of his coming?" (2 Peter 3:4.) But to return: the Scriptures represent Christ as the lord of the vineyard, (see Matthew 8:20; Mark 12:9; Luke 20:13, 15; Jacob 5; D&C 101:52, 55.) as the "heir" that was killed; (see Matthew 21:38; Mark 12:7-8; Luke 20:14-15) as the "sower of the seed" in the world; (see Matthew 12:24-30; Luke 8:5; Jeremiah 31:27) as the "destroyer of the wicked husbandmen;" (see Matthew 21:40-41; Mark 12:9; Luke 20:15-16) as coming to "rule the nations with a rod of iron," (Revelations 12:5, 19:15) etc.; and to take possession of the kingdom. Daniel says, "I saw in the night visions, and behold, one like the Son of man came with the clouds of heaven, and came to the Ancient of Days, and they brought him near before him. And [76] there was given him dominion, and glory, and a kingdom, that all people, nations, and languages, should serve him; his dominion is an everlasting dominion, which shall not pass away, and his kingdom that which shall not be destroyed." (Daniel 7:13-14.) Zechariah says, "And his feet shall stand in that day upon the Mount of Olives, which is before Jerusalem on the East; and the Mount of Olives shall cleave in the midst thereof toward the east and toward the west, and there shall be a very great valley; and half of the mountain shall remove toward the north, and half of it toward the south. And ye shall flee to the valley of the mountains; for the valley of the mountains shall reach unto Azal; yea, ye shall flee, like as ye fled from before the earthquake in the days of Uzziah, king of Judah: and the Lord my God shall come, and all the saints with thee."...."And the Lord shall be king over all the earth: in that day shall there be one Lord, and his name one." (*Ibid.* 14:4-5, 9.) These and many other things must be fulfilled if the Scriptures be true. These designs of God, which were the hope of the ancient Saints, and of which poets sung, and prophets wrote, were the consolation of all the faithful Saints, Prophets, and Patriarchs,—Jews and Christians. Take these away, and the world, to the Saints, is a miserable blank; the hope of the righteous futile, and the Word of God a farce.

Fourthly.—It would frustrate the designs of God, in regard to the spirits of the righteous, the dead, the progression of the world, and its final exaltation; and also the exaltation of man.

When the Lord created this world, as we have already stated, he had an object in view, not only in regard to the world, and its future destiny, but also as it regards the spirits which were then in existence. Those great and eternal purposes which our heavenly Father, in his consummate wisdom, had in view, when he issued his Divine Mandate, and this world was created, cannot be frustrated unless he cease to be God. And those enlivening hopes which cheered his sons; those spirits that lived with him, when they saw this beautiful orb fashioned, this earth made as the place for their habitation, as their possession, as the place where they should take bodies, where they should live, rule, and reign, not only in time, but in eternity, must not, cannot be destroyed. And yet what avails it all to them, if Satan triumph, the wicked rule, and God's kingdom be not established! [77] They could not "have shouted for joy" (Job 38:7) at the prospect of this world continuing under the dominion of Satan; at the blight, degradation, misery, and ruin that have overspread it. But if we trace the matter still further, and look at the righteous dead, their position would be any thing but enviable under those circumstances. It was the hopes of the resurrection that made them endure, and it was God that implanted them in their bosoms; but if they are not raised, and if Christ's kingdom is not established, and they do not reign with him, their hopes are vain, their sufferings useless, and the purposes of God are frustrated. In vain did they bear a faithful testimony in opposition to a depraved world; in vain they endured, as seeing him that is invisible; in vain they wandered about in sheep skins, and in goat skins; in vain they looked for a city which hath foundations, as a recompense of reward; and false and deceptive are the testimonies of all the prophets who have testified of the restitution of all things, from the foundation of the world. Take away this, and our highest, and most exalted hopes are blighted; we live like fools, and die like dogs. If the world is always suffered to continue as it is, then is the hope of the righteous vain, the promises of God fail, Satan triumphs, and God's purposes are frustrated.

All the designs of God concerning this world and the work of creation, were perfected in his mind before this world rolled into existence, or "e'er the morning stars sang together for joy." (See Job 38:7.) When this world was formed, God intended it as the final dwelling place of those bodies which should inhabit it. And when "the sons of God shouted for joy," (*Ibid.*) it was at the prospect of that exaltation, that they would be capable of obtaining, in consequence of this creation, which they then saw come into existence. And if, as Jesus, they had to descend below all things, in order that they might be raised above all things; still this was the medium, or channel, through which they were to obtain their ultimate exaltation, and glorification. It was by the union of their spirits, which came forth from the Father as the "Father of Spirits," (Hebrews 12:9) with earthly bodies, that perfect beings were formed, capable of continued increase and eternal exaltation; that the spirit, quick, subtle, refined, lively, animate, energetic, and eternal, might have a body through which to operate, that might be compared to the steam to an engine; the electric fluid to the [78] telegraphic wire; for, notwithstanding that spirit, steam, or electricity are the powerful, quickening, energetic principles, employed; yet without the engine, the telegraphic wire, or the matter, they would be comparatively useless; these elements might wander in empty space; spend their force at random, or remain dormant, or useless, without those more tangible, material objects, through which to exercise their force. When steam was first applied to practical purposes; when the operation of the magnetic needle, and the mode of communication through the electric telegraph, were discovered; when railroads and steam boats were first invented, something of importance was discovered, and of great value to the human family. The men who made these discoveries and applications are deservedly looked upon at the present time as men of great genius, and as the benefactors of the world; but what was it they did? they did not create the elements, those already existed; steam, magnetism, electricity, iron, coals, water, existed before, and had existed from the beginning of creation. What was it these geniuses discovered? It was simply a method of organizing this matter, the making use of gross inanimate materials to confine the more subtle, refined, elastic, energetic, and powerful, that their combined power and energy might be brought into effect; and that through the union of two powerful agencies, which had lain dormant, their forces might be united, and be brought into active and powerful operation. Thus, then, was the body formed as an agent for the spirit. It was made of grosser materials than the spirit, which proceeded from God, but was necessary as an habitation for it that, it might be clothed with a body, perfect in its organization, beautiful in its structure, symmetrical in its proportions, and in every way fit for an eternal intelligent being; that through it, it might speak, act, enjoy, and develope its power, its intelligence, and perpetuate its species. Hence as the discoveries of those geniuses already referred to, were hailed with pleasure by the inhabitants of the world, on account of the benefits conferred upon men, so when God created this earth, and organized men upon it, "the morning stars sung together for joy;" they looked upon it as God looked upon it, as a work perfect, magnificent, and glorious, through which they saw their way to exaltation, glory, thrones, principalities, powers, dominions, and eternal felicity. They [79] had the intelligence before, but now they saw a way through which to develope it. Through the world's great Architect, their Father, they discovered a plan fraught with intelligence and wisdom, reaching from eternity to eternity, pointing out a means whereby, through obedience to celestial laws, they might obtain the same power that he had. And if, in fallen humanity, they might have to suffer for a while, they saw a way back to God, to eternal exaltations, and to the multiplied, and eternally increasing happiness of in numerable millions of beings. And if, as Jesus, they had to descend below all things, it was that they might be raised above all things, and take their position as sons of God, in the eternal world; that overcoming the world they might sit down with Christ upon his throne, as he overcame and sat down upon the Father's throne. (Revelation 3:21.)

But again; this creation is unlike the works of man, which, however excellent, and useful, all bear the marks of humanity, all are more or less imperfect in their structure, and liable to a thousand contingences, are more or less clumsy, cumbrous, and unwieldy, and must be governed by numerous very limited laws; as for instance, you can convey intelligence, but it must be exactly on the line of the electric wire, you cannot go beyond its limits; you can make an engine work, but it must be stationary; or if moving, must be confined to rails, depth of water, and a thousand other contingences. None of these things possess intelligence, nor the principles of life within themselves, neither can they impart, nor perpetuate it to others, they are merely machines, to be acted upon by man, and without man they cease to exist; when one is worn out, or broken, another must be made at the same toil and labour; possessing not the principles of life, they cannot impart their likeness; whereas man, beasts, fish, fowl, and all the animate works of God can. Man's works in comparison with God's, are like comparing a child's wooden horse to the beautiful creature God has made, or rather his penny whistle to the music of heaven, or the larger boy's billiards to the motions of the planetary system. They possess no intelligence, no powers, no reflection, no agency. The works of man are merely made to be acted upon; are short lived, temporary, perishable things. Man, however, bears the impress of Jehovah, is made after his image, in his likeness, and possesses the principles of intelligence within himself, and the medium of conveying it to others. [80] He possesses also, power to perpetuate his species, as also to communicate his thoughts, his intelligence, genius, and power to others, that are formed like him. He received his intelligence, his spirit, from God, he is a part of himself,

"A spark of Deity

Struck from the fire of his eternal blaze;"

He came from God as his son, he bears the impress of Jehovah, even in his fallen degenerate corrupted state. His powerful intellect, his stately genius, his grasping ambition, his soaring, and in many instances, exalted hopes, display, though he be fallen, the mark of greatness; he bears the impress of Deity and shows that he is of divine origin.

Unlike the works of man, the work of God in relation to this earth was destined to be eternal, not subject to be controlled by any little contingencies; nor was it dependent upon fluctuation, or change. Man's works might fluctuate, change, or be destroyed, but not so with God's, they were, and are eternal; eternal mind, and eternal matter; organized and created according to the unsearchable intelligence of that eternal unfathomable mind; that fountain of intelligence, forethought, wisdom, and energy, that dwells with God. And this earth, and man in their destination, and all the works of this creation, are as unchangeable as the sun, moon, or stars, and as unalterable as the throne of God. Satan may deceive men, for a season; their minds may be blinded by the god of this world, but God's purposes will be unchanged. Who is Satan? A being powerful, energetic, deceptive, insinuating; and yet necessary to develope the evil, as there are bitters, to make us appreciate the sweet; darkness, to make us appreciate light; evil and its sorrows, that we may appreciate the good; error that we may be enabled to appreciate truth; misery, in order that we may appreciate happiness. And as there are in the works of creation opposing, mineralogical substances which in chemical processes are necessary to develope certain properties of matter, and produce certain effects; as fire is necessary to purify silver, gold, and the precious metals, so it is necessary to instruct, and prepare man for his ultimate destiny—to test his virtue, develope his folly, exhibit his weakness and prove his incompetency without God to rule himself or the earth; or to make himself happy or exalt himself in time, or in eternity. But [81] again, who is Satan? He is a being of God's own make, under his control, subject to his will, cast out of Heaven for rebellion; and when his services can be dispensed with, an angel will cast him into the bottomless pit. Can he fight against and overcome God? verily, No! Can he alter the designs of God? verily, No! Satan may rage; but the Lord can confine him within proper limits. He may instigate rebellion against God, but the Lord can bind him in chains.

Shall the purposes of the Lord be frustrated? verily, No! The nations of the earth may be drunken, and rush against each other like inebriates; but the Lord's purposes are unchanged. Thrones may be cast down, kingdoms depopulated; and blood, sword, and famine may prevail, yet the Lord lives, and will accomplish his own designs. Man may forget God, but God does not forget man: man may be ignorant of his calling, but not so with God. Man may not reflect upon the designs of God, in relation to this earth, but God must and does; and if in man's madness, his infidelity, his hypocrisy, or his ignorance, he cannot find time here to reflect upon these things, he will find ample leisure hereafter, and the purposes of God will roll on; and perhaps when he shall be preached to, as the rebellious Antediluvians, after receiving the punishment of his deeds, he may know something more of the power, justice, and purposes of God, and be glad to hear the Gospel in prison which he rejected on this earth. But to suppose that the purposes of God will be frustrated in relation to his designs in the formation of this earth, is altogether folly. They will roll on as steadily as the sun or moon in their courses. And as surely as we look in the east for the rising of the sun in the morning to display his gorgeous glory, light up the beauties of creation, and waken sleepy man; so surely will "the sun of righteousness arise with healing in his wings," (Malachi 4:2) so surely will the sleeping dead burst from their tombs, and the glorified bodies with their spirits re-unite, so surely will a reign of justice, truth, equity, and happiness—the reign of God, supersede the barbarous oppression, and corrupt governments of this world, so surely will that long night of darkness, ignorance, crime, and error be superseded by the glorious day of righteousness; and so surely will this earth become as the Garden of the Lord, the kingdom and reign of God be established, and the Saints of the Most High take the kingdom and possess it for ever and ever. The time of the resti[82]tution of all things will be ushered in; the earth resume its paradisiacal glory, and the dead and the living Saints possess the full fruition of those things for which they lived, and suffered, and died. These are the hopes that the ancient Saints enjoyed; they possessed hopes that bloomed with immortality and eternal life; hopes planted there by the Spirit of God, and conferred by the ministering of Angels, the visions of the Almighty, the opening of the Heavens, and the promises of God. They lived and died in hopes of a better resurrection. How different to the narrow, conceited, grovelling views of would-be philosophers, of sickly religionists, and dreaming philanthropists!

Therefore, as we have said, anything short of this would render inutile the hopes of the Saints; would fail to accomplish the *expectation* of millions of spirits; and cause Satan to triumph, and frustrate the designs of God. This earth, after wading through all the corruptions of men, being cursed for his sake, and not permitted to shed forth its full lustre and glory, must yet take its proper place in God's creations; be purified from that corruption under which it has groaned for ages, and become a fit place for redeemed men, angels, and God to dwell upon. The Lord Jesus will come and dispossess the usurper; take possession of his own kingdom; introduce a rule of righteousness; and reign there with his Saints, who, together with him, are the rightful proprietors. [83]

CHAPTER 10

WILL GOD'S KINGDOM BE A LITERAL OR A SPIRITUAL KINGDOM?

It would be almost unnecessary to answer such a question as the above, were it not for the opinions that are entertained in the world concerning a purely spiritual kingdom, particularly as in a preceding chapter I have clearly pointed out a literal kingdom, rule, and reign. But I have introduced this merely to meet some questions that exist in the minds of many, relative to a spiritual kingdom, arising from certain remarks of our Saviour's, where he says, "My kingdom is not of this world;" (John 18:36) and again, the "kingdom of heaven is not meat and drink, but righteousness, and peace, and joy in the Holy Ghost;" (Romans 14:17) and again, "the kingdom of God is within (or among) you." (Luke 17:21.)

The kingdom of God, as I have already stated, is the government of God, whether in the heavens, or on the earth. Hence Jesus taught his disciples to pray, "Thy kingdom come, thy will be done on earth, as it is done in heaven." (Matthew 6:10.) And when the kingdom of God is established on the earth, and prevails universally, then will the will of God exist on the earth, as it now does in heaven. It is this reign we are speaking of, a reign of righteousness. But whenever God's laws are established, or his kingdom is organized, and officers selected, and men yield obedience to the laws of the kingdom of God; to such an extent does God's kingdom prevail. John preached the kingdom of God, or, heaven nigh at hand. Jesus said, the kingdom of heaven is within you. Jesus compared the kingdom of heaven to a [84] husbandman who sowed wheat, and when he went to his field, he found tares also. (Matthew 13.) Now what was this field? The field was the world, or in other words, God's rightful possession, where he ought to govern; the good seed are the children of the kingdom, or those who receive and obey the laws of the kingdom of heaven. The tares are the children of the wicked one; or those who rebel against God and his laws. The tares are to be gathered out of his kingdom, and burned; and then are the righteous to shine as the sun in the kingdom of their Father. Again, the kingdom of Heaven is likened unto a treasure that a man found in a field, and sold all his possessions, in order that he might possess himself of that field and treasure; and a pearl of great price, for which a man did likewise; thus Abraham, Noah, Lot, Moses, and many of the Prophets purchased this treasure at the sacrifice of all things. And why? they discovered the pearl, the treasure, and had respect unto the recompense of reward; enduring as seeing him who is invisible. And what was it all for? for the purpose of obtaining present blessings, earthly enjoyments, the pleasures of sense? No! they all died in faith *not having* received the promises; but having seen them afar off; they knew of the treasure, and sold all for it; they "looked for a city which hath foundations, whose builder and maker is God." (See Hebrews 11:10.) Wherefore it is said, God is not ashamed to be called their God, for he hath prepared for them a city. They looked for a reign of righteousness —the government of God—they were inspired with the same hope as that of all the Prophets who had prophesied since the world begun, viz., the hope of the restitution of all things. John the Baptist, and Jesus would have introduced the kingdom; but the people would not have it; still, as the apostle John says, to as many as did believe, "to them gave he power to become the Sons of God, even to them that believe on his name." (John 1:12.) They became sons of God. Yes, say some spiritually, and I say literally too. They made a literal covenant with God to keep his laws; they were administered to literally by officers of the kingdom of God; they believed literally; were baptised literally, and received the gift of the Holy Ghost literally; and became literally the servants or sons of God. But what was their hope? Was it in this world? Yes, but not at the present. They expected the promise of Jesus to be fulfilled to them: "Blessed are the meek, for they shall inherit the earth." (Matthew 5:5.) And [85] they looked, with Peter, and all the ancient Saints, for a new Heaven and a new Earth, wherein dwelleth righteousness. They looked with Paul, and the Saints to whom he wrote, for a kingdom, not ariel or visionary, but one "which hath foundations, whose builder and maker is God." (Hebrews 11:10.)

The world, as we have before stated, although it belongs to God, has never been under his control. His vineyard has brought forth briars and thorns; tares have been sown in his field; but there has been some wheat, and that wheat represents the children of the kingdom, who have kept his laws and observed, in the same proportion has his kingdom prevailed. Christ, therefore, organized his kingdom with Apostles, Prophets, Pastors, Teachers, Evangelists, etc.; officers and administrators of his laws, which laws were given by the Lord; they baptized for the remission of sins, laid on hands for the gift of the Holy Ghost, and introduced members into the kingdom of God on earth, and as they were empowered to bind on earth, and in heaven, to seal on earth, and in heaven, these persons, not only became members of the Church here, but also of the kingdom of heaven, and participators in all its blessings here and hereafter. They were now Sons of God; but it did not fully appear yet what they should be, only they should be like him. If he conquered death, so should they; if he overcame, so should they; if he sat down upon his Father's throne, he would give to them that overcame, power to sit down upon his throne, as he overcame and sat down upon his Father's throne. And if Jesus comes to reign on the earth, he will also bring his Saints with him, and they shall live and reign with him. These things are spiritual, but they are literal; they are temporal, but they are also spiritual and eternal. Hence with God all things are temporal; all things are spiritual; and all things are eternal. These are only our phrases to specify certain ideas, which ideas in themselves are very often incorrect: we have bodies and spirits, but it takes both to be a perfect man. We talk about time and eternity,—what is time? A portion of eternity; eternity was, before time was, and will continue to exist when time shall be no more. Spiritual and temporal things are only so, as we form ideas of them. What is our body?—temporal, material? Yes, matter; but the [86] matter of which it is made is eternal, and it will yet be spiritual like unto Christ's glorious body. What is our spirit?—material, spiritual and eternal also? But more subtle and elastic than our corporeal bodies.

Having said so much on this subject, we now come to some of our questions. "The kingdom of Heaven is not meat and drink, but righteousness, and peace, and joy, in the Holy Ghost." (Romans 14:17.) What are we to understand by this? that righteousness composes a kingdom? Righteousness is an attribute, a principle, a state of being, not a government; peace and joy are the result of this attribute. God is righteous, and consequently righteousness flows from him. There may be also a righteous man; but we do not say that God is a kingdom, or that a righteous man is a kingdom, but that the kingdom of God is a righteous kingdom. You can say a righteous kingdom, a kingdom of righteousness; but you cannot say righteousness is a kingdom. A kingdom may be governed by righteous laws; its laws may be righteous, its administrators righteous, its people righteous; but to say righteousness is a kingdom, is nonsense. The kingdom of God is a righteous kingdom; it is made up of higher enjoyments than eating and drinking; it is more refined and elevated; it is a kingdom of holiness, virtue, purity; of "righteousness, peace, and joy in the Holy Ghost,"—principles that exist in part now, as far as the kingdom extends. When the kingdom of God is universal, it will, like the kingdom in the heavens, be all "righteousness, peace, and joy in the Holy Ghost;" yet, it will have its laws, officers, and administrators, and will be a literal, tangible thing. The Spirit of the Lord shall be poured upon all flesh; the will of God will be done on earth as it is in heaven, and the joy and peace which result from righteousness, will be experienced by all the world. What did Jesus mean, then, when he said, "The kingdom of Heaven is within you," or "among you." (Marginal reading of Luke 17:20-21.) There certainly must be some mistake here, for Jesus was speaking to Pharisees, whom he had denounced as corrupt men, hypocrites, whited walls, painted sepulchres, etc. Now, who will say they had the kingdom of God within them? The kingdom of God was among them. And it did not come with observation, nor with ostentation or pomp; [87] they might have seen it, but their eyes were blinded, that they could not see; their ears were stopped that they could not hear. Many of us suppose that if we had lived in their day, we should have recognized it among the miracles, signs, and powers that were manifested by him. But Jesus said, "My sheep hear my voice, and know me, and follow me, but others do not." (See John 10:27.) If any man do his will, says Jesus, "he shall know of the doctrine whether it be of God, or whether I speak of myself." (John 7:17.) But if they do not, what then? They have eyes, but see not; ears, but hear not. The God of this world blinds their eyes, lest the light of the gospel should shine in upon them. Jesus says, "Except a man be born again; he cannot see the kingdom of God." And "except he is born of water and the spirit, he cannot enter into it." (John 3:3, 5.) It therefore cometh not with observation; the Scriptures are clear on the point, and show to the last that when God's kingdom shall be more fully established on the earth, the inhabitants of the earth will be as ignorant of it as the Jews were, that Jesus was the Messiah; for the nations of the earth, with their kings, will yet be gathered together against the people of the Lord, to battle, when the Lord himself will go and fight against them, and there will be one of the most terrible slaughters that ever took place on the earth. It cometh *not with observation.* (Luke 17:20.) It is a righteous kingdom, and righteous men can see it, and appreciate it, and those only.

I have demonstrated, in a preceding chapter, to which I refer my readers, more fully on this subject, that the kingdom of God would be literally established on the earth; it will not be an ariel phantom, according to some visionaries, but a substantial reality. It will be established, as before said, on a literal earth, and will be composed of literal men, women, and children; of living saints who keep the commandments of God, and of resurrected bodies who shall actually come out of their graves, and live on the earth. The Lord will be king over all the earth, and all mankind literally under his sovereignty, and every nation under the heavens will have to acknowledge his authority, and bow to his sceptre. Those who serve him in righteousness will have communications with God, and with Jesus; will have the ministering of Angels, and will know the past, the present, and the future; and other people, who may not yield full obedience to his [88] laws, nor be fully instructed in his covenants, will, nevertheless, have to yield full obedience to his government. For it will be the reign of God upon the earth, and he will enforce his laws, and command that obedience from the nations of the world which is legitimately his right. Satan will not then be permitted to control its inhabitants, for the Lord God will be king over all the earth, and the kingdom and greatness of the kingdom under the whole heaven will be given to the saints. This may properly be called the day of reckoning, the time when the world's accounts will be settled; when things that have been going wrong for ages, will be put right; when injustice and misrule will no more be permitted; when the usurper shall be cast out; when the rightful heir shall possess the kingdom; when unrighteousness will be banished, and justice and judgment bear sway; when the wicked shall be rooted out of the earth, and the saints possess it; when God's designs shall be accomplished on the earth, and men resume their proper position. It is the fulfilment of the promises of the Lord to his people, or in scriptural words, "The dispensation of the fulness of times, when God will gather together all things in one." (See Ephesians 1:10.) Satan has had his dominion, and has deceived, corrupted, and cursed the human family; but then his dominion will be destroyed, and he will be cast into the bottomless pit; men will no longer be under the influence of his spirit, be decoyed by his wiles, or imposed upon by his deceptions. Religion, and the fear of God, will no longer be painted in dismal colours, or be dressed in the sable drapery of sanctimonious priests, or sacerdotal gloom; nor yet in the forbidding costumes of hermits, monks, and nuns. But, stript of all this religious masquerade, and superstitious mummery, the fear of God, and the observance of his laws, will be looked upon in their proper light. God will be seen, feared, and worshipped as our Father, Friend, and Benefactor; his laws will be kept as being those framed by infinite wisdom, and the most conducive to the happiness of the human family. Virtue, truth, and righteousness, will appear in their native loveliness, beauty, simplicity, glory, and magnificence, for God alone will be exalted in that day. [89]

CHAPTER 11

THE ESTABLISHMENT OF THE KINGDOM OF GOD UPON THE EARTH

How will the kingdom of God be established? We have already shown very clearly, that none of the means which are now used among men are commensurate with the object designed, and that all the combined wisdom of man must, and will fail, in the accomplishment of this object; that the present forms of political and religious rule cannot effect it; that philosophy is quite as impotent; and that as these have all failed for ages, as a natural consequence they must continue to fail. We have portrayed the world broken, corrupted, fallen, degraded and ruined; and shown that nothing but a world's God can put it right.

The question is, what course will God take for the accomplishment of this thing? and as this is a matter that requires more than human reason, and as we are left entirely to Revelation, either past, present, or to come, it is to this only that we can apply. We will enquire, therefore, what the Scriptures say on this subject. It is called the kingdom of God, or the kingdom of heaven. If, therefore, it is the kingdom of heaven, it must receive its *laws, organization,* and *government,* from heaven; for if they were earthly, then would they be like those on the earth. The kingdom of heaven must therefore be the government, and laws of heaven, on the earth. If the government and laws of heaven are known and observed on the earth, they must be communicated, or revealed from the heavens to the earth. These things are plain and evident, if we are to have any kingdom of heaven,

[90] for it is very clear, that if it is not God's rule, it cannot be his *government*, and it is as evident that if it is not revealed from heaven it cannot be the *kingdom of heaven*. That such a kingdom will be set up is evident from the following, "And in the days of these kings shall the God of Heaven set up a kingdom, which shall never be destroyed, and the kingdom shall not be left to other people;" (Daniel 2:44) and again, "I saw in the night visions, and behold one like the son of man came with the clouds of Heaven, and came to the Ancient of Days; and they brought him near before him. And there was given him dominion, and glory, and a kingdom that all people, nations, and languages, should serve him; his dominion is an everlasting dominion, which shall not pass away; and his kingdom that which shall not be destroyed." (Daniel 7:13-14.) From the above we learn two things: First—that God will set up a kingdom which shall be universal; and, that that kingdom shall not be given into the hands of other people; and secondly—that the Saints of God shall take possession of that kingdom. The Angel which announced to Mary the birth of Jesus said, "He shall be great, and shall be called the Son of the Highest; and the Lord God shall give unto him the throne of his Father David; and he shall reign over the house of Jacob for ever, and of his kingdom there shall be no end." (Luke 1:32-33.)

It may not be improper here to notice an opinion that has very generally prevailed throughout the Christian world, that Christ's kingdom was a spiritual kingdom; that it was set up at the time our Saviour was upon the earth; and that Christianity as it now exists, is that kingdom. After what I have already written on the subject of a literal reign and kingdom, this would seem superfluous; but as this opinion is almost universal in the Christian world, my readers must excuse me, if, in this instance, I digress a little. Several writers in the Catholic church, as well as the Rev. David Simpson, M.A., Bishop Burnett, the Rev. John Wesley, and many others among the Protestants, have advocated the above opinion. The substance of their ideas is as follows: that Daniel, by the figure of an image of gold, silver, brass, iron, clay, in chap. 2—and by the figures of the four beasts, in chap. 7, represented a spiritual kingdom; that this kingdom was set up in the days of the Saviour, and his disciples; that Christianity, as it now exists, is that kingdom, and that it will become universal over all the [91] earth. They state that the four great empires, the Babylonian, Persian, Grecian, and Roman, are represented by the head, breast, belly, and legs of the Image, and by the four Beasts, in chapter 7; and that the kingdom of God was to be set up under the dominion of the fourth, which, as they correctly state, was the Roman. They state, moreover, that the declaration and prophecy of the Angel to Mary, above quoted, were also fulfilled in the first coming of the Messiah; in his preaching, in his gospel, and in the organizing of the church, etc. Many other passages are made to bear the same signification, which it would be foreign from my present purpose to notice. I have referred to the above, as some of the most prominent. Now, with all deference to the gentlemen who have written on this subject (and education, respectability, and talent, entitle their opinions to some respect) I must beg leave to differ from them, and consider, that in trying to support a favorite dogma, they have been led into error; for it seems to me that nothing can be more foreign to the meaning of these scriptures than the above interpretation. Now concerning the four great monarchies being represented as above, I consider it is perfectly correct; but to state that the kingdom was to be set up under the fourth monarchy, or under the dominion of the fourth beast, is stretching the thing too far; and putting a construction upon it which it evidently will not bear. The text reads, "in the days of those kings shall the God of Heaven set up a kingdom." (Daniel 2:44.) The question is, What kings? I am answered, during the reign of one of the four; and that as Christ came during the reign, and dominion of the Roman empire, it evidently refers to that. But let me again ask a question, Under the reign of what kings was this kingdom to be set up? Under the reign of the fourth? Verily, No. Let Daniel speak for himself. After describing the fourth kingdom, which was the Roman, which is compared to iron, and which in the Image was represented by the legs, he then refers to other kingdoms and powers, as being compared to iron and clay. There were also feet and toes, as well as a *body*, which were compared to powers or kings. This is clearly exemplified in the seventh chapter of Daniel, for after speaking of the four kings, he describes ten horns, of which the ten toes in the Image above referred to, are typical. Those ten horns, he says, are ten kings. It was, then, in the days of those kings, or while those kingdoms should be in ex[92]istence, that the God of Heaven should set up a kingdom; and not during the power of the fourth kingdom; to which, with any degree of truthfulness, the figure could not apply in either case. But again, it could not apply to the first coming of our Saviour for the following reasons:—

First.—The stone hewn out of the mountain without hands was to smite the Image on the toes; whereas, according to the interpretation of the divines before referred to, the toes were not yet in existence, for they state that this kingdom was set up during the fourth monarchy, which was the Roman, and which is represented in the legs of the Image. Now, as the powers composing the feet and toes were not yet formed, how could the little stone smite that which was not in existence? For it will be observed that after the whole Image was made, the stone was hewn out of the mountains without hands which smote it.

Secondly.—When this kingdom is set up, it is stated "it *shall not be left to other people*;" (2:44) but we are told in Daniel 7, that after the fourth monarchy which was the time, according to the aforesaid interpretation, for the setting up of the kingdom of God, a certain "horn," or king, should make war with the Saints, and prevail against them;" (v. 21) and that "he should think to change times and laws—and that they should be *given into his hand*." (v. 25.) Nothing can be more obvious than this; for this power, after the first coming of the Messiah, not only thinks to change times and laws, but "they" are actually "given into his hand," (v. 25) which will not be the case, when the kingdom above referred to is set up.

Thirdly.—When the kingdom of God was to be set up, it was to be "given to the Saints of the Most High;" (v. 27) and all nations, kindreds, people, and tongues, were to obey the Lord, which has not taken place, and never can under the present state of things.

Fourthly.—There is no more similarity between christianity, as it now exists, with all its superstitions, corruptions, jargons, contentions, divisions, weakness, and imbecility, and this KINGDOM OF GOD, as spoken of in the Scriptures, than there is between light and darkness; and it would no more compare with things to come, than an orange would compare with the earth, or a taper with the glorious luminary of day. [93]

Fifthly.—The kingdom of God, as spoken of by Daniel, was to become universal, which christianity has not, and cannot, as it now exists.

Sixthly.—The Angel's testimony to Mary has not yet been fulfilled. It is stated, that "The Lord shall give unto him the throne of his father David, and he shall reign over the House of Jacob for ever, and of his kingdom there shall be no end;" (Luke 1:32-33.) whereas he did not sit upon David's throne, nor does he now; he did not reign over the house of Jacob, nor does he now, for the ten tribes are yet outcasts; "the house of Judah is scattered and without a king," and Jesus himself, when asked to divide an inheritance, demanded, "Who made me a ruler or king."[5] (See Luke 12:13-14.) He, indeed was a king; "but in his humiliation his judgment was taken away." (Acts 8:33.)

From the whole of the above it is very evident that the kingdom, of which these divines speak, was not, and could not be the one referred to by Daniel, or by the angel to Mary; as we have before stated, it was a literal kingdom, and not a spiritual one only. I would further remark here, that a certain power was to "make war with the Saints, and to prevail against them until the Ancient of Days came;" and then, and not till then, was "judgment given to the Saints of the Most High." (Daniel 7:21-22.)

We will now return from our digression, and after stating that the kingdom of God is a literal kingdom; that it will be great, powerful, glorious, and universal, and that it will extend from sea to sea, and from the rivers unto the ends of the earth; that all kingdoms will be in subjection to it, and all powers obey it, we will proceed to examine how it will be established. It is compared to a small stone "hewn out of the mountain without hands," (*Ibid.* 2:45) and yet the God of Heaven is to set up this kingdom. Isaiah in his eleventh chapter, to which I refer my readers, in speaking of the establishment of this kingdom, says, "In that day there shall be a root of Jesse, which shall stand for an ensign of the people; to it shall the Gentiles seek, and his rest shall be glorious. And it shall come to pass in that day, that the Lord shall set his hand again the second time to recover the remnant of his people, which shall be left, from Assyria, and from Egypt, and from Pathros, and from Cush, and from Elam, and from Shinar, and from Hamath, and from the islands of the sea. And he shall set up an ensign for the nations, and shall assemble the outcasts of Israel, [94] and gather together the dispersed of Judah from the four corners of

---

5 The actual wording of this verse is "Man, who made me a *judge* or a *divider* over you?"—Compiler's Note.

the earth." (Isaiah 11:10-12.) From the above it would seem, that an ensign or standard is to be raised to the nations; that the Gentiles shall seek to it; and that the ten tribes return, as well as the Jews to their land; that the dispersed of Judah, and the outcasts of Israel are to return. Now, a standard, or ensign, is a nation's colours, flag, or rallying point; it is one of those appendages to a kingdom that is always respected by its inhabitants. It is used in a variety of ways, and for different purposes; sometimes by the emperor, king, governor, or general, to signify his presence; sometimes by vessels to specify their nation; and sometimes by estates, cities, corporations, or clubs; and always by armies and navies, to represent whom they belong to. If a king had a proclamation to make, and wished to rally his subjects, or try their fidelity, he might send a flag, or standard, and all that rallied to it would be considered his liege subjects.

But here the God of Heaven sets up a standard. The world, as we have before stated, is his; it is his right to possess it. Satan has held the dominion for some time, and the Lord now comes to dispossess him, to take possession of his rightful inheritance, and to rule his own kingdom. In order to do this, he issues his mandate, makes a proclamation, lifts up a standard, and invites all to join it. Those who do may be considered as his servants, as the citizens of his kingdom; those who do not, as being in opposition to him, his government, and laws. As the Father of the human family, as the prince and king, he lifts up an ensign, and calls the world's attention. Now the only rational way for the Lord to accomplish this, is to form a communication with man, and to make him acquainted with his laws. We cannot conceive of him thundering from the heavens and terrifying the inhabitants of the earth, nor yet sending angels with flaming swords to coerce obedience. This would be using physical power to control the mind; but as man is a free agent, he uses other means to act upon his mind, his judgment, and his will; and by the beauty and loveliness of virtue, purity, holiness, and the fear of God, to captivate his feelings, control his judgment, and influence him to render that obedience to God which is justly his due; not until these means fail, will others be exercised. [95]

As the world are ignorant of God and his laws, not having had any communication with him for eighteen hundred years; and as all those great and important events must transpire, and as the Lord says he will "do nothing but what he reveals to his servants the Prophets," (Amos 3:7) it follows, that there must be revelations made from God; and if so, as a necessary consequence, there must be prophets to reveal them to. How did God ever reveal his will and purposes to Enoch, Noah, Abraham, Moses, the Prophets, Jesus, and his Disciples, and they to the people. God's messengers made known his will, and the people obeyed, or rejected it. If they were punished by floods, fire, plagues, pestilence, dispersions, death, etc., it was in consequence of their disobedience. As God has dealt in former times, so will he in the latter, with this difference, that he will accomplish his purposes in the last days; he will set up his kingdom; he will protect the righteous, *destroy* Satan, and his works, purge the earth from wickedness, and bring in the restitution of all things. The above, while it is the only rational way, is evidently the only just and scriptural way. Some people talk about the world being burned up, about plagues, pestilence, famine, sword, and ruin, and all these things being instantaneous. Now it would not be just for the Lord to punish the inhabitants of the earth without warning. For if the world are ignorant of God, they cannot altogether be blamed for, it; if they are made the dupes of false systems, and false principles, they cannot help it; many of them are doing as well as they can while, as we have before stated, it would be unjust for the world to continue as it is. It would at the same time be as unjust to punish the inhabitants of the world for things that they are ignorant of, or for things over which they have no control. Before the Lord destroyed the inhabitants of the old world, he sent Enoch and Noah to warn them. Before the Lord destroyed Sodom and Gomorrah, he sent Lot into their midst. Before the Children of Israel were carried captive to Babylon, they were warned of it by the Prophets; and before Jerusalem was destroyed, the inhabitants had the testimony of our Lord, and his Disciples. And so will it be in the last days; and as it is the world that is concerned, the world will have to be warned. We will therefore proceed to examine the scriptural testimony on this subject. John says in the Revelations, "And I saw another angel fly in the midst of [96] Heaven, having the everlasting gospel to preach unto them, that dwell on the earth; and to every nation, and kindred, tongue, and people, saying with a loud voice, Fear God, and give glory to him, for the hour of his judgment is come, and worship him that made heaven and earth, the sea, and the fountains of waters. And there followed another angel, saying, Babylon the great is fallen." (Revelation 14:6-8.) Here, then, a light bursts forth from the heavens; a celestial messenger is deputed to convey to men tidings of salvation; the everlasting gospel is again to be proclaimed to the children of men; The proclamation is to be made to "every nation, kindred, people, and tongue." (v. 6.) Associated with this, was to be another declaration, "Fear God, and give glory to him, for the hour of his judgment is come." (v. 7.) Thus, all were to have a fair warning, and afterwards Babylon falls—not before. From the above it is evident, that the everlasting gospel will be restored, accompanied with a warning to the world. Now, if the everlasting gospel is restored, there must be the same principles, laws, officers, or administrators, and ordinances. If, before, they had Apostles, they will again have them; the same laws and ordinances will be introduced, and the same method for receiving members into the kingdom. They will also have Prophets, Pastors, Teachers, and Evangelists. If they baptised by immersion for the remission of sins, and laid on hands for the gift of the Holy Ghost, they will again do the same things. If the gift of the Holy Ghost formerly brought things past to the saints' remembrance, led them into all truth, and showed them things to come, it will do the same again, for it is the everlasting gospel. If formerly it caused men to dream dreams, and to see visions, it will do the same again; if to one was given the gift of tongues, to another the gift of healing, to another power to work miracles, to another the gift of wisdom, the same will exist in latter days, for it is the everlasting gospel which is to be restored. If it put men in possession of a knowledge of God, and of his purposes, and brought life and immortality to light in former days, it will do the same again. If it dispelled the clouds of darkness, unveiled the heavens, put men in possession of certainty, and gave them a hope that bloomed with immortality and eternal life, it will do the same again. If it caused men to know the object of their creation, their relationship to God, their position on the earth, and their final [97] exaltation and glory, it will do the same agin, for it is the everlasting Gospel. In short, it is the will of God to man, the government of God among men, and a portion of that light, glory and intelligence, which exist with God and angels, communicated to mortals, and obtained through obedience to his laws and ordinances. If the Gospel formerly was to be proclaimed to all nations, so it is now, with this difference associated with it, there is to be a cry, "Fear God, and give glory to him, for the hour of His judgment is come." (Revelation 14:7.) From this, then, we may expect a proclamation to be made to all people; messengers to go forth to every nation, and the same principles which once existed to be again restored in all their fulness, power, glory, and blessings. The above is the way pointed out in the Scriptures, and is the only just and rational way to deal with rational, intelligent beings; for intelligence must be appealed to by intelligence, and it would be unjust to punish the world indiscriminately, without first appealing to their reason, judgment, and intelligence. But not only will the everlasting Gospel be again restored, and be preached in its fulness as formerly, and go as a messenger to all the world; not only will there be a spiritual kingdom and organization; but there will also be a literal kingdom, a nation, or nations, a Zion, and the people will gather to that. We will here insert a prophecy of David on this subject: "But thou, O Lord, shalt endure for ever; and thy remembrance unto all generations. Thou shalt arise, and have mercy upon Zion: for the time to favor her, yea, the set time, is come. For thy servants take pleasure in her stones, and favor the dust thereof. So the heathen shall fear the name of the Lord, and all the kings of the earth thy glory. When the Lord shall build up Zion, he shall appear in his glory. He will regard the prayer of the destitute, and not despise their prayer. This shall be written for the generation to come: and the people which shall be created shall praise the Lord. For he hath looked down from the height of his sanctuary; from heaven did the Lord behold the earth; to hear the groaning of the prisoner; to loose those that are appointed to death; to declare the name of the Lord in Zion, and his praise in Jerusalem; when the people are gathered together, and the kingdoms to serve the Lord." (Psalms 102:12-22.) Here we find, First, that a literal Zion is to be built up; Secondly, that when that [98] Zion is built up, the Lord will come—will appear in his glory; Thirdly, that it is something which concerns the nations of the earth, and the whole world, for there shall the people be gathered together, and the kingdoms to serve the Lord.

It may be proper here to remark, that there will be two places of gathering, or Zions; the one in Jerusalem, the other in another place; the one is a place where the Jews will gather to, and the other a mixed multitude of all nations. Concerning the house of Israel, Jeremiah says,

"Therefore, behold, the days come, saith the Lord, that it shall no more be said, The Lord liveth, that brought up the children of Israel out of the land of Egypt; but, the Lord liveth, that brought up the children of Israel from the land of the north, and from all the lands whither he had driven them: and I will bring them again into their land that I gave unto their fathers." (Jeremiah 16:14-15.) According to this passage, and many others, there will evidently be a great display of the power of God manifested towards the house of Israel in their restitution to their former habitations. Another Scripture says, that "Jerusalem shall be inhabited in her own place, even in Jerusalem." (Zechariah 12:6.) Here I would remark, that there was a Zion formerly in Jerusalem; but there is also another spoken of in the Scriptures. Hence, in the passage which we quoted from the Psalms, the Kingdoms are to be gathered together in Zion, and the people to serve the Lord; and not only the Jews, but the Heathens are to fear the name of the Lord, and all the kings of the earth his glory. The law is to issue from Zion, and the word of the Lord from Jerusalem. Again—"The Lord God that gathereth the outcasts of Israel, says, yet will I gather others unto me besides these." (See Isaiah 56:8.) It is very evident from these passages that there are two places of gathering, as well as from many others that might be quoted. For example, Joel in speaking of the troubles of the last days, says, There shall in the last days be deliverance in Mount Zion, and in Jerusalem. (See Joel 2:32.) Now, he never could say with propriety in Mount Zion, and in Jerusalem, if these were not two places. The ancient Zion was in Jerusalem. It would not be proper to say in London, and in London; but you could say in London and in Edinburgh, in New York and in Philadelphia, in Frankfort and in Brussels; and so you can say in Zion and in Jerusalem But again, the Jews are to be gathered to Jerusalem in [99] unbelief, as spoken of in Zechariah; and when the Messiah appears among them, being ignorant of Jesus, they shall ask, "What are these wounds in thy hands?" Then he shall answer, "Those with which I was wounded in the house of my friends." (Zechariah 13:6.) And then a fountain shall be opened for the house of David, and the inhabitants of Jerusalem, and they will enter into the covenant by baptism. (v. 1.) But the people of Zion the Lord will take them one of a city, and two of a family, and bring them there, and give them pastors after his own heart, that shall feed them with knowledge and understanding.

(Jeremiah 3:14-15.) The people there are to be all righteous. It is the last Zion that we wish more particularly to speak of at present, as associated with the kingdom of God; and, as we are now searching out the manner in which the kingdom of God will be established, it is to us a matter of great importance. There are very great judgments spoken of in the last days, as the consequence of man's departure from God; these we have already referred to in part; but as we have mentioned, the Gospel must again be preached as a warning unto all nations, and accompanied with it is to be a proclamation, "Fear God, and give glory to him, for the hour of his judgment is come." (Revelation 14:7.) But the people would very reasonably be heard to enquire, what can we do? What hope have we? If war comes, we cannot either prevent or avoid it. If plague stalks through the earth, what guarantee have we of deliverance. You say you have come as messenger of mercy to us, and as the messengers of the nations. What shall we do? Let Isaiah answer: he has told the tale of war, and defined the remedy. This shall be the answer of the messenger of the nations, that "the Lord hath founded Zion, and the poor of his people shall trust in it." (Isaiah 14:32.) Yes, says Joel, when this great and terrible day of the Lord comes, there shall be deliverance in Mount Zion, and in Jerusalem, as the Lord hath said, and in the remnant whom the Lord shall call. (See Joel 2:32.) Yes, says Jeremiah, He will take them one of a city, and two of a family, and bring them to Zion, and give them pastors after his own heart, that shall feed them with knowledge and understanding. (Jeremiah 3:14-15.) The proclamation to the world will be the means of establishing this Zion, by gathering together multitudes of people from among all nations. For there are multitudes among all [100] nations who are sincerely desirous to do the will of God, when they are made acquainted with it; but having been cajoled with priestcraft and abominations so long, they know not which course to steer, and are jealous of almost everything. As it was formerly, so will it be in the latter times. Jesus said, "My sheep hear my voice, and know me, and follow me, and a stranger they will not follow, for they know not the voice of strangers." (See John 10:3-5.) Those who love truth, and desire to be governed by it, will embrace it, and enter into the covenant which the Lord will make with his people in the last days, and be gathered with them; they will be taught of the Lord in Zion, will form his kingdom on the earth, and will be prepared for the Lord when he comes to take possession of his kingdom. For "when the Lord shall build up Zion, he shall appear in his glory," (Psalms 102:16) and not before. But if Zion is never built up, the Lord never will come, for he must have a people, and a place to come to. The prophets hailed this day with pleasure, as the ushering in of those glorious times, which were to follow. Micah says, "But in the last days it shall come to pass, that the mountain of the house of the Lord shall be established in the top of the mountain of the house of the Lord shall be established in the top of the mountains, and it shall be exalted above the hills; and people shall flow unto it. And many nations shall come, and say, Come, and let us go up to the mountain of the Lord, and to the house of the God of Jacob; and he will teach us of his ways, and we will walk in his paths; for the law shall go forth of Zion, and the word of the Lord from Jerusalem." (Micah 4:1-2; see also Isaiah 2:2-3.) Isaiah with rapture gazed upon the scene, and in ecstacy cried out, "Who are these that fly as a cloud, and as the doves to their windows? Surely the isles shall wait for me, and the ships of Tarshish first, to bring thy sons from afar, their silver and their gold with them, unto the name of the Lord thy God, and to the Holy One of Israel, because he hath glorified thee. And the sons of strangers shall build up thy walls, and their kings shall minister unto thee." (Isaiah 60:8-10.) You will find by reading the 14th verse, that this place is to be called "The City of the Lord; the Zion of the Holy One of Israel." Here then we find, that the Lord will have a house built; that it shall be upon the tops of the mountains, and be exalted above the hills; that many nations shall go there, to learn the will of the Lord, and that the law shall go forth from Zion. That the people shall come as clouds to it; that they shall take their silver and gold [101] with them; that God's worship will be known, and the religion of the Lord will lose its forbidding aspect. And God, and his religion, be popular among the nations of the earth.

    This brings us to another means that will be made use of, for the establishment of the kingdom of God; for, before this, he will rebuke strong nations that are *afar off. And before they "beat their swords into ploughshares, and their spears into pruning hooks, and nations shall have war no more*," (Isaiah 2:4.)[6] there will be a time of terrible

---

6 If any one wish further information on this subject, I refer them to O. Pratt's "New Jerusalem."—Liverpool: S. W. Richards.

trouble, and distress, of war and calamity, such as never has been before on the earth. Having noticed in the above that a standard will be raised to the nations, that the Gospel will be preached again to all people and a proclamation be made to all nations; that a literal Zion will be built; that the righteous will flock to that Zion, and be taught of the Lord, and be prepared for his coming; that great multitudes will flow to Zion, and the blessing of God dwell there; we now come to point out another way that the kingdom of God will be established, viz., by judgments, that the nations may be purified and prepared for an universal reign.

Before the Lord destroyed the old world, he directed Noah to prepare an ark; before the cities of Sodom and Gomorrah were destroyed, he told Lot to "flee to the mountains;" (See Genesis 19:17) before Jerusalem was destroyed, Jesus gave his disciples warning, and told them to "flee out of it;" (See Matthew 24:16; Mark 13:14; Luke 21:21) and before the destruction of the world, a message is sent; after this, the nations will be judged, for God is now preparing his own kingdom for his own reign, and will not be thwarted by any conflicting influence, or opposing power. The testimony of God is first to be made known, the standard is to be raised; the Gospel of the kingdom is to be preached to all nations, the world is to be warned, and then come the troubles. The whole world is in confusion, morally, politically, and religiously; but a voice was to be heard, "Come out of her, my people, that you partake not of her sins, and that ye receive not of her plagues." (Revelation 18:4.) John saw an angel having the everlasting Gospel to preach to every nation, kindred, people, and tongue. And afterwards there was another cried, "Babylon is fallen." (*Ibid.* 14:8.) Isaiah, after describing some of the most terrible calamities that should [102] overtake that people, says, "The noise of a multitude in the mountains, like as of a great people; a tumultuous noise of the kingdoms of nations gathered together: the Lord of hosts mustereth the host of the battle. . . . Pangs shall take hold of them, and they shall be in pain, as a woman that travaileth." That "the day of the Lord cometh, cruel both with wrath and fierce anger, to lay the land desolate, and shall destroy the sinners thereof out of it; for the stars of heaven, and the constellations thereof, shall not give their light: the sun shall be darkened in his going forth; and the moon shall not cause her light to shine. And I will punish the world for their evil, and the wicked for their iniquity, and I will cause the arrogancy of the proud to cease, and will lay low the haughtiness of the terrible. I will make a man more precious than fine gold." (Isaiah 13:4, 8, 9-12.) After enumerating many other things concerning Babylon and Assyria, as types of things to come, he says, "This is the purpose that is purposed upon the whole earth: and this is the hand that is stretched out upon all the nations." (*Ibid.* 14:26.) He says again, "Behold the Lord maketh the earth empty, and maketh it waste, and turneth it upside down, and scattereth abroad the inhabitants thereof. And it shall be, as with the people so with the priest; as with the servant, so with his master. . . . The land shall be utterly emptied, and utterly spoiled: for the Lord hath spoken this word. . . . The earth also is defiled under the inhabitants thereof, because they have transgressed the laws, changed the ordinance, broken the everlasting covenant." (*Ibid.* 24:1-3, 5.) From the above, it would seem that terrible judgments await the inhabitants of the world; that there will be a general destruction; the world will be full of war, and confusion, the nations of the earth will be convulsed, and the wicked hurled out of it. Jesus said, when on the earth, "For nation shall rise against nation, and kingdom against kingdom; and there shall be famines and pestilences and earthquakes in divers places; men's hearts shall fail them for fear of those things that are coming on the earth." (See Matthew 24:7; Luke 21:6; also Mark 13:8.) Jesus came first as the babe of Bethlehem; he will come again, "and rule nations with a rod of iron, and dash them in pieces like a potter's vessel." (See Psalms 2:9; also Revelation 2:27.) Isaiah says, "There shall come forth a rod out of the stem of Jesse, and a Branch shall grow out of his roots. And the Spirit of the Lord shall rest upon him, the spirit of wisdom and understanding, the spirit of counsel and might, the spirit [103] of knowledge and of the fear of the Lord; and shall make him of quick understanding in the fear of the Lord; and he shall not judge after the sight of his eyes, neither reprove after the hearing of his ears; but with righteousness shall he judge the poor, and reprove with equity for the meek of the earth; and he shall smite the earth with the rod of his mouth, and with the breath of his lips shall he sly the wicked, and righteousness shall be the girdle of his loins, and faithfulness the girdle of his reins." (Isaiah 11:1-5.) The first of this was fulfilled when our Saviour came on this earth before; the second will be when he comes again, "he will smite the earth with the rod of his mouth, and with the breath of his lips will he slay the wicked." (v. 4.) The spirit of the Lord will be withdrawn from the nations, and after rejecting the truth, they will be left in darkness, to grope their way, and being full of the spirit of wickedness, they will rage and war against each other, and finally, after dreadful struggles, plagues, pestilence, famine, etc., instigated by the powers of darkness, there will be a great gathering of the nations against Jerusalem, for they will be infuriated against its inhabitants, and mighty hosts will assemble, so that they will be like a cloud to cover the land, and the Lord will appear himself to the deliverance of his people and the destruction of the wicked. Zechariah 14. Let any one compare this chapter with Ezekiel 38 and 39, and he will find one of the most terrible destructions described, that is possible to conceive of; and then turn to the second Psalm, where David describes the kings of the earth taking counsel against the Lord, and against his anointed. He says, "He that sitteth in the heavens shall laugh; the Lord shall have them in derision. . . . That he will set his king upon his holy hill in Zion, that he will give him the heathen for his inheritance, and the uttermost parts of the earth for his possession. . . . That he will break them with a rod of iron, and dash them in pieces like a potter's vessel; and then he concludes by saying, Be wise, therefore, O ye kings; be instructed, ye judges of the earth, serve the Lord with fear, and rejoice with trembling; kiss the son, lest he be angry, and ye perish from the way, when his wrath is kindled but a little. (See verses 4, 6, 8-12.)

In making a brief summary of what we have said before in relation to the means to be employed for the establishment of the Kingdom of God, we find the following:—[104]

1st.—That it will be not only a spiritual kingdom, but a temporal and literal one also.

2nd.—That if it is the Kingdom of Heaven, it must be revealed from the heavens.

3rd.—That a standard is to be lifted up, by the Lord, to the nations.

4th.—That an Angel is to come with the everlasting Gospel, which is to be proclaimed to every nation, kindred, people, and tongue; that it is to be the same as the ancient one, and that the same powers and blessings will attend it.

5th.—That not only will the Ancient Gospel be preached, but

there will accompany it a declaration of judgment to the nations.

6th.—That there will be a literal Zion, or gathering of the Saints to Zion, as well as a gathering of the Jews to Jerusalem.

7th.—That when this has taken place, the Spirit of God will be withdrawn from the nations, and they will war with and destroy each other.

8th.—That judgments will also overtake them, from the Lord, plague, pestilence, famine, etc.

9th.—That the nations, having lost the Spirit of God, will assemble to fight against the Lord's people, being full of the spirit of unrighteousness, and opposed to the rule and government of God.

10th.—That when they do, the Lord will come and fight against them himself; overthrow their armies, assert his own right, rule the nations with a rod of iron, root the wicked out of the earth, and take possession of his own kingdom. I might here further state, that when the Lord does come to exercise judgment upon the ungodly, to make an end of sin, and bring in everlasting righteousness, he will establish his own laws, demand universal obedience, and cause wickedness and misrule to cease. He will issue his commands, and they must be obeyed; and if the nations of the earth observe not his laws, "they will have no rain." (See Zachariah 14:17-18.) And they will be taught by more forcible means than moral suasion, that they are dependant upon God; for the Lord will demand obedience, and the Scriptures say, time and again, that the wicked shall be rooted out of the land, and the righteous and the meek shall inherit the earth. The Lord, after trying man's rule for thousands of years, now takes the reins of government into his own hands, and makes use of the only possible means of [105] asserting his rights. For if the wicked never were cut off, the righteous never could rule; and if the Devil was still suffered to bear rule, God could not, at the same time; consequently after long delay, he whose right it is, takes possession of the kingdom; and the kingdom, and the greatness of the kingdom under the whole heavens, shall be given to the Saints of the Most High God; and the world will assume that position for which it was made. A King shall rule in righteousness, and Princes shall decree judgment. The knowledge of the Lord will spread, and extend under the auspices of this government. Guided by his counsels, and under his direction, all those purposes designed of Him, from the commencement, in relation to both living and dead, will be in a fair way for their accomplishment.

CHAPTER 12

The Effects of the Establishment of Christ's Kingdom, or the Reign of God Upon the Earth

Having said so much pertaining to the Kingdom, we come to our last proposition, and enquire, What will be the effects of the establishment of Christ's kingdom, or the reign of God on the earth?

This is, indeed, a grand and important question, and requires our most serious and calm deliberation. If, after all this distress, tribulation, war, bloodshed, and sacrifice of human life, the condition of the world is no better, man is certainly in a most unhappy, hopeless situation. If it is nothing more than some of the changes contemplated by man, from one species of government to another, and we [106] must still have war, bloodshed, and disorder, and be subject to the caprices of tyrants, or the anarchy of mobs, our prospects are indeed gloomy, and our hopes vain; we may as well "eat and drink, for tomorrow we die;" (See Isaiah 22:13; 2 Nephi 28:7) for, as we have already proven, under the most improved state of human governments we should still be subject to all the ills which flesh is heir to, without any redeeming hope. But this is not a transient, short-lived change; it is something decreed by God in relation to the earth and man, from before the commencement of the world; even the dispossessing of Satan, the destruction of the ungodly, and the reign of God; or in other words, putting the moral world in the same position in which the physical world is—under the direction of the Almighty. It is the doing away with war, bloodshed, misery, disease, and sin, and the ushering in of a kingdom of peace, righteousness, justice, happiness, and prosperity. It is the restoration of the earth and man to their primeval glory, and pristine excellence; in fact, the "restitution of all things spoken of by all the prophets since the world began." (See Acts 3:21.)

Now, restoration signifies a bringing back, and must refer to something which existed before; for if it did not exist before, it could not be restored. I cannot describe this better than Parley P. Pratt has done in his "Voice of Warning," and shall therefore make the following extract:—

"This is one of the most important subjects upon which the human mind can contemplate; and one perhaps as little understood, in the present age, as any other now lying over the face of prophecy. But however neglected at the present time, it was once the ground-work of the faith, hope, and joy of the Saints. It was a correct understanding of this subject, and firm belief in it, that influenced all their movements. Their minds once fastening upon it, they could not be shaken from their purposes; their faith was firm, their joy constant, and their hope like an anchor to the soul, both sure and steadfast, reaching to that within the veil. It was this that enabled them to rejoice in the midst of tribulation, persecution, sword, and flame; and in view of this, they took joyfully the spoiling of their goods, and gladly wandered as strangers and pilgrims on the earth. For they sought a country, a city, and an inheritance, that none but a Saint ever thought of, understood, or even hoped for. [107]

"Now, we can never understand precisely what is meant by restoration, unless we understand what is lost or taken away; for instance, when we offer to restore any thing to a man, it is as much as to say he once possessed it, but had lost it, and we propose to replace or put him in possession of that which he once had; therefore, when a prophet speaks of the restoration of all things, he means that all things have undergone a change, and are to be again restored to their primitive order, even as they first existed.

"First, then, it becomes necessary for us to take a view of creation, as it rolled in purity from the hand of its Creator; and if we can discover the true state in which it then existed, and understand the changes that have taken place since, then we shall be able to understand what is to be restored; and thus our minds being prepared, we shall be looking for the very things which will come, and shall be in no danger of lifting our puny arm, in ignorance, to oppose the things of God.

"First, then, we will take a view of the earth, as to its surface, local situation, and productions.

"When God had created the heavens and the earth, and separated the light from the darkness, his next great command was to the waters, Genesis 1:9,—'And God said, let the waters under the heaven be gathered together into *one place*, and let the dry land appear: and it was so.' From this we learn a marvellous fact, which very few have ever realized or believed in this benighted age; we learn that the waters, which are now divided into oceans, seas, and lakes, were then all gathered together, into *one* vast ocean; and, consequently, that the land, which is now torn asunder, and divided into continents and islands, almost innumerable, was then *one* vast continent or body, not separated as it is now.

"Second, we hear the Lord God pronounce the earth, as well as every thing else, very good. From this we learn that there were neither deserts, barren places, stagnant swamps, rough, broken, rugged hills, nor vast mountains covered with eternal snow; and no part of it was located in the frigid zone, so as to render its climate dreary and unproductive, subject to eternal frost, or everlasting chains of ice,—

"Where no sweet flowers the dreary landscape cheer,

Nor plenteous harvests crown the passing year; [108]

"But the whole earth was probably one vast plain, or interspersed with gently rising hills, and sloping vales, well calculated for cultivation; while its climate was delightfully varied, with the moderate changes of heat and cold, of wet and dry, which only tended to crown the varied year, with the greater variety of productions, all for the good of man, animal, fowl, or creeping thing; while from the flowery plain, or spicy grove, sweet odours were wafted on every breeze; and all the vast creation of animated being breathed nought but health, and peace, and joy.

"Next, we learn from Genesis 1:29-30,—'And God said, Behold, I have given you every herb bearing seed, which is upon the face of *all* the earth, and every tree, in which is the fruit of a tree, yielding seed; to you it shall be for meat. And to every beast of the earth, and to every fowl of the air, and to every thing that creepeth upon the earth, wherein there is life, I have given every green herb for meat: and it was so.' From these verses we learn, that the earth yielded neither nauseous weeds nor poisonous plants, nor useless thorns and thistles; indeed, every thing that grew was just calculated for the food of man, beast, fowl, and creeping thing; and their food was all vegetable; flesh and blood were never sacrificed to glut their souls, or gratify their appetites; the beasts of the earth were all in perfect harmony with each other; the lion ate straw like the ox—the wolf dwelt with the lamb—the leopard lay down with the kid—the cow and bear fed together, in the same pasture, while their young ones reposed, in perfect security, under the shade of the same trees; all was peace and harmony, and nothing to hurt nor disturb, in all the holy mountain.

"And to crown the whole, we behold man created in the image of God, and exalted in dignity and power, having dominion over all the vast creation of animated beings, which swarmed through the earth, while, at the same time, he inhabits a beautiful and well-watered garden, in the midst of which stood the Tree of Life, to which he had free access; while he stood in the presence of his Maker, conversed with him face to face, and gazed upon his glory, without a dimming veil between. O reader, contemplate, for a moment, this beautiful creation, clothed with peace and plenty; the earth teeming with harmless animals, rejoicing over all the plain; the air swarming with delightful birds, whose never ceasing notes filled the air with varied melody; [109] and all in subjection to their rightful sovereign who rejoiced over them; while, in a delightful garden—the Capitol of creation,—man was seated on the throne of his vast empire, swaying his sceptre over all the earth, with undisputed right; while legions of angels encamped round about him, and joined their glad voices, in grateful songs of praise, and shouts of joy; neither a sigh nor groan was heard, throughout the vast expanse; neither was there sorrow, tears, pain, weeping, sickness, nor death; neither contentions, wars, nor bloodshed; but peace crowned the seasons as they rolled, and life, joy, and love, reigned over all his works. But, O! How changed the scene.

"It now becomes my painful duty, to trace some of the important changes, which have taken place, and the causes which have conspired to reduce the earth and its inhabitants to their present state.

"First, man fell from his standing before God, by giving heed to temptation; and this fall affected the whole creation, as well as man, and caused various changes to take place; he was banished from the presence of his Creator, and a veil was drawn between them, and he was driven from the garden of Eden, to till the earth, which was then cursed for man's sake, and should begin to bring forth thorns and thistles; and with the sweat of his face he should earn his bread, and in sorrow eat of it, all the days of his life, and finally return to dust. But as to Eve, her curse was a great multiplicity of sorrow and conception; and between her seed, and the seed of the serpent, there was to be a constant enmity; it should bruise the serpent's head, and the serpent should bruise his heel.

"Now, reader, contemplate the change. This scene, which was so beautiful a little before, had now become the abode of sorrow and toil, of death and mourning: the earth groaning with its production of accursed thorns and thistles; man and beast at enmity; the serpent slily creeping away, fearing lest his head should get the deadly bruise; and man startling amid the thorny path, in fear, lest the serpent's fangs should pierce his heel; while the lamb yields his blood upon the smoking altar. Soon man begins to persecute, hate, and murder his fellow; until at length the earth is filled with violence; all flesh becomes corrupt, the powers of darkness prevail; and it repented Noah that God had made man, and it grieved him at his heart, because the Lord should come out in vengeance, and cleanse the earth by water. [110]

"How far the flood may have contributed, to produce the various changes, as to the division of the earth into broken fragments, islands and continents, mountains and valleys, we have not been informed; the change must have been considerable. But after the flood, in the days of Peleg, the earth was divided, (See Genesis 10:25) a short history, to be sure, of so great an event; but still it will account for the mighty revolution, which rolled the sea from its own place in the north, and brought it to interpose between different portions of the earth, which were thus parted asunder, and moved into something near their present form; this, together with the earthquakes, revolutions, and commotions which have since taken place, have all contributed to reduce the face of the earth to its present state; while the great curses which have fallen upon different portions, because of the wickedness of men, will account for the stagnant swamps, the sunken lakes, the dead seas, and great deserts.

"Witness, for instance, the denunciations of the prophets upon Babylon, how it was to become perpetual desolations, a den of wild beasts, a dwelling of unclean and hateful birds, a place for owls; and should never be inhabited, but should lie desolate from generation to generation. Witness also the plains of Sodom, filled with towns, cities, and flourishing gardens, well watered: but O, how changed! a vast sea of stagnant water alone marks the place. Witness the land of Palestine; in the days of Solomon it was capable of sustaining millions of people, besides a surplus of wheat, and other productions, which were exchanged with the neighbouring nations; whereas, now it is desolate, and hardly capable of sustaining a few miserable inhabitants. And when I cast mine eyes over our own land, and see the numerous swamps, lakes, and ponds of stagnant waters, together with the vast mountains and innumerable rough places; rocks having been rent, and torn asunder, from centre to circumference; I exclaim, Whence all this?

"When I read the Book of Mormon, it informs me, that while Christ was crucified among the Jews, this whole American continent was shaken to its foundation, that many cities were sunk, and waters came up in their places; that the rocks were all rent in twain; that mountains were thrown up to an exceeding height; and other mountain became vallies: the level roads spoiled; and the whole face of [111] the land changed.—I then exclaim, These things are no longer a mystery; I have now learned to account for the many wonders, which I everywhere behold, throughout our whole country; when I am passing a ledge of rocks, and see they have all been rent and torn asunder, while some huge fragments are found deeply imbedded in the earth, some rods from whence they were torn, I exclaim, with astonishment, These were the groans! the convulsive throes of agonizing nature! while the Son of God suffered upon the cross!

"But men have degenerated, and greatly changed, as well as the earth. The sins, the abominations, and the many evil habits of the latter ages, have added to the miseries, toils, and sufferings of human life. The idleness, extravagance, pride, covetousness, drunkenness, and other abominations, which are characteristics of the latter times, have all combined to sink mankind to the lowest state of wretchedness and degradation; while priestcraft and false doctrines, have greatly tended to lull mankind to sleep, and caused them to rest, infinitely short of the powers and attainments which the ancients did enjoy, and which are alone calculated to exalt the intellectual powers of the human mind, to establish noble and generous sentiments, to enlarge the heart, and to expand the soul to the utmost extent of its capacity. Witness the ancients, conversing with the Great Jehovah, learning lessons from the angels, and receiving instruction by the Holy Ghost, in dreams by night, and visions by day, until at length the veil is taken off, and they permitted to gaze, with wonder and admiration, upon all things past and future; yea, even to soar aloft amid unnumbered worlds; while the vast expanse of eternity stands open before them, and they contemplate the mighty works of the Great I AM, until they know as they are known, and see as they are seen.

"Compare this intelligence, with the low smatterings of education and worldly wisdom, which seem to satisfy the narrow mind of man in our generation; yea, behold the narrow-minded, calculating, trading, overreaching, penurious sycophant, of the nineteenth century, who dreams of nothing here, but how to increase his goods, or take advantage of his neighbour; and whose only religious exercises or duties consist of going to meeting, paying the priest his hire, or praying to his God, without expecting to be heard or answered, supposing that God has been deaf and dumb for many centuries, or altogether stupid [112] and indifferent like himself. And having seen the two contrasted, you will be able to form some idea of the vast elevation from which man has fallen; you will also learn, how infinitely beneath his former glory and dignity, he is now living, and your heart will mourn, and be exceedingly sorrowful, when you contemplate him in his low estate—and then think he is your brother; and you will be ready to exclaim, with wonder and astonishment, O man! how art thou fallen! once thou wast the favourite of Heaven; thy Maker delighted to converse with thee, and angels and the spirits of just men made perfect were thy companions; but now thou art degraded, and brought down on a level with the beasts; yea, far beneath them, for they look with horror and affright at your vain amusements, your sports and your drunkenness, and thus often set an example worthy of your imitation. Well did the apostle Peter say of you, that you know nothing, only what you know naturally as brute beasts, made to be taken and destroyed. (See 2 Peter 2:12.) And thus you perish, from generation to generation. While all creation groans under its pollution; and sorrow and death, mourning and weeping, fill up the measure of the days of man. But O my soul, dwell no longer on this awful scene: let it suffice, to have discovered in some degree, what is lost. Let us turn our attention to what the Prophets have said should be restored.

"The Apostle Peter, while preaching to the Jews, says, 'And he shall send Jesus Christ, which before was preached unto you, whom the heavens must receive, until the times of restitution (restoration) of all things which God hath spoken, by the mouth of all the holy prophets, since the world began.' (Acts 3:20-21.) It appears from the above, that all the holy prophets from Adam, and those that follow after, have had their eyes upon a certain time, when all things should be restored to their primitive beauty and excellence. We also learn, that the time of restitution was to be at or near the time of Christ's second coming; for the heavens are to receive him, until the times of restitution, and then the Father shall send him again to the earth.

"We will now proceed to notice Isaiah 40:1-5. 'Comfort ye, comfort ye my people, saith your God. Speak ye comfortably to Jerusalem, and cry unto her, that her warfare is accomplished, that her iniquity is pardoned: for she hath received of the Lord's hand, double for all her sins. The voice of him that crieth in the wilderness, [113] Prepare ye the way of the Lord, make straight in the desert a highway for our God. Every valley shall be exalted, and every mountain and hill shall be made low: and the crooked shall be made straight, and the rough places plain: and the glory of the Lord shall be revealed, and all flesh shall see it together: for the mouth of the Lord hath spoken it.'

"From these verses we learn, first, that the voice of one shall be heard in the wilderness, to prepare the way of the Lord, just at the time when Jerusalem has been trodden down of the Gentiles long enough to have received, at the Lord's hand, double for all her sins, yea, when the warfare of Jerusalem is accomplished, and her iniquities pardoned; then shall this proclamation be made as it was before by John, yea, a second proclamation, to prepare the way of the Lord, for his second coming; and about that time every valley shall be exalted, and every mountain and hill shall be made low, and the crooked shall be made straight, and rough places plain, and then the glory of the Lord shall be revealed, and all flesh shall see it together, for the mouth of the Lord hath spoken it.

"Thus you see, every mountain being laid low, and every valley exalted, and the rough places being made plain, and the crooked places straight, that these mighty revolutions will begin to restore the face of the earth to its former beauty. But all this done, we have not yet gone through our restoration; there are many more great things to be done, in order to restore all things.

"Our next is Isaiah 35th chapter, where we again read of the Lord's second coming, and of the mighty works which attend it. The barren desert should abound with pools and springs of living water, and should produce grass, with flowers blooming and blossoming as the rose, and that, too, about the time of the coming of their God, with vengeance and recompense, which must allude to his second coming; and Israel is to come at the same time to Zion, with songs of everlasting joy, and sorrow and sighing shall flee away. Here, then, we have the curse taken off from the deserts, and they become a fruitful, well-watered country.

"We will now inquire whether the islands return again to the continents, from which they were once separated. For this subject we refer you to Revelation 6:14,—'And every mountain and island [114] were moved out of their places.' From this we learn that they moved somewhere; and as it is the time of restoring what had been lost, they accordingly return and join themselves to the land whence they came.

"Our next is Isaiah 13:13-14, where 'The earth shall move out of her place, and be like a chased roe which no man taketh up.' Also, Isaiah 62:4, 'Thou shalt no more be termed forsaken; neither shall thy land any more be termed desolate; but thou shalt be called Hephzibah, and thy land Beulah: for the Lord delighteth in thee, and thy land shall be married.'

"In the first instance, we have the earth on a move like a chased roe; and in the second place, we have it married. And from the whole, and various Scriptures, we learn, that the continents and islands shall be united in one, as they were on the morn of creation, and the sea shall retire and assemble in its own place, where it was before; and all these scenes shall take place during the mighty convulsion of nature, about the time of the coming of the Lord.

"Behold! the Mount of Olives rend in twain:
While on its top he sets his feet again,
The islands at his word, obedient, flee;

While to the north, he rolls the mighty sea;
Restores the earth in one, as at the first,
With all its blessings, and removes the curse.

"Having restored the earth to the same glorious state in which it first existed; levelling the mountains, exalting the valleys, smoothing the rough places, making the deserts fruitful, and bringing all the continents and islands together, causing the curse to be taken off, that it shall no longer produce noxious weeds, and thorns, and thistles; the next thing is to regulate and restore the brute creation to their former state of peace and glory, causing all enmity to cease from off the earth. But this will never be done until there is a general destruction poured out upon man, which will entirely cleanse the earth, and sweep all wickedness from its face. This will be done by the rod of his mouth, and by the breath of his lips; or, in other words, by fire as universal as the flood. 'But with righteousness shall he judge the poor, and reprove with equity for the meek of the [115] earth: and he shall smite the earth with the rod of his mouth, and with the breath of his lips shall he slay the wicked. The wolf also shall dwell with the lamb, and the leopard shall lie down with the kid; and the calf, and the young lion, and the fatling together; and a little child shall lead them. And the cow and the bear shall feed; their young ones shall lie down together; and the lion shall eat straw like the ox. And the sucking child shall play on the hole of the asp, and the weaned child shall put his hand on the cockatrice's den. They shall not hurt nor destroy in all my holy mountain: for the earth shall be full of the knowledge of the Lord, as the waters cover the sea.' (Isaiah 11:4, 6-9.)

"Thus, having cleansed the earth, and glorified it with the knowledge of God, as the waters cover the sea, and having poured out his Spirit upon all flesh, both man and beast becoming perfectly harmless, as they were in the beginning, and feeding on vegetable food only, while nothing is left to hurt or destroy in all the vast creation, the prophets then proceed to give us many glorious descriptions of the enjoyments of its inhabitants. 'They shall build houses and inhabit them; they shall plant vineyards, and drink the wine of them; they shall plant gardens and eat the fruit of them; they shall not build and another inhabit; they shall not plant and another eat; for as the days of a tree are the days of my people, and mine elect shall long enjoy the work of their hands. They shall not labour in vain, nor bring forth in trouble; for they are the seed of the blessed of the Lord, and their offspring with them; and it shall come to pass, that before they call I will answer, and while they are yet speaking I will hear.' (Isaiah 65:21-24.) In this happy state of existence it seems that all people will live to the full age of a tree, and this too without pain or sorrow, and whatsoever they ask will be immediately answered, and even all their wants will be anticipated. Of course, then, none of them will sleep in the dust, for they will prefer to be translated; that is changed in the twinkling of an eye, from mortal to immortal; after which they will continue to reign with Jesus on the earth." (Pages 110-122.)

A great council will then be held to adjust the affairs of the world, from the commencement, over which Father Adam will preside as head and representative of the human family. There have been in different ages of the world, communications opened between [116] the heavens and the earth. Those powers have been separated, and have acted in different spheres, until the present. The kingdom of God on the earth has been small, weak, unpopular, trampled under foot of men, and none but men of noble minds, firm hopes, and daring resolution, have advocated its principles. These men, being possessed of intelligence from the heavens by the ministering of angels, the communications of the spirits of the just, and the manifestation of eternal things, knew of the approaching day of glory, the reign of God on the earth; they understood their destiny, and lived, and died, in the hopes of inheriting these things. Those communications from the heavens developed the purposes of God to them; and in all their moves, they were regulated by the prospect of the future. In the Mosaic Dispensation they had to make earthly things according to the pattern of heavenly. Hence it was said to Moses, "See that thou make all things according to the pattern shewn thee in the Mount." (Hebrews 8:5; Exodus 25:40.) The ark was made, therefore, after a heavenly pattern, and so was the Temple of Jerusalem. Jerusalem was a figure of the heavenly. The sacrifices of the Aaronic Priesthood referred to the expiation of Christ, who appears as the earthly High Priest of the Jews, and as our eternal High Priest and Intercessor in the heavens. His Priesthood was an eternal one, and is after the order of Melchisedek, and Melchisedek's was after his order, and they both were after the order that exists in the heavens. This priesthood with the Gospel, brought life and immortality to light, put men in possession of certainty, and unveiled the future; they knew the divine laws and ordinances, and acted with a reference to them; and being commissioned of God, they had power to bind and loose, etc.

Then they will assemble to regulate all these affairs, and all that held keys of authority to administer, will then represent their earthly course. And, as this authority has been handed down from one to another in different ages, and in different dispensations, a full reckoning will have to be made by all. All who have held keys of Priesthood, will then have to give an account to those from whom they received them. Those that were in the heavens, have been assisting those that were upon the earth; but then, they will unite together in a general council to give an account of their stewardships, and as in the various ages men have received their power to adminis[117]ter, from those who had previously held the keys thereof, there will be a general account. Those, under the authorities of the Church of Jesus Christ of Latter-day Saints, have to give an account of their transactions to those who direct them in the Priesthood; hence the Elders give an account to Presidents of Conferences; and Presidents of Conferences to Presidents of Nations. Those Presidents and the Seventies give an account to the Twelve Apostles; the Twelve to the First Presidency; and they to Joseph, from whom they, and the Twelve, received their Priesthood. This will include the arrangements of the last dispensation. Joseph delivers his authority to Peter, who held the keys before him, and delivered them to him; and Peter to Moses and Elias, who endued him with this authority on the Mount; and they to those from whom they received them. And thus the world's affairs will be regulated and put right, the restitution of all things be accomplished, and the Kingdom of God be ushered in. The earth will be delivered from under the curse, resume its paradisiacal glory, and all things pertaining to its restoration be fulfilled.

Not only will the earth be restored, but also man; and those promises which, long ago, were the hope of the saints, will be realised. The faithful servants of God who have lived in every age, will then come forth and experience the full fruition of that joy, for which they lived, and hoped, and suffered, and died. The tombs will deliver up their captives, and re-united with the spirits which once animated, vivified, cheered, and sustained them while in this vale of tears, these bodies will be like unto Christ's glorious body. They will then rejoice

The Government of God

in that resurrection for which they lived, while they sojourned below. Adam, Seth, Enoch, and the faithful who lived before the flood, will possess their proper inheritance. Noah and Melchisedek will stand in their proper places. Abraham, with Isaac and Jacob, heirs with him of the same promise, will come forward at the head of innumerable multitudes, and possess that land which God gave unto them for an everlasting inheritance. The faithful, on the continent of America, will also stand in their proper place; but, as this will be the time of the restitution of all things, and all things will not be fully restored at once; there will be a distinction between the resurrected bodies, and those that have not been resurrected; and as the Scriptures say that flesh and blood cannot inherit the kingdom of God, [118] neither doth corruption inherit incorruption; and although the world will enjoy just laws—an equitable administration, and universal peace and happiness prevail as the result of this righteousness; yet, there will be a peculiar habitation for the resurrected bodies. This habitation may be compared to Paradise, from whence man, in the beginning, was driven.

When Adam was driven from the Garden, an angel was placed with a flaming sword to guard the way of the tree of life, lest man should eat of it, and become immortal in his degenerate state, and thus be incapable of obtaining that exaltation, which he would be capable of enjoying through the redemption of Jesus Christ, and the power of the resurrection, with his renewed and glorified body. Having tasted of the nature of the fall, and having grappled with sin and misery, knowing like the gods both good and evil, having like Jesus overcome the evil, and through the power of the atonement, having conquered death, hell, and the grave, he regains that Paradise, from which he was banished, not in the capacity of ignorant man, unacquainted with evil, but like unto a god. He can now stretch forth, and partake of the tree of life, and eat of its fruits, and live and flourish eternally in possession of that immortality which Jesus long ago promised to the faithful: "To him that overcomes, will I grant to sit with me in my throne; and eat of the tree of life which is in the midst of the Paradise of God." (Revelation 3:21; 2:7.)

THE FOLLOWING

ITEMS ON PRIESTHOOD

ARE PRESENTED TO

THE LATTER-DAY SAINTS

BY

PRESIDENT JOHN TAYLOR

SALT LAKE CITY, UTAH

1881

C O N T E N T S
───────

INTRODUCTION. 323

CHAPTER 1: The Aaronic Priesthood. 325

CHAPTER 2: Principally on the Aaronic Priesthood or Bishopric. 338

CHAPTER 3: The Levitical Priesthood.................. 356

INTRODUCTION

As there is more or less uncertainty existing in the minds of many of the bishops and others in regard to the proper status and authority of the Bishopric and what is denominated the "Aaronic or Levitical" Priesthood, I thought it best to lay before the brethren a general statement of the subject, as contained in the Bible and Book of Doctrine and Covenants.

With this in view, I have made copious extracts from both of the above sacred records, and so arranged them that they can be readily comprehended by those who hold the Priesthood and are conversant with the holy order of God; adding only such remarks, for explanation, as the plain statements warranted; preferring to give generally the simple quotations, and to let them speak for themselves.

In the elucidation of this subject I have necessarily had to refer, more or less, to the Melchizedek Priesthood, as the two Priesthoods are inseparably united, the one with the other. I have also given a brief Scriptural synopsis of the Levitical Priesthood, as record in the Old Testament. [2]

The following views have been submitted to the Council of the Twelve and have received their sanction; they were also laid before the Priesthood Meeting at the Semi-Annual Conference, held in the Assembly Hall, Salt Lake City, October 9th, A.D. 1880, and were unanimously accepted by the large body of Priesthood present on that occasion.

CHAPTER 1

THE AARONIC PRIESTHOOD

AS CONTAINED IN THE BIBLE

First.—The Aaronic, or Levitical Priesthood, spoken of in the revelations as being "lesser" than the Melchizedek; Aaron was made the mouthpiece of Moses, while Moses was as a God to Aaron. The Lord having called Moses to deliver Israel, the Prophet realized his weakness and plead to be excused. We quote from the Scriptures:

"And the anger of the Lord was kindled against Moses, and he said, Is not Aaron the Levite thy brother? I know that he can speak well. And also, behold, he cometh forth to meet thee: and when he seeth thee, he will be glad in his heart. And thou shalt speak unto him, and put words in his mouth: and I will be with thy mouth, and with his mouth, and will teach you what ye shall do. And he shall be thy spokesman unto the people: and he shall be, even he shall be to thee *instead of a mouth*, and thou shalt be to him instead of God." (Exodus 4:14-16.)

It would seem from the foregoing that the Lord was angry with Moses, because he doubted the ability of God to sustain him and to enable him to speak: "And the Lord said unto him, Who hath made man's mouth? or who maketh the dumb, or deaf, or the seeing, or the blind? Have not I the Lord? Now therefore go, and I will be with thy mouth, and teach thee [3] what thou shalt say. And he said, O, my Lord, send, I pray thee, by the hand of *him whom* thou wilt send."

(Exodus 4:11-13.)

The Lord further says: "And thou shalt take this rod in thine hand, wherewith thou shalt do signs." (Exodus 4:17.)

"And the Lord said to Aaron, Go into the wilderness to meet Moses. And he went, and met him in the Mount of God, and kissed him. And Moses told Aaron all the words of the Lord who had sent him, and all the signs which he had commanded him." (Exodus 4:27-28.)

"These are that Aaron and Moses, to whom the Lord said, Bring out the children of Israel from the land of Egypt according to their armies. These are they which spake to Pharaoh, king of Egypt, to bring out the children of Israel from Egypt: these are that Moses and Aaron." (Exodus 6:26-27.) "And the Lord spake unto Moses and Aaron in the land of Egypt." (Exodus 12:1.)

It may be noticed that Aaron was with Moses, that God called him and spake to him and Moses, and that he assisted in bringing the message to Pharaoh, and was a prophet to Moses before he held the Aaronic Priesthood, or before that Priesthood known to us as the Aaronic or Levitical Priesthood was given. But it would seem also that the Lord spake to Aaron himself;— how and on what principle? The Lord also said to Moses, "I will be with thy mouth, and with his mouth, and will teach you what ye shall do." (Exodus 4:15.) And Aaron spake all the words which the Lord had spoken unto Moses, and did the signs in the sight of the people. The Lord had before spoken to Moses on this subject; he now spake to Aaron. Hence Paul says, "No man taketh this honor unto himself: but he that is called of God as was Aaron." (Hebrews 5:4.) What did the Lord say to him? "Go into the wilderness to meet Moses." (Exodus 4:27.) And then Moses told Aaron all the words of the Lord, who had sent him. Moses was thus his instructor and guide, [4] or in other words, acted as a God to him. Thus, Aaron being selected to assist Moses and to be his mouthpiece, went with him to Egypt, and was with him in his intercourse with Pharaoh, and in the deliverance of the children of Israel from Egypt. But Moses always took the lead, and when Moses' father-in-law, Jethro, met him, "Moses sat to judge the people (not Aaron): and the people stood by Moses, from the morning unto the evening." (Exodus 18:13.) And when Jethro saw the excessive labors of Moses, he counseled him, If *God should command him*, to choose able men to be rulers of thousands, of hundreds, of fifties, and of tens; to judge the smaller cases, while Moses should have charge of the most important. Thus Moses, and not Aaron, was the most prominent personage in these matters.

We further find that Aaron was permitted to go up to Mount Sinai. "And the Lord said unto him [Moses], Away, get thee down, and thou shalt come up, thou, and Aaron with thee: but let not the Priests and the people break through to come up unto the Lord, lest he break forth upon them." (Exodus 19:24.) It may be here asked, Who were these Priests? for the Aaronic Priesthood, as we know it, was not then introduced. But Moses was his leader, and it was he who obtained the word of the Lord, and it was he with whom the Lord conversed. For we find, "And Moses went up unto God, and the Lord called unto him out of the mountain, saying, Thus shalt thou say to the house of Jacob, and tell the children of Israel. . . . And the Lord came down upon Mount Sinai, on the top of the mount: and the Lord called Moses up to the top of the mount; and Moses went up. And the Lord said unto Moses, Go down, charge the people lest they break through unto the Lord to gaze, and many of them perish." (Exodus 19:3, 20-21.) Moses always took the lead: "And he said unto Moses, Come up unto the Lord, thou, and Aaron, Nadab, and Abihu, and seventy of the Elders of Israel; and worship ye afar off. And Moses alone shall come near the Lord: but [5] they shall not come nigh; neither shall the people go up with him." (Exodus 24:1-2.) They *saw God* and did eat and drink: "And upon the nobles of the children of Israel he laid not his hand: also they saw God, and did eat and drink." (v. 11.) And afterwards Moses was with the Lord forty days. "And Moses went into the midst of the cloud, and got him up into the mount: and Moses was in the mount forty days and forty nights." (v. 18.) By what power did Aaron see God? May we not suppose it was by the power of the Melchizedek Priesthood? for without that no man can see the face of God and live. It, the Melchizedek, holds the keys of the mysteries of the Kingdom, even the key of the knowledge of God. (D&C 84.) Moses had these keys; but Aaron also saw God, as well as the seventy Elders of Israel, and the people saw his glory and heard his voice. (Exodus 20:22; Deuteronomy 4:36.)

It would seem that Aaron and the seventy Elders of Israel then had the Melchizedek Priesthood, and the Aaronic was about being combined with it, as we have them now. Moses held the keys of the Melchizedek Priesthood, and presided over the whole. Aaron was then in possession of the Melchizedek Priesthood; but another or lesser Priesthood was about to be conferred upon him, which was done soon after. We quote, "And take thou unto thee Aaron thy brother, and his sons with him, from among the children of Israel, that he may minister unto me in the Priest's office, even Aaron, Nadab and Abihu, Eleazar and Ithamar, Aaron's sons. And thou shalt make holy garments for Aaron thy brother, for glory and for beauty." (Exodus 28:1-2.)

Does it not seem probable that Aaron, when he received this lesser Priesthood, was in the same position (as to Priesthood) that our Presiding Bishop is, holding the Melchizedek and lesser Priesthoods, but presiding over the latter, and Moses presiding over all—the Melchizedek as well as the Aaronic or Levitical, the latter being an appendage to the former? For we read [6] that the law was added because of transgression; added to what? Was there anything but the Gospel to add it to? The children of Israel, at this time, had the Gospel and the pattern of the ark, and the commandments were given under its auspices. And the Lord spake unto Moses, saying, "And look that thou make them after their pattern, which was shewed thee in the mount." (Exodus 25:40; See also the whole chapter.) And further, the words of the Lord, the book of the covenant or law of the Lord were given under the Gospel. (See Exodus 24:1-8.) And the sacrifices and burnt offerings were also performed under the Gospel; and as the great Presiding High Priest, Moses, gave directions concerning the sacrifices, and himself sprinkled half of the blood upon the altar, and put half into basins, hence we have the following:

"And Moses took half of the blood, and put it in basins; and half of the blood he sprinkled on the altar. And he took the book of the covenant, and read in the audience of the people: and they said, All the Lord hath said will we do, and be obedient. And Moses took the blood, and sprinkled it on the people, and said, Behold the blood of the covenant, which the Lord hath made with you concerning all these words." (Exodus 24:6-8.) Moses was with the Lord forty days in the mount receiving these things, viz., the laws and covenants, the pattern of the ark and tabernacle, and the tables. (See Exodus 24-32.)

We here have a statement of the manner in which Aaron and his sons were set apart to administer in the Aaronic Priest's office, while yet under the Gospel; for we read, "And Aaron and his sons thou shalt bring unto the door of the tabernacle of the congregation, and shalt wash them with water. And thou shalt take the garments, and put upon Aaron the coat, and the robe of the ephod, and the ephod, and the breastplate, and gird him with the curious girdle of the ephod: and thou shalt put the mitre upon his head, and put the holy crown upon the mitre. Then shalt [7] thou take the anointing oil, and pour it upon his head, and anoint him. And thou shalt bring his sons, and put coats upon them. And thou shalt gird them with the girdles, Aaron and his sons, and put the bonnets on them: and the *Priest's office shall be theirs for a perpetual statute*: and THOU shalt consecrate Aaron and his sons." (Exodus 29:4-9.)

Further, "And thou shalt anoint them, as thou didst anoint their father, that they may minister unto me in the Priest's office: for their anointing shall surely be *an everlasting Priesthood throughout their generations*." (Exodus 40:15.) We find that in all this Moses was the chief actor. Sometime after, for certain reasons specified, Aaron was to be gathered to his people, and not to be permitted to enter the land, as stated. "Aaron shall be gathered unto his people: for he shall not enter into the land which I have given unto the children of Israel, because ye rebelled against my word at the water of Meribah. Take Aaron and Eleazar his son, and bring them up unto Mount Hor: and strip Aaron of his garments, and put them upon Eleazar his son: and Aaron shall be gathered unto his people, and shall die there. And Moses did as the Lord commanded: and they went up into Mount Hor in the sight of all the congregation. And Moses stripped Aaron of his garments, and put them upon Eleazar his son; and Aaron died there in the top of the mount: and Moses and Eleazar came down from the mount." (Numbers 20:24-28.)

What the sin was that Moses and Aaron committed does not distinctly appear, except it was in taking glory to themselves instead of giving God the glory. For God had commanded Moses to take the rod, he and Aaron, and smite the rock, which he did. In doing this, however, Moses said: "Hear now, ye rebels: must we fetch you water out of this rock? . . . And the Lord spake unto Moses and Aaron, Because ye believed me not, to sanctify me in the eyes of the children of Israel, therefore ye shall not bring this [8] congregation into the land which I have given them." (Numbers 20:10-12.) This is the water of Meribah (or strife) because the children of Israel strove with the Lord and he was sanctified in them. David, in referring to this, says: "They angered him also at the waters of strife, so that it went ill with Moses for their sakes: because they provoked his spirit, so that he spake unadvisedly with his lips." (Psalms 106:32-33.)

The same judgment afterwards overtook Moses, and also for the same reason. For, "The Lord said unto Moses, get thee up into this mount Abarim, and see the land which I have given unto the children of Israel. And when thou hast seen it, thou also shalt be gathered unto thy people, as Aaron thy brother was gathered. For ye rebelled against my commandment in the desert of Zin, in the strife of the congregation, to sanctify me at the water before their eyes, that is the water of Meribah, in Kadesh, in the wilderness of Zin." (Numbers 27:12-14; Deuteronomy 32:48-52.)

Moses plead with the Lord to have this sentence reversed, but the Lord would not grant his prayer. He said, "I pray thee, let me go over, and see the good land that is beyond Jordan, that goodly mountain, and Lebanon. But the Lord was wroth with me for your sakes, and would not hear me: and the Lord said unto me, Let it suffice thee; speak no more unto me of this matter, Get thee up into the top of Pisgah, and lift up thine eyes westward, and northward, and southward, and eastward, and behold it with thine eye; for thou shalt not go over this Jordan." (Deuteronomy 3:25-27.) And when Moses found that the Lord would not permit him to go to the goodly land, he still felt interested about the welfare of the people. For we read: "And Moses spake unto the Lord, saying, Let the Lord, the God of the spirits of all flesh, set a man over the congregation, which may go out before them, and which may go in before them, and which may lead them out, and which may bring them in; [9] that the congregation of the Lord be not as sheep which have no shepherd. And the Lord said unto Moses, Take thee Joshua, the son of Nun, a man in whom is the spirit, and lay thine hand upon him; and set him before Eleazar the Priest, and before all the congregation; and give him a charge in their sight. And thou shalt put *some* of thine honor upon him, that all the congregation of the children of Israel may be obedient. And he shall stand before Eleazar the Priest, who shall ask counsel for him after the judgment of Urim before the Lord: at his word shall they go out, and at his word they shall come in, *both* he, and all the children of Israel with him, even all the congregation. And Moses did as the Lord commanded him: and he took Joshua, and set him before Eleazar the Priest, and before all the congregation: and he laid his hands upon him, and gave him a charge, as the Lord commanded by the hand of Moses." (Numbers 27:15-23.)

In his day Moses was the law-giver and leader of the children of Israel. When he died some of Moses' honor was conferred upon Joshua, not all; Joshua then was to be under the priestly direction of Eleazar, the son of Aaron, who was to ask counsel for him after the judgment of Urim. Thus the lesser Priesthood began to bear rule in the person of Eleazar, the son of Aaron, although in operation it did not bear rule in Aaron's time. And while the keys and powers of the Melchizedek Priesthood was maintained in all its powers in the person of Eleazar. Joshua indeed led the people, but had not the gifts and powers of the Priesthood which Moses had, holding indeed the Melchizedek Priesthood, but possessing only *some of Moses' honor*.

Moses died, according to the chronological record of the Bible, in the year B.C. 1451. Upwards of three hundred years afterwards we find Eli officiating as Priest; and although he was a good man, he did not control his [10] sons, nor stop their iniquitous practices; for which he and his sons were reproved by the Lord. And Samuel took his place, and he selected and anointed Saul, who had, as Joshua, part of Moses' honor. And the Aaronic Priesthood continued to exercise its priestly power, more or less, until Christ; of which as appears, John was the *last legitimate High Priest*.

In the new translation the removal of the Melchizedek Priesthood is clearly defined as follows: "And the Lord said unto Moses: Hew thee two other tables of stone, like unto the first, and I will write upon them also, the words of the law, according as they were written at first on the tables which thou brakest: but it shall not be according to the first, for I will take away the priesthood out of their midst; therefore my holy order [or the Melchizedek], and the ordinances thereof, shall not go before them; for my presence shall not go up in their midst, lest I destroy them. But I will give unto them the law as at the first, but it shall be after the law of a carnal commandment; for I have sworn in my wrath, that they shall not enter into my presence, into my rest, in the days of their pilgrimage." (JST Exodus 34:1-2.)

The Lord said unto Moses: "Thou canst not see my face at this time, lest mine anger is kindled against thee also, and I destroy thee and thy people; for there shall no man among them see me at this time and live; for they are exceeding sinful. And no sinful man hath at any time; neither shall there be any sinful man at any time, that shall see my face and live." (JST Exodus 33:20.) He did, however, place him in the cleft of a rock, and covered him with His hand, and permitted him to see His back parts; but not His face. A little while before this, Moses and Aaron, Nadab and Abihu, and seventy of the Elders of Israel saw God, and did eat and drink. (Exodus 24:9-11.) But now Moses even, could not see his face, nor any of the people go near him, and when Moses had been a second time on the mount [11] and his face shone so that they could not look upon him, Moses had to put a veil on his face. (Exodus 34:29-35.)

Paul in referring to this says: "And not as Moses, which put a veil over his face, that the children of Israel could not steadfastly look to the end of that which is abolished: but their minds were blinded; for until this day remaineth the same veil untaken away in the reading of the Old Testament; which veil is done away in Christ. But even unto this day, when Moses is read, the veil is upon their heart. Nevertheless when it shall turn to the Lord, the veil shall be taken away." (2 Corinthians 3:13-16.)

From the foregoing, and from the whole history of the Aaronic Priesthood until the coming of Christ, it appears that, with the exception of some prominent prophets who held the Melchizedek Priesthood, as the direct gift of God, without, it would seem, the power to confer it upon others—not having an organization—there was very little of the manifestation of the gift and power of God among the people of the Jews, so that it might truly be said, "There arose not a prophet since in Israel like unto Moses, whom the Lord knew face to face, in all the signs and the wonders which the Lord sent him to do in the land of Egypt, to Pharaoh, and to all his servants, and to all his land; and in all that mighty hand, and in all that great terror, which Moses showed in the sight of all Israel." (Deuteronomy 34:10-12.)

From the foregoing it is evident:

First.—That the Melchizedek Priesthood was greater than the Aaronic, and that while it ruled, it controlled all matters pertaining to the government and instruction of the people, and that it organized and directed the Aaronic Priesthood, which was in reality an appendage to the greater.

Second.—That when the Melchizedek Priesthood was in a great measure withdrawn, as there was no regular organization of that Priesthood, it was left to a great extent to the guidance and direction of the Lord, [12] who, from time to time, inspired different men as Prophets, who came to the people with the word of the Lord, receiving their inspiration and calling directly from him, as Ezekiel, Isaiah, Jeremiah, Daniel and others. But that a portion of Moses' spirit rested upon Joshua, upon the seventy Elders of Israel, upon the Prophets in the days of Elijah, Elisha and others.

Third.—That the Aaronic Priesthood continued in its full force, having a complete organization, which it received under the hands of Moses, or through the Melchizedek Priesthood.

Fourth.—That the Aaronic Priesthood, being continued, it held the Urim and Thummim, and gave direction to Joshua, who was set apart by Moses, and to Saul, David, Solomon and others, who were anointed and set apart to their kingly power, and to rule over and to lead and direct Israel, and that this state of things continued until Christ. The High Priests of the Aaronic Priesthood being the acknowledged representatives of God, holding the priestly power: whilst the kings were anointed by them, or by their priestly authority, and the kings and rulers had to get the word of the Lord from the Aaronic Priesthood, or through the Urim and Thummim.

Fifth.—It is further evident that this Priesthood became, in many instances, very corrupt, and incurred the displeasure of God, and that many of the kings also, though anointed, perverted their office and calling, and instead of being the protectors and saviors of Israel, helped to lead them astray.

Sixth.—It is evident that all the Aaronic Priesthood did not have the Urim and Thummim, nor did they call, anoint and direct kings, or bear rule in the nation. But only the High Priest—one man—and that one man presided over and directed the action of the kings, telling them when to go out to war, and when not to go, and giving unto them the word of the Lord through the Urim and Thummim. [13]

Seventh.—That they only had one tabernacle, one ark of the covenant, or one temple at one time; and not as we, many stakes, many temples, and many services. But then they, when Moses left, were under the Aaronic, and we are under the Melchizedek Priesthood; they were under the law and the Mosaic dispensation; we are under the Gospel, and in the dispensation of the fullness of time, and have consequently labors and duties to perform which did not belong to them.

It may be proper here to remark that there was a council, called a "senate of the children of Israel." (Acts 5:21.) The High Priest called this council together. The council, it is said, was composed of seventy men or judges, and to have taken its rise from the installment of the seventy Elders spoken of in Numbers 11:16-17. They were to be known by Moses to be Elders of the people and officers over them—"Able men, such as fear God, men of truth, hating covetousness"—a portion of Moses' spirit was to be given unto them, and they were to help him to bear the burdens of the people. As Saul was anointed by Samuel to be captain over the Lord's inheritance, and the Spirit of the Lord was to come upon him, and he was to prophesy and be turned into another man. (See 1 Samuel 10:6.) And God gave him another heart, and all the signs came to pass that day, and he prophesied.

This senate or council was known by the name of the Sanhedrin, and it is said, sat in the form of a half moon. This council is spoken of in John 11:47-52. "Then gathered the Chief Priests and Pharisees a council. . . . And one of them named Caiaphas, the High Priest, said . . . it is expedient for us that one man should die for the people. . . . And this spake he not of himself; but being High Priest that year, he prophesied that Jesus should die for that nation, and not for that nation only; but that also he should gather together in one the children of God that [14] were scattered abroad." "Now Caiaphas was he which gave counsel to the Jews, that it was expedient that one man should die for the people." (John 18:14.) This council had not the power of death. (v. 31; See also Acts 4, 5 and 6.) About this Sanhedrin there is little or nothing said in the Old Testament nor of the organization of this court. It is thought by some it existed after the captivity, or in the days of the Maccabees only.

There is another remarkable thing about the Aaronic Priesthood, or at least about the only action of Aaron, as an associate of Moses. When Moses was first called upon to deliver Israel from Egyptian

ITEMS ON THE PRIESTHOOD 335

bondage, he told the Lord that they would not believe him, nor hearken unto his voice, and Moses was told to cast his rod upon the ground, and it became a serpent, and he fled from before it; but when the Lord told Moses to take it by the tail, and he caught it, it became a rod again. Then the Lord told him to put his hand into his bosom, and when he took it out it was leprous. He was told to put it into his bosom again, and it was restored and like his other flesh. Still, Moses was unconvinced and said, "O my Lord, I am not eloquent, neither heretofore, nor since thou hast spoken unto thy servant; but I am slow of speech and of a slow tongue. And the Lord said unto him, Who hath made man's mouth? or who maketh the dumb, or deaf, or the seeing, or the blind? have not I the Lord? Now therefore, go, and I will be with thy mouth, and teach thee what thou shalt say." (Exodus 4:10-12.) Yet Moses was not satisfied and shrank from his mission, and said: "O my Lord, send, I pray thee, by the hand of *him* whom thou wilt send. And the anger of the Lord was kindled against Moses, and he said, Is not Aaron the Levite thy brother? I know that he can speak well. And also, behold, he cometh forth to meet thee: and when he seeth thee, he will be glad in his heart. And thou shalt speak unto him, and put words in his mouth: and I will [15] be with thy mouth, and with his mouth, and will teach you what ye shall do. And he shall be thy spokesman unto the people: and he shall be, even he shall be to thee instead of a mouth, and thou shalt be to him instead of God. And thou shalt take this rod in thine hand, wherewith thou shalt do signs." (See the whole of Exodus chapter 4.)

From the above it would seem that if Moses would have done as the Lord requested him, Aaron would not have been called. Moses shrank from the responsibility; and though the Lord was angry with him yet he gave unto him a helper in Aaron. A revelation through the Prophet Joseph Smith says: "Now this Moses plainly taught to the children of Israel in the wilderness, and sought diligently to sanctify his people that they might behold the face of God; but they hardened their hearts and could not endure his presence, therefore, the Lord in his wrath (for his anger was kindled against them) swore that they should not enter into his rest while in the wilderness, which rest is the fullness of his glory. Therefore he took Moses out of their midst, and the Holy Priesthood also; and the lesser Priesthood continued, which Priesthood holdeth the key of the ministering of angels and the preparatory Gospel, which Gospel is the Gospel of repentance and of baptism, and the remission of sins, and the law of carnal commandments, which the Lord in his wrath, caused to continue with the house of Aaron among the children of Israel until John, whom God raised up, being filled with the Holy Ghost from his mother's womb; for he was baptized while he was yet in his childhood, and was ordained by the angel of God at the time he was eight days old unto this power, to overthrow the kingdom of the Jews, and to make straight the way of the Lord, before the face of his people to prepare them for the coming of the Lord, in whose hand is given all power." (D&C 84:23-28.) Again, Paul says, "If therefore perfection were [16] by the Levitical Priesthood, (for under it the people received the law,) what further need was there that another Priest should rise after the order of Melchizedek, and not be called after the order of Aaron? For the Priesthood being changed, there is made of necessity a change also of the law." (Hebrews 7:11-12; See also chapters 8, 9 and 10.) John the Baptist came as the forerunner of Christ, and baptized him as stated. "Then cometh Jesus from Galilee to Jordan unto John, to be baptized of him. But John forbade him, saying, I have need to be baptized of thee, and comest thou to me? And Jesus answering said unto him, Suffer it to be so now: for thus it becometh us to fulfill all righteousness. Then he suffered him. And Jesus, when he was baptized, went up straightway out of the water: and lo, the heavens were opened unto him, and he saw the spirit of God descending like a dove, and lighting upon him: and lo, a voice from heaven, saying, This is my beloved Son, in whom I am well pleased." (Matthew 3:13-17.) On inquiry being made, Jesus said of John the Baptist, "Verily I say unto you, Among them that are born of women, there hath not risen a greater than John the Baptist; notwithstanding he that is least in the kingdom of heaven is greater than he." (Matthew 11:11.) Again Jesus said, "And if ye will receive it, this is Elias which was for to come. He that hath ears to hear, let him hear." (vs. 14-15.) But they would not receive it: they beheaded John and crucified Jesus; hence the restoration, the mission of Elias was postponed until he appeared to Joseph Smith and Oliver Cowdery in the Kirtland Temple. (D&C 110.) At which time Elijah came, as Malachi says: "Behold, I will send you Elijah the prophet before the coming of the great and dreadful day of the Lord: and he shall turn the heart of the fathers to the children, and the heart of the children to the fathers, lest I come and smite the earth with a curse." (Malachi 4:5-6.)

It seems from the foregoing that Moses had the [17] greater or Melchizedek Priesthood; that when he was taken, the keys went with him; that the Aaronic Priesthood ruled until Christ, and the people were under the law; that when Christ came he introduced a better covenant and restored the Gospel; and that the Bishopric was, and the Aaronic Priesthood is, under the Melchizedek, and an appendage thereto, as are also all Elders appendages to the Melchizedek Priesthood; and it is also evident that the Presidency of that Priesthood presides over all, as did Melchizedek, Moses, Joseph Smith, etc., with Jesus at the head, as the great Presiding High Priest.

But if, as Paul says, the Priesthood being changed, then is made of necessity a change also of the law; or in other words, a change from the law of carnal commandments and ordinances to the law of the Gospel. Yet the Aaronic Priesthood, as the Melchizedek is an everlasting Priesthood, as before exhibited, and continueth forever as an appendage to the Melchizedek Priesthood; and hence in the old apostolic days, when under an organization of the Melchizedek, the latter is the most prominent, and very little is said about the Levitical or Aaronic: probably on account of the peculiar traditions and superstitions of the Jews, which made it almost impossible for them to comprehend the greater or Melchizedek. Yet the Aaronic cannot be ignored, and in the dispensation of the fullness of times it again comes forth, as one of the grand aids or appendages to the Melchizedek Priesthood; and hence in the ushering in of this dispensation, John the Baptist appears on the stage and confers the Aaronic Priesthood upon Joseph Smith and Oliver Cowdery.

Having therefore traced out these two Priesthoods, principally from the old Scriptures, we now turn to the revelations given by Joseph Smith in the introduction of the Priesthood, as revealed by the Latter-day Prophet in the ushering in of the dispensation of the fullness of times. [18]

CHAPTER 2

PRINCIPALLY ON

THE AARONIC PRIESTHOOD OR BISHOPRIC

THE AARONIC PRIESTHOOD CONFERRED

Words of the Angel, John, (the Baptist,) spoken to Joseph Smith, Jr., and Oliver Cowdery, as he (the angel) laid his hands upon their heads and ordained them to the Aaronic Priesthood, in Harmony, Susquehanna County, Pennsylvania, May 15, 1829:

"Upon you, my fellow servants, in the name of Messiah, I confer the Priesthood of Aaron, which holds the keys of the ministering of angels, and of the Gospel of repentance, and of baptism by immersion for the remission of sins; and this shall never be taken again from the earth, until the sons of Levi do offer again an offering unto the Lord in righteousness." (D&C 13.)

We quote from some of the first revelations given to the Prophet Joseph Smith upon this subject. "Every President of the High Priesthood (or Presiding Elder,) Bishop, High Councilor, and High Priest, is to be ordained by the direction of a High Council or General Conference. Presiding Elders, Traveling Bishops, High Councilors, High Priests, and Elders, may have the privilege of ordaining where there is no branch of the Church." (D&C 20:67-66.) At this time

Presidents of the High Priesthood, Presiding Elders, Bishops, High Councilors, and High Priests were placed on the same footing. It may be observed that Traveling Bishops are here referred to. These were given for the regulation of the newly organized branches or churches.

From the above we learn: That before the appointment of Bishops there were revelations given [19] and arrangements made for this office. Whilst the following teaches us:

That certain men among the Saints should be appointed by the voice of the Church to look after the poor and needy, and to govern the affairs of the property of the Church. "And now I give unto the Church in these parts, a commandment that certain men among them shall be appointed, and they shall be appointed by the voice of the Church; and they shall look to the poor and the needy, and administer to their relief, that they shall not suffer; and send them forth to the place which I have commanded them." (D&C 38:34-35.) The place referred to at that time was Kirtland, Geauga Co., Ohio. (v. 32.)

Edward Partridge was ordained a Bishop—the first Bishop in the Church–and was called February 4, 1831. He was to *spend all his time in the labors of the Church*. We quote: "And again, I have called my servant Edward Partridge, and give a commandment, that he should be appointed by the voice of the Church, and ordained a Bishop unto the Church, to leave his merchandise and to spend all his time in the labors of the Church: to see to all things as it shall be appointed unto him, in my laws in the day that I shall give them." (D&C 41:9-10.) He was to "see to all things, as it *shall be appointed unto him, in my laws*" [Who was to give these laws?] "in the day that I shall give them."

Newel K. Whitney was the second Bishop—called *to be* a Bishop, December 4, 1831. "And now, verily I say unto you, my servant Newel K. Whitney is the man who shall be appointed and ordained unto this power. Even so. Amen." (D&C 72:8.) "And again, I say unto you, that my servant Edward Partridge shall stand in the office wherewith I have appointed him. And it shall come to pass, that if he transgresses, another shall be appointed in his stead. Even so. Amen." (D&C 42:10; February 9, 1831.) [20]

Property was to be consecrated for the poor, and laid before the Bishop and his counselors, who are to be two Elders or High Priests. (See D&C 42:30-31.) The residue was to be kept in a storehouse for the poor and needy, as shall be appointed by the High Council and the Bishop and his Council and for *purchasing Church lands, building houses of worship,* building up the New Jerusalem; of course he was to act as a general Bishop of the Church (he was not confined to a ward), to receive and distribute property, appoint stewardships, etc. It will be perceived that the High Council then had a voice in these matters. It is written:

"And inasmuch as ye impart of your substance unto the poor, ye will do it unto me, and they shall be laid before the Bishop of my Church and his Counselors, two of the Elders, or High Priests, such as he shall or has set apart for that purpose. And it shall come to pass, that after they are laid before the Bishop of my Church, and after that he has received these testimonies concerning the consecration of the properties of my Church, that they cannot be taken from the Church agreeable to my commandments; every man shall be made accountable unto me, a steward over his own property, or that which he has received by consecration, inasmuch as is sufficient for himself and family. And again, if there shall be properties in the hands of the Church, or any individuals of it, more than is necessary for their support, after this first consecration, which is a residue to be consecrated unto the Bishop, it shall be kept to administer to those who have not, from time to time, that every man who has need may be amply supplied, and receive according to his wants. Therefore the residue shall be kept in my storehouse, to administer to the poor and the needy, as shall be appointed by the High Council of the Church, and the Bishop and his Council. And for the purpose of purchasing lands for the public benefit of the Church, and building houses of worship, and building up of [21] the New Jerusalem which is hereafter to be revealed." (D&C 42:31-35.)

The Bishop was to receive his support, and also his Counselors, or a remuneration for services. We read: "And the Elders, or High Priests who are appointed to assist the Bishop, as Counselors in all things, are to have their families supported out of the property which is consecrated to the Bishop, for the good of the poor, and for other purposes, as before mentioned; or they are to receive a just remuneration for all their services, either a stewardship or otherwise, as may be thought best or decided by the Counselors and Bishop, and the Bishop, also, shall receive his support, or a just remuneration for all his services in the Church." (D&C 42:71-72.)

"And unto the Bishop of the Church, and unto such as God shall appoint and ordain to watch over the Church, and to be Elders unto the Church, are to have it given unto them to discern all those gifts." (D&C 46:27.) Certain gifts were here referred to. Not only Bishops but Elders were to have this power. We further find that Edward Partridge was to appoint unto this people their portion—every man equal, giving him a writing—and every man was to deal honestly, and be and receive alike; one Church must not use the money of another Church without making arrangements to pay it. A storehouse was to be appointed. The Bishop was to receive unto himself and family what was needed for his wants, and for those of his family. This was to be an example unto Edward Partridge, and to all Churches.

"And let my servant, Edward Partridge, when he shall appoint a man his portion, give unto him a writing that shall secure unto him his portion. . . . And let that which belongeth to this people not be taken and given unto that of another Church; wherefore, if another Church would receive money of this Church let them pay unto this Church again according as they shall agree; and this shall be done through [22] the Bishop or the agent which shall be appointed by the voice of the Church. And again, let the Bishop appoint a storehouse unto this Church, and let all things, both in money and in meat, which is more than is needful for the want of this people, be kept in the hands of the Bishop. And let him also reserve unto himself for his own wants, and for the wants of his family, as he shall be employed in doing this business. And thus I grant unto this people a privilege or organizing themselves according to my laws; and I consecrate unto them this land for a little season, until I, the Lord, shall provide for them otherwise, and command them to go hence; and the hour and the day is not given unto them, wherefore let them act upon this land as for years, and this shall turn unto them for their good. Behold this shall be an example unto my servant Edward Partridge, in other places, in all Churches." (D&C 51:4, 10-18.)

First.—From the above we find that bishops were first spoken of as early as April, 1830. (See D&C 20.)

Second.—Certain men were to be appointed to look after the poor and administer to their relief and govern the affairs of the property of the Church. (See D&C 38: 34-36, January 2, 1831.)

Third.—Edward Partridge was called to be the first Bishop, (See D&C 41:9, February 1831,) "and to spend *all his time* in the labors of the Church."

Fourth.—That Newel K. Whitney was called and appointed to this office as the second Bishop of this Church.

Fifth.—After this, besides Bishops' agents, there were other Bishops appointed. George Miller was appointed to the Bishopric, and had it sealed upon his head.

"I therefore say unto you, I seal upon his head the office of a Bishopric, like unto my servant Edward Partridge, that he may receive the consecrations of mine house, that he may administer blessings upon the [23] heads of the poor of my people, saith the Lord. Let no man despise my servant George, for he shall honor me." (D&C 124:21.)

Also, "He who is appointed to administer spiritual things, the same is worthy of his hire, even as those who are appointed to a stewardship to administer in temporal things." (D&C 70:12.)

There seems to be a difference in the duties of Bishops; Brother Miller's was to be like Edward Partridge's whose duties are distinctly marked out as follows: "And again, verily I say unto you, my servant George Miller is without guile; he may be trusted because of the integrity of his heart; and for the love which he has to my testimony I, the Lord, love him." (D&C 124:20; See also verse 21.)

At the same time and in the same manner Vinson Knight, Samuel H. Smith, and Shadrach Roundy were appointed to preside over the Bishopric.

"And again, I say unto you, I give unto you Vinson Knight, Samuel H. Smith, and Shadrach Roundy, if he will receive it, to preside over the Bishopric; a knowledge of said Bishopric is given unto you in the Book of Doctrine and Covenants." (D&C 124:141.) Vinson Knight was a Bishop, the two others were of course his Counselors.

We find from the foregoing and from what follows that there were several kinds of Bishops, as well as Bishops' agents. Bishop Edward Partridge was appointed to preside over the Saints in Zion, to purchase lands, divide inheritances, and sit as a judge in Israel, as a general Bishop to that district of country, and he had a special agent to assist him, viz., Sidney Gilbert.

Items on the Priesthood 343

Bishop Whitley was appointed Bishop in Kirtland, Ohio, yet he had charge of all the Churches in the eastern country, as a general Bishop. Neither of these, at that time, were presiding Bishops over the Bishopric. George Miller was appointed to fill the place of Edward Partridge and officiate in the same order of Bishopric. [24]

Vinson Knight was appointed to preside over the Bishopric with Samuel H. Smith and Shadrach Roundy for counselors, and at the same time that George Miller was appointed to take the place of Edward Partridge. Then there were Alanson Ripley and others. Sidney Gilbert was to be an agent unto this Church in the place that shall be appointed by the Bishop. (D&C 53:4.)

"And let my servant Sidney Gilbert stand in the office which I have appointed round about, inasmuch as can be in righteousness, and as wisdom shall direct. . . . And again, verily I say unto you, let my servant Sidney Gilbert plant himself in this place, and establish a store, that he may sell goods *without fraud*, that he may obtain money to buy lands for the good of the Saints, and that he may obtain whatsoever things the disciples may need to plant them in their inheritances." (D&C 57:6, 8.)

The Lord says Edward Partridge was also to "stand in the office which I have appointed him, to divide the Saints their inheritance, even as I have commanded; and also those whom he has appointed to assist him. . . . Let the Bishop and the agent make preparations for those families which have been commanded to come to this land, as soon as possible, and plant them in their inheritance." (D&C 57:7, 15.) "I have selected my servant Edward Partridge, and have appointed unto him his mission in this land; but if he repent not of his sins, which are unbelief and blindness of heart, let him take heed lest he fall. Behold his mission is given unto him, and it shall not be given again. And whoso standeth in his mission is appointed to be a judge in Israel, like as it was in ancient days, to divide the lands of the heritage of God unto his children, and to judge his people by the testimony of the just, and by the assistance of his Counselors, according to the laws of the king[25]dom which are given by the Prophets of God; for verily I say unto you, my law shall be kept on this land. Let no man think he is ruler, but let God rule him that judgeth, according to the counsel of his own will; or, in other words him that counseleth or sitteth upon the judgment seat." (D&C 58:14-20.) "Let the residue of the Elders . . .

hold a conference;" and Edward Partridge was empowered to direct the conference which should be held by certain Elders. (D&C 58:61-62.)

"And let my servant Edward Partridge impart of the money which I have given him, a portion unto mine Elders who are commanded to return." (D&C 60:10-11.) If not able, they were not required to return it.

"Let my servant Newel K. Whitney retain his store, or in other words, the store yet for a little season. Nevertheless let him impart all the money which he can impart, to be sent up unto the land of Zion. Behold these things are in his own hands, let him do according to wisdom. Verily I say, let him be ordained as an agent unto the disciples that shall tarry, and let him be ordained unto this power." (D&C 43:42-45.) It would seem from the above that Bishop Whitney was not yet a Bishop when he was ordained to be an agent.

"And even the Bishop, who is a judge, and his Counselors, if they are not faithful in their stewardships, shall be condemned, and others shall be planted in their stead." (D&C 64:40.)

We find from the following that Bishops must be selected from the High Priests and be set apart to the Bishopric.

"There remaineth hereafter, in the due time of the Lord, other Bishops to be set apart unto the Church, to minister even according to the first; wherefore they shall be High Priests who are worthy, and they shall be appointed by the First Presidency of the Melchizedek Priesthood, except they be literal descendants of [26] Aaron. And if they be literal descendants of Aaron, they have a legal right to the Bishopric, if they are the first born among the sons of Aaron; for the firstborn hold the right of the *Presidency* over this Priesthood, and the *keys* or authority of the same. No man has a legal right to this office to hold the *keys* of this Priesthood, except he be a literal descendant and the firstborn of Aaron; but as a High Priest of the Melchizedek Priesthood has authority to officiate in all the lesser offices, he may officiate in the office of Bishop when no literal descendant of Aaron can be found, provided he is called, and set apart and ordained unto this power under the hands of the First Presidency of the Melchizedek Priesthood. And a literal descendant of Aaron, also, must be designated by this Presidency and found worthy, and anointed, and ordained under the hands of this Presidency, otherwise they are not legally authorized to officiate in their Priesthood; but by virtue of the decree concerning their right of the Priesthood descending from father to son, they may claim their anointing, if at any time they can prove their lineage, or do ascertain it by revelation from the Lord under the hands of the above named Presidency. And again, no Bishop or High Priest who shall be set apart for this ministry, shall be tried or condemned for any crime save it be before the First Presidency of the Church; and inasmuch as he is found guilty before this Presidency, by testimony that cannot be impeached, he shall be condemned." (D&C 68:14-23.)

We may here notice, as elsewhere referred to, that it is the Presidency of the Aaronic Priesthood that is above spoken of, that must be set apart by the First Presidency, and also tried by them, whether of lineal descent or High Priests. Newel K. Whitney was appointed and ordained a Bishop. (See D&C 72:8.) "Let my servant Newel K. Whitney, and my servant Joseph Smith, Jr., and my servant Sidney Rigdon, sit in council with the Saints which are in Zion." (D&C 78:9.) [27] Thus it seems that though Bishop Whitney was Bishop of Kirtland, he sat in council with the Saints which were in Zion, associated with Joseph Smith and Sidney Rigdon, thus showing that he was not a ward but a general Church Bishop.

"Therefore, verily I say unto you, that it is expedient for my servant Alam, and Ahashdah, (Newel K. Whitney,) Mahalaleel, and Pelagoram, (Sidney Rigdon,) and my servant Gazelam, (Joseph Smith,) and Horah, Olihah, (Oliver Cowdery,) and Shalemanasseh and Mehemson, (Martin Harris,) to be bound together by a bond and covenant that cannot be broken by transgression, (*except judgment shall* immediately follow,) in your several stewardships, *to manage the affairs of the poor, and all things pertaining to the Bishopric*, both in the land of Zion and in the land of Shinehah (Kirtland.)" (D&C 82:11-12.)

This proves that President Joseph Smith and his Counselor Sidney Rigdon were authorized to supervise temporal matters in the Church as well as the Bishop or with him. Here the Melchizedek Priesthood is united with the Aaronic to manage the Bishopric in both lands. We continue our quotations: "Every man seeking the interest of his neighbor, and doing all things with an eye single to the glory of God." (D&C 82:19.)

"Which Abraham received the Priesthood from Melchizedek who received it through the lineage of his fathers, even till Noah and from Noah till Enoch, through the lineage of their fathers; and from Enoch to Abel, who was slain by the conspiracy of his brother who received the Priesthood by the commandments of God, by the hand of his father Adam, who was the first man—which Priesthood continueth in the Church of God in all generations, and is without beginning of days or end of years. And the Lord confirmed a Priesthood also upon Aaron and his seed, throughout all their generations—which Priesthood also continueth and abideth forever with the Priesthood, which is after the [28] holiest order of God. And this greater Priesthood administereth the Gospel and holdeth the key of the mysteries of the Kingdom, even the key of the knowledge of God; therefore, in the ordinances thereof, the power of Godliness is manifest, and without the ordinances thereof, and the authority of the Priesthood, the power of Godliness is not manifest unto men in the flesh; for without this no man can see the face of God even the Father, and live. Now this Moses plainly taught to the children of Israel in the wilderness, and sought diligently to sanctify his people that they might behold the face of God; but they hardened their hearts and could not endure his presence, therefore the Lord in his wrath (for his anger was kindled against them) swore that they should not enter into his rest while in the wilderness which rest is the fullness of his glory. Therefore he took Moses out of their midst, and the Holy Priesthood also." (D&C 84:14-25.)

We have already shown that there was a Priesthood conferred upon Aaron and his seed throughout all their generations. It becomes a question what Priesthood Aaron had before he had bestowed upon him what is termed the Aaronic Priesthood, when he administered with Moses? "The greater Priesthood administereth the Gospel and holdeth the key of the mysteries of the Kingdom even the key of the knowledge of God." (v. 19.)

Frederick G. Williams was called and appointed a High Priest and Counselor to Joseph Smith. His call reads as follows:

"Verily, verily I say unto you, my servant Frederick G. Williams, listen to the voice of him who speaketh, to the word of the Lord your God, and hearken to the calling wherewith you are called, even to be a High Priest in my Church and a Counselor unto my servant Joseph

Smith, Jr., unto whom I have given the keys of the Kingdom, *which belongeth always unto the Presidency of the High Priesthood*: therefore, verily, I acknowledge him and will bless [29] him and also thee, inasmuch as thou art faithful in counsel, in the office which I have appointed unto you in prayer always vocally and in thy heart, in public and in private, also in thy ministry in proclaiming the Gospel in the land of the living, and among thy brethren." (D&C 81:1-3.)

From the following we find that God took Moses from the midst of the children of Israel and also the Holy or Melchizedek Priesthood, leaving the lesser, or the Aaronic Priesthood. "Therefore, he took Moses out of their midst, and the Holy Priesthood also; and the lesser Priesthood continued, which Priesthood holdeth the key of the ministering of angels and the preparatory Gospel, which Gospel is the Gospel of repentance and of baptism, and the remission of sins, and the law of carnal commandments, which the Lord in his wrath, caused to continue with the house of Aaron among the children of Israel until John, whom God raised up, being filled with the Holy Ghost from his mother's womb; for he was baptized while he was yet in his childhood, and was ordained by the angel of God at the time he was eight days old unto this power, to overthrow the kingdom of the Jews, and to make straight the way of the Lord before the face of his people, to prepare them for the coming of the Lord, in whose hand is given all power. And again, *the offices of Elder and Bishop are* necessary appendages belonging unto the High Priesthood." (D&C 84:25-29.) From this, it would seem that the law of carnal commandments was a curse. Paul said the law was added because of transgression. ("It was added because of transgressions till the seed should come to whom the promise was made." Galatians 3:19.) And that it was a yoke which neither they nor their fathers were able to bear; and that Christ came to fulfill the law and introduce the Gospel which was greater—a higher law and a greater Priesthood, viz: the Melchizedek.

Both Elders and Bishops are appendages to the [30] High Priesthood. "And again, the offices of Teacher and Deacon are necessary appendages belonging to the lesser Priesthood." (D&C 84:30); thus Elders and Bishops are appendages to the High Priesthood, while Teachers and Deacons are appendages to the lesser, which lesser is an appendage to the higher or Melchizedek. "Therefore, as I said concerning the sons of Moses—for the sons of

Moses, and also the sons of Aaron shall offer an acceptable offering and sacrifice in the house of the Lord, which house shall be built unto the Lord in this generation, upon the consecrated spot as I have appointed." (D&C 84:31.) When both of these Priesthoods are carried out and united in their purity, the glory of the Lord will be manifested upon Mount Zion, in the Lord's house, both operating according to their callings, position and authority. For it is written, "And the sons of Moses and Aaron shall be filled with the glory of the Lord, upon Mount Zion, in the Lord's house, whose sons are ye; and also many whom I have called and sent forth to build up my Church; for whoso is faithful unto the obtaining these two Priesthoods, of which I have spoken, and the magnifying their calling are sanctified by the Spirit unto the renewing of their bodies; they become the sons of Moses and of Aaron and the seed of Abraham, and the Church and Kingdom, and the elect of God; and also all they who receive this Priesthood receiveth me, saith the Lord; for he that receiveth my servants receiveth me; and he that receiveth me receiveth my Father; and he that receiveth my Father receiveth my Father's Kingdom; therefore all that my Father hath shall be given unto him; and this is according to the oath and covenant which belongeth to the Priesthood. Therefore, all those who receive the Priesthood, receive this oath and covenant of my Father which he cannot break, neither can it be moved; but whoso breaketh this covenant, after he hath received it, and altogether turneth therefrom, shall not have forgiveness [31] of sins in this world nor in the world to come. And all those who come not unto this Priesthood which ye have received, which I now confirm upon you who are present this day, by mine own voice out of the heavens, and even I have given the heavenly hosts and mine angels charge concerning you." (D&C 84:32-42.)

"And let all those who have not families, who receive moneys, send it up unto the Bishop in Zion, or unto the Bishop in Ohio, that it may be consecrated for the bringing forth of the revelations and the printing thereof, and for establishing Zion." (D&C 84:104.)

In the same revelation "unto Joseph Smith, Jun., and six Elders," it is written: "Therefore, take with you those who are ordained unto the lesser Priesthood, and send them before you to make appointments, and prepare the way, and to fill appointments that you yourselves are not able to fill. Behold, this is the way that mine

Apostles, in ancient days, built up my Church unto me.[1] Also the body hath need of every member, that all may be edified together, that the system may be kept perfect." (D&C 84:107-108, 110.)

We further quote: "For the body is not one member, but many. . . . And the eye cannot say unto the hand, I have no need of thee: nor again the head to the feet, I have no need of you." (1 Corinthians 12:14, 21.)

"And the Bishop, Newel K. Whitney, also, should travel round about and among all the Churches, searching after the poor to administer to their wants by humbling the rich and the proud; he should also employ an agent to take charge and to do his secular business as he shall direct." (D&C 84:112-113.) Thus High Priests, Seventies, Elders, Bishops, and all men holding the Priesthood were to be actively engaged in magnifying their Priesthood. [32]

"It is the duty of the Lord's clerk, whom he has appointed, to keep a history, and a General Church Record of all things that transpire in Zion, and of all those who consecrate properties, and receive inheritances legally from the Bishop; and also their manner of life, their faith, and works; and also of all the apostates who apostatize after receiving their inheritances. It is contrary to the will and commandment of God, that those who receive not their inheritance by consecration, agreeably to his law, which he has given, that he may tithe his people, to prepare them against the day of vengeance and burning, should have their names enrolled with the people of God; neither is their genealogy to be kept, or to be had where it may be found on any of the records or history of the Church; their name shall not be found, neither the names of the fathers, nor the names of the children written in the book of the law of God, saith the Lord of Hosts. Yea, thus saith the still small voice, which whispereth through and pierceth all things, and often times it maketh my bones to quake while it maketh manifest, saying: And it shall come to pass that I, the Lord God, will send one mighty and strong, holding the sceptre of power in his hand, clothed with light for a covering, whose mouth shall utter words, eternal words; while his bowels shall be a fountain of truth, to set in order the house of God, and to arrange by lot the inheritances of the Saints, whose names are found, and the names of their fathers, and of their children, enrolled in the book of the law of

---

1 Why should not this be the way now?

God: while that man, who was called of God and appointed, that putteth forth his hand to steady the ark of God, shall fall by the shaft of death, like as a tree that is smitten by the vivid shaft of lightning; and all they who are not found written in the book of remembrance, shall find none inheritance in that day, but they shall be cut asunder, and their portion shall be appointed them among unbelievers, where are wailing and gnashing of teeth. These things I say not of myself; there[33]fore, as the Lord speaketh, he will also fulfill. And they who are of the High Priesthood, whose names are not found written in the book of the law, or that are found to have apostatized, or to have been cut off from the Church; as well as the lesser Priesthood, or the members, in that day, shall not find an inheritance among the Saints of the Most High; therefore it shall be done unto them as unto the children of the Priest, as will be found in the second chapter and sixty-first and second verses of Ezra." (D&C 85.)

"And let the Bishop search diligently to obtain an agent, and let it be a man who has got riches in store, a man of God, and of strong faith, that thereby he may be enabled to discharge every debt; that the storehouse of the Lord may not be brought into disrepute before the eyes of the people." (D&C 90:22-23.)

"Nevertheless, I am not well pleased with many things, and I am not well pleased with my servant William E. McLellin, neither with my servant Sidney Gilbert, and the Bishop also, and others have many things to repent of; but verily I say unto you, that I, the Lord, will contend with Zion, and plead with her strong ones, and chasten her until she overcomes and is clean before me; for she shall not be removed out of her place. I, the Lord, have spoken it. Amen." (D&C 90:35-37.)

"My servant Newel K. Whitney, also a Bishop of my Church, hath need to be chastened and set in order his family, and see that they are more diligent and concerned at home, and pray always, or they shall be removed out of their place." (D&C 93:50.)

"Therefore let my servant Newel K. Whitney take charge of the place which is named among you, upon which I design to build mine holy house; and again, let it be divided in lots according to wisdom, for the benefit of those who seek inheritances, as it shall be [34] determined in council among you." (D&C 96:2-3.)

"And again, I say unto you, it is contrary to my commandment and my will, that my servant Sidney Gilbert[2] should sell my storehouse which I have appointed unto my people, into the hand of mine enemies. Let not that which I have appointed be polluted by mine enemies, by the consent of those who call themselves after my name; for this is a very sore and grievous sin against me, and against my people, in consequence of those things which I have decreed and are soon to befall the nations. Therefore, it is my will that my people should claim, and hold claim upon that which I have appointed unto them, though they should not be permitted to dwell thereon." (D&C 101:96-99.)

"There are, in the Church, two Priesthoods, namely, the Melchizedek, and Aaronic, including the Levitical Priesthood. Why the first is called the Melchizedek Priesthood is because Melchizedek was such a great High Priest. Before his day it was called *the Holy Priesthood after the order of the Son of God*; but out of respect or reverence to the name of the Supreme Being, to avoid the too frequent repetition of his name, they, the Church, in ancient days, called that Priesthood after Melchizedek, or the Melchizedek Priesthood. *All other authorities or offices* in the Church *are appendages* to this Priesthood: but there are two divisions or grand heads—one is the Melchizedek Priesthood, and the other is the Aaronic or Levitical Priesthood. The office of an Elder comes under the Priesthood of Melchizedek. The Melchizedek Priesthood holds the right of Presidency, and has power and authority over all the offices in the Church, in all ages of the world to administer in spiritual things. *The Presidency of the High Priesthood, after the order of Melchizedek, have a right to officiate in all the offices in the Church.*" (D&C 107:1-9.) [35]

Thus the Melchizedek Priesthood holds the right of Presidency, and has power and authority over all the offices in the Church, to administer in spiritual things, while the Presidency of the High Priesthood has a right to officiate in ALL the offices in the Church.

"This is the duty of a Bishop who is not a literal descendant of Aaron, but has been ordained to the High Priesthood after the order of Melchizedek. Thus shall he be a judge, even a common judge among the inhabitants of Zion, or in a Stake of Zion, or in any branch of the Church where he shall be set apart unto this ministry, until the

---

2 This is the Bishop's Agent

borders of Zion are enlarged, and it becomes necessary to have other Bishops or judges in Zion, or elsewhere." (D&C 107:73-75; See all of this section.)

He was to be a common judge among the inhabitants of Zion, or in a Stake of Zion, or in a branch of the Church, *when he shall be set apart unto his ministry*. His Bishopric is sufficient for any of these places when set apart: and he can only fill those offices for which he is set apart. But a literal descendant of Aaron has a legal right to the Presidency of this Priesthood, to *the keys* of this ministry, to act in the office of Bishop, without Counselors, except in a case when a President of the High Priesthood is tried.

We have the following on tithing: "Verily, thus saith the Lord, I require all their surplus property to be put into the hands of the Bishop of my Church of Zion, for the building of mine house, and for the laying of the foundation of Zion, and for the Priesthood, and for the debts of the Presidency of my Church; and this shall be the beginning of the tithing of my people: and after that, those who have been thus tithed, shall pay one-tenth of all their interest annually; and this shall be a standing law unto them forever, for my Holy Priesthood, saith the Lord. Verily I say unto you, it shall come to pass, that all those who gather unto the land of Zion shall be tithed of their surplus properties, and shall observe this law, or [36] they shall not be found worthy to abide among you. And I say unto you, if my people observe not this law, to keep it holy, and by this law sanctify the land of Zion unto me, that my statutes and my judgments may be kept thereon, that it may be most holy, behold, verily I say unto you, it shall not be a land of Zion unto you; and this shall be an example unto all the Stakes of Zion. Even so. Amen." (D&C 119:1-7.)

"A revelation making known the disposition of property tithing:

"Verily, thus saith the Lord, the time is now come, that it shall be disposed of by a Council, composed of the First Presidency of my Church, and of the Bishop and his Council, and by my High Council; and by mine own voice unto them, saith the Lord. Even so. Amen." (D&C 120.)

"That when he shall finish his work, I may receive him unto myself, even as I did my servant David Patten, who is with me at this time, and also my servant Edward Partridge, and also my aged servant Joseph Smith, Sen., who sitteth with Abraham at his right hand, and blessed and holy is he, for he is mine." (D&C 124:19.)

First.—We find from the above that there are two distinctive general Priesthoods, namely, the Melchizedek and Aaronic, including the Levitical Priesthood.

Second.—That they are both conferred by the Lord; that both are everlasting, and administer in time and eternity.

Third.—That the Melchizedek Priesthood holds the right of Presidency, and has power and authority *over all the offices in the Church*, in all ages of the world, *to administer in spiritual things*.

Fourth.—That the second Priesthood is called the Priesthood of Aaron; because it was conferred upon Aaron and his seed throughout all their generations.

Fifth.—That the lesser Priesthood is a part of, or an appendage to the greater, or the Melchizedek Priest[37]hood, and has power in administering outward ordinances. The lesser or Aaronic Priesthood can make appointments for the greater, in preaching, can baptize, administer the sacrament, attend to the tithing, buy lands, settle people on possessions, divide inheritances, look after the poor, take care of the properties of the Church, attend generally to temporal affairs; act as common judges in Israel, and assist in ordinances of the Temple, under the direction of the greater or Melchizedek Priesthood. They hold the keys of the ministering of angels and administer in outward ordinances, *the letter of the Gospel*, and the baptism of repentance for the remission of sins.

Sixth.—That there is a Presidency over each of these Priesthoods, both over the Melchizedek and the Aaronic.

Seventh.—That while the power of the higher, or Melchizedek is to hold the keys *of all the* spiritual *blessings of the Church*, to have the privilege of receiving the mysteries of the Kingdom of heaven, to have the heavens opened to them, to commune with the general assembly and Church of the Firstborn and to enjoy the communion and presence of God the Father, and Jesus the Mediator of the new covenant, and to preside over all the spiritual officers of the Church, yet the *Presidency* of the High Priesthood, after the order of Melchizedek, have a right to officiate in *all the offices in the Church*, both spiritual and temporal.

"Then comes the High Priesthood, which is the greatest of all; wherefore it must needs be that one be appointed of the High

Priesthood to preside over the Priesthood, and he shall be called President of the High Priesthood of the Church; or, in other words, the Presiding High Priest over the High Priesthood of the Church." (D&C 107:64-66.)

It is thus evident that this Priesthood presides over all Presidents, all Bishops, including the Presiding Bishop, over all Councils, organizations and authorities in the whole Church, in all the world. [38]

That the Bishopric is the Presidency of the Aaronic Priesthood, which is "an *appendage* to the greater or Melchizedek Priesthood," (D&C 107:14) and that no man has a legal right to hold the KEYS of the Aaronic Priesthood, which presides over all Bishops and all the lesser Priesthood, except he be a literal descendant of Aaron. But, that "as a High Priest of the Melchizedek Priesthood has authority to officiate in all the lesser offices, he may officiate in the office of Bishop . . . if *called, set apart and ordained unto this* power by the hands of the Presidency of the Melchizedek Priesthood." (v. 17.)

We may here notice that John the Baptist conferred this Priesthood upon Joseph Smith, and that therefore, as he held it, he had the power to confer it upon others.

Eighth.—That there are Bishops holding different positions: Bishop Partridge was a general Bishop over the land of Zion; while Bishop Whitney was a general Bishop over the Church in Kirtland, Ohio, and also over all the eastern Churches until afterwards appointed as Presiding Bishop. That there are also ward Bishops, whose duties are confined to their several wards. That there are also Bishops' agents, such as Sidney Gilbert and others.

That the position which a Bishop holds, depends upon his calling and appointment, and that, although a man holding the Bishopric is eligible to any office in the Bishopric, yet he cannot officiate legally in any, except by selection, calling and appointment.

Ninth.—That the power and right of selecting and calling of the Presiding Bishop and general Bishops is vested in the First Presidency, who also must try those appointed by them in case of transgression, except in the case of a literal descendant of Aaron; who, if the firstborn, possesses a legal right to the keys of this Priesthood; but even he must be sanctioned and appointed by the First Presidency. This arises from the fact that the Aaronic is an appendage to the

Melchizedek Priesthood. [39]

That the Presiding Bishop, who presides over all Bishops, and all of the lesser Priesthood, should consult the First Presidency in all important matters pertaining to the Bishopric.

Tenth.—That in regard to the appointment and trial of ward Bishops, it appears that they stand in the same relationship to the Presidents of Stakes as the early Bishops did to the First Presidency, who presided over the Stake at Kirtland; but that those Presidents should consult with the First Presidency on these and other important matters, and officiate under their direction in their several Stakes.

That in regard to the office and calling of Bishops it is very much like the office and calling of High Priests. All High Priests are eligible to any office in the Church, when called, ordained and appointed to fill such office. The First Presidency are High Priests. The Twelve are High Priests, High Councilors are High Priests, Presidents of Stakes are High Priests, and all their Counselors; Bishops and their Counselors are High Priests: but it does not follow that all High Priests are First Presidents, members of the Twelve Apostles, Presidents of Stakes, High Councilors, Bishops or Bishops' Counselors, they only obtain these offices by selection and appointment from the proper source, and when not appointed to any specific calling, they are organized in a Stake quorum, under a President and Council.

So although the Bishopric is eligible to fulfill any office to which they may be appointed, all are not presiding Bishops, all are not general Bishops, or special Bishops, or ward Bishops, or even Bishops' agents; they occupy their several offices, as do the High Priests, by selection, appointment, as well as ordination, and that the Presidency of the Melchizedek Priesthood presides over, calls, directs, appoints, and counsels all. It is further evident that as the Melchizedek Priesthood holds the keys of all the spiritual blessings of the Church, and that the Presidency thereof has a right to officiate in all the offices of the Church, therefore that [40] Presidency has a perfect right to direct or call, set apart and ordain Bishops, to fill any place or position in the Church that may be required for that ministry to perform in all the Stakes of Zion, or throughout the world. Thus, after going through the whole matter, we come back to a term frequently used among us: Obey counsel!

CHAPTER 3

THE LEVITICAL PRIESTHOOD

As the Levitical Priesthood is referred to in the Old Testament scriptures, as well as in the book of Doctrine and Covenants, the following quotations and remarks may throw some light upon the subject:

LEVITES AND LEVITICAL PRIESTHOOD

"And the Lord spake unto Moses, saying: Bring the tribe of Levi near, and present them before Aaron the Priest, that they may minister unto him. And they shall keep his charge, and the charge of the whole congregation, before the tabernacle of the congregation, to do the service of the tabernacle. And they shall keep all the instruments of the tabernacle of the congregation, and the charge of the children of Israel, to do the service of the tabernacle. And thou shalt give the Levites unto Aaron and to his sons, they are wholly given unto them out of the children of Israel. And thou shalt appoint Aaron and his sons, and they shall wait on their Priest's office; and the stranger that cometh nigh shall be put to death." (Numbers 3:5-10.)

Aaron and his sons held the Aaronic Priesthood, and the Levites were given unto them to minister unto them to keep his charge, the charge of the congrega[41]tion, to do the service of the tabernacle, keep the instruments of the tabernacle, and the charge of the children of Israel.

"And I, behold, I have taken the Levites from among the children of Israel instead of all the firstborn that openeth the matrix among the children of Israel; therefore the Levites shall be mine; because all the firstborn are mine; for on the day that I smote all the firstborn in the land of Egypt I hallowed unto me all the firstborn in Israel, both man and beast: mine they shall be: I am the Lord." (Numbers 3:12-13.)

All the firstborn the Lord claimed as belonging to him, because when he destroyed the firstborn of the Egyptians, he spared the firstborn of the Israelites. But the Levites were appointed to fill the place of the firstborn of all Israel, and they were commanded to be numbered, viz., all the males from a month old and upward, to assist Aaron and his sons in the service of the tabernacle; at that time there were twenty-two thousand of them. (v. 39.)

"And the Lord spake unto Moses, saying: Take the Levites instead of all the first born among the children of Israel, and the cattle of the Levites instead of their cattle; and the Levites shall be mine: I am the Lord." (v. 44-45.)

The remainder of the Israelites had to redeem their firstborn, and the money for the redemption was given by Moses to Aaron and his sons according to the word of the Lord. (v. 50-51.)

They seemed to have been an appendage to the Aaronic Priesthood to assist in the service of the tabernacle and other duties. Aaron and his male descendants were selected for the Priesthood, and the other Levites as assistants, or an appendage.

The Levites had forty-eight cities and their suburbs provided for them from among the possessions of the other tribes: First came by lot the children of Aaron: "And the children of Aaron the Priest, which were of the Levites, had by lot out of the tribe of Judah, and out of the tribe of Simeon, and out of the tribe of Benjamin, thirteen cities." (Joshua 21:4; See the whole of the chapter for a division of cities to the remainder of the Levites, or the tribe of Levi, who were thus provided for as distinct from the other tribes.) "All the cities of the Levites within the possession of the children of Israel were forty and eight cities with their suburbs." (Joshua 21:41.)

It may here be observed that both Moses and Aaron belonged to the tribe of Levi, and that the Levites had a tithing given to them. "And the Lord spake unto Aaron, Thou shalt have no inheritance in their land, neither shalt thou have any part among them: I am thy part and thine inheritance among the children of Israel. And, behold, I have given the children of Levi all the tenth in Israel for an inheritance, for their service which they serve, even the service of the tabernacle of the congregation." (Numbers 17:20-21; See also the chapter.)

There is a peculiarity about this tithing, for while one-tenth was given to the Levites, they, the Levites, were commanded to give one-tenth of the tithe to Aaron.

"And the Lord spake unto Moses, saying, Thus speak unto the Levites, and say unto them, When ye take of the children of Israel the tithes which I have given you from them for your inheritance, then ye shall offer up an heave offering of it . . . for the Lord, even a tenth part of the tithe . . . and ye shall give thereof the Lord's heave offering to Aaron the Priest." (Numbers 18:25-28.)

It would seem that while the Levites were called "to do the service of the tabernacle of the congregation" (v. 6), that the Priest's office belonged especially to Aaron and his family. The Lord, in speaking to Aaron, says, "And I, behold, I have taken your brethren the Levites from among the children of Israel: to you they are given as a gift for the Lord, to do [43] the service of the tabernacle of the congregation." (Numbers 18:6.)

It furthermore appears that while the Levites were given to Aaron, that Aaron and his sons were to hold the Priest's office. "Therefore thou and thy sons with thee shall keep your Priest's office for everything of the altar, and within the veil; and ye shall serve: I have given your Priest's office unto you as a service of gift: and the stranger that cometh nigh shall be put to death." (Numbers 18:7.)

In the case of Korah, Dathan and Abiram, whom the earth opened and swallowed up for assuming the Priest's office, "Moses said unto Korah, hear, I pray you, ye sons of Levi: Seemeth it but a small thing unto you, that the God of Israel hath separated you from the congregation of Israel, to bring you near to himself to do the service of the tabernacle of the Lord, and to stand before the congregation to minister unto them? And he hath brought thee near to him, and all thy brethren the sons of Levi with thee: *and seek ye* the Priesthood also?" (Numbers 16:8-10.) And also the whole chapter, in which is depicted the terrible judgment of God upon them for assuming the Priest's office.

From the above it would seem—

First.—That the Levites were selected in the place of the firstborn whom the Lord called his own.

Second.—That they were given to Aaron to assist him in the minor or lesser duties of the Priesthood; but that Aaron and his sons officiated in the leading offices of the Priesthood, and not the Levites.

Third.—That there was a tithing paid to them by the whole house of Israel for their sustenance.

Fourth.—That they paid a tithe of this to Aaron.

Fifth.—That on assuming the higher duties of the Priesthood of Aaron, the judgments of God overtook them.

Sixth.—That their Priesthood was only an appendage to the Aaronic Priesthood, and not that Priesthood itself as held by Aaron and his sons.

SUCCESSION IN THE PRIESTHOOD

A DISCOURSE

BY

PRESIDENT JOHN TAYLOR

DELIVERED AT THE

Priesthood Meeting, held in the Salt Lake Assembly Hall, Friday Evening, October 7th, 1881.

REPORTED BY GEORGE F. GIBBS

There are two or three things that I wish to speak about for the information of the elders of Israel. Since the death of President Joseph Young, of the First Seven Presidents of the Seventies, the question has been asked who shall occupy his place. There are a number of men pretty well up in years who are associated with the First Seven Presidents over the Seventies. Some have been of the opinion, as these men are aged, that it would be perhaps better to have some younger person appointed to fill the vacancy as presiding President over the Seven Presidents of Seventies, occasioned by Brother Joseph Young's death. However, there seems to be an order in the Priesthood pertaining [2] to these matters that we cannot well ignore. It has been usual heretofore, in cases of this kind, both in regard to the Quorum of the Twelve and also in regard to High Councils—not always, perhaps, carried out in regard to High Councils, but acted upon in numerous instances—that is, that the members preside according to priority of ordination and seniority of age, and the two, I think, would probably go together. The Twelve, when they were first organized, were directed to have the oldest man selected for their President, who was Thomas B. Marsh. There were similar arrangements made in many instances in regard to High Councilors, and in such cases they were regulated, if my memory serves me aright, in the same way. This is my understanding of the order in the early history of the church. This has been the case in regard to the Twelve, and there may be other circumstances that I may refer to connected with this order; but I wish to speak of this subject before I come to the other, in order that we may have a just and clear conception of the position we occupy in relation to these matters.

Joseph Young, Sen., who was known as President Joseph Young, occupied the position of President over the First Seven Presidents of the Seventies from the time of their organization until his death. I wish to remark that a peculiar connection exists between the Seventies and the Twelve. The Twelve are a travelling High Council, whose business it is to preach the Gospel, or to see it preached, in all the world; that is their special calling and appointment by revelation. The Seventies also possess a mission of a similar nature. This mission is to preach the Gospel to all the world. They are placed under the direction of the Twelve, who are authorized to call upon them to go forth to the nations of the earth; thus their mission in this respect is similar to the mission of the Twelve. The same responsibilities rest upon them in regard to these duties as those which rest upon the Twelve, so far as their Priesthood and calling go. The High Priesthood, as you are aware, [3] differs from the Priesthood of the Seventies in this respect—the High Priests are expected to preside. It is a part of their office and calling to do that. Their organization in a Quorum capacity is, as stated, an ordinance "instituted for the purpose of qualifying those who shall be appointed standing Presidents or servants over different Stakes scattered abroad." (D&C 124:134.) It is not the special business of the Seventies to preside, but to preach the Gospel, and we understand that it is their duty, whenever called upon, to go forth and fulfil missions under the directions of the Twelve. And it is so far imperative upon them that the Twelve are told first to call upon the Seventies,[1] and, in the event of their not being prepared to perform this labor, then they may call upon others. But the Seventies seem to be the especial helps, assistants, and fellow-laborers of the Twelve. This being the case, if a rule of the kind that has been referred to in regard to age and priority of ordination exists among the Twelve, the question would naturally arise: Would it not be quite as proper that the same principle should exist among the Seventies, who possess a mission and calling so similar in its duties and responsibilities to that of the Twelve? This seems to be reasonable, proper, and correct. There is a fitness about many of these things that it is well for us to comprehend. Joseph Young died awhile ago, that is, what we call death. But he lives; and where is he? He has gone behind the veil. Are there any other Seventies gone behind the veil before him? I think there are a great many. Do they expect to hold their Priesthood and position behind the veil? Yes, if they understand themselves they do, just as much as here. For if the Priesthood is everlasting and administers in time and in eternity, then what has been sealed upon the earth by the proper authorities upon the heads of men is also sealed in the heavens. I so read it. And if it is sealed in the heavens, then Joseph Young would [4] take his place in the heavens and operate in his calling and Priesthood there, as he did here, and preside over the Seventies who have been ordained in this dispensation in their administrations in the other world.

If we look at some statements made in the Doctrine and Covenants, we find these things very plainly set forth—that is, the same ideas; and they are principles that are understood by all intelligent elders of Israel. However, there is no harm to speak about them that we may all see eye to eye and comprehend alike.

The Doctrine and Covenants, in referring to the Twelve, mentions their names and that of their President. It then mentions the names of the presiding officers in the Seventies. It mentions the names of the members of the High Council that was then organized. And in speaking about David Patten, one of the Twelve, it is written: "behold, his Priesthood no man taketh from him; but, verily I say unto you, another may be appointed unto the same calling." (D&C 124:130.) But his being dead made no difference in regard to his Priesthood. He held it just the same in the heavens as on the earth. There is another

---

[1] See D&C 107:38 and 124:139, 140.

man mentioned. Referring to the High Council, it is stated: "Seymour Brunson I have taken unto myself; no man taketh his Priesthood, but another may be appointed unto the same Priesthood in his stead." (D&C 124:132.) Then there is something said concerning Joseph Smith, Sen., the father of the Prophet Joseph Smith, of whom it is said that he sitteth with Abraham, at his right hand. (See D&C 124:19.) Who was Abraham? A Patriarch. Who was Father Joseph Smith? A Patriarch. It is quite fitting, therefore, that he should associate with Abraham, who was and is also a Patriarch; and, perhaps, if we had the full details given, we should have an account of other Patriarchs as well. But here is a place alluded to, where he went when he left this world.

I have now referred to men holding three different [5] callings in the Priesthood on the earth who are indicated as being provided for in their proper positions in the heavens. If the Priesthood administers in time and in eternity, and if Quorums of this kind are organized upon the earth, and this Priesthood is not taken away, but continued with them in the heavens, we do not wish, I think, to break up the order of the Priesthood upon the earth; and it would seem to be necessary that these principles of perpetuity or continuity should be held sacred among us. There is nothing new in this: we are told that Moses and Elias, who held the Priesthood on the earth, came from the heavens, where they still officiated, to administer to Jesus, Peter James and John on the Mount. We are elsewhere told that a mighty Angel was seen by John on the Isle of Patmos, who communicated to him many great and important things. John was about to fall down and worship this holy messenger, but he forbade him, saying: "See that thou do it no; I am thy fellow servant, and of thy brethren that have the testimony of Jesus: worship God: for the testimony of Jesus is the spirit of prophecy." (Revelation 19:10.) This mighty angel held the Priesthood on the earth; he now held it in the heavens and came to administer to John. The same may be said of personages who came to administer to the Prophet Joseph Smith, such as Moroni, Nephi, John the Baptist, Peter, James, John, Elijah, Elias, Moses; and such ministrations have been made by Michael or Adam, Gabriel or Noah, and others; as instanced in the case of Gabriel, who came to earth to announce the approaching birth of John the Baptist and of Jesus Christ. This principles confirmed by the Prophet Joseph Smith in an address to the Saints, embodied in the Doctrine and Covenants: He writes:

"And again, what do we hear? Glad tidings from Cumorah! Moroni, an angel from heaven, declaring the fulfilment of the prophets—the book to be revealed. A voice of the Lord in the wilderness of Fayette, Seneca county, declaring the three witnesses to bear record of the book! The voice of Michael on the banks of the [6] Susquehanna, detecting the devil when he appeared as an angel of light! The voice of Peter, James, and John in the wilderness between Harmony, Susquehanna county, and Colesville, Broome county, on the Susquehanna river, declaring themselves as possessing the keys of the kingdom, and of the dispensation of the fulness of times!

"And again, the voice of God in the chamber of old Father Whitmer, in Fayette, Seneca county, and at sundry times, and in divers places through all the travels and tribulations of this Church of Jesus Christ of Latter-day Saints! And the voice of Michael, the archangel; the voice of Gabriel, and of Raphael, and of divers angels, from Michael or Adam down to the present time, all declaring their dispensation, their rights, their keys, their honors, their majesty and glory, and the power of their priesthood; giving line upon line, precept upon precept; here a little, and there a little; giving us consolation by holding forth that which is to come, confirming our hope!" (D&C 128:20-21.)

Now, because some of these brethren of the First Seven Presidents of Seventies are feeble, aged, or infirm, it is not for us to deprive them of their rights and privileges, and put some others in their places while they remain true and faithful and good members in the church. And, therefore, the proper way, as I understand it, would be to take the senior member of that Quorum, that is, the senior President of the Seven Presidents of Seventies, and allow him to preside. The senior President is Levi W. Hancock. Let these brethren then get together and consult over these things, the senior President taking his place among them, and whatever business they may have to transact associated with the Seventies, they can all operate together, each performing in his own duties as directed by counsel, as when President Joseph Young was here, each retaining his proper standing, office, calling, and Priesthood. I presume my counselors agree with me in that. [Presi[7]dents George Q. Cannon and Joseph F. Smith both answered, "Yes, sir."] The First Presidency are agreed; and I presume the Twelve would be. This seems to be the proper way, that all may be respected and honored in their office.

Another subject that I wished to speak about is in regard to the Twelve, and the changes that have taken place from time to time in the church since the organization of that Quorum. I desire to show the reason for these changes, that we may understand things properly and intelligently.

As I stated, the Twelve, when they were called, were placed on the same footing that I have referred to, and Thomas B. Marsh was the senior in that Quorum. Hence he was appointed and he is spoken of in the revelations as their President.

At the time of his apostasy, there was another change made. David W. Patten would have been the next, had he lived, but he was killed in Missouri before Thomas B. Marsh apostatized. Had he lived, he would have been President of the Twelve, instead of Brigham Young. But he died, and consequently Brigham Young, being the senior member of the Twelve, was appointed in his place.

Now, in regard to the apostasy of Thomas B. Marsh, I will get Brother Reynolds to read in what his apostasy consisted. It was a horrible affair, as I look at it.

The affidavit of Thomas B. Marsh was then read, as follows:

"*Affidavit of Thomas B. Marsh*"

"They have among them a company, considered true Mormons, called the Danites, who have taken an oath to support the heads of the Church in all things that they say or do, whether right or wrong. Many, however, of this band are much dissatisfied with this oath, as being against moral and religious principles. On Saturday last, I am informed by the Mormons, that they had a meeting at Far West, at which they appointed a [8] company of Twelve, by the name of the Destruction Company, for the purpose of burning and destroying, and that if the people of Buncombe came to do mischief upon the people of Caldwell, and committed depredations upon the Mormons, they were to burn Buncombe; and if the people of Clay and Ray made any movement against them, this destroying company were to burn Liberty and Richmond.

"The plan of said Smith, the Prophet, is to take this state; and he professes to his people to intend taking the United States, and ultimately the whole world. This is the belief of the Church, and my own opinion of the Prophet's plans and intentions. The Prophet inculcates the notion, and it is believed by every true Mormon that Smith's prophecies are superior to the laws of the land. I have heard the Prophet say that he would yet tread down his enemies, and walk over their dead bodies; that if he was not let alone, he would be a second Mohammed to this generation, and that he would make it one gore of blood from the Rocky Mountains to the Atlantic Ocean; that like Mohammed, whose motto in treating for peace was 'the Alcoran or the Sword,' so should it be eventually with us, 'Joseph Smith or the Sword.' These last statements were made during the last summer. The number of armed men at Adam-Ondi-Ahman was between three and four hundred.

"Thomas B. Marsh

"Sworn to and subscribed before me, the day herein written.

"Henry Jacobs,

"J. P., Ray County, Missouri.
"Richmond, Missouri, October 24, 1838. [9]

"*Affidavit of Orson Hyde*

"The most of the statements in the foregoing disclosure I know to be true; the remainder I believe to be true.

"Orson Hyde

"Richmond, October 24, 1838.
"Sworn to and subscribed before me, on the day above written.

"Henry Jacobs, J. P."

Testimonies from these sources are not always reliable, and it is to be hoped, for the sake of the two brethren, that some things were added by our enemies that they did not assert, but enough was said to make this default and apostasy very terrible.

I will here state that I was in Far West at the time these affidavits were made, and was mixed up with all prominent church affairs. I was there when Thomas B. Marsh and Orson Hyde left there; and there are others present who were there at the same time. And I know that these things, referred to in the affidavits, are not true. I have heard a good deal about Danites, but I never heard of them among the Latter-day Saints. If there was such an organization, I never was made acquainted with it. The fact of a President of the Twelve, who ought to be true to his trust, Apostleship, and calling, and the guardian and protector of the people, making such statements, is truly infamous and is to be deplored by all correct feeling people. It is not unusual for lawyers to say, when speaking of any crime, that such a man, instigated by the devil, did so and so. Thomas B. Marsh was unquestionably "instigated by the devil" when he made this statement which has been read in your hearing. The consequence was, he was cut off the church. When he was cut off, he seemed to have lost all the spirit and power and manhood that he once enjoyed. I was acquainted with him before this. I was acquainted with him soon after I came into the church. With the Prophet Joseph Smith and Sidney Rigdon, he visited Upper Canada at the time I was presiding there, in the year 1837. I was with them for some time. I procured from a sister, a carriage, which was a very good one, and Brother Joseph Horne, who may be present, supplied the team, and, I think, [10] acted as teamster. In it we visited the churches. I rode with them in the same carriage. They were with us for some time, visiting the various churches and holding meetings and conferences. Thomas B. Marsh many of you knew as he was here in the valleys, and some of you perhaps knew him at that time. At that earlier period, he was a pretty fair average man in regard to intelligence, speech, good, sound reason, etc. I have heard some people say he was a fool, but I did not so understand it. [Brother Woodruff said: "I did not, either."] Until the time of his apostasy, he was a fair average man in regard to intelligence. But when he took the steps he did, it was a shocking course for a man to pursue, occupying the position that he did. I remember a circumstance that occurred. A number of us had been out to a place called Di-Ahman. Its proper name was Adam-Ondi-Ahman. In coming into Far West, I heard about him and Orson Hyde having left. It would be here proper to state, however, that Orson Hyde had been sick with a violent fever for some time, and had not yet fully recovered therefrom, which, with the circumstances with which we were surrounded and the influence of Thomas B. Marsh, may be offered as a slight palliation for his default. Brother Heber C. Kimball and I were together, and I said to him: "I have a notion to take a team and follow after these brethren, and see if I cannot persuade them to come back," speaking particularly of Brother Marsh. "Well," said he, "if you knew him as well as I do, you would know that if he had made up his mind to go, you could not turn him." With that I gave up the idea, knowing that Brother Kimball was better acquainted with him than I was, and I did not go. The result was that he did this deed. I am here reminded of the words of Joseph in exhorting the Twelve. He said:

"O ye Twelve, and all Saints, profit by this important key, that in all your trials, troubles, and temptations, afflictions, bonds, imprisonment and death, see to it [11] that you do not betray heaven, that you do not betray Jesus Christ, that you do not betray your brethren, and that you do not betray the revelations of God, whether in the Bible, Book of Mormon, or Doctrine and Covenants, or any of the word of God. Yes, in all your kicking and floundering, see to it that you do not this thing, lest innocent blood be found on your skirts, and you go down to hell. We may ever know by this sign that there is danger of our being led to a fall and apostasy, when we give way to the devil so as to neglect the first known duty. But, whatever you do, do not betray your friends." (*History of Joseph Smith*, June 2, 1839.)

Thomas B. Marsh, of course, was cut off from the church for this, as he ought to be, and so was Orson Hyde. I will give you a little further history of Thomas B. Marsh. On my way, I think, from a mission in Europe—I do not now remember the time—I met him in Florence, Nebraska. He hunted me up, and he looked a broken-down man. He spoke to me and asked me about affairs in the mountains, and told me what a wretched position he was in, in consequence of the course he had taken, and said he: "I want to go out there, and I would like to have your opinion as to how the people will receive me." I replied: "In regard to that, I do not think the people will entertain any hard or harsh feelings about you; they realize your position as you realize it; they would feel disposed to treat you properly and kindly; but as regards your ever occupying the position you once held, that to me would be impossible." He answered: "I do not look for anything of that kind," and I do not know but what he said that he did not deserve anything of the kind. I don't remember, however. But he did say: "I want to have a place among the brethren there. I want to stand in the position of a private member, or anywhere that shall be allotted to me. I want to die there." His circumstances were poor, and I relieved, in part, his present necessities. After his arrival here, I remember [12] hearing him talk in the Fourteenth Ward meetinghouse. It seemed to me about the most foolish and ridiculous talk, devoid of common sense, common intelligence, and common manhood, that I had heard for a long time. Said I to myself: "There is a specimen of apostasy." I remember I was once driving north out of the city. I think it was rather cold. I saw a man tottering along, I thought he was hardly fit to be out in such weather, and when I drew near to him, I found it was Brother Marsh. I asked him to get into my carriage. He had started for Bountiful, but I do not think he could have reached there alone. He appeared to be so weak and feeble. Perhaps you remember, in the Old Tabernacle, he got up when something was said in regard to apostasy, and said: "If any of you want to see the effects of apostasy, look upon me." You will perhaps remember that. [A number of voices in the congregation, "Yes, sir."] He lived in that way, and died in that way. He might have been at the head of the church, but he died in that miserable condition. I refer to this, because all of these things, when you reflect upon them, have a bearing upon our history, and on the propriety of the course that has been taken in these matters. Did the Twelve feel bad towards him? No. I remember that on learning that he was in poor circumstances, they proposed to give him a new suit of clothes, and assist in relieving his wants. But President Young, hearing of it, desired to do it himself, and he supplied his necessities. These are some little reminiscences associated with him. It was real apostasy, and I wanted his affidavit read to show that it was apostasy, that there was nothing wrong or unjust in regard to the treatment that he received. After his apostasy, President Young, by reason of his seniority, necessarily took the position of President of the Twelve.

When the Twelve arrived in England, a meeting of the Quorum was held in Preston. Brother Woodruff has an account of the whole concern. [Brother Woodruff—"Yes, sir."] And there was a vote taken by the [13] Twelve at that meeting, and the vote was unanimous, that Brigham Young should be accepted as the President of the Twelve Apostles. Afterwards, you will find, in a revelation given concerning the Twelve, that President Young's name is mentioned as being President of the Twelve. It is in that revelation given concerning the Nauvoo House, January 19th, 1841. His name is mentioned as being

President of the Twelve, and then follow the names of the other members then belonging to that Quorum.

I will now go a little back and trace up some other things associated with this subject.

There was a time when there was a large amount of apostasy in Kirtland; it was in 1837, I think. There was a very bitter feeling gotten up by a number of men who had apostatized. Parley P. Pratt was one who was affected. He, however, did not go to the length that some did; and Orson Pratt had partaken more or less of that spirit. I speak of these things as facts. Parley mentions it himself in his own autobiography, which he published, or at least prepared for publication. And then he speaks about his bitter repentance and his reconciliation with Joseph Smith, when the thing was made right. He says:

"About this time, after I had returned from Canada, there were jarrings and discords in the Church at Kirtland, and many fell away and became enemies and apostates. There were also envyings, lyings, strifes, and divisions, which caused much trouble and sorrow. By such spirits I was also accused, misrepresented, and abused. And at one time, I also was overcome by the same spirit in a great measure, and it seemed as if the very powers of darkness which war against the Saints were let loose upon me. But the Lord knew my faith, my zeal, my integrity of purpose, and he gave me the victory.

"I went to Brother Joseph Smith in tears, and with a broken heart and contrite spirit, confessed wherein I had erred in spirit, murmured, or done or said amiss. [14] He frankly forgave me, prayed for me, and blessed me. Thus by experience I learned more fully to discern and to contrast the two spirits, and to resist the one and cleave to the other. And being tempted in all points, even as others, I learned how to bear with and excuse and succor those who are tempted." (*Autobiography of Parley P. Pratt*, page 183.)

But there were four of the Twelve who did apostatize.—William E. McLellin, Luke Johnson, John F. Boynton, and Lyman Johnson. When they apostatized, the following revelation was given:

"*Revelation given through Joseph Smith, the Prophet, at Far West, Missouri, July 8th, 1838, in response to the supplication: Show us thy will, O Lord, concerning the Twelve, etc.*"

"Verily, thus saith the Lord: Let a conference be held immediately;

let the Twelve be organized; and let men be appointed to supply the place of those who are fallen.

"Let my servant Thomas remain for a season in the land of Zion, to publish my word.

"Let the residue continue to preach from that hour, and if they will do this in all lowliness of heart, in meekness and humility, and long-suffering, I, the Lord, give unto them a promise that I will provide for their families; and an effectual door shall be opened for them, from henceforth.

"And next spring let them depart to go over the great waters, and there promulgate my Gospel, the fulness thereof, and bear record of my name.

"Let them take leave of my saints in the city Far West, on the twenty-sixth day of April next, on the building-spot of my house, saith the Lord.

"Let my servant John Taylor, and also my servant John E. Page, and also my servant Wilford Woodruff, and also my servant Willard Richards, be appointed to fill the places of those who have fallen, and be officially notified of their appointment." (D&C 118.)

I will state that I was living in Canada at the [15] time, some three hundred miles distant from Kirtland. I was presiding over a number of churches in that region, in fact, over all of the churches in Upper Canada. I knew about this calling and appointment before it came, it having been revealed to me. But not knowing but that the devil had a finger in the matter, I did not say anything about it to anybody. [Brother Woodruff here spoke up and said that he was on the Fox Islands, which were farther away still; and also knew, by the Spirit, that he would be called to the Apostleship.] A messenger came to me with a letter from the First Presidency, informing me of my appointment, and requesting me to repair forthwith to Kirtland, and from there to go to Far West. I went according to the command. When I reached Far West, John E. Page, another one mentioned in the revelation just read to you, was there also. John E. Page and I were ordained into the Quorum of the Twelve at the same meeting. Brother Woodruff was ordained, after the scenes of the war at Far West; but I think it was right in the midst of the war when Brother Page and I were ordained. Brother Woodruff was ordained on the cornerstone of the foundation of the temple in Far West, on the 26th of April, 1839, when we went to fulfil this same revelation that you have heard read, and I helped to ordain him. Brother George A. Smith was ordained at the same time, and I am informed that he took the place of Thomas B. Marsh, who apostatized. I had not retained this fact in my memory, but I think it is correct. There were two other men ordained at the same time, one by the name of Darwin Chase, the other Norman Shearer. The former joined Conner's company and was in the fight on Bear River, where he was shot and shortly afterwards died at Camp Douglas. These are some reminiscences associated with this affair. Now we come to some other events. When the Twelve were reorganized, there were some changes made. For instance, in the case of John E. Page, it was not long before he apostatized. Willard Richards [16] was ordained into the Twelve at Preston in Lancashire, England, at the same time and place as President Young was voted for and accepted as President of the Twelve. Through some inadvertence, or perhaps mixed up with the idea of seniority of age taking the precedence, Wilford Woodruff's name was placed on the records of the time, and for many years after, before that of John Taylor. This matter was investigated some time afterwards by President Young and his Council, sanctioned also by the Twelve, whether John Taylor held the precedence and stood in gradation prior to Brother Wilford Woodruff, and it was voted on and decided that his name be placed before Wilford Woodruff's, although Wilford Woodruff was the older man. The reason assigned for this change was that although both were called at the same time, John Taylor was ordained into the Twelve prior to Wilford Woodruff; and another prominent reason would be that as John Taylor assisted in the ordination of Elder Wilford Woodruff, he therefore must precede him in the Council. Another question arose afterwards on this same subject: Orson Hyde and Orson Pratt had both of them been disfellowshipped and dropped from their Quorum, and when they returned, without any particular investigation or arrangement, they took the position in the Quorum which they had formerly occupied, and as there was no objection raised, or investigation had on this subject, things continued in this position for a number of years. Some ten or Twelve years ago, Brother George A. Smith drew my attention to this matter. I think it was soon after he was appointed as counselor to the First Presidency; and he asked me if I had noticed the impropriety of the arrangement.

He stated at the same time that these brethren having been dropped from the Quorum could not assume the position that they before had in the Quorum; but that all those who remained in the Quorum when they had left it must necessarily take the precedence of them in the Quorum. He stated, at the same time, that these questions might become very seri[17]ous ones, in case of change of circumstances arising from death or otherwise; remarking also, that I stood before them in the Quorum. I told him that I was aware of that, and of the correctness of the position assumed by him, and had been for years, but that I did not choose to agitate or bring up a question of that kind. Furthermore, I stated that, personally, I cared nothing about the matter, and, moreover, I entertained a very high esteem for both the parties named; while, at the same time, I could not help but see, with him, that complications might hereafter arise, unless the matters were adjusted. Some time after, in Sanpete, in June, 1875, President Young brought up the subject of seniority, and stated that John Taylor was the man that stood next to him; and that where he was not, John Taylor presided. He also made the statement that Brother Hyde and Brother Pratt were not in their right positions in the Quorum. Upon this statement, I assumed the position indicated.

Thus our positions at that time seemed to be fully defined; and what had been spoken of by Elder George A. Smith, without any action of mine, was carried out by President Young. I occupied the senior position in the Quorum, and occupying that position, which was thoroughly understood by the Quorum of the Twelve, on the death of President Young, as the Twelve assumed the Presidency, and I was their President, it placed me in a position of President of the church, or, as expressed in our conference meeting: "As President of the Quorum of the Twelve Apostles, as one of the Twelve Apostles, and of the Presidency of the church of Jesus Christ of Latter-day Saints." In this manner, also, was President Brigham Young sustained, at the general conference held in Nauvoo, in the October following the martyrdom of the Prophet Joseph Smith. We find the following recorded in the minutes of that conference: "Elder W. W. Phelps moved that we uphold Brigham Young, the President of the Quorum of [18] the Twelve, as one of the Twelve, and First Presidency of the Church." Thus I stood in the same position that President Young did when called to occupy the same place at the death of the Prophet

Joseph Smith.

It may be proper here to again say a few words with regard to Brother Orson Hyde, whose endorsement of the terrible charges made by Thomas B. Marsh, in his affidavit, has already been read. Suffice it to say, in addition to what has previously been stated, he was cut off the church, and of course lost his Apostleship; and when he subsequently returned, and made all the satisfaction that was within his power, he was forgiven by the authorities and the people, and was again re-instated in the Quorum. But having been cut off from the Quorum, and having remained in that condition for some time, he of course lost his former position as to seniority, and that necessarily placed me in advance of him.

Orson Pratt also had some difficulties while we were in Nauvoo, arising out of the introduction of the celestial order of marriage. It seems, from remarks made in a conversation that I had with him afterwards, that he did not fully realize or comprehend the situation. But, at the time of the occurrence, when I saw that he was very severely tried, as I had always held pleasant relations with him, I took every pains that I possibly could to explain the situation of things, to remove his doubts, and to satisfy his feelings, but without avail. At one time I talked with him for nearly two hours, to prevent, if possible, his apostasy or departure from the church. But he was very sorely tried, and was very self-willed and stubborn in his feelings, and would not yield. His feelings were bitter towards the Prophet Joseph Smith and others, and the result was that he was dropped from his position in the Quorum. But I am not aware of his ever having written or published anything against the church. On the contrary, when Dr. John C. Bennett, who had apostatized, sent a letter to Sidney Rigdon, wherein he denounced President Smith, [19] and stated that he was a villain and a scoundrel, and that a requisition would be made for him by the State of Missouri, and requested him to show this letter to Orson Pratt; although Sidney Rigdon, who was the First counselor to Joseph, did not show this statement unfolding this conspiracy to him [the Prophet], yet, as soon as Sidney Rigdon handed the letter to Orson Pratt, he immediately took it to the Prophet Joseph. And thus, while Sidney Rigdon withheld this information from one to whom he was in honor and duty bound, as his first counselor, to make it known, yet Orson Pratt, although at the time disfellowshipped, immediately made Joseph acquainted with the conspiracy that was being plotted against him, and thus exhibited a manhood and integrity that were so woefully deficient in Sidney Rigdon. In reference to Brother Pratt's severance from the Council of the Twelve, the following items from the life of President Young are interesting:

"August 8, 1842.—Assisted by Elders H. C. Kimball and George A. Smith, I spent several days laboring with Elder Orson Pratt, whose mind became so darkened by the influence and statements of his wife, that he came out in rebellion against Joseph, refusing to believe his testimony or obey his counsel. He said he would believe his wife in preference to the Prophet. Joseph told him if he did believe his wife and follow her suggestions, he would go to hell.

"We reported to the Prophet that we had labored with Brother Orson diligently, in a spirit of meekness, forbearance, and long-suffering. He requested us to ordain Brother Amasa Lyman in Brother Orson's stead. After receiving these instructions, we met Brother Orson near my house, and continued to labor with him. He said to us: 'There is Brother Amasa Lyman in your house, Brother Young; he has been long in the ministry: go in and ordain him in my stead.'

August 20.—Brother Orson Pratt was cut off from the Church, and, according to the Prophet's direction, Brothers H. C. Kimball, George A. Smith, and I ordained [20] Brother Amasa Lyman in his stead." (*History of Brigham Young.*)

Of Brother Pratt's integrity, indefatigable labors, purity of life, zeal for the cause of God, and untiring devotion in proclaiming the word of the Lord, I cannot speak in terms of too high praise or affectionate regard; and these other matters, painful though they be, are only mentioned now because they are necessary to make plain to your minds an important principle, and without these details you would not so readily nor fully understand my position, and the position of the Twelve, at the present time.

Having said so much on these matters, I will talk a little on some other things.

We are told in the Doctrine and Covenants, that when the people are united, or the Priesthood are united, and are moved upon by the Holy Ghost, their teachings "shall be scripture, shall be the will of the Lord, shall be the mind of the Lord, shall be the word of the Lord, shall be the voice of the Lord, and the power of God unto salvation."

(D&C 68:4.) That is the case, and I have not seen greater unanimity than we have had, both in the selection of the Twelve and in that of the First Presidency afterwards. And if the united voice of a few elders is the will of God, and the word of God, and the law of God, the question is, is not the voice of the whole Church the law of God and the will of God? I speak of this for your information, that you may comprehend the ground upon which you stand, speaking not of persons, but of the principle. Speaking of myself, who am I? Just like you. Who are you? Just like me—poor, feeble, weak, erring humanity. Can I do anything without the aid of the Almighty? No; I could not leave this stand without his assistance, nor could any of you leave this house if God was to say, no, and was to withdraw the breath which you breathe, which you received from him. But God has called all of us to a high calling; and there is a regular organization in the church and kingdom of God which ought to be respected. [21]

There are some things which I have disliked to mention; I do not like to mention anything unpleasant about Brother Marsh, or Brother Pratt, or Brother Orson Hyde. Brother Hyde, as I stated, had his weaknesses, as we all have; but he was received back again, after making a humble acknowledgment; and so was Brother Marsh; but then Brother Marsh could never again occupy the position of an apostle; and it was a hard struggle at times for Brother Hyde, but he got along, and I am thankful for it. Did other men have their weaknesses? I think they had, and I think, too, that they themselves did not consider it improper to speak of them. I think that Peter, on a certain occasion, when Jesus was telling what poor, weak creature they were, said, "Though all men forsake thee, yet will not I." Why, you would if God did not sustain you. Said the Savior, "Peter, before the cock crows twice, thou shalt deny me thrice." (See Matthew 26:33-34; Mark 14:29-30.) And so he did. But afterwards Peter went out and wept bitterly. And so did Brother Hyde weep bitterly. He came to me on a certain occasion, after Mr. Colfax came out here and quoted this affidavit which Marsh had made, and told me he would give his life over and over again, if it were possible, to wipe out the recollection of that act; but I think, as I said before, that Brother Hyde was scarcely in his right mind: he was laboring under a fever and was hardly himself. I would gladly hope it was so. And I mentioned, in my reply to Colfax, that Peter had his weaknesses, and afterward went out and wept bitterly; and that so did Brother Hyde. But that Peter, after this, stood up manfully for the cause of truth, sustaining the Gospel and all the principles thereto; and so did Brother Hyde. He went on a mission to Jerusalem and to other places, and proved himself as faithful as he knew how to be. But he was not, I think, the man that he as before. Such things affect men. And I say, brethren, never, under any circumstances whatever, betray your honor nor the truths of the Gospel of Jesus Christ. Whenever you do that, you will find it hard to retrace your steps. [22]

We all hold important positions before God. We are called to build up the Church of God; we are called to build up the Kingdom of God; we are called to introduce and maintain the government of God; and God expects it at our hands; and He expects that we shall be true to Him and to our Priesthood, and true to our calling; and if we are, there are thrones and principalities and powers and dominions, exaltations and increase, worlds without end; and if we are not there will be sorrow and mourning and lamentation and woe. It behooves us, therefore, to consider and ponder well the path of our feet. As Elders in Israel, the Kingdom of God ought to be the first and the last, the beginning, the middle and the end, of all our acts. We are not called upon to seek for our own glory, our own emolument, our own honor, our own family, our own wealth; but God has committed to us eternal treasures, treasure of intelligence, treasures that the Gods inherit in the eternal worlds; treasure that will exalt us in time, and bring us to associate with the Gods in eternity. And if we are faithful and true to our trust, everything that God has promised will be fulfilled to us, and to our generation after us, if they are faithful, just as sure as God lives. But we have to learn to do the will of God. We have to follow the counsel and advice of those whom God has given for our guidance. Every one of us has to walk in the line that God has marked out. If we are Teachers, Priests, or Deacons, we must be subject to the counsel of our Bishops, and we must seek their counsel, and then be governed by it. If we are Bishops, we must ask the counsel of our Presidents and the counsel of the presiding Bishopric. And then, in peculiar cases, the counsel of the First Presidency or Twelve, as the case may be. If we are High Councillors, we must act in uprightness and in honor, and administer justice in righteousness and with integrity of heart, dealing out justice and equity to all men, and must seek for the Holy Spirit to help us to do these [23] things. If we are Bishops, we want the spirit of righteousness within us, not to hold any man's person in admiration, but to do justly and equitably to all men, according the to circumstances in which they may be placed, and act as judges in Israel, judging in all righteousness. If we are Presidents of Stakes, we ought to feel a fatherly care over the Stakes, even as a Bishop should watch over his Ward, and know the position of every man in it. If there be any danger of defalcations in anything, try to meet these difficulties in the right way and act as saviors to men; and then, in cases of difficulty, applying to the First Presidency or the Twelve, as the case may be; if it be the Twelve, they have to be in subjection to their file leaders in the same way. If it be the Presidency, it is for them to seek to God for help. And I call upon you, my brethren, for help also, for your faith and prayers; for we need it; that the whispering of His Spirit may descend upon the proper authorities, and that that Spirit may permeate the hearts of all the Elders of Israel; all of whom have rights, as individuals, to approach God in the name of Jesus Christ, to have their prayers heard. But God has organized His Church and Kingdom for the accomplishment of His purposes upon the earth.

Well, let every man act in his place, and honor his calling. Let no man set the world before his Maker, for if he does, I tell you, in the name of God, he will have his reward; and if it is the world he wants, he will have it; but when he does he will be without the other and greater reward. Take which you like. We shall have both if we do right and magnify our Priesthood and calling and honor our God, and we shall have riches in this world and riches in the worlds to come. But love not the world nor the things that are in the world, for any man loving the world, the love of the Father is not in him. I say, O God, pour upon thy Elders thy Holy Spirit, that they may appreciate the principles of truth and honor, and that they may be prepared to receive the riches of [24] this world, and be able to build up they Kingdom and establish righteousness, and raise up Zion and establish it upon the earth, and prepare the earth and the people thereof for the time when the bursting heavens shall reveal the Son of God, and all creation shall feel His power, and every creature in the heavens and on the earth and under th earth be heard to say, Blessing and glory and honor and power, might, majesty and dominion be ascribed to Him that sits upon the throne, and to the Lamb forever. Amen.

ON MARRIAGE

A PAMPHLET

BY

PRESIDENT JOHN TAYLOR

Published in Salt Lake City, Utah, in 1882.

Marriage is the legitimate union of the sexes. God made male and female, not only of man, but of all animals, fowls, fishes, and, as stated, everything that creepeth upon the earth; and endued them with organs and power to propagate their own species. He also endued the herbs, plants, flowers, trees, grasses, and all the vegetable kingdom with fecundity, whose seed (as expressed in the scriptures) should be in itself. Thus everything in the animal and vegetable kingdoms was prepared to propagate, increase, and perpetuate its own species. That principle, and the organs and media necessary for its development, have continued intact from the commencement up to the present time and it is a fact that all life in this creation, animal or vegetable, possesses the inherent power within itself fully to maintain and perpetuate its own species. This principle applies to the lower as well as to the higher grades of creation. The most repulsive animal and venomous reptile possess this power, as well as those that are the most refined, symmetrical, beautiful, or intellectual; and the most noxious and poisonous weeds or plants possess this fecundity, in common with the most lovely, sweet, nutritive, aromatic, or life-sustaining species. So that this grand, life-giving, preserving, and perpetuating power exists among all life, whether vegetable or animal.

There are certain laws or principles regulating all these operations. The animals mingle together by their natural impulses and instincts, without any moral law or code to regulate their sexual intercourse or associations; and provision having been made for the plants, herbs and flowers to have the seed, as expressed, within themselves, they are also without any law, other than the natural [2] law which was implanted in the originals, which law has continued throughout all time; and impelled by which the plant struggles for its perpetuity and existence as much as do the members of the animal creation.

Man stands at the head of creation. God gave unto him dominion over the fish of the sea, the fowls of the air, the beasts of the field, and every creeping thing that creepeth upon the face of the earth. He is lord of all. We are told also that man became a living soul. We are further told that "the body and the spirit is the soul of man;" (D&C 88:15) he is therefore a compound being and has a dual capacity—has both a spiritual and fleshly or temporal existence, and, of course, occupies a more exalted sphere than that of the animal or vegetable creations.

Pertaining to the flesh, his faculties, sympathies, instincts, fecundity, organs, and powers of propagation are similar, in many respects, to those of the animal world. A command was giving to him to be fruitful and multiply, and replenish the earth. All other animals, possessing like powers of fecundity, are under to oral or written law in relation to the propagation of their species, other than what may be termed the law of nature, implanted by the Almighty and inherent in themselves, which law, attraction, affinity, or impulse alone leads to the propagation of their kind. In this respect, man occupies a different position from that of all other created life. In addition to his natural impulses, instincts and sympathies, a law is given to him, commanding him to be fruitful and multiply, and to replenish the earth; and to so far replenish it that he, as the head of creation, possessing a superior intelligence, may so increase, spread and grow, that according to the eternal fitness of things he may not only have, but also retain, the dominion over all created beings, as at first contemplated by his and their Creator. This command was given to Adam and eve, before the Fall, whilst they were in the Garden of Eden, as an eternal [3] law, emanating from the Almighty. But when man fell, he placed himself in other conditions, both in his relationship to and communication with god, his possession of the Garden of Eden, and his subjecting himself to the penalty of death. Nevertheless, the natural instincts of men, as in animals, have continued through all past time from then until the present, in all ages, among all nations and peoples, extending over the whole earth. Nor has the religious or political condition of men made much difference in regard to the association of the sexes; for while one was a law of God pertaining to the eternal exaltation of the human species, the other arose from the natural impulses connected with the organization of the human family as it has existed in all ages.

The Gospel, when introduced and preached to Adam after the fall, through the atonement of Jesus Christ, placed him in a position not only to have victory over death, but to have within his reach and to possess the perpetuity, not only of earthly, but of heavenly life; not only of earthly, but also of heavenly dominion; and through the law of that Gospel enabled him (and not him alone, but all his posterity) to obtain, not only his first estate, but a higher exaltation on earth and in the heavens, than he could have enjoyed if he had not fallen; the powers and blessings associated with the atonement being altogether in advance of and superior to any enjoyment or privileges that he could have had in his first estate. Hence, he and his partner became the father and mother of lives—lives temporal, lives spiritual, and lives eternal, and were placed in the position to become Gods, yea, the sons and daughters of God, and to the increase and extent of their dominion there was to be no limit; worlds without end. But it became necessary that Adam should obey, observe, and keep the law of the gospel, and it also became necessary that his posterity, who would possess the same exaltation and blessings, should also keep and observe the same law; and if they did not, they could not obtain the blessings [4] of celestial lives and exaltations in the eternal worlds. But, while this was the law pertaining to celestial affairs, man was not deprived of the power, the right, and the privilege, the faculties and instincts of the association of the sexes, nor of the propagation of his own species; and hence, when man had transgressed the law of God and had corrupted himself to such a degree that it is said of him that his thoughts were only evil, and that continually; and when it had become an act of justice with the Almighty, in reference to the unborn spirits, in consequence of the extreme degradation of the human family, to introduce a better race, man possessing the power, while living, to propagate his own species, he could only accomplish and bring about this design by destroying that corrupt race, and appointing a selected and chosen race for the above named purpose.

The law before referred to was the law of the gospel. When the gospel is lived up to and enjoyed, its powers and blessings are also enjoyed, pertaining both to time and eternity; but when the law of the gospel is not lived up to, yet the principle of procreation and the association of the sexes still continues as a principle separate and distinct from that of the gospel; and the nearer we can approach pure and correct principles, whereby the chastity of the race may be preserved, in our marital relations, the more will our actions be acceptable to our Heavenly Father. Hence, it has always been considered, among all intelligent and right thinking people in the nations, both in a social and political capacity, that it is in the interests of humanity that the marital relations should be sustained, that virtue and chastity should be preserved, and that in proportion as these principles are disregarded has the elevation or degradation of the race been manifested.

Paul, in speaking on this subject, tells us that "marriage is honorable in all, and the bed undefiled," (Hebrews 13:4) and in another place he says:

"Now the Spirit speaketh expressly, that in the latter times some shall depart from the faith, giving heed to [5] seducing spirits, and doctrines of devils; speaking lies in hypocrisy; having their conscience seared with a hot iron; forbidding to marry." (1 Timothy 4:1-3.)

Whilst in writing to the Corinthians he enters into a lengthy argument on the subject of marriage. (See Corinthians 7:1-16.)

Statesmen, in different ages, without reference to any particular law of God, have inculcated the principle of martial relations, and in some instances have compelled their peoples to marry; and thus, outside of the more elevated principles of the Gospel law, whether among the Jews, Christians, or Pagans, the sanctity of the marital relations has been sacredly guarded and protected.

The Lord has revealed unto us the ancient law, which was revealed to Adam through the gospel, and which is called the law of celestial marriage. This, as before stated, applies only to certain conditions of men, and can only be enjoyed by parties who have obeyed the everlasting gospel. It is one of the eternal principles associated therewith, uniting mortal and immortal beings by eternal covenants that will live and endure forever. Outside of this covenant, statesmen have, in many instances, enacted laws sanctioning the plurality of wives, but this, of course, has nothing to do with eternal covenants or eternal relations of man, any more than the monogamic relations have; those covenants only having a reference to time, and not to eternity; and to such an extent has this principle prevailed that it may almost with propriety be called the normal condition of man. But with regard to the law of celestial marriage, there are certain safeguards thrown around it, as there always were, and those safeguards are, and always were, in the hands of the proper authorities and Priesthood, delegated by God to man for the protection and preservation and right use of this most important, sacred, exalting, and eternal ceremony or covenant. These things are clearly defined in the revelation on celestial marriage, and can rightly only be enjoyed and participated in by such as are considered worthy, according to the [6] laws, rites, privileges, and immunities connected therewith. But while this is the case in relation to this everlasting covenant, men and women do now, outside of this arrangement, posses the same instincts, affinities, passions, fecundity and powers of procreation as they have done in other ages and at other times; for, as before stated, this is one of those natural laws and instincts which God has placed in the human system. It therefore has become and is a question of what shall be done with those who do not fulfil the obligations of the Gospel, and are not prepared to assume the responsibilities and obligations connected therewith. Is the order of God to be violated? Are the barriers placed around this sacred institution to be broken down and trampled underfoot? And are unworthy characters who do not fulfil the requirements of the gospel to have conferred upon them the blessings of eternal lives, of thrones, and powers, and principalities in the celestial kingdom of God? We emphatically answer, No!

On the other hand, are men and women, who, while nothing immoral can be laid to their charge, and who are considered worthy of a standing in the church, but who may be thoughtless, careless, and indifferent in regard to many religious matters, and who either do not comprehend the gospel, or who do not appreciate the privileges conferred by the celestial law of marriage connected therewith—are they, while they cannot enjoy the greater privileges of the gospel, to be deprived of the privileges and blessings arising from the marital relations, and of the proper exercise of the impulses and instincts of nature? We as emphatically answer, No! There ought to be placed within the reach of the young of both sexes a full and fair opportunity of correctly fulfilling the perpetuation of their species, free and untrammelled, leaving it for themselves to embrace or reject the higher or more exalted law, as all men are left free to receive or reject the gospel; thus preserving the free agency of man in this as in all other things. While the parties themselves do [7] not take a course to embrace and enjoy the higher privileges of the gospel, it is not for us to throw barriers in their way, but to encourage, by all possible means, our youth to enter into such marital relations as they are capable or worthy of enjoying, leaving it for them in the future to receive or reject the fulness of the gospel; and thus preserve the virtue, chastity and purity of our youth.

Before the Law of Celestial Marriage was given, Joseph Smith gave instructions relative to the marital relations, as contained in the Book of Doctrine and Covenants, wherein he enjoins chastity, virtue and an adherence to the covenants entered into between men and women, according to the laws and usages that then existed in the Christian world. But these covenants and arrangements referred only to time, and had no bearing upon or relation to eternal unions. When the revelation pertaining to Celestial Marriage was given, that revelation superseded everything else that had previously been practised among the Saints, and thoroughly defined the relations of the sexes to each other pertaining both to time and eternity.

JOHN TAYLOR

The following is a matter of counsel and expediency under the existing state of things, in view of the situation of persons who are not prepared to fully comply with the requirements of the Gospel, yet cannot be denied, as above mentioned, the privilege of participating in the marital relations.

The question arises, what shall be done in regard to those persons, who being members of the church, are not worthy to enter into those sacred and eternal relations of which we have been speaking? This is probably a question that concerns our civil polity rather than our religion, but we have deemed it worthy of our consideration, and after due deliberation have determined that in cases where recommends cannot be justifiably given for the blessings of the House of the Lord, the parties desiring marriage be united by the Bishop, [8] inasmuch as they are worthy of the recognition of their brethren and sisters and have not forfeited their right to be esteemed members of the church, though not sufficiently valiant in the cause of righteousness to be deemed altogether worthy of those weightier blessings that belong to the new and everlasting covenant. But that holier order to which we have referred is the law of marriage as it exists in its fulness, in its completeness, in the strength and beauty of its purity, without end or change, but eternal as the existence of the soul, abiding forever.

This recommendation, with regard to those who cannot live the higher law, who do not possess much faith, but possess a little faith, is given as a means of purification among some of our youth and others, who, while they are desirous to marry and fulfil the great law of nature and be fruitful and multiply, are not justly and consistently entitled to those blessings which the fulness of the gospel covenant provides. It has therefore been deemed best by myself and council, as well as by the council of the Apostles, under our present circumstances, to place them in the hands of the Bishops, rather than to have them go for the performance of the marriage ceremony to justices of the peace and others, who, in their operations, do not carry the weight of blessing and responsibility which belongs of right to the Priesthood in all its ministrations and labors.

The foregoing ideas and considerations were submitted by me to the council of the Apostles, and were approved by that body, and have already been read from the manuscript to assemblies of the Priesthood or saints in Salt Lake City and other places. They are now presented to the presiding authorities in the various stakes and wards, and unity of action and concord of feeling may exist on this as on all other subjects in which we, as the servants of the Lord, and all the saints, are directly concerned.

JOHN TAYLOR
President of the Church of Jesus Christ of Latter-day Saints.

THE ORIGIN AND DESTINY OF WOMAN

AN ARTICLE

BY

JOHN TAYLOR

TAKEN FROM

The Mormon, *August 29th Issue, 1857.* The Mormon *was a newspaper Elder Taylor published in New York while serving as President of the Eastern States Mission.*

The Latter-day Saint have often been ridiculed on account of their belief in the pre-existence of spirits, and for marrying for time and all eternity, both being Bible doctrines. We have often been requested to give our views in relation to these principles, but considered the things of the kingdom belonged to the children of the kingdom, therefore not meet to give them to those without. But being very politely requested by a lady a few days since (a member of the Church) to answer the following questions, we could not consistently refuse, viz.:

"Where did I come from? What am I doing here? Whither am I going? And what is my destiny after having obeyed the truth, if faithful to the end?"

For her benefit and all others concerned, we will endeavor to answer the questions in brief, as we understand them. The reason will be apparent for our belief in the pre-existence of spirits, and in marrying for time and all eternity.

Lady, whence comest thou? Thine origin? What are thou doing here? Whither are thou going, and what is thy destiny? Declare unto me if thou hast understanding. Knowest thou not that thou are a spark of Deity, struck from the fire of His eternal blaze, and brought forth in the midst of eternal burnings?

Knowest thou not that eternities ago thy spirit, pure and holy, dwelt in thy Heavenly Father's bosom, and in His presence, and with thy mother, one of the queens of heaven, surrounded by thy brother and sister spirits in the spirit world, among the Gods? That as thy spirit beheld the scenes transpiring there, and thou grewest in intelligence, thou sawest worlds upon worlds organized and peopled with thy kindred spirits who took upon them tabernacles, died, were resurrected, and received their exaltation on the redeemed worlds they once dwelt upon. Thou being willing and anxious to imitate them, waiting and desirous to obtain a body, a resurrection and exaltation also, and having obtained permission, madest a covenant with on thy kindred spirits to by thy guardian angel while in mortality, also with two others, male and female spirits, that thou wouldst come and take a tabernacle through their lineage, and become one of their offspring. You also chose a kindred spirit whom you loved in the spirit world (and who had permission to come to this planet and take a tabernacle), to be your head, stay, husband and protector on the earth and to exalt you in eternal worlds. All these were arranged, likewise the spirits that should tabernacle through your lineage. Thou longed, thou sighed and thou prayed to thy Father in heaven for the time to arrive when thou couldst come to this earth, which had fled and fallen from where it was first organized, near the planet Kolob. Leaving thy father and mother's bosom and all thy kindred spirits thou camest to earth, took a tabernacle, and imitated the deeds of those who had been exalted before you.

At length the time arrived, and thou heard the voice of thy Father saying, go daughter to yonder lower world, and take upon thee a tabernacle, and work out thy probation with fear and trembling and rise to exaltation. But daughter, remember you go on the condition, that is, you are to forget all things you ever saw, or knew to be transacted in the spirit world; you are not to know or remember anything concerning the same that you have beheld transpire here; but you must go and become one of the most helpless of all beings that I have created, while in your infancy, subject to sickness, pain, tears, mourning, sorrow and death. But when truth shall touch the cords of your heart they will vibrate; then intelligence shall illuminate your mind, and shed its lustre in your soul, and you shall begin to understand the things you once knew, but which had gone from you; you shall then begin to understand and know the object of your creation. Daughter, go, and be faithful as thou hast been in thy first estate.

Thy spirit, filled with joy and thanksgiving, rejoiced in thy Father, and rendered praise to His holy name, and the spirit world resounded in anthems of praise to the Father of spirits. Thou bade father, mother and all farewell, and along with thy guardian angel, thou came on this terraqueous globe. The spirit thou hast chosen to come and tabernacle through their lineage, and your head, having left the spirit world some years previous, thou came a spirit pure and holy. Thou hast obeyed the truth, and thy guardian angel ministers unto thee and watches over thee. Thou hast chosen him you loved in the spirit world to by thy companion. Now crowns, thrones, exaltations and dominions are in reserve for thee in the eternal worlds, and the way is opened for thee to return back into the presence of thy Heavenly Father, if thou wilt only abide by and walk in a celestial law, fulfill the designs of thy Creator and hold out to the end that when mortality is laid in the tomb, you may go down to your grave in peace, arise in glory, and receive your everlasting reward in the resurrection of the just, along with thy dad and husband. Thou wilt be permitted to pass by the Gods and angels who guard the gates, and onward, upward to thy exaltation in a celestial world among the Gods. To be a Priestess queen upon thy Heavenly Father's throne, and a glory to thy husband and offspring, to bear the souls of men, to people other worlds (as thou didst bear their tabernacles in mortality) while eternity goes and eternity comes; and if you will receive it, lady, this is eternal life. And herein is the saying of the Apostle Paul fulfilled, "That the man in not without the woman, neither is the woman without the man in the Lord." (1 Corinthians 11:11.) "That the man is the head of the woman, and the glory of the man is the woman." (See Ephesians 5:23; 1 Corinthians

11:7.) Hence, thine origin, the object of thy ultimate destiny. If faithful, lady, the cup is within thy reach; drink them the heavenly draught and live.

INDEX

AARON
    may not have been called if Moses had done as the Lord commanded, 334, 335
    Moses was an instructor and guide to, 326
    Moses was his leader, 327
    probable that, held both Aaronic and Melchizedek Priesthoods, 327, 328
    selected to assist Moses and to be his mouthpiece, 326
    was a prophet to Moses before he held the Aaronic Priesthood, 326

ABEL, 186
    same spirit that killed, manifested against all servants of God, 70

ABINADI, 111-113

ABRAHAM, 98-101, 242-244, 251
    covenant God made with, 100, 101
    offered sacrifices, 98, 99
    understood the saving value of the atonement, 98
    was in possession of the principles of the Gospel, 98

ACCOUNTABILITY OF MAN TO GOD, 246-253
    as a moral agent, man is accountable for his acts, 254
    God as proprietor has a right to bless or curse nations, 250
    God has a perfect right to dictate what laws He pleases, 247
    God never gave man unlimited control of the affairs of the world, 248
    man held responsible when he thwarts the design of God, 247
    man is God's agent, 248
    man's actions are subject at all times to the law of God, 257
    man's dominion given him by the Lord, 248
    power subject to conditions imposed by the owner of the property, 248
    the earth and man are the Lord's, 247
    those who have no law will be judged without law, 251
    why the Lord destroys the wicked, 252, 253, 383, 384

ADAM-ONDI-AHMAN
    Adam here probably offered sacrifices for himself and posterity, 71
    Joseph Smith identifies altar that Adam used, 71

Joseph Smith identifies location of, 71

ADOPTION, 133, 140

AGENCY, 228, 249, 255, 256, 293, 386
Christ endured the results of giving man his, 137
God has never coerced or forced the human mind, 254
God has never controlled the human mind, 256
God sets before man blessings and cursings, 249
if deprived of, man could not be tempted by Satan or any power, 94
if man had no, it would be unjust to punish him for his acts, 246
if people were punished, it was because of their disobedience, 294
intelligence must be appealed to by intelligence, 296
man could not be exalted without, 137
man is a free agent with power to act, 248, 249
man is a moral agent with power to do good or evil, 250
man, in part, is the arbiter of his own destiny, 205
man's, has placed the world where it is, 224, 256
Satan wanted to deprive men of, 94, 96, 137
the abuse of, 252
there are many circumstances over which man has no control, 250
when influence has failed, God will use other means, 293
without, all would have been compelled to do God's will, 94
without, man would have been deprived of the power to do wrong, 94

ANGLES
difference between, and ministering spirits, 77

ANIMALS, 202-204
all peculiarly adapted to their situation, 203
so many marked evidences of forethought, intelligence and power, 202

APOSTASY, 179-182, 185
Elder Hyde not the same man that he was before, 378
Joseph Smith's warning about, 369
man prone to, 185
Thomas B. Marsh as an example of, 366-370

ATONEMENT, THE
a ransom provided, 105
all the attributes of Deity harmonize in this great act, 164
Christ beneath the intense and incomprehensible load, 144, 145
Christ bore the weight of the sins of the whole world, 143
Christ's sufferings affected nature, 145, 146
covered more than the transgression of Adam, 146
doctrine of, understood in every dispensation, 179-181
fully adequate to meet the demands of justice, 156
great connecting link between the past and the future, 122
how men are benefitted by, 170, 171
important to understand why Christ needed to suffer, 18
incomprehensible and inexplicable, 143
interests the whole human family, 16
is a righteous act because all requirements and debts are met, 164
made it possible for us to obtain exaltation, 132, 133
meets the requirements of justice,

INDEX

105
more than simply the suffering of personal death, 144
provided a way whereby death could be overcome, 124
provided at the beginning of creation for the redemption of man, 105
results of, 163, 164, 169
the sacrifices offered prefigured and typified the, 63
what is required of man to receive benefits of, 171-173
what was lost by Adam was restored by Christ, 170
why, needed to be infinite, 139, 140

AUTHORITY TO RULE, 257-267
all the kingdoms of the earth are merely temporary arrangements, 265
if the world is the Lord's, he has a right to govern it, 257
king or queen must be appointed by God, 258
kingdoms adapted to the weakness, ignorance & wickedness of man, 265
man has no authority except that which is delegated to him, 257
man is not authorized to act independent of God, 257
only Christ has a right to rule, 271
people are given wicked rulers as chastisement and punishment, 261
the authority the Lord has given to kings to reign, 260
the authority to anoint kings and queens, 258, 259
the kings God anointed to rule over Israel, 261-265
the Lord gives the people kings according to their deserts, 260
the Lord sets up wicked kings to trouble the nation, 260, 261
the monarchy of Israel originated in rebellion and pride, 263, 264
the two things necessary to make authority legal, 258
there are no kings who are legally appointed of God on the earth, 267
wicked kings are used to punish corrupt nations, 261

BAPTISM, 173

BISHOP, 338-355
a difference in the duties of, 342, 343, 354
a man can not officiate legally as, unless called and appointed, 354
are to be tried for any crimes by the First Presidency, 345, 354
are to have power to discern gifts, 341
are to look after the poor and administer to their relief, 339
counselors are to be Elders or High Priests, 339
Edward Partridge was the first, in the Church, 339
firstborn of Aaron's sons holds the right to the Presidency, 344
govern the affairs of the property of the Church, 339
High Priests have authority to officiate in all lesser offices, 344, 354
literal descendant of Aaron must also be ordained by Presidency, 344
literal descendants of Aaron have a legal right to the Bishopric, 344, 352
Melchizedek Priesthood is also to supervise in temporal matters, 345
must be selected from the High Priests, 344, 345
power and right to select a, is vested in the First Presidency, 354
to be a common judge, 352
was to receive support for his

services, 340
BODY, 277-279
   one of greatest curses is not to have a body, 231
   Satan seeks to occupy a, of man in order to posses greater power, 232
   the object of man's taking a, 232
   the spirit requires a, to develop and exalt itself, 231
CAIN, 65, 66, 69, 70
   like Satan, rebelled against his father and his God, 70
CENTURION
   testimony of, 145
CHASTITY, 234-236
CHILDREN
   all, are saved who have not arrived at the age of accountability, 147
   are placed in a state of salvation without any act of their own, 142
   Book of Mormon on baptism of, 147
   more than half have died before the age of accountability, 142, 143
   visiting the iniquities of the parents upon the, 146
COUNCIL AT THE COMMENCEMENT OF MILLENNIUM, 315, 316
   a great council will be held to adjust the affairs of the world, 315
   all who held keys will then give an account of stewardships, 316
   Father Adam will preside, 315
   the order of accounting, 316
COUNCIL IN HEAVEN
   Christ entered into a covenant with God to atone for sins, 96
   Christ wished the glory be given to the Father, 93
   Genesis infers that God counseled with others, 92, 93
   God was originator and designer of the plan, 93
   Lucifer coveted and asked for a power that belonged to God, 97
   Lucifer presents his plan, 93
   Lucifer probably wanted to avoid responsibilities of position, 95
   Lucifer wanted to go contrary to the will of the Father, 94
   man could not be exalted if they adopted Lucifer's plan, 94, 96
   not so fully exhibited in the O.T. as in the book of Abraham, 92
   question arose upon what principle should salvation be brought, 93
   Satan likely refused to take responsibilities of being redeemer, 96
   Satan may have wanted to force men to atone for their own acts, 96
   Satan's plan was rejected, 96
   the Father accepted the offer of His Well Beloved, 95
   the plan of salvation was probably duly considered in the, 93
   we should infer that all that Christ wanted to do was God's will, 93
COVENANT
   if the people fulfill their, the Lord is bound to fulfil His, 249
   making of a, naturally implies two parties, 249
CRUCIFIXION
   antediluvians in same condition as those who crucified Christ, 34
   concerning forgiveness of those who crucified Christ, 34
CURSE
   it is their misfortune not an individual offense they are under, 251
DANITES, 367
EARTH, 241, 242
   destined to be purified and become celestial, 236
   is man's eternal inheritance, 236
   is not man's possession but is the Lord's, 246
   no man can have a lasting claim

unless given him of God, 242
represented as laboring under a curse, 274
shall become as the Garden of Eden, 274
there is something that draws and binds man to the, 241

ELIJAH, 152, 153
holds keys to administer in all the ordinances of the Priesthood, 117

ENOCH, 73-76, 79-81, 190
Bible gives a meager history, 73
by his word the earth trembled and obeyed his word, 80
City of, was translated, 81
commanded of the Lord to preach repentance and to baptize, 80
Lord dwelt among, and his people, 80
Lord showed, the world and its future, 80
saw the days of the Son of Man in the flesh, 80
saw the Lord and talked with him face to face, 80
very important figure among the antediluvians, 73

ENSIGN OR STANDARD
God will set up an, 293
how God lifts an, to the people, 293
what is an, and what is it used for, 293

ETERNAL LIFE
bringing about the, of man is God's purpose, 88
Christ was provided so that man may have, 88

EVOLUTION
different qualities are inherent in different species, 158
in the resurrection man will retain the same image and likeness, 158
man not from a chaotic mass of matter but a son of God, 157
primitive organisms are in same form as when first created, 157
principles do not change as represented by evolutionists, 157
there are some modifications but they are slight, 157, 158

FAITH, 172

FALL, THE, 124-130, 146, 147, 317
Adam brought death, Christ restored life, 170
Christ assumed responsibility that would have devolved upon Adam, 142
earth before, 205, 206
if not for, children could not have existed, 142, 146
man could not have obtained a knowledge of good and evil without, 177
man placed himself in other conditions, 382, 383
placed man in a position to enjoy a higher exaltation, 383
what was lost by Adam was restored by Christ, 170

FAMILY, 234

GATHERING
Jews are to be gathered to Jerusalem in unbelief, 297

GOD, THE FATHER
and His religion will be popular among the nations of the earth, 299
could not impart what He did not know, 201
derogatory to, for the world to yield obedience to another power, 272
has offered his services and instructions from time to time, 254
mercy and long-suffering of, 269, 270
no sinful man can see the face of, and live , 332
plan of, in relation to man, 177

purposes of, cannot be frustrated, 280, 281
recognized Christ as His beloved Son, 17
sustainer of all life, 159

GOSPEL, THE
applies to the living and the dead, 172
benefits of, 178
Christ came to fulfil the Law of Moses, and introduce, 347
Christ taught, to the Nephites, 178
conditions required of man, 172, 173
faith, repentance, baptism...etc. are introductory principles of, 173
fully understood by the Nephites, 176, 177
has been the same in all ages and among all nations, 173, 174
Jesus taught further truths to Nephites because of greater faith, 178
privilege of all men to partake of salvation, 172
short history of, 173-178
that world might be benefitted by, Christ called Apostles, 171
the proclamation of, will be the means of establishing Zion, 298
the same as in the past, 178, 295, 296
there are many among all nations who desire to do God's will, 298
those who love truth and want to be governed by it will embrace, 298
through, is how men can receive benefits of the atonement, 171
when, is lived its powers and blessing are enjoyed, 384

GOVERNMENT OF GOD
after long delay, God will take possession of the kingdom, 303
all things under His dominion, subject to His laws, 199
as God has dealt in former days, so will He in latter, 294
beauty and harmony are effects of God's wisdom, 199
concerning the manuscript, 197
God has a right to punish the guilty, 254, 255
God offers rewards to the faithful, 256
God will not force man, but He can punish in order to teach them, 255
His moral government, 200, 201
if God's creations did not work by law, 207, 208
is that over which God has sole control, 200
moral world will be under the direction of the Almighty, 305
nothing gloomy in the works of God, only harmony, beauty...etc., 229
perfect in operation, for all mandates of God are carried out, 200
planets upheld, sustained, directed and controlled by His will, 199
the effects of the reign of God on the earth, 305-318
the Kingdom of God is the, 199, 282
the part God has played in moral government, 254-256
two kinds of rule: government of God's work and moral government, 199, 200
when the will of God will exist on earth as it does in heaven, 282
will bring peace, righteousness, justice, happiness & prosperity, 305
will do away with war, bloodshed, misery, disease, and sin, 305
world belongs to God but has never been under His control, 284

INDEX

GOVERNMENT OF MAN, 205-225
    after trying man's rule, the Lord will take the reins, 303
    all human means used to ameliorate the world must fail, 214
    any rule not given to man from God is not sanctioned by Him, 257
    Communism, 220
    dispositions of nations, kings, ruler and people are the same, 219
    evils that exist are the consequence of man's departure from God, 214, 251
    examples of, 208-211
    if men ruled by principles instead of passions, 209
    if the fountain is impure, the stream must be impure, 218
    man found the earth an Eden & has filled it with misery and woe, 206
    man has kept the world in one continual ferment and commotion, 206, 207
    man has taken it upon himself to reign and rule without God, 214
    man is not authorized to act independent of God, 257
    only Christ has a right to rule, 271
    only God can correct the evils we have created, 213, 214, 219, 224
    Socialism, 220
    the efforts man have made to improve the world, 214-225
    the influence of Christianity, 215-218
    the means used are not adequate to the end designed, 219, 220
    the past shows that any effort with the same means is useless, 225
    the two things necessary to authorize man to act for God, 257, 258
    there are some things over which man has no control, 228
    there is much uprightness, sincerity and honest zeal, 225
    this state of things is merely permitted for a season, 269-271
    want of a great, governing, ruling principle, 209
    what has man not done to satisfy his cravings or desires, 206
    when nations & rulers set a pattern, people follow their example, 211, 212
    who can look at the world and say man has acted wisely?, 250
    why the world cannot remain as it is, 268-281

GOVERNMENTS OF GOD AND MAN COMPARED, 199-204
    in God's there is order, harmony, beauty, grandeur...etc., 200
    in Man's there is confusion, disorder, instability, death...etc., 200
    works of God show His skill, workmanship, glory and intelligence, 204

HAPPINESS, 220, 221
    is a gift from God, 223

HEATHEN NATIONS
    derived their religious ideas from Christianity not vice versa, 179, 185, 191
    Egypt, 181-184
    Egyptians had great faith in the advent of a son of God, 184
    further back we trace ancient religious belief the purer it is, 184, 185
    ideas entertained by, of atonement, redemption, and God, 181-191
    knowledge of atonement and a Savior was wide spread, 186-188
    Mexicans had a knowledge of the life of the Savior, 188, 189
    mixing and mingling of ideas and people, 187

women claiming their children were offspring of a god was common, 183
HEAVEN, 236-241
   a place of reward for the righteous, 239
   location of, 239-241
   Paradise is not, 238
HEAVENS, 201, 202
   also means the planetary system, 201
   beautiful regularity and precision of whole elegant machinery, 202
   worlds are governed by principles independent of man, 201
HIGH PRIEST, 355
HOLY GHOST, GIFT OF, 173
ISAAC, 101
JACOB, 101
JESUS CHRIST
   all power given to, explained, 163, 164
   all the Prophets testified of the coming of, 20
   ancients almost as acquainted with the life of, as we are, 179, 180
   angels, authorities and powers subject unto, 37
   as first born, inherited the right to be God's representative, 132
   as first born, inherited the right to be Savior of the world, 132
   as first born, inherited the right to carry out designs of God, 132
   Author of salvation to all creation, 62
   baptism of, 17
   Book of Mormon statement about brazen serpent confirms with NT, 50
   Book of Mormon texts concerning, and atonement, 45-57
   bread and wine are a representation of the body and blood of, 84
   by right, becomes director on earth and heaven of man, 164
   by, we obtain every blessing, power, right, immunity & salvation, 140
   came in accordance to preconceived ideas, 16
   came to do the will of the Father, 16, 17
   comparison between, and the other children of God, 131-133
   created all things, 88-90
   Doctrine and Covenants texts concerning, and atonement, 58-62
   drink fruit of the vine with resurrected saints in heaven, 123
   every knee shall yet bow to, 123
   express image of the Father, 131
   first born of every creature, 36
   first fruits of them that slept, 123
   has power to raise himself from the dead, 131, 141
   has power to restore life to mankind, 131
   in, are the attributes and power of the Father, 133
   is the mediator between God and man, 164
   is the Resurrection and the Life, 131, 141
   many types, shadows and forms which He was the great prototype, 120
   New Testament texts concerning, 27-40
   New Testament texts concerning the birth of, 27-29
   no other name given whereby salvation may come, 105, 106
   Old Testament prophecies concerning the coming and life of, 20-26
   Pearl of Great Price and JST texts concerning, and his atonement, 41-44

representative of God in the interests of humanity, 36
sacrifices, prophecies, & prominent acts of ancients centered in, 122
stands next to the Father, 37
subject to man, 137
temptations of, by Satan, 66-68
the agency through which the Father would communicate to man, 133
the Grand Medium through which all blessings flow, 36
the how and why we must become like, 140
through, we might become the sons of God, 132
was the Lamb slain from before the foundation of the world, 123
was the Lamb spoken of by the Prophets, 123
why, needed to descend below all things, 139, 144, 145

JESUS CHRIST, BLOOD OF
redemption obtained through the, 36

JESUS CHRIST, SECOND COMING OF, 274, 275
after the, the nations will be taught by more forcible means, 303
all will have a fair warning, 295
come to claim His rights, dispossess the usurpers, and to rule, 273, 293
Lord will establish His own laws, and demand universal obedience, 303
man must be warned before the Lord destroys wicked at His coming, 294-296

JEWS
as a nation are cursed, 250

JOSHUA
possessed only some of Moses' honor, 330, 331

JUDGMENT, THE, 148-150, 242
Christ at the head, then His Apostles, then the Saints, 150
Christ judges those who died without the law, 149
reasonable that brother of Jared and Jared will judge Jaredites, 150
Saints will judge the world, 150
the combined Priesthood will hold destiny of man in their hands, 150
the Twelve Apostles will judge the twelve tribes of Israel, 149
the Twelve Nephite Disciples will judge Nephi's seed, 149
those who have no law will be judged without law, 251
Twelve Nephite Disciples under Twelve Apostles, 150

JUDGMENTS OF GOD
a time of troubles, such as never has been before on the earth, 299
after rejecting the truth, the nations will be left in darkness, 302
are a consequence of man's departure from God, 298
deliverance from the, will only be found in Zion, 298
Gospel is to be preached, the nations warned, then come troubles, 300
if the wicked never were cut off, the righteous could not rule, 303
man must get a fair warning of the, 294, 295
nations are purified and prepared by the, for an universal reign, 300
there will be a general destruction, 301
very great judgments are spoken of in the last days, 298

JUSTICE, 164-168
is satisfied and the debt paid, 164
it would be unjust to punish man for things they are ignorant of, 294

man could not be redeemed from spiritual or temporal death, 168
would not be just of God to punish man without warning, 294

KINGDOM OF GOD, 282
a brief summary concerning the establishment of the, 302-304
all hold important positions before God, 378
as the world is ignorant of God & His laws, they must be reveled, 293
concerning the idea that the, is solely righteousness, 285
concerning the scripture, "the kingdom of heaven is within you", 285
establishment of the, and the vision of Daniel, 289-292
everyone in the, must walk the line that God has marked out, 378, 379
God is to set up this kingdom, 292
God must be originator and controller or it will fail, 214
how to see and recognize the, 285, 286
is a righteous kingdom, 285
is the government of God, 199, 282
literal kingdom, not just spiritual, 282-287, 296
must be governed by the laws of heaven, 288
must receive its laws, organization, and government from heaven, 288
no similarity between the, and Christianity as it now exists, 291
righteousness, peace, and joy exist as far as the, extends, 285
Saints of God will posses the, 289
shall be given to the Saints of the Most High, 291
the object of the, is to re-establish all holy principles, 234
the wheat and the tares and the, 283
to the extent that man obeys the laws of God, does the, prevail, 282
we are called to build up, 378
we are not called to seek our own glory, honor, or riches, 378
will be established by judgments, 300
will be great, powerful, glorious, and universal, 292

KINGS AND PRIESTS, 151, 152

LAW, 155-162
all the works of God are strictly governed by, 156
corrupt persons will always find means to evade, 235
do to unchanging, scientists can apply tests & learn properties, 156
God could not be God without fulfilling, 161
God has a perfect right to dictate what, he pleases, 247
God is the giver and sustainer of all, 160
God is unchangeable, so are His laws, 160
impossible for God to violate, 160
is a product of God's comprehensive, intelligent, infinite mind, 159
man under a simple, but fraught with the gravest consequences, 124
matter of which the earth is composed is governed by strict, 156, 157
no power can resist a law of God, 161
observance of, would secure eternal life, 124
penalty of transgression of, was the death of the body, 124, 170
required that the penalty of broken, to be paid for, 163
same principle of unchangeableness dwells in God

himself, 158
there are some apparent deviations from, 159, 160
there is regularity, exactitude, and order in all worlds, 156
without, man could not have been tested, 124
would have been a violation of, to let the cup pass from Christ, 161

LAW OF MOSES, 315, 316
a yoke the ancients were unable to bear, 347
apostate Nephites ceased to keep the, 107, 114
Christ came to fulfil the, and introduce the Gospel, 347
Christ fulfilled the, 115
Christ fulfilled the law and made it honorable, 121
Christ introduced a better covenant, 337
facts concerning, in connection with the ancient Nephites, 107, 108
it would seem the law of carnal commandments was a curse, 347
Nephites understood the, though some erred, 110-113
strictly observed by the Nephites, 107
the Gospel was a greater and higher law, 347
understood better by the Nephites than the Jews, 108
was in force until the death of Christ, 120
we have duties to perform that did not belong to those under the, 334
when, was given, sacrificial ceremonies were revealed in detail, 120

LEVITES
the tithing of the children of Israel was given to the, 357
were appointed to fill the place of the first born of Israelites, 357
were provided for as distinct from the other tribes, 357

MAN
a compound being that has a dual capacity, 382
a difficult thing to persuade men that they are deceived, 250
an eternal being, 227, 228
as animals propagate their own species so God perpetuates His, 157
beautifully constructed, 134
by himself, can only rise to the stature of a man, 136, 140
can do nothing without the aid of God, 377
can only use the powers which are possessed by man, 134
capable of using and subjugating the forces of nature, 134
comparison between Jesus Christ and, 131-133
destined to be great, dignified, and exalted, 270
for, to come to the state of a God is why atonement was made, 135
God sustains the life of man from day to day, 268
has left God and submitted himself to the Evil One, 249
has within him the germs of greatness, 270
if men do not copy the good, they generally copy the evil, 211
if, understood true position and eternal consequences of actions, 236
is endued with intelligence and capacity for improvement, 205
it is the corruption of the world that has made, unhappy, 229
lost sight of the object of his creation and his future destiny, 249

monarch of the universe, 134
object of man's existence, 231-236
occupies a more exalted sphere than the animal or vegetable, 382
offspring of God, 157
once stood proudly, now is weak, immoral, and degraded, 212
order, beauty, workmanship, skill...etc in construction of, 203
our relationship to God, 229, 230
posses power to reflect, reason, and comprehend, 134
possess in an embryotic state all the faculties of a God, 157
power to be like God must come from a being other than man, 135, 136, 139, 140
relationship to the earth, 236-245
requires both body and spirit to make a perfect, 227, 231
shouted for joy at the prospect of exaltation, 277
stands at the head of creation, 134, 205, 229, 382
subject to weakness, infirmity, disease, and death, 135
the blessings of providence were made for, and his enjoyment, 229
the dependence of, on God, 269
the medium or channel through with, is to obtain exaltation, 277
the weakness and dependence of, 268, 269
though fallen, bears the impress of Deity, 279
when progressed to maturity, will be like his Father, 157
why God allows, to wallow in his corruption, 269, 270

MARRIAGE, 381-387
if one does not obey the Gospel they should not be deprived of, 385, 386
is the legitimate union of the sexes, 381

MARRIAGE, CELESTIAL
can only be enjoyed by those who obey the Gospel, 385
has safeguards thrown around it, 385
revelation of, superseded everything previously before practiced, 386
uniting mortal and immortal beings by covenant forever, 385

MARRIAGE, CIVIL, 386, 387
best to send to the Bishop instead of justice of peace, 387
not sufficiently valiant to be worthy of weightier blessings, 387

MARRIAGE, PLURAL
may be more the normal condition of man than monogamic relations, 385

MARSH, THOMAS B., 366-370
a specimen of apostasy, 370

MELCHIZEDEK, 84-86
administers the bread and wine to Abraham, 84
was a High Priest after the same order held by Christ, 84

MERCY
simply claimeth her own, 164

MILLENNIUM
all nations will have to acknowledge Lord's authority and rule, 286
during the, religion will be looked upon in its proper light, 287
God alone will be exalted, 287
may properly be called the day of reckoning, 287

MOSES, 102-104, 152, 153
Aaron may not have been called if, had done as Lord commanded, 334, 335
doubted God's ability to sustain him and enable him to speak, 325
held the keys of the gathering dispensation, 152

INDEX

the Presiding High Priest, 328
NOAH, 82-84
    first act after flood was to recognize the atonement, 83
    the rainbow is the token of God's covenant with, 83
OBEDIENCE
    God's requirements cannot be evaded or changed, 156
OLD TESTAMENT
    has various and detailed utterances concerning coming of Messiah, 20
PARENTING, 233, 234
    actions of fathers have a bearing on children in eternity, 251
    Lord feels strongly about the perpetuation of correct principles, 251, 252
    the conduct of fathers has a great influence over the children, 251
PASSOVER, THE, 102-106, 120-122
    blood sprinkled on the door was a type of the blood of Christ, 104
    centered in Christ, 122
    Christ himself was the great expiatory offering, 122
    Christ was the embodiment of, 121
    it was through the atonement that the Israelites were saved, 106
    Lord accepted the tribe of Levi in lieu of the first-born, 106
    Lord made a claim on the first-born of the Israelites, 106
    the act of the atonement was the fulfilment of, 122
PEACE
    is a gift from God, 218, 223
PEARL OF GREAT PRICE AND THE INSPIRED VERSION OF THE BIBLE
    replace some of the "plain and precious" parts take from Bible, 41
PRATT, PARLEY P.
    quote from "Voice of Warning", 244, 245, 306-314

PRAYER
    all individuals have the right to approach God and have, heard, 379
PRIESTHOOD
    both, are everlasting, 353
    Christ is our President and great High Priest, 88
    close connection between operations of, in heaven and, on earth, 148
    God stands at the head of the, 88
    operates in time and eternity, 148-154, 363-365
    proceeds from Christ, through the atonement, to man, 87
    the inspired and united voice of the, is the will and law of God, 376, 377
    the, in heaven and on earth work together, 151, 152
    there is a Presidency over each Priesthood, 353
    though men die, they continue to officiate in the, 152-154
PRIESTHOOD, AARONIC, 325-359
    "lesser" than the Melchizedek Priesthood, 325
    assist in ordinances of Temple, under direction of M. Priesthood, 353
    attends generally to temporal affairs, 353
    called the, because it was conferred upon Aaron and his seed, 353
    cannot be ignored, 337
    continues forever as an appendage to the Melchizedek Priesthood, 337
    first born of Aaron's sons has a legal right to Presidency of, 344
    has power to administer outward ordinances, 353
    in Apostolic days very little is said about, 337

is an appendage to the Melchizedek Priesthood, 337, 347, 353
is under the Melchizedek Priesthood, 337
John was the last legitimate High Priest, 331
one of the great aids to the Melchizedek Priesthood, 337
only the High Priest had the Urim and Thummim, 333
only the High Priest presided, anointed kings, etc., 333
ruled from Eleazar, the son of Aaron, until Christ, 331, 337
Teachers and Deacons are appendages to the, 347
when the, ruled, it held the Urim and Thummim, 333

PRIESTHOOD, KEYS OF
Peter, James and John are legitimate custodians of the, 150

PRIESTHOOD, LEVITICAL, 356-359
not the Priesthood held by Aaron and his sons, 359
Priest's office belonged to Aaron and his family, 358
seems to have been an appendage to the Aaronic Priesthood, 357
to assist in the service of the tabernacle and other duties, 356, 357

PRIESTHOOD, MELCHIZEDEK
Elders and Bishops are appendages to the, 347
has power and authority over all the offices in the Church, 351
holds the keys of all the spiritual blessings of the Church, 355
holds the right of Presidency, 351, 353
is also authorized to supervise in temporal matters, 345
is greater than Aaronic Priesthood, 333

Jesus is at the head, as the great Presiding High Priest, 337
keys of, were taken with Moses, 337
organized and directed the Aaronic Priesthood, 333
Presidency of, has right to officiate in all the offices, 351
Presidency of, presides over all, 337
removal of, 331
when withdrawn, there was no regular organization of the, 333
without the, no man can see the face of God and live, 327

PRIESTHOOD, POWER OF
exercised by faith, 86, 88
is delegated power from the priesthood in the heavens, 88
is simply the power of God, 88
manifest to the world by a number of the servants of God, 86, 87
we'll have more, as we subject ourselves to Priesthood in heaven, 88
without the atonement the, could not have existed, 88

PROCREATION
all life posses this power, whether plant or animal, 381, 382
in addition to his impulses, man is been given a law to multiply, 382
in animal life, the natural impulse alone leads to, 382
there are certain laws that regulate this power, 382
when the Gospel is not obeyed, the principle of, still continues, 384

QUETZALCOATL, 188-190

REMISSION OF SINS
why there is no, without shedding blood is beyond comprehension, 143

REPENTANCE, 172, 173

RESTORATION

postponed until Joseph Smith, 336
signifies bringing back something which existed before, 306
there will be a memorial or evidence of matters and events, 118, 119
will embrace all systems, doctrines, ordinances, priesthood..etc, 118

RESTORATION OF ALL THINGS, 306-318
all things will not be fully restored at once, 317
earth's curse will be removed and resume its paradisiacal glory, 316
man will regain Paradise and partake of the Tree of Life, 317
the faithful servants of God will receive the joy they lived for, 316

RESTORATION OF THE HOUSE OF ISRAEL
great power will be displayed in the, to their former lands, 297

RESURRECTION, THE
Adam brought death, Christ restored life, 170
atonement of Christ brought about, 169
Christ is the means of the resurrection of all men, 141
how far does, extend and to whom is it applicable, 169, 170
how men are benefitted by, 170
is one part of the restoration, the restoration of the body, 170
Jesus Christ is, and the Life, 141
man has not power under any circumstance to resurrect himself, 141
the power of, does not belong to man in and of himself, 141
there will be a place of habitation for resurrected persons, 317
will not all take place at once, 170
without the atonement, could not be brought about, 124

RIGHTEOUSNESS
God is, and consequently, flows from him, 285
is an attribute, a principle, a state of being, not a government, 285
peace and joy are a result of, 285

ROAD TO EMMAUS, 15

SACRAMENT, THE, 120-123
a great memorial of Christ, 122
Christ was the embodiment of, 121
to commemorate Christ's great crowning act of redemption, 121
we partake of, in remembrance of Christ's sacrifice, 122

SACRIFICES, 122
ancient, were acceptable to the Lord, 99
blood of the animals was merely a shadow of Christ's sacrifice, 121
continued until Christ offered his own body for all, 65
corrupt ideas about, 185-187
details of ancient, cannot now fully be defined, 118
every ordinance and, will be restored and attended to, 118
evident that Abraham offered, in token of the atonement, 99
full details of the mode offering, in ancient times is not given, 99
how can there be a restitution of all things without restoring, 118
Law of Moses not to be restored but those, which existed prior, 118
Lehi offered, to the Lord like his forefathers, 108
Lehi's, were occasions of thanksgiving and praise, 108
Lord commanded Adam and Eve to worship him and offer, 64
Nephites understood that, had value because of the atonement, 109
not entirely consumed, 117, 118

offered as a memorial or type of the sacrifice of Christ, 122

offered as a token and remembrance of covenants entered into, 105

offering of, has ever been a part of duties of the Priesthood, 117

prefigured and typified the sacrifice of the Son of God, 63, 120

prefigured the atonement, 163

prefigured the plan of salvation, 164

sons of Levi will offer an acceptable offering unto the Lord, 116, 117

the Bible references to, are limited and somewhat obscure, 64

though not mentioned it is assumed Adam's posterity offered, 70

to Nephites, not unmeaning, burdensome, spiritless performances, 109

until instructed Adam did not know reason for offering, 64

used to manifest to God their faith in the plan of redemption, 119

SALVATION

many things concerning final, of man we do not yet comprehend, 116

many things concerning final, of man will yet be revealed, 116

of those who died without the law, 148, 149

SANHEDRIN OR THE "SENATE OF THE CHILDREN OF ISRAEL", 334

SATAN, 65-68, 255, 286, 287

God's purposes cannot be carried out unless, is bound, 250

has important role to play upon the earth, 65

his dominion will be destroyed and he will be cast out, 287

is only a usurper, 271

knows he has but a short time, 68

leader of rebellious spirits who did not their first estate, 70

occupied a very prominent role in the premortality, 65

office of, is to deceive and to blind men, 97

on earth, still manifests same animus and spirit as in heaven, 70

origin of rebellion in heaven, 70

presents his plan, 93

why, is necessary, 280

will continue opposition until bound & cast into bottomless pit, 65, 66

SETH

did not rebel, 70

God gave Adam, in order to perpetuate the chosen seed, 69

stood in place of or represented Abel, 69

SHEREM, 111

SONS OF GOD

power to become, 283, 284

STEPHEN, 70

SUCCESSION, 361-380

preside according to priority of ordination and age, 361, 362, 365, 366

seniority takes precedence over age, 373

TEMPLE, 151, 152

"saviors on Mount Zion", 151

first thing Nephites did on arrival at their new home was build, 109

Nephite, built after Jerusalem, because used for same purposes, 109

Nephites could not keep all the Lord's commandments without a, 109

TESTIMONY OF JESUS

is the principle, essence and power of the spirit of prophecy, 20

INDEX

TRANSLATION
    delivers one from the tortures and sufferings of the body, 76
    doctrine of, 76-78
    Melchizedek and his people seemed to possess the power of, 86
    power which belongs to the Priesthood, 76
    resurrected Lord ministered to translated and resurrected beings, 77
    there is a place of habitation prepared for translated beings, 76
    translated beings may visit other worlds, 77-79
    translated bodies are designed for future missions, 77
    translated residents of Enoch's city under direction of Christ, 77

TRUTH
    fulness of, only revealed to highly favored persons, 93
    many desire to know the, 298

WAR IN HEAVEN
    could not have happened without agency, 94
    Lucifer could not rebel against a plan that had not been given, 94
    Lucifer not only rebelled but sought to destroy man's agency, 94
    Lucifer rebelled against God's will concerning agency, 94
    Lucifer was cast out of Heaven for his rebellion, 94
    power to cast Lucifer out was conferred by God upon Christ, 97
    rebellion in heaven was transmitted to a rebellion on earth, 70
    rebellion signifies a violation of law, command, or authority, 94
    rebellious spirits cast down to the earth, 70
    Satan's plan would have deprived men of exaltation, 138
    Satan's plan would have frustrated the designs of God, 138

WEALTH, 222
    the form of government will not materially affect the people, 222, 223

WOMAN, 389-392
    destiny of, 391, 392
    origin of, 390

WORK FOR THE DEAD, 151, 152
    Priesthood and others who passed on are working with the dead, 151

WORKS OF GOD
    could not be without a purpose, 231, 246, 247
    God as proprietor has a right to bless or curse nations, 250
    whole creation is represented as groaning and travailing in pain, 274

WORKS OF MAN, 277-279

WORLD, CONDITION OF
    why the, cannot remain as it is, 268-281
    would be unjust to allow the, to continue, 271-273

YOUNG, BRIGHAM
    Christ is the author of salvation of every living creature, 62

ZION
    a literal, will be built up, 296, 300
    called "The City of the Lord; the, of the Holy One of Israel", 299
    Lord will have a house built upon the tops of the mountains, 299
    people there are to be all righteous, 298
    shall be exalted above the hills, 299
    the righteous will flock to, 299, 300
    there will be two, 296-299
    will be built before the Lord comes in glory, 299

Made in the USA
Middletown, DE
25 April 2023